Contents

PENGUIN BOOKS

UNFINISHED EMPIRE

'The depth of Darwin's learning is impressive . . . [his] tone throughout is admirably detached and scholarly . . . a sharp, thoughtful, enjoyable and level-headed book'
The New York Times Book Review

'Mr Darwin's informative and intelligent book is ably written, and it is brimming with interesting statistics and acute observations' *Wall Street Journal*

'A remarkable history of the empire . . . immensely important and useful. As an Englishman, Darwin declines to be either boastful or self-lacerating about the empire his country presided over, but simply examines it with a clear eye. This he has achieved to a laudable and indeed remarkable degree'
Jonathan Yardley, *Washington Post*

'Comprehensive . . . Darwin's erudition allows him to skirt around the narrow orthodoxies of apologist v critic and provide an insightful account of Britain's unlikely period of global hegemony' *Sunday Times*

'John Darwin has crafted a brilliant historical account of what the British empire was, stripped of the ideological fog that usually clouds the subject, and how we still live in its shadow'
Timothy Brook, author of *Vermeer's Hat: The Seventeenth Century and the Dawn of the Global World*

'In his sweeping new book *Unfinished Empire: the Global Expansion of Britain*, John Darwin reminds us that empires are created by people. This is the story of the British Empire from the perspective of the men and women who built and ran it. As such it provides a new and sober look at the complex workings of one of the longest lived and most influential empires in world history from a pre-eminent authority on imperial history. Those interested in an accessible, comprehensive, and up-to-date survey of the British Empire need look no further'
Timothy Parsons, Washington University in St. Louis,
author of *The Rule of Empires*

'A sweeping, non-dogmatic study of the gradual and not always secure development of the British Empire . . . The author does an excellent job delineating the remarkable British rule in India . . . An even-handed, erudite book that finds the work of empire building more nuanced than catastrophic'
Kirkus Reviews

ABOUT THE AUTHOR

John Darwin's interest lies in the history of empires, both their rise and fall. He has written extensively on the decline of Britain's empire and teaches imperial and global history at Oxford, where he is a Fellow of Nuffield College. Most recently he is the author of *After Tamerlane: The Rise and Fall of Global Empires, 1400–2000*, which won the Wolfson History Prize, and *The Empire Project: The Rise and Fall of the British World-System, 1830–1970*.

JOHN DARWIN

Unfinished Empire

The Global Expansion of Britain

PENGUIN BOOKS

PENGUIN BOOKS

Published by the Penguin Group
Penguin Books Ltd, 80 Strand, London WC2R ORL, England
Penguin Group (USA), Inc., 375 Hudson Street, New York, New York 10014, USA
Penguin Group (Canada), 90 Eglinton Avenue East, Suite 700, Toronto, Ontario, Canada M4P 2Y3
(a division of Pearson Penguin Canada Inc.)
Penguin Ireland, 25 St Stephen's Green, Dublin 2, Ireland (a division of Penguin Books Ltd)
Penguin Group (Australia), 707 Collins Street, Melbourne, Victoria 3008, Australia
(a division of Pearson Australia Group Pty Ltd)
Penguin Books India Pvt Ltd, 11 Community Centre, Panchsheel Park, New Delhi – 110 017, India
Penguin Group (NZ), 67 Apollo Drive, Rosedale, Auckland 0632, New Zealand
(a division of Pearson New Zealand Ltd)
Penguin Books (South Africa) (Pty) Ltd, Block D, Rosebank Office Park, 181 Jan Smuts Avenue,
Parktown North, Guateng, South Africa 2193

Penguin Books Ltd, Registered Offices: 80 Strand, London WC2R ORL, England

www.penguin.com
First published by Allen Lane 2012
Published in Penguin Books 2013

005

Copyright © John Darwin, 2012

The moral right of the author has been asserted

Typeset in Sabon LT Std by Palimpsest Book Production Limited, Falkirk, Stirlingshire
Printed in Great Britain by Clays Ltd, St Ives plc

A CIP catalogue record for this book is available from the British Library

978-1-846-14089-1

www.greenpenguin.co.uk

Just for Caroline

List of Maps

List of Maps

Preface

Few subjects in history evoke stronger opinions than the making of empire. Indeed, some historians of empire still feel obliged to proclaim their moral revulsion against it, in case writing about empire might be thought to endorse it. Others like to convey the impression that writing against empire is an act of great courage: as if its agents lie in wait to exact their revenge or an enraged 'imperialist' public will inflict martyrdom on them. These are harmless, if rather amusing, conceits. But they reveal something interesting: that for all the ink spilt on their deeds and misdeeds, empires remain rather mysterious, realms of myth and misconception.

This is partly the result of thinking in monoliths. 'Empire' is a grand word. But behind its façade (in every place and time) stood a mass of individuals, a network of lobbies, a mountain of hopes: for careers, fortunes, religious salvation or just physical safety. Empires were not made by faceless committees making grand calculations, nor by the 'irresistible' pressures of economics or ideology. They had to be made by men (and women) whose actions were shaped by motives and morals no less confused and demanding than those that govern us now. This was certainly true of the British overseas empire. Far from being the mere handiwork of kings and conquistadors, it was largely a private-enterprise empire: the creation of merchants, investors, migrants and missionaries, among many others. Building an empire was not just an act of will or an imaginative impulse, though both were essential. It required a long chain of mundane activities to bring it about: the reconnoitring of 'targets'; the founding of bridgeheads; the raising of money; the recruiting of sailors, soldiers, emigrants and adventurers; the rallying of allies (not least at court or in government);

the writing of rules (not least about property in 'newfound' lands); the regulation of trade as well as of moral behaviour in exotic locations; the framing of governments. It is not hard to see how much could go wrong. One of the most difficult tasks, but also one of the most vital, was settling the terms on which indigenous peoples and their leaders would become the allies, the clients or the subjects of empire. It is easily forgotten that across much of the world empire was 'made' as much if not more by the local auxiliaries that 'empire-builders' recruited as by the imperialists themselves. The result was an empire of hybrid components, conflicting traditions, and unsettled boundaries between races and peoples: a source of constant unease as well as extraordinary energy.

It was also, and crucially, an unfinished empire. When we stare at old maps of the world with their masses of British imperial pink, it is easy to forget that this was always an empire-in-making, indeed an empire scarcely half-made. As late as 1914 (sometimes imagined as the 'high noon' of empire), the signs of this were everywhere: in the derelict state of some of Britain's oldest possessions; in the exiguous strands of settlement that made up Canada and Australia; in the skeletal administration of tropical Africa, soon to be even more skeletal in the 1930s depression; in the chronic uncertainty over what kind of Raj would secure British control and appease Indian unrest; in the constant avowals that there would be no further imperial expansion, and the no less constant advances, a pattern that continued even after 1945; in the fuming and fretting of imperialists at home that public opinion was not imperial-minded enough. Indeed, the most ardent Edwardian imperialists believed that far from constructing a durable edifice that needed only periodic attention, the Victorian makers of empire had bequeathed their successors little more than a building site and a set of hopelessly defective plans.

If empire on closer inspection betrayed its improvised and provisional character, there were good reasons for this. Firstly, no single vision of empire had inspired its founders. Instead, society at home threw up a mass of competing interests and lobbies that pursued different versions of expansion and empire. Colonizing (with British migrants), civilizing (with British officials), converting (with British missionaries) and commerce (preferably without migrants, officials or missionaries) coexisted in uneasy and often quarrelsome partnership as the 'objects' of empire. Colonial politics were the cockpit where the local protagonists of these parties struggled for mastery. Secondly, the 'command and control' of this empire was always ramshackle and quite often chaotic. To suppose that an order uttered in London was obeyed round the world by zealous proconsuls is an historical fantasy (although a popular one). For this was an empire that depended on the cooperation of local elites, on the loyalty of settlers and the (often grudging) acquiescence of British officials, impatient of Whitehall's demands. None of these could be tested too far. Each was susceptible to myriad local pressures and problems unsuspected in London. Imperial governance was by necessity a series of compromises, some of them forced by the explosive rebellions – Irish, American, Canadian, Indian and African – that periodically blew it on to the rocks. Empire in practice required the continual adaptation of the methods of rule. 'Constitutional reform' was an elegant term for bringing new players on to the political pitch, widening (or narrowing) the goal, or changing the shape of the ball. Its aim was not to achieve a 'final solution' but to ensure the empire's survival as a going concern – to keep the game going. Who was subject to which laws remained, in many colonies, a quagmire of uncertainty. Thirdly, this intraimperial activity could not exist in a closed sphere of its own. Perhaps more than most empires, that of the British was exposed to external influences: the ideological claims and religious appeals that attracted its subjects; the effects of economic competition and crisis; and (most dangerously) the appearance of geostrategic challenge. The price of empire was constant attention to the unpredictable impact of geopolitical change, and a constant reshuffling of plans and priorities as new dangers or prospects appeared.

In this unstable world, no version of empire could be final, no imperial 'end-state' more than a temporary respite. Nor – until it happened – could the end of empire be realistically envisaged, let alone planned for. Indeed, until the very last moment, the British themselves (certainly some of their leaders) went on believing that their empire could survive in some form, however reduced. Much of their policy in the era of decolonization (1945–1965) was meant to preserve an invisible empire of economic and political influence. Mundane reality was cruel to this dream. But its effects – as that of empire itself – linger still.

This book is meant to be read as a study in the processes of empire-building spread, in Britain's case, over three centuries of expansion beyond Europe, and with their roots in the history of medieval English imperialism.

A book such as this could hardly be written without the assistance of a vast body of scholarship inadequately acknowledged in the references that accompany its chapters. I am also greatly indebted to my colleagues at Oxford and elsewhere from whose knowledge and insights I have tried to learn. In framing some of the questions that have shaped this book, I have been guided by the curiosity of both undergraduate and postgraduate students – confirming the old adage that to teach is to learn. A particular mention is needed of the late Freddie Madden, whose monumental study of the constitutional practices of the British Empire from the medieval period to the end of empire is fundamental to understanding its byzantine workings. It is a work of extraordinary scholarship.

It is a pleasure to acknowledge the help and advice of the numerous libraries and archives in Britain and abroad on whose materials I have drawn, directly and indirectly, in writing this book. A particular word of thanks is due to the excellent museum and archive of Puke Ariki in New Plymouth, New Zealand and its most helpful staff.

The writing of this and two previous books would have been very much harder without the support and stimulus that Nuffield College offers its Fellows. There can be few better places to attempt works of research and reflection. For this, and for the patience of my family, I am most grateful.

Not for the first time, I owe my warmest thanks to Simon Winder of Penguin for enthusiasm, support and wise advice. I would also like to thank Bela Cunha who copy-edited the manuscript, Richard Duguid who superintended production and made an invaluable suggestion, and James Pullen. Jeff Edwards drew the maps.

I

Imagining Empire

IN HISTORY'S REAR WINDOW

We live in a world that empires have made. Indeed, most of the modern world is the relic of empires: colonial and pre-colonial, African, Asian, European and American. Its history and culture is riddled with the memories, aspirations, institutions and grievances left behind by those empires. The largest if not grandest of these was the empire laboriously assembled by the British across more than three centuries. No less than one quarter of today's sovereign states were hewn from its fabric. For that reason alone, its impact was second to none.

Its history has aroused deep and bitter disagreement: it could hardly be otherwise. A century ago, when the British Empire appeared as a great going concern with an indefinite future, the judgement of historians was usually positive. Mistakes had been made, injustice inflicted, abuses indulged in. Reform had come late. Misunderstanding had flourished. But all, or much, had come right in the end. For at the heart of the empire lay a self-correcting device: a liberal constitution through which political power answered to enlightened opinion. Indeed, this benevolent outcome seemed the best justification for the murkier aspects of the imperial story. The record of conquest and settlement, of the displacement and subjugation of peoples, so it was argued, could be seen as the price paid for progress among the barbarous and backward, trapped in their 'stationary states' and unable to grasp what was in their own interests. Redeeming peoples from superstition and savagery was bound to be messy and quite often bloody.

The history of empire contained a further assurance. For it showed that the British themselves had undergone a moral improvement. In a huge fit of conscience, they had thrown over the system of slavery that had made them so rich and launched a furious global crusade against those who upheld it. They had also abandoned the futile endeavour to impose London's central control on settler societies and by granting self-government won over their loyalty. Most wisely of all, according to liberal opinion, they had rejected commercial protection and embraced the path of free trade. Virtue and self-interest had been rewarded together. Free trade was the secret of British prosperity and was also the best lever for promoting world peace. It was perhaps hardly surprising that H. E. Marshall's popular history, published in 1908 as *Our Empire Story*, was relentlessly upbeat.

Indeed, that positive view was to last a long time – almost as long as the empire itself. A powerful lobby existed to promote the idea that, despite some imperfections, the British Empire was a 'force for good' in the world. When the 'white dominions' became sovereign states (a status made formal in 1931) while remaining part of the empire, this was held up as a model for international cooperation, of how a league of nations should work.[1] This started to change in the depressed 1930s. The Marxist attack on capitalism's failings became much more appealing and it became intellectually fashionable to denounce empire as the tool of financiers and industrialists. John A. Hobson's great polemic, *Imperialism: A Study*, had made little impact when originally published in 1902 but now found an eager new readership. A black historian from Trinidad (later its prime minister), Eric Williams, then a research student at Oxford, wrote a doctoral thesis in support of the claim that Britain's Industrial Revolution – the principal source of its wealth and power – had been built on the profits of slavery, the labour system of empire.[2] These were straws in the wind, but their wider influence was limited. A more reliable gauge of contemporary views was the reputation of Cecil Rhodes, the great 'empire-builder'. Rhodes, who died in 1902, had not entirely escaped his detractors.[3] But his heroic status was sanctioned by royal approval. His grave near Bulawayo (in modern Zimbabwe) was visited by the Prince of Wales in 1925, and by the future George VI in 1934. The centenary of his birth in 1953 was marked by the visit there of the Queen Mother and the Queen's sister, Princess Margaret, amid a large gathering of dignitaries, and by the unveiling of a memorial tablet in

Westminster Abbey.[4] In *Rhodes of Africa* (1936), cinema-goers were regaled with a vision of Rhodes as gruff, manly and masterful, a true maker of empire.

After 1960, a great reaction set in. The dismantling of empire, foreshadowed in the independence of India in 1947, was now well advanced. Colonial rule had lost what remained of its moral legitimacy as a form of enlightened trusteeship. The postwar idea of world order, embodied in the United Nations' Charter, rejected all forms of colonialism in favour of the universal ideal of the sovereign nation-state. To progressive opinion in Britain, the imperial tradition now seemed an incubus. Its outdated values of order and hierarchy blocked cultural change and social mobility. The burdens of rule had wasted resources far better spent on modernizing Britain's economy. The 'soft' markets of empire had feather-bedded manufacturing with disastrous long-term effects. It was easy to see the history of empire as irrelevant at best; at worst a disturbing reminder of an obsolete vision that had left Britain beached in a post-empire world. This mood of disillusion was highly receptive to the genre of 'nationalist' history that decolonization encouraged in the newly independent societies. Just as imperial history in Britain had once celebrated the acquisition of empire and the deeds of its makers, so nationalist histories applauded the achievement of nationhood and the arduous struggle for freedom against the imperialist oppressor. In a happy consensus, historians on high horses could break their lance on the cold corpse of empire.

Indeed, the further that empire receded from view the more severe grew the verdict. In the 1970s, the apparent dislocation of the global economy lent renewed credibility to a Marxian history of exploitation and class conflict. Scrutinized in this light, the imperial past seemed an extreme version of this universal travail. Colonialism had imposed a cruel yoke of economic dependency that locked much of what became the 'third world' into exchanging ever cheaper raw produce for imported manufactures in a cycle of growing impoverishment. Revolution and class war were the only escape. In settler societies, where indigenous labour and land were seized by the colonists, exploitation and empire seemed perfectly fused. For historians of (and in) South Africa, the inhuman apparatus of apartheid in all its manifold forms was the more or less inevitable consequence of white colonization.[5] What South Africa's grim history also revealed – indeed this might be proclaimed as its principal 'lesson' – was that colonization and empire were invariably constructed on a platform of racial privilege and oppression. In a decolonized world in which race discrimination and inequality were still deeply entrenched (not least in the West's richest and strongest society), the evil of racism became empire's great legacy, the ideological core that drove all imperial endeavour, the vital ingredient of the imperial economy, and the guiding principle of imperial rule.

This depiction of empire as (more than anything else) a system of *racial* oppression was the sharpest prong of a much wider attack. Here empire became a systematized means of imposing repression on a range of 'subaltern' groups (the term was borrowed from the Italian Marxist revolutionary Antonio Gramsci). Subaltern history described the social and economic injustice sanctioned by empire against those without access to political power: peasant communities; marginal groups, such as 'tribals', forest-dwellers, and out-castes in India; migrant labourers in Africa; nomads, travellers and transients; women workers and prostitutes; and women more generally.[6] Empire represented a pragmatic conspiracy between a locally dominant class and the imperial regime. This subaltern formula could be extended to the empire 'at home'. Here too was a mass population taken in by the wiles of an imperialist elite, paying in taxes and blood for the prestige, profits and pleasure enjoyed by the few. Here was a world of disempowered women, whose secondary status in a male-dominated society was reinforced by the masculine ethos of pioneer settlement, colonial wars and imperial rule.

Subaltern history raised another large issue. Its exponents insisted that coercion was central to imperial authority, and brutality more commonplace than sanitized histories of empire admitted. But it was obvious that the use of force or its threat could not be the whole explanation for the acquiescence in empire, at home and abroad. In Britain's South Asian Raj, Europeans were hugely outnumbered by Indians and except in 1857–8 faced only very localized rebellions, and not many of them. It would be even harder to claim that the 'imperial idea' depended on coercion at home, either against women or any other subaltern group. But this explanatory gap could be filled, so ran a new argument, by invoking the impact of Britain's 'cultural imperialism'. This suggestion derived from the insight, highly influential elsewhere, that command over how people and ideas were *represented* was the secret of social and political power. Accepted prescriptions of what it meant to be criminal or insane, moral or immoral, progressive or primitive, could exert a silent dictatorship over thought and behaviour. They could also be manipulated by a cultural elite to protect its own privileges. It was easy to see how this could be extended to empire.

Histories of cultural imperialism portrayed empire as the systematic disparagement of the values, social practices and religious beliefs of its subject peoples, and of 'oriental' peoples in general (a category that included almost all non-Western societies). The transparent intention of this cultural assertiveness was to justify rule by outsiders as a triumph of truth, progress and freedom over superstition, stagnation, despotism and slavery, the elements of barbarism. Cultural imperialism's founding precept was the patent superiority of the European (in this case the British) over the non-European 'Other'. Generations of scholastic ingenuity and pragmatic double-think had ensured that almost every dimension of a given colonial society was screwed up and squeezed into an illustration of backwardness. This was the task (to take one example) of colonial ethnography and its official practitioners, the authors of the gazetteers and reports, surveys and censuses, at which the British in India excelled. In a vast work of imaginative re-creation, they constructed an image of stagnant or regressive communities, saved from disaster by imperial intervention, but too unprogressive to be released into freedom for an indefinite time. As a charter for mastery (and an excuse for rough methods) this was bad enough. What made it worse, so the argument ran, was cultural imperialism's pervasive effect upon the peoples ruled over. For in destroying the authority of indigenous cultures, and imposing its own, it wrecked the self-confidence and creative capacity of local elites and drove a deep wedge between a collaborative minority seduced by the charms of imported ideas and the rest of society. Here then was empire at its most durably destructive. It erected a false notion of 'traditional' society and shored up its allies against social or political change. Even more damagingly, it created an 'educated' elite of Westernized poodles, while condemning indigenous cultures to a frozen, fragmented and inferior existence, the exotic remains of an immobile past.

As all this suggests, in histories of empire the sound and fury of the ideological battlefield are rarely absent for long. We should not complain about this. Since histories were first written, the aim of the writer has invariably been to 'correct' our view of the past, and to align it more closely with the writer's view of the present, and the way it was reached. The remotest of times have been annexed and 're-conquered' in such 'history wars'.[7] For many of those who have written (and still write) about empire, there has been a missionary purpose. It springs from a deep sense of moral unease about the impact of empire, and often from the presumption that the worst ills of our time (racism in particular) can be traced to its influence. On this view of its task, the history of empire should adopt a strict method and present a clear message. It should treat the historical evidence that the imperialists bequeathed – official documentation, private papers and records, scholarly works of the period, newspapers, maps, paintings and photographs and all other forms of visual representation – as unavoidably tainted by an imperialist agenda: the relentless insistence upon their racial and cultural superiority, upon their right to rule and control, and upon Europe's world-historical role as the source of civilization and progress. Instead imperial history should set out to show that this imperialist mentality was deluded and false and deeply immoral. It should strip away the nostalgia that still colours our image of empire and reveal the imperial assumptions that still pervade British and Western thinking about non-Western peoples. A truly post-colonial history would allow us to see the imperial past for what it was: a shameful record of economic exploitation, cultural aggression, physical brutality (and periodic atrocity) and divisive misrule. Indeed for some Western historians, it remains *de rigueur* to insist that for them, empire was 'evil'.

There is no need to take up a dogmatic position on the truth or untruth of these various claims (some of which are discussed later) to see their limitations as a depiction of empire and of Britain's in particular. The underlying assumption, on which almost all else hangs, is that empires are abnormal, a monstrous intrusion in a usually empire-free world. No error could be more basic, or perhaps more revealing of an unconscious Eurocentrism. Empire – as the assertion of mastery (by influence or rule) by one ethnic group, or its rulers, over a number of others – has been the political rule of the road over much of the world and over most of world history: the default mode of state organization.[8] Nor was it just the modern world that was created by empire. This suggests that the conditions that give rise to empires are neither peculiarly modern, nor peculiarly rooted in European behaviour, technology or values. It also suggests – unless we dispense with our view of historical change as a whole – that empires cannot be seen as the inveterate enemies of cultural and material advance among those they ruled over. Indeed, historians of pre-modern or non-European empires show few qualms in conceding that, whatever their shortfall in political freedom, they were often culturally creative and materially beneficial. It seems strange to withhold this more balanced approach from the European empires as a matter of doctrine (of course an empirical *finding* might turn out to be negative). It leads (an additional problem) to a history in stereotypes; to a cut-and-dried narrative in which the interests of rulers and ruled are posed as stark opposites, without the ambiguity and uncertainty which define most human behaviour. It denies to the actors whose thoughts and deeds we trace more than the barest autonomy, since they are trapped in a thought-world that determines their motives and rules their behaviour. It treats the subjects of empire as passive victims of fate, without freedom of action or the cultural space in which to preserve or enhance their own rituals, belief-systems or customary practices. It imagines the contact between rulers and ruled as a closed bilateral encounter, sealed off from the influence of regional, continental or global exchange. Most strangely of all, given how much we know, it turns Britain itself into a cultural and political monolith, obsessed not just with empire but with imposing one version of it: cultural domination, economic extraction, coercive control.

Whatever its merits as a 'tract for our times', such history is a poor guide to the past, and a misleading base from which to imagine the future. We need a history of empire that explains more convincingly how Britain's imperial world was constructed. It will need to do justice to the extraordinary variety of colonial societies – and hence to the variety and complexity of their post-colonial successors. Barbados, Uganda, South Africa, Singapore, New Zealand and India were all British colonies. The British occupation of Egypt lasted for more than seventy years. It would not be easy to argue that their shared experience of empire has produced similar outcomes. A British history of empire also needs to acknowledge the pluralism and diversity of British society. The social and cultural complexity (the product of internal and external influence) sustained within the bounds of a single sovereign state may go far to explain Britain's global pre-eminence during the long nineteenth century before 1914. What made the British so adept as empire-builders was, in part, the exceptional range and variety of the interests, skills and activities mobilized by the prospect of expansion abroad. It was this versatility – in method, language and object – that gave the 'British connection' (the contemporary phrase used by colonizers and colonized) its kaleidoscopic significance, as a source of attraction to some and repulsion to others. But it also denied to British imperialism the ideological coherence and political solidarity with which monolithic accounts of 'imperial Britain' naively endow it.

Most of all, perhaps, we need an imperial history that pays close attention to the terms and conditions on which British interests and influence entered a particular region in search of trade or dominion. This was almost never possible without some form of local alliance or understanding with the rulers and peoples who claimed or controlled the area concerned. Indeed, there was rarely much point in going to a place that had (or was thought to have) no inhabitants unless to dump convicts: a barren land without people to trade with or produce to buy had little to offer. The bridgeheads the British established, sometimes extending no more than a mile from the beach, might be hemmed in by locals, determined to stop them from capturing their trade with the peoples and markets inland (for long the case in West Africa, India and China) and with the military means to prevent them. In this situation, it required a drastic upsetting of this local balance of power before the British could be more than a puny mercantile presence, usually a convenience for local rulers and traders, sometimes a nuisance, but almost never a threat. Sometimes this upset occurred because governments in London decided that British control must be real, and provided the force to make this effective. But this rarely occurred as a unilateral or spontaneous decision. The usual scenario was much more complex – and had much more complex results.

This was because the British were in almost all cases only one element in a much larger equation. The places they went to were not pristine locations, untouched by time and untroubled by change. In the Middle East, India, Southeast Asia, China and East and West Africa, they encountered vigorous, highly organized commercial economies, and – in India and China especially – highly organized states. These were regions already drawn into the highways of commerce, often responding dynamically to the impact of trade. These were regions in motion, as much as Europe itself. In them a change in the pattern of economic activity – like the changes we think of today as 'globalization' – could often unsettle the political order. New sources of wealth rewarded new social groups, expanding their power and prestige while demoting others. New skills (and perhaps values) challenged the possessors of old, or threatened their status. New concentrations of power and new kinds of states began to emerge, some precariously dependent upon the new flows of trade and the revenues it brought in. If things were to go wrong, if trade was depressed or disrupted, and with it the revenue that financed the regime, a grand crisis would follow. This was not the only danger that loomed. A crisis that came 'from the sea' – that arose from local involvement in maritime commerce – posed one kind of threat. But in many parts of the world, a crisis 'from the land' was almost equally likely. Inland empires with faraway rulers in Delhi, Beijing, Ava (in Burma) or Kumasi (in Asante in modern-day Ghana) might claim coastal dominion and resent the appearance of new mercantile states. Or they might themselves be caught up in a great political struggle against outside invasion and internal revolt: the fate of the Mughals in eighteenth-century India. Thus, social and cultural tensions of which they were barely aware, or events taking place far beyond their local horizon, could transform the conditions in which the British bridgehead or beachhead existed. British traders might be ruined by rebellions and wars in which they were merely third parties, and they themselves might be seen as the sinister allies of parvenu rulers, or suspected of plotting their downfall. It was situations like these that the British confronted after 1740 in India and to which they had to react, or cut their losses and leave.

There was one further complication they faced, in India and elsewhere. They were rarely alone. Other European states, often represented by great chartered monopolies such as the French or Dutch East India Companies, were usually present, drawn to the spot by the same commercial incentive. They competed for influence and commercial advantage. When the local crisis began, they were just as determined as the British to protect their position and exploit any chance to expand and enhance it. The result was a struggle in which European rivalry was mixed up in the conflicts of local rulers and leaders, and whose outcome depended (as far as the British were concerned) upon the success of their allies and friends. Unless, that is, they were willing themselves to commit their resources to the diplomatic and military contest – and could persuade their masters in London that the effort was worth it. London was willing over India, although its help was largely confined to sending naval assistance. But even in India, the key to British success in expanding their bridgehead and building a wider dominion was the tenacious infiltration of local sources of power, conscripting local resources and adapting their message and methods to Indian conditions. To become the rulers of India, the British became 'Anglo-Indians' – the term used to describe the British in India until *c*. 1900.

As a result, the British did not so much impose their control over local societies as tunnel their way into them. Even where they made a forced entry through a settler invasion (the American pattern), their prospects depended on coming to terms with indigenous 'first peoples': as vendors of land, as partners in trade and as allies in war. Settlers had to adjust to new kinds of landscape, new kinds of production, new kinds of warfare. Both the tools and equipment and the institutions and values that they had carried ashore had to be modified to local conditions – sometimes quite drastically. The acute problem of labour in the plantation economies of the Caribbean was solved by the import of slaves from West Africa, creating a racial Grand Canyon and a coercive machine utterly different from social

conditions at home. In settler communities, as in other colonial societies, empire was not just a story of domination and subjection
(although both might be present) but something more complicated:
the creation of novel or hybrid societies in which notions of governance, economic assumptions, religious values and morals, ideas about
property, and conceptions of justice, conflicted and mingled, to be
reinvented, refashioned, tried out or abandoned. For colonial societies
were not forged in an instant, at the moment of conquest. Throughout
the period of this book, they were works in progress whose politics,
economics and social structures were in more or less constant
upheaval.

How can we capture the cocktail of changes that colonization
brought with it? Some fifty years ago, two of the shrewdest historians
of Europe's imperialisms, John Gallagher and Ronald Robinson,
sketched out a 'road map' of Britain's route to world empire after
1815.[9] At the heart of their argument lay two crucial assertions: that
the British constantly sought the least effortful way of pursuing their
interests in every part of the world, partly because of their system of
government with its inbuilt constraint on public expenditure; and
that this led them, wherever they could, to rely upon cooperation
('collaboration') with the local elites into whose backyards they
strayed. The logic of collaboration was to find a working arrangement with which both sides could live. The British had no wish to
inject more resources (of manpower and force) than they thought
their interests required, while for the local elite calculated collaboration would limit the scale of intrusion, preserve the substance of
power and might even yield benefits. The result was a complex historical pattern. For in some parts of the world, the British could secure
an open door for their trade by an energetic diplomacy that left local
sovereignty more or less intact: this was the Latin American model. In
less cooperative regions, a more coercive approach was adopted: if
the locals would not open the door, the lock would be forced and the
door battered down. Between 1839 and 1842, the British applied this
to China, demanding free entry to its markets, and blocking the
Yangtze – China's main artery – with their steamers until Beijing gave
way. Thereafter, with a fistful of 'treaty ports' (where foreign merchants were exempt from Chinese authority), a flotilla of gunboats

and a grand harbour at Hong Kong (now a British possession), the British hoped to exploit the Chinese 'eldorado', but without the huge burden of imposing their rule. But sometimes it happened that armed intervention and the treaty port model could not guarantee the commercial regime that the British demanded. Or (often in places without commercial appeal) they wanted exclusive control over strategic locations overlooking the sea-lanes that tied their spheres of interests together. Here, they went the whole hog: British rule was imposed; local rulers deposed; a governor installed; the map coloured pink. Yet even here, where empire was 'formal', collaboration logic was followed. It was wise to seek out the local power-brokers and enlist their support because governing by coercion was clumsy and dangerous, and importing large numbers of Britons to man the bureaucracy a futile extravagance. As is well known, the British ruled India (population 250 millions) with an administrative cadre of under 1,000.

Gallagher and Robinson's brilliant historical insights remain the point of departure for most serious work on the history of empire. What we can add is an emphasis upon the multiple viewpoints and sometimes conflicting activities of all those individuals and interests in Britain – merchants, missionaries, migrants, soldiers, sailors, shipowners, scientists, diplomats, humanitarians, investors and would-be career-builders – for whom empire represented either a valuable asset or a desirable prospect. For it turns out on inspection that the 'empires' they wanted were often quite different. The 'empire of slavery' was abolished by law in the early nineteenth century: the wealthy slaveowning interest was crushed by the weight of reforming opinion at home.[10] The 'empire of migrants' – instinctively protectionist and truculently self-governing – had little in common with the wider 'empire of free trade' on which exports, employment and profits depended. Neither looked much like the 'empire of Christ' – the open sea of Christian faith – into which Britain's Protestant missionaries hoped to draw the whole world. The 'empire of coaling stations, bases and fortresses' was different again. The quarrels and squabbles of these rival imperialists meant that no single imperial ideology ruled the Victorian roost: they also gave succour to subject peoples in search of friends in high places and held out the faint hope that one day freedom would come.

There is something else we can add: it is the main theme of this book. The history of Britain's expansion took shape as a series of imperial encounters that started with contact and ended with the emergence of colonial societies. This was the making of empire. But to follow the action, we must see it in slow motion: breaking it down into components and phases; digging out the ideas that made empire seem 'reasonable'; tracing the methods on which empire rulers relied; explaining the grievances that led to revolt; tracking the means by which revolt was usually suppressed; following the missionary trail (and travail); dissecting the impact of empire on the sense of place and identity. Making contact, taking possession, unleashing war, settling in (or trying to), buying and selling (by fair means or foul), ruling, rebelling, repressing, converting, reinventing identities: all these and more went into the making of empire.

VISIONS OF EMPIRE

The idea of empire in Britain went back a long way. From its earliest beginnings, it was an uneasy and sometimes contradictory amalgam of territorial ambition, administrative practice, legal procedure and cultural pretensions. Much of what became the institutional framework of empire was laid down in England long before Columbus had crossed the Atlantic. A fundamental conception was that of a unitary monarchy to rule all English possessions. Sovereignty and allegiance were ruthlessly centralized and the Crown brooked no competition. However, allegiance was softened by a second great principle: that the Crown's dependencies could retain their own laws and customs unless these were deliberately and specifically changed. It was also established by habit and precedent that laws could be made for dependent possessions by the Crown acting through Parliament (making 'statutes'), or by the 'king-in-council'. In fact, the second of these routes became much the more common, because much the more flexible. The so-called 'order-in-council' was an executive act, authorized by the Privy Council, originally the body of the king's closest advisers, but in more recent times an administrative formality. The right of the king to hear legal appeals from his 'subjects' in all and every possession was firmly entrenched: indeed its shadow survives in our post-colonial age in appeals to the Judicial Committee of the Privy Council, which some independent Commonwealth countries have maintained as a legal convenience. This blend of common allegiance and (in practice) decentralized law-making framed English (later British) ideas about empire from beginning to end.[11]

There were other inventions that the English reproduced later in America and Asia. As early as 1363 the Crown delegated powers of self-government to twenty-six English merchants of Calais, then a key English possession (and the last to be lost on the European mainland). In the following century, in the Calais Staple Act of 1423, it granted a cartel of merchants in Calais a monopoly over the sale of English wool abroad, and established the precedent for the monopolies later given to the East India Company, the Levant Company, the Hudson's Bay Company, the Royal Africa Company and (the last of a long line) Cecil Rhodes's British South Africa Company. In 1381, a 'navigation act' tried to restrict (but not very successfully) trade in and out of England to ships owned and manned by Englishmen. Here was the kernel of the system of commercial exclusion perfected (so far as it could be) in the transatlantic empire of the seventeenth and eighteenth centuries.

It was not just a set of legal and administrative expedients that later empire-builders inherited from medieval policymakers. From the 900s onwards (and perhaps even earlier) English kings laid claim to 'high kingship' over the whole British archipelago. Edward the Confessor styled himself *rex totius Britanniae* – king of all Britain.[12] The 'Norman century' (1066–1154) marked an interlude (when English sea power declined), but from the later twelfth century onward there was a vigorous assertion of English authority over Ireland (where Henry II assumed the 'Lordship of Ireland' in 1172) and Wales, the scene of Edward I's conquests and castle-building – as well as less successful attempts to bring Scotland to heel. In the struggle with over-mighty settlers in Ireland (as well as the indigenous Irish) and in the planting of English settlers in Wales (recruited in East Anglia and given municipal privileges),[13] we can see the dilemmas and tactics of a later colonialism. What this pattern of English expansion also revealed was a stark confrontation between English ideas of 'civility' – the qualities of an ordered and peaceful society – and those that prevailed on the British 'peripheries'. The English model presumed: a well-peopled countryside of compact village communities; a landscape of manors, common-fields and a corn-growing agriculture; a peasantry under the thumb of a landowning class and its ecclesiastical allies; a network of towns, markets and fairs; an active land market, permitting some social mobility; and above all a monarchy that supplied peace, founded towns, levied taxes and fostered trade.[14] But in Ireland and Wales, the social system was different. These were kin-centred communities where allegiance and loyalty were owed not to the king, but to kinsmen and clan leaders. They were mobile and pastoral, not fixed and crop-growing. Their notions of property were loose and informal. The conflict between clans (the inevitable consequence, said some English observers, of a cattle-herding economy) encouraged plunder and slavery. Towns were few and far between; money was scarce. Manners were worse. A world of hard-riding herders had no use for tables to dine on or elaborate social decorum. Without the strict social discipline the English priest imposed on the parish, their clan culture encouraged trial marriage, divorce and the recognition of children born out of wedlock. To English observers, these were lawless, chaotic, thug-ridden societies, where political life was reduced to a protection-racket. Order and progress must be imposed from outside. The English in Ireland must not be allowed to 'go native' – the purpose of the 1366 Statute of Kilkenny, which forbade (among other things) the fashion for Irish-style haircuts. The powerful equation between cultural advantage and imperial over-rule was born close to home.

Of course medieval English ambition was not confined to the British Isles. The Norman and Plantagenet dynasties brought with them territorial interests and claims on the European mainland. Normandy was lost to the kings of France in 1204. But the English kings upheld their claim to a vast swathe of what is now south-western France in Poitou and Aquitaine, and drew a large revenue from the wine-exporting region of Gascony and its capital at Bordeaux: the Gascon wine duty alone yielded as much as the entire English customs revenue. English garrisons peppered Brittany, whose strategic importance on the sea-route to Gascony foreshadowed that of Egypt on the sea-route to India 500 years later.[15] However, dynastic rule on the mainland did not exert the same influence on English visions of empire as their experience of Ireland and Wales. This was partly because the English monarch's authority (as duke of Aquitaine) required formal allegiance to the kings of France (and thus narrowed the scope for creating new institutions); partly because the claims of English civility made little sense in a wealthy dependency with a highly organized government and a rich commercial economy; but mainly because, by 1453, the English had been driven out of the mainland except the enclave of Calais.

The timing, however fortuitous, proved very significant. It meant that the course of English expansion in the following century, when the scope of English aims and ambitions was extended dramatically, was archipelagic and maritime and not continental. Indeed, the consolidation of Spain and France as dynastic states, and the family alliance between Austria and Spain (both ruled by Habsburgs), threw the English on the defensive in Europe. This sense of vulnerability was sharpened by the crisis over England's religious alignment from the time of Henry VIII's quarrel with Rome over his marriage, through the Catholic 'restoration' under Mary (1553–8), and Elizabeth's Protestant settlement after 1558, which appeared to pit England against the most powerful European and oceanic state of the age, the Spain of Philip II. It was Henry's vehement assertion of his right to religious autonomy that prompted the claim in the Appeals Act of 1533 that England was an empire – and thus free of any allegiance to other earthly rulers. The fear that English-style Protestantism would be overthrown from within by a coup or from without by invasion (the purpose of the Spanish Armada of 1588) became obsessive and chronic. The need for popular vigilance against a Catholic takeover, bringing despotism, persecution and England's subjection to Spain (later France), became a well-spring of patriotism and Protestant English identity. After the Union of 1707, it helped smooth the mutual antipathy of English and Scots into a sense of shared 'Britishness'.[16] At the Victorian apogee of British world power, it still had the strength to incite public alarm and to fuel missionary fervour. But it was only one element, however explosive, in the Elizabethans' vision of empire.

Just as important was the widening conception of geostrategic security after *c.* 1560. Fear of foreign invasion drove home the vital importance of controlling both the Narrow Seas between England and the Low Countries – the most likely launch-pad for a Spanish assault – and the Western Approaches, the sea-gate leading from the Atlantic into the Irish Sea and the Channel. By 1560, a distinct 'Queen's navy' had come into being, with an administrative system to maintain and supply it.[17] The defeat of the Spanish Armada in 1588 brought a temporary respite. But in the 1590s, Elizabeth's government sent expeditionary forces to the Netherlands and Brittany to forestall a renewed Spanish attack. The Reformation in Scotland eased English fears of attack from the north. But the evident failure of the Protestant Reformation in Ireland, the vulnerability of the Pale, the supposedly safe zone around Dublin, and the danger that Ireland might offer a base for a back-door invasion of England, caused growing alarm among Elizabeth's ministers. Between the 1560s and 1580s, the English garrison rose steadily from 1,500 men to over 8,000.[18] In the 1590s, the drastic decision was taken to embark on a great war of conquest, to re-make Gaelic Ireland to an English design. Here, as in Europe, success was transient and costly. But the 'lesson' that English security depended upon the active naval surveillance of north-western Europe, and effective control over the whole island of Ireland, was now indelibly printed on the strategic imagination of governments in London, and remained firmly lodged there until after the Second World War.

The third crucial influence was England's wider turn to the ocean. As is often remarked, the English were latecomers to Atlantic exploration and conquest, trailing behind the Portuguese, Spanish and French. They were spurred into action by commercial disaster. Bristol merchants had grown rich on the Gascon wine trade, sending cloth and grain to Bordeaux. The collapse of English rule in 1453 disrupted this trade and forced them to look south, towards Portugal and Spain. Here they learned of the new seafaring knowledge that carried Portuguese and Spanish navigators to the Caribbean and West Africa. Bristol sailors began to search for the 'island of Brazil' (probably Newfoundland) somewhere in the Atlantic. John Cabot, a Genoese like Columbus, was commissioned to seek a 'newfound land' in the north Atlantic, perhaps to replace the Icelandic fishery from which

Bristol men had been driven by Hanseatic competition.[19] At first little came of this. But from the 1550s, West Country seamen and their mercantile backers exploited the new maritime knowledge to challenge the Atlantic predominance of the Portuguese and Spanish. In 1562, John Hawkins arrived on the West African coast to buy slaves to sell in Spanish America. His kinsman and protégé, Francis Drake, adopted Hawkins's technique of trading at gunpoint in Spanish American ports: the bonus was plunder.[20] English ministers 'disapproved'. But they also rejected the claim by the Spanish and Portuguese that the papal 'donation' of 1494 had shared the Atlantic between them and excluded everyone else. Instead they and their propagandists insisted on the doctrine of *mare liberum*: 'seeing therefore that the sea and trade are common by the lawe of nature and nations, it was not lawfull for the Pope, nor is it lawfull for the Spaniards, to prohibit other nations for the communication and participation of this lawe'.[21] Imagining themselves as outsiders struggling to break into the closed trading systems of the Spanish, Portuguese, Dutch and (later) Chinese, and invoking the 'freedom of the seas' as their doctrine, became one of the most durable elements of British imperialism. Its influence was still felt well into the twentieth century.

The great would-be empire-builder of the age was Walter Ralegh (1554–1618), the 'pushy outsider'[22] whose gallant appearance and talent for verse helped him become one of Elizabeth's court favourites, duly rewarded with office, income and property. Ralegh was one of the Devonshire gentry, for whom the maritime conflict with Spain and Elizabeth's troubles in Ireland offered rich pickings. Ralegh's half-brother was Humphrey Gilbert whose career had flowered after a spectacularly brutal campaign to suppress a rebellion in Ireland in the 1570s. Gilbert was convinced that a north-west passage to China could be found and favoured founding an American colony to relieve English poverty. In 1583 he sailed to Newfoundland and, with a patent from Elizabeth, laid claim to the harbour and environs of what became St John's. When Gilbert was lost on this voyage, Ralegh took up his cause. It was at his instigation that Richard Hakluyt wrote his *Discourse of Western Planting* in 1584, the first great manifesto of English imperialism overseas.[23] It denied Spanish claims to North America, denounced the cruelty with which they had treated the

Amerindians and urged systematic colonization as a cure for unemployment, overpopulation and commercial depression at home. 'All the commodities of our old and dangerous trades in Europe, Africa and Asia . . . may in short space for little or nothing . . . be had in that part of America which lieth between 30 and 60 degrees of northerly latitude,' he claimed. The object should be to import raw produce and export finished goods '. . . to the employment of a wonderful multitude of the poor subjects of this realm in return . . . what in the number of things to go out wrought and to come in unwrought, there need not one poor creature to steal, to starve or to beg as they do . . .'[24] Like Gilbert, Ralegh combined soldiering in Ireland, where he was granted an enormous estate from forfeited lands, with his American ventures. Raising money from merchants in London, and with the practical help of Thomas Hariot, the leading mathematician-astronomer of the day, he dispatched two expeditions to Roanoke (on the coast of today's North Carolina) in 1585 and 1587 as a base for trade, but also to attack the Spanish treasure fleet that returned each year via the Florida Strait. For, like many leading figures at Elizabeth's court, Ralegh believed that cutting off Spain's supply of bullion was a vital means of lessening its European primacy – and the threat that this posed to Protestant England. 'It is his Indian gold that endangereth and disturbeth all the nations of Europe . . .' he remarked of Philip II.[25]

By the end of the century, the English were still the outsiders of empire. Their attempt to found a colony at Roanoke had failed calamitously. They had nothing to compare with Spain's silver-rich empire in Mexico and Peru, or with Portugal's *Estado da India* with its capital at 'Golden Goa'. The Dutch had beaten them to the spice islands of the East Indies: their Vereenigde Oost-Indische Compagnie, or 'VOC', would prove more than a match for its London-based rival. But the prospect of riches in the Atlantic beyond was now firmly anchored in English imaginings. The ambition was there and so, more and more, were the commercial resources to fund overseas ventures. In the year of the Armada, Richard Hakluyt had sat down to write his *Principall Navigations . . . of the English People*, published the following year. He followed this up with his enormous compendium *The Principal Navigations, Voyages, Traffiques and Discoveries of the English Nation* (1598–1600), an epic celebration of England's maritime past. The defeat of the Spanish Armada in 1588 vindicated Hakluyt and Ralegh's claim that Spain could be challenged in the Americas. War and plunder in the 1590s encouraged further attempts, including Ralegh's own venture to what he called 'the Large, Rich and Bewtiful Empire of Guiana' in 1595. This too came to nothing. But in 1607, a London-based syndicate established a precarious American bridgehead with just sufficient resilience and supply to survive the disasters that had overwhelmed the English at Roanoke. This was Virginia.

The long seventeenth century up to 1713 was an age of revolution and war in England, Scotland and Ireland. By its end, the English had transformed their position both in Europe and beyond. At home they had achieved a precarious constitutional settlement which survived the fierce party strife in the reign of Queen Anne (1702–14).[26] The conquest of Ireland that had eluded Elizabeth was carried through with a vengeance after 1690. The union with Scotland (soon to be tested by the Jacobite Rising of 1715) averted the danger of a divided succession on the mainland of Britain. The War of the Spanish Succession (1702–13) confirmed England's status as a great naval and military power, now with two naval bases (Gibraltar and Minorca) in the western Mediterranean. At the end of that war, they acquired in the peace treaty the right to sell slaves into Spanish America, the so-called *asiento*, puncturing at long last the continent's commercial seclusion. And they had acquired their own empire of 'plantations' and 'factories': the sprinkling of settlements along the North American coast and among the Caribbean islands; the Levant and East India Companies' depots and enclaves at Izmir, Aleppo, Basra, Bandar Abbas, Surat, Bombay, Madras and Calcutta. They controlled much of the fishery on the Grand Banks off Newfoundland. Their Hudson's Bay fur trade rivalled that of the French. They were deep in the slave trade. They had even begun to buy tea at Canton in China.

No single vision of empire lay behind this expansion. But there was agreement on one thing: that the point of expansion was to make England richer. Merchants venturing to the Near East and India would discover new markets. Founding American colonies would create them. Exotic goods from the East could be resold at a profit to

European customers. Refining raw produce that was grown in the colonies would increase employment at home, add to its value, provide a valuable export, and profit both merchants and shipping. Disagreement began over how best to achieve this roseate vista. The Levant and East India merchants (an overlapping group) insisted that without a monopoly the costs and risks of their trade would make it unprofitable. Those outside the circle denounced this self-serving claim, and challenged the Crown's right to grant such a favour. A more damaging criticism, aimed at the East India Company, was that the imports it brought in could be purchased only by the export of bullion, and thus, it was argued, by decreasing the supply of money at home and with it demand. Private profit was made at the public expense. The most effective defence was to show that goods brought from India were re-exported to Europe, and that the mark-up on price was more than enough to cover the cost of the silver sent east to pay for it. By the late seventeenth century this entrepot doctrine had become well entrenched.

Perhaps its most fluent exponent was the Bristol merchant John Cary (?1650–?1720). In his *Essay on the State of England in Relation to its Trade, its Poor and its Taxes* (1695), Cary emphasized the value of the plantations in creating employment and trade.

> For I take England and all its Plantations to be one great Body, those being the so many Limbs or Counties belonging to it, therefore when we consume their Growth we do as it were spend the Fruits of our own Land and what thereof we sell to our Neighbours for Bullion, or such Commodities as must pay for therein, brings a second Profit to the Nation . . . This was the first Design of settling Plantations abroad, that the People of England might better maintain a Commerce and Trade among themselves, the chief Profit was to redound to the Centre . . .[27]

But if the centre was to profit most, it followed, so most contemporaries thought, that colonial trade must be regulated – in the interests first and foremost of English shipping. At a moment of financial and military crisis for the post-Revolution regime in 1696, the Navigation Laws were reinforced. A stringent system (although laxly enforced) was imposed to ensure that the raw produce of the Caribbean and American colonies came first to Britain, and in British ships, whatever its ultimate market. Britain would grow wealthy and strong as the great entrepot of the Atlantic world.[28]

This 'entrepot imperialism' became the dominant view from the Glorious Revolution of 1688 until the great American crisis of the 1770s and 1780s. It masked a wide range of imperial assumptions as well as colonial dissent. It proclaimed, in effect, that the only empire worth having was one whose commodities were exported exclusively to Britain and were then re-exported for the profit of its merchants and the benefit of its revenues. It imposed a commercial straitjacket on colonial economies that was deeply resented as an infringement of freedom – by the Protestant Anglo-Irish as well as by planters in Barbados: 'Free Trade is the life of all colonies,' declared the Barbados governor rebelliously.[29] Its supporters at home longed to smash open Spain's American empire but were restrained by the need to show prudence in Europe. As a political doctrine, it combined formal recognition of the right to self-government by settlers and planters with the spasmodic assertion of the British Parliament's right to make their laws if it chose: a view fiercely resisted by colonial assemblies. Neither did the English at home waste any sentiment on the settlers and planters as heroic empire-builders. An English visitor to Barbados (then England's most valuable colony) remarked in 1655 that 'this Island is the dunghill whereon England doth cast forth its rubbish: rogues and whores and such like people . . .'[30] The view from Barbados was understandably different: 'British blood runs in our veins and the spirit of Englishmen in our hearts,' declared a local patriot.[31] The ideological claim, that a seaborne empire of commerce was the secret of freedom – that 'Britons never shall be slaves' – was smoothly reconciled with a frank recognition that the African slave trade and slavery were its real engine of growth. 'No African trade, no negroes; no negroes, no sugars, gingers, indicoes [indigo] etc.; no sugars etc. no islands; no islands no continent; no continent no trade,' was how Daniel Defoe put it in 1713.[32] Far from restraining the planters' demand for more slaves, London vetoed the efforts of colonial assemblies (fearful of slave insurrection) to limit the influx.[33]

As far as India went, entrepot imperialism showed no interest at all in schemes of conquest or rule, for the very good reason that they would have been absurdly impractical. The East India Company had survived the removal in 1694 of its monopoly rights by a Whig-controlled House of Commons (dismissed by its chief executive Josiah Child as 'the nonsense of a few ignorant country gentlemen who have hardly enough wit to manage their own private affairs . . .')[34] and absorbed its rival New Company some fourteen years later. The Company's defeat of free trade marked a recognition that English commerce in Asia was 'different'. There was no naval power to protect it, no means to defend it against unfriendly rulers, no legal tribunal to provide arbitration. The Company must fend for itself and carry the overheads: its heavily armed 'East Indiamen', its forts and garrisons, its mercantile hierarchy of men on the spot. The price of such continuous investment by joint stock investors was the exclusion of interlopers and free-riders from the long-distance trade between England and India. But to an extent barely noticed until the second half of the century, this Indian 'exception' created a powerful new interest with a mind of its own. Too big to fail, too far away to control, it turned into the kernel of a mighty new empire.

NEW EMPIRES FOR OLD?

For all its contradictions, it had been possible to think of Britain's Atlantic empire as a unity. Its (white) inhabitants had shared (as 'free-born Englishmen') the right to representative government in their own colonial assemblies. They owed a common allegiance to the British Crown. They enjoyed British protection against any threat from without. They were bound to obey the laws that Parliament passed for the trade of the empire. In theory at least, their place in the imperial economy was a guarantee of prosperity in an age of commercial exclusion. In this 'British' world, the awkward fact of a huge slave population could be simply ignored by treating slaves as property. This was the empire celebrated by Edmund Burke as 'a great political union of communities'[35] and the one he defended against London's wrongheaded attempts to impose direct taxes (the Stamp Tax) on self-governing colonies. It was largely destroyed by a great settler rebellion with eager assistance of Britain's European rivals. But even as it broke up, a new 'global' vision of Britain's place in the world began to take shape. New schemes of conquest, new doctrines of empire and a new apparatus of rule soon arose in its wake.

Indeed, far from heralding the implosion of British imperial power, the loss of America was the prelude to a colossal expansion of its scale and ambition. Dismantling Spain's American empire and its commercial controls remained the great prize: its silver-rich colonies still seemed to glitter with promise. The British had captured Havana (Spain's Caribbean 'Gibraltar') in 1762, but reluctantly handed it back to secure a peace treaty. However, Cook's exploration of the Pacific (begun in 1769) showed their determination to challenge Spain's claim to a Pacific monopoly, and to search out new markets and trades in the rumoured southern land (*terra australis*). Perhaps the grandest ambition was to open up China. The foundation of Botany Bay as a faraway gaol in 1788 was at least partly inspired by hopes of an 'Australian' sea-route to China. Four years later, in 1792, a high-powered delegation under Lord Macartney, a former ambassador, was dispatched to Beijing to establish diplomatic relations and open China fully to trade. On this occasion at least, the British had to take no for an answer. But from the outset of their war against France in 1793, the British seized every chance to further their global expansion. They took the Cape and Ceylon from the Dutch to strengthen their grip on the sea-route to India, and then French-held Mauritius. Spain's alliance with France was punished by the loss of Trinidad in 1796. An expedition from India occupied the island of Java, the jewel in the crown of the Dutch overseas empire. When the Portuguese king, in fear of the French, removed his court to Brazil, the price of British protection was to open the country to British mercantile enterprise. The British even attempted to 'liberate' Spanish-ruled Buenos Aires in 1807, but that was a fiasco. And although they handed back some of their prizes in 1815 (the most important was Java to help prop up a new Kingdom of the Netherlands against French aggression in Europe), the results of the war set in motion a drastic re-ordering of British ideas about empire.

The most fundamental revision (because it underwrote almost everything else) was the realization that their entrepot imperialism could now be pursued on a global scale, and largely without the costly defences required up till then. Its real foundation was the achievement of maritime primacy. The rough balance of sea power between Britain on one side and her rivals in Europe (chiefly, France, Spain and the Dutch) on the other had been overthrown. Nelson's victory at Trafalgar in 1805 meant that no other *European* power now had the strength to exclude Britain from markets in the rest of the world. The age of rival mercantilisms, of closed trading zones barred to imperial outsiders, was finished. The greatest of these, Spain's American empire, was already dissolving. The British could now see themselves as the entrepot, not just of their empire, but of much of the world. It was a staggering enlargement of scale and of mental horizons that took some time to sink in. It underpinned the extraordinary self-confidence (not to say arrogance) with which they approached both commerce and politics in Asia and Africa. But it went hand in hand with a second revelation that had gradually dawned on them since the crisis-ridden 1770s.

This was the prospect opened up by what Robert Clive called the 'revolution' in India: the East India Company's conquest of Bengal after 1757. The Company's move had been made out of fear that French machinations and the local ruler's hostility would drive it altogether from the richest market in India: the meaning it drew from the attack on Calcutta in 1756 and the notorious 'Black Hole' into which its agents were thrown. But the first reaction in Britain had been one of alarm and disgust at the astonishing windfall that this brought the so-called 'nabobs' – the get-very-rich-very-quick Company servants in the age of Indian kleptocracy between 1750 and 1790. The Company's later misfortunes in war, its imminent bankruptcy (threatening a financial crisis in London), and the need (as it seemed) to restrain the reckless adventurism of its men on the spot, drove home the necessity of some greater control by the government in Britain. The abuses of power, highlighted in Burke's famous onslaught on the governor-general Warren Hastings,[36] demanded administrative reform on the ground, not least to enable the Company government to collect more of its revenue. So London took command, in theory at least, of the Company's 'political' side including the right to choose the governor-general. A new class of officials, now completely barred from commercial activity, and from which Indians and Eurasians were strictly excluded, was recruited to administer the districts the

Company had conquered. The chronic anxiety after 1793 that France might lend critical help to the Company's Indian enemies (Napoleon's occupation of Egypt in 1798 appeared to signal this aim) completed the 'rehabilitation' of India from being seen as a lawless 'Wild East' threatening moral and financial contagion into an invaluable asset of empire. To a hard-pressed government in London, facing French domination of Europe, the Company's army and navy became a vital resource. Its strategic thinking became global and Anglo-Indian – a habit that persisted until after the Second World War. For middle-class (and especially Scottish middle-class) opinion, administrative service in India became a respectable career opportunity. Commercially, the realization that India's exports of opium to China would permit a colossal expansion of British trade in the East, now made it the pivot of what promised to be a zone of unparalleled promise. Ruling Indians directly and collecting the taxes that paid for that rule, had become an indispensable part of an emerging world-system that was managed from London.

By the early nineteenth century, then, the British had begun to experiment with three different visions of empire – and three different versions. They had acquired a new empire of conquest, above all in India, for which a new ideology of enlightened reform and disinterested trusteeship was being gradually fashioned. It was based on the claim that British control brought a 'rescue from chaos', and offered escape from superstition, predation and violence towards the sunlit uplands of order. Its most brilliant exponent was the politician-historian Thomas Macaulay, who served a term as India's highest legal official. With the start of the Company's rule, he proclaimed, 'commenced a great, a stupendous process – the reconstruction of a decomposed society' wrecked by 'all the evils of despotism and the evils of anarchy'.[37] Its subtlest philosopher was the great liberal thinker John Stuart Mill, who defended Britain's despotism in India as the only sure means of its social and cultural improvement.[38] In stagnant or regressive societies, so the argument ran, progress required the injection of external energy, free from the incubus of local inertia. Much the same arguments justified the imposition of authoritarian rule in the numerous 'little Indias' acquired after 1790. Representative government on the old Atlantic model was unsuited to peoples without freeborn English traditions; if it was granted to the (usually) tiny minority of whites, they would abuse it and cause trouble. Better by far to preserve executive power in the hands of officials who would be answerable to London.

An empire of enlightened officialdom, conscientiously serving ignorant colonial masses, was an extraordinary idea to have arisen in Britain where (unlike in France or Germany) there was no established tradition of bureaucratic authority. It coincided with the rise of the utilitarian philosophy associated with Jeremy Bentham (1748–1832) which imagined the construction of an ideal society by the systematic application of the vital criterion: did a law or institution serve the greatest happiness of the greatest number. A corps of administrative experts, imbued with this principle, would be the agents of change. Bentham's influence could be seen in the spate of administrative reform in Early Victorian Britain. But it really took root in the 'civil service' founded in India after *c.* 1790.[39] Here it was mixed with, and was often at odds with, an older quasi-military tradition of aristocratic paternalism, whose outlook was far more conservative and mistrustful of blueprints for change. Nevertheless, utilitarianism was imprinted on the official ideology of British-ruled India (the annual reports of its government were titled *The Moral and Material Progress of India*) for much of the century. It surmounted the challenge of rejection and failure by indigenous peoples (the clear implication of the great Indian revolt of 1857) by insisting that the timescale of change was now infinitely long, that the need for enlightened outsiders was more obvious than ever, and that local intransigence made 'robust' methods necessary.[40] In its somewhat gloomier Late Victorian version, much of this imperialist credo survived into the era of decolonization in the 1950s and 1960s.

An empire administered by expatriate officials recruited in Britain and taught to command could not have been more different from the 'first' British empire against which Jefferson and his friends had raged in the 1770s. Yet that old semi-self-governing empire had not disappeared. It survived in Canada, and reappeared in the settler communities of Australia and New Zealand. In the 1830s and 1840s, it came under huge strain, worst of all in Quebec, where political friction was sharpened by religious and racial antipathy (see ch. 8). In British radical circles, a solution was framed: settlers should be granted 'responsible government', with executive power being transferred from the governor to a cabinet of elected politicians, on the Westminster model. By the late 1840s, this had been adopted pragmatically by the imperial government in London as the least-worst of outcomes, although it was still widely assumed that no halfway house between dependency and separation could last very long: the colonies would soon go their own way as the American colonies had once done. In fact, a new and remarkable vision of empire sprang up in the settler societies as well as at home. It celebrated what was seen as the unique British talent for the colonization of new lands and proclaimed its moral validity as contribution to progress. Settlers were not to be treated as rejects or 'refuse'. Instead, it was important to cherish the connection, to see settler societies as parts of a new 'Greater Britain'. 'In 1866 and 1867 I followed England round the world,' was how the radical politician Charles Dilke described his world tour.[41] Settler societies, claimed the historian-publicist James Anthony Froude, re-created the lost yeoman virtues of a stable, agrarian England at a time when 'old England' was becoming raucous, industrial and decadent.[42] In his hugely influential 1883 account of *The Expansion of England* (an enormous bestseller), John Robert Seeley, a Cambridge professor, portrayed the settlement countries as the natural extension of England. Twenty years later, Joseph Chamberlain launched his campaign for an imperial federation to hold them to Britain. Even those who rejected his political formula acknowledged that Greater Britain was Britain's real empire. Most Australians, New Zealanders and English-speaking Canadians and South Africans took the same view. But the empire they imagined was an empire of partners and equals, not of dependents and subjects.

For many Victorians, however, it was the third kind of empire that served Britain best and returned the largest moral dividend. Its outline was sketched in Adam Smith's hymn to free trade, *The Wealth of Nations* (1776). In the 'empire of free trade' (not a term Smith used), rule was, or should be, redundant. Free commercial relations would allow the free passage of ideas. It was easy to think that complementary economies would become complementary cultures as well, and that the world's richest, most complex and most diversified culture would export its institutions and values alongside its manufactures. 'Not a bale of merchandise leaves our shores,' declared the great Victorian free trader Richard Cobden, 'but it bears the seeds of intelligence and fruitful thought to the members of some less enlightened community . . . Our steamboats . . . and our miraculous railroads are the advertisements and vouchers of our enlightened institutions.'[43] The force of commercial and cultural attraction would make Britain the centre of a great cooperative commonwealth, promising peace and prosperity to the British at home and their partners abroad. By contrast, so free traders believed, the empire of rule, on display in India, was wasteful and violent, a saga of futile belligerence as an obsolete aristocracy clung on to power.[44] It was a seductive prospectus and far from absurd. The idea of free trade was closely allied with the idea of free labour and the attack on the slave trade and slavery. It was the ideological spearhead of British 'soft power'. It encouraged the British to see themselves as liberators, opening up 'closed' societies, and freeing their peoples to become producers and consumers. It was the key justification behind the onslaught on China in the first Opium War in 1839–42. But as that conflict revealed, Richard Cobden's assumption that the ideal of free trade would win universal acceptance was too optimistic. To his political nemesis, Lord Palmerston, it was blindingly obvious that if free trade was resisted, the British should act to impose its acceptance in the interests of all – but especially themselves. 'It may be true in one sense,' he wrote with characteristic brio, 'that Trade ought not to be enforced by Cannon Balls, but on the other hand Trade cannot flourish without security, and that security may often be unattainable without the Protection of physical force.'[45]

That the empire of rule subserved the great cause of free trade was hard to dispute. After all, it was empire that wedged India open as the largest market for Lancashire and its vast output of textiles. Up to 1914, British opinion still regarded free trade as the vital ingredient of British prosperity. By that time, however, it was widely accepted that free trade was under general attack and that it would be hard for the British to defend their huge stake in a world now all but divided between five Western powers and the cadet power of Japan. In Kipling's gloomy poem 'Recessional' (1897), a decaying Great Britain stared into the pit. A more sober pronouncement was that of Halford Mackinder, the influential geographer, half a dozen years later. The world had changed, said Mackinder. Command of the sea, which had made Britain great, was no longer the key to world power. Now it was railways that united vast spaces, resources and manpower. For the first time in history since the age of Columbus, the 'heartland' of Eurasia would be able to master the vast landmass of the world, and drive the sea power to the margins.[46] Russia's defeat by Japan in 1905 seemed to belie any imminent risk. But in 1918, when the German conquest of Russia briefly threatened a domination of Europe as complete as anything that Hitler was to strive for, Mackinder's vision of a British empire at the end of its tether became, for a few months, frighteningly real. That vision recurred, in an even more nightmarish form, in June 1940.

THE UNDERTOW OF DISSENT

Jonathan Swift's view of empire was characteristically unsparing:

> A crew of pirates are driven by a storm, they know not whither; at length a boy discovers land from the top-mast; they go on shore to rob and plunder; they see a harmless people, are entertained with kindness; they give the country a new name; they take formal possession of it for the king; they set up a rotten plank or a stone for a memorial; they murder two or three dozen of the natives, bring away a couple more by force for a sample, return home, and get their pardon. Here commences a new dominion, acquired with a title by divine right. Ships are sent . . . the natives driven out or destroyed; their princes tortured to discover their gold; a free licence given to all acts of inhumanity and lust; the earth reeking with the blood of its inhabitants: and this execrable crew of butchers employed in so pious an expedition is a modern colony sent to convert and civilize an idolatrous and barbarous people.[47]

Of course, there had almost always been those who rejected imperial visions of wealth, power and prestige, and the moral flannel they were wrapped in. The violence involved in the colonization of America aroused moral unease, not least because the English had made much of the sadistic brutality of Spanish imperialism – the so-called 'black legend' – to justify their own 'milder' presence. The troubling realization that plantations – a harmless-sounding word – involved dispossession by force lay behind the anxiety to frame the best moral case. This anxiety persisted, partly because the moral case was always ambiguous at best, and was subject to constant subversion by unwelcome reports of colonial realities. It was fuelled by the chronic disputes over whether British expansion should *absorb* other peoples by conciliation and inclusion, or *exclude* them as the alien and unassimilable relics of an obsolete past; and whether inclusion required a long (?indefinite) period of subjection before equal status was safe. Missionaries (as we will see) were especially perplexed by this question. But they also believed that social degradation (by alcoholism and sexual exploitation) and violence were commonplace wherever the frontier of European expansion (and its predatory white men) lacked close control. The loss of aboriginal 'innocence', doubling and redoubling the task of Christian salvation, was the huge moral debt that empire incurred. Extreme moral discipline was required to redeem it.

But for most of those who resisted the allure of an imperial future, the fate of the conquered was a secondary matter. Their mistrust was partly inspired by dislike for the British abroad. The British at home found it hard to shake off the suspicion that colonial wealth was ill-gotten gain. The nabobs and the West Indian planters were equally suspect. Respectable British opinion seethed at the thought of what the planters could do with the bodies (especially the female bodies) of their slaves.[48] Such unrestrained licence, like that of the nabobs, meant moral corruption. When nabobs and planters came home, this corruption would spread like a virus. Indeed, it was precisely the danger that empire at home would distort or derail Britain's domestic affairs that lay behind the most articulate criticism. Burke's great polemic against nabob abuses in India exploited the fear that returning 'East Indians' would buy their way into Parliament and power. Richard Cobden's attack on Britain's Indian Raj turned on his claim that the aristocracy used this patronage empire to hang on to power. By sucking Britain into its futile wars of expansion and obsolete rivalry (in this case with Russia), said Cobden, India upset Europe's peace and delayed the triumph of free trade and reform.[49] His fellow radical

Goldwin Smith, a professor at Oxford, warned that the strain of garrisoning India against a second Mutiny would force Britain into conscription and a great 'standing army', that universal anathema.[50] In J. A. Hobson's *Imperialism: A Study* (1902), the most eloquent tract against empire before 1914, Cobden was updated by casting financiers as the manipulative force behind imperial expansion, and proconsular wars (such as the war in South Africa) as their ruse to subvert by jingo distractions the advance of social reform. Empire diverted British savings abroad: it put off the day when the price of so much under-consumption at home – and the skewed distribution of wealth from which it derived – would have to be paid. For Hobson, like Cobden, the great objection to empire was that it served as the prop for reaction, the barrier to political and social progress at home. This grievance endured. In the last days of empire in the 1950s and 1960s, it was denounced as a drag on the postwar modernization of British society.

Yet the point should be made that the critics of empire hardly ever commanded more than marginal backing. They worked as a goad, the prickings of conscience, not as the champions of an alternative policy. Moreover, they rarely opposed British expansion as such: only those forms they saw as serving a sectional interest or obstructing Britain's own social needs. 'He was as anxious as anyone that the English race should spread itself over the earth,' Richard Cobden told the House of Commons in 1843.[51] Even Hobson regarded Britain's settlement colonies as 'healthful expansions of nationality': their democratic institutions and egalitarian ethos were examples to follow. Cobdenites looked forward to universal free trade and expected representative government to emerge in its wake. British anti-imperialists expected that their nationalist friends would treat liberal Britain as their model and ally. For the critics of empire, like the most ardent imperialist, it was Britain's manifest destiny to lead from the centre, as the liberator, protector, transformer and (some said) evangelist of the world beyond Europe. Here was the grandest of imaginary empires, the one that lived longest and survived many defeats.

2

Making Contact

It was one thing to imagine an empire. It was quite another to make one. Of course, the claims of would-be empire-builders were meant to create the illusion that constructing a presence on alien soil was straightforward and simple, requiring only practical skills and a measure of will-power. Indeed, until surprisingly recently, historians were generally willing to echo this view, as if the intruders' success was a foregone conclusion. Looking back, we can see that, as long as empires remained the great fact of the present, and the likely shape of the future, they cast a large shadow over how the past was conceived. Yet the tradition of what might be called 'intruder triumphalism' (usually in the guise of 'frontier history') was most widely endorsed, and lasted the longest, in the United States, the richest and strongest of the world's settler societies.[1]

At first sight, a fundamental difference appears between the enterprise of founding a 'colony' – the permanent occupation of a patch of someone else's land while retaining a continuous connection with the mother country or metropole – and that of setting out to trade with a distant market about which little was known, with which there had been no continuous contact, or where the usual commercial intermediaries were lacking. Thus we might distinguish between two almost simultaneous ventures: the colonizing of Virginia from 1607 and the East India Company's attempt to set up a 'factory' – a combined warehouse and residence – on the west coast of India. But this distinction breaks down if we look a little more closely. This is partly because what turned into a colony did not always begin as an agricultural as opposed to a trading settlement. Those who arrived there did not necessarily intend to stay very long. It was equally true that

33

in what may have been meant as a trading station of sojourners rather than settlers, dealing with powerful or well-organized states on the spot imposed from the beginning certain 'colonial' characteristics on the aliens. They might find it essential to preserve a distinct 'corporate' identity, with their own internal regulations and hierarchy. They might need some means of defence, if on a limited scale, against predation or disturbance. They might also find that local tradition, as well as their own preference, encouraged residential segregation and the setting apart of their factory from indigenous settlement.[2]

Whatever its purpose, the beginnings of contact followed a similar pattern and posed similar problems for the English intruders. They had to decide in advance how to deal with the local inhabitants and hope that they had guessed right about their political system and commercial desires. They had to choose the best place to make their first landing and establish a beachhead. On getting ashore, they had to make sense of the immediate environment as quickly as possible and try to master its hazards. Unless they brought with them a large cargo of food, or had a convenient source of supply, they would need local assistance before the growing season was out to build up their rations and guard against famine (at Botany Bay, famine remained a recurrent danger even twenty years after the penal colony's foundation in 1788). Whether or not their purpose was mainly commercial, the intruders had to establish the terms of exchange with the locals, a tricky negotiation and (as we will see) one that could easily unravel. They had to decide on the *political form* of their relations with the peoples they met, and how this should be presented symbolically. They had to find the right formula for making agreements and settling disputes – which meant making some effort to understand the locals' world-view, ideology, political structure and spiritual life. They had to accept some adaptation to the physical setting and material culture in which they now found themselves, if only for reasons of cost, convenience and health. Typically, the quest for sexual companionship drew them out of their beachhead community, where women were absent or few. But they had to weigh the advantages of adjusting their diet and dress, their leisure pursuits and private morality, or their acceptance of new kinship connections, against the need to enjoy the trust of their comrades, maintain solidarity with them, and preserve an embattled identity – in case they went home. Finally, unless they could hope for large-scale reinforcements from home, they had to reach equilibrium in their local relations, and hope that any disturbance would not threaten their interests or safety.

If the problems of contact were universal, we can see, nevertheless, two broadly different patterns emerging from the effort to solve them. Between 1600 and 1750, the British established a whole series of bridgeheads in the Atlantic and Asia. By the early eighteenth century, they had created an 'English Atlantic' – a connected system of empire based on plantations and settlements.[3] In Asia, meanwhile, they remained a commercial sea people, with a modest scattering of factories. Their trade was dependent on the goodwill of rulers whose power it seemed futile to challenge. A revolution in India, only partly of their making, brought the British a subcontinental empire in the second half of the century. But this was an empire quite different from the one they had fashioned in the English Atlantic: an empire of conquest and rule, but far more dependent on local agents and allies, and far less attractive to British settlers and migrants. The early pattern of contact was to cast a long shadow.

ATLANTIC FRONTIERS

By the late 1600s, the English (before the 1707 union Scots were largely excluded) were busying themselves along a huge arc of activity from Gambia and the 'Slave Coast' (modern Benin) in West Africa, through Barbados and Jamaica in the English Caribbean, to the Carolinas, the Chesapeake and New England on the North American mainland, and as far north as Newfoundland with its enormous cod fisheries. The Caribbean was the pivot around which all this revolved. The English had been drawn there as if by a magnet. Their Atlantic expansion had begun in the wake of the Spanish. They hoped to find on the islands or on the mainland nearby the treasure of silver and gold on which the Spanish had stumbled – this had been the point of Ralegh's expeditions to the Orinoco in modern Venezuela. As well as finding their own, they were also determined to steal as much as they could of the bullion the Spanish took home, by raiding their convoys. It was the Caribbean's special geography that made this worthwhile.

It was a matter of access. Once Columbus had shown how, it was quite easy to reach the West Indies from Europe, and certainly much easier than sailing straight across the Atlantic against the prevailing westerlies. Once in the region of the Azores or Madeira, a ship sailing from Europe picked up the trade winds that would carry it quite quickly (in five or six weeks) to the Windward and Leeward Islands (or Lesser Antilles), the eastern fringe of the Caribbean. The Spanish had disdained these small islands and Barbados and pressed on to Hispaniola and Cuba, from where they had launched their *entrada* to Mexico. If the silver of Mexico, and that of Spanish Peru (brought up to Panama for shipment to Europe) aroused English avarice, it was Caribbean geography that dictated English tactics. Facing Spain's network of forts and its strong naval presence, they had no hope of establishing a base close to the central American mainland. As if reflecting their weakness, their first permanent settlements were far out on the edge, at St Kitts in 1624 and Barbados in 1627. Neither was much good for intercepting the convoys of silver since the favoured return passage to Europe lay through the Florida Strait between Cuba and Florida (where ships could pick up the Gulf Stream) and then north and east along the North American mainland until the prevailing westerlies carried them Europe-wards. The Florida Strait was guarded by Havana, Spain's great citadel, carefully sited to protect the most valuable and vulnerable leg of the sea voyage home.

The North American mainland was thus almost an afterthought. Gilbert and Ralegh had dreamed of an American colony. But Ralegh's choice of Roanoke Island in modern North Carolina was a more precise calculation. It lay just far enough north to be out of range of Spain's Florida posts, but might still serve as a base from which to pillage its convoys.[4] The site chosen for Jamestown in 1607 reflected the same need for protection from Spanish attack (it was well away from the sea coast) and perhaps the same hope of preying on Spain's homeward shipping. The English also brought to their mainland

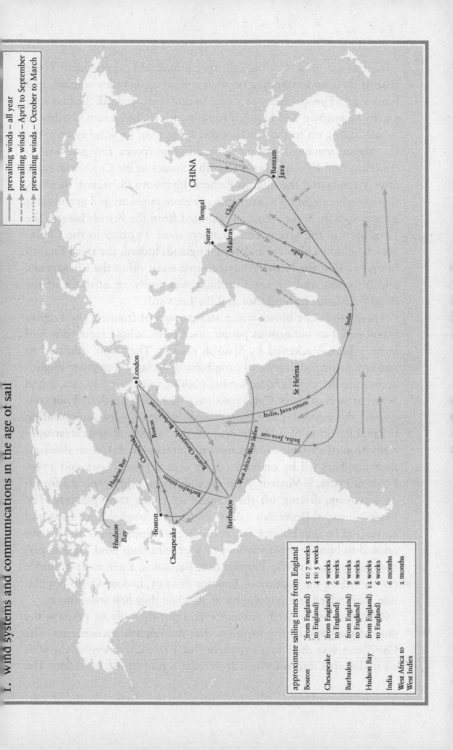

1. Wind systems and communications in the age of sail

| prevailing winds – all year |
| prevailing winds – April to September |
| prevailing winds – October to March |

approximate sailing times from England		
Boston	(from England)	5 to 7 weeks
	(to England)	4 to 5 weeks
Chesapeake	(from England)	9 weeks
	(to England)	6 weeks
Barbados	(from England)	9 weeks
	(to England)	8 weeks
Hudson Bay	(from England)	12 weeks
	(to England)	6 weeks
India		6 months
West Africa to West Indies		2 months

adventures a set of 'Caribbean' expectations and experiences.[5] These
shaped their understanding of what sort of colony they wanted, and
what kind of peoples they expected to find there. Indeed, the first voyage to Jamestown had lingered for a month in the eastern Caribbean
before sailing on to the Chesapeake. Because of its wind system, the
Caribbean remained for most practical purposes the gateway to
America. And although most English colonies in the Caribbean came
after Virginia and the Pilgrim Fathers' Plymouth Plantation of 1620,
they swiftly caught up to attract many more migrants and promise far
greater wealth. Some 210,000 migrated from the British Isles to the
Caribbean in the seventeenth century; some 175,000 to the Chesapeake, 'middle colonies' and New England. Indeed, the third English
bridgehead on the North American east coast (after the Chesapeake
and New England) in the Carolinas was really an offshoot of the
'English' islands of Barbados and the Leewards.

The English Caribbean was a strange sort of frontier. The English
encountered an indigenous people, the Caribs, whose reputation had
already been blackened by Spanish reports. They were addicted to
sodomy, incest, adultery and cannibalism, declared a popular English
account in the early 1600s, leaving nothing to chance.[6] In fact, it had
been partly because of Carib resistance that the Spanish had not conquered the eastern Caribbean islands where English colonization
began. Like other New World peoples, the Caribs suffered catastroph-
ically from their lack of immunity to Eurasian and African diseases:
their numbers fell by perhaps 90 per cent between 1492 and 1700.
But in St Lucia, St Vincent, Barbuda and Antigua they proved a formidable enemy, driving off the English or killing their planters. The
English invaded Dominica – the main Carib stronghold – in 1675 and
massacred its inhabitants, but resistance continued, since the Caribs
refused to become servile labour or part with their land.[7] It was perhaps fortunate for the English that Barbados, their most valuable
colony before the capture of Jamaica in 1655, had no Carib population, nor indeed any population at all when they first went there.

The frontier of Carib resistance was not the only or perhaps the
most demanding of the frontiers that the English encountered. The
Caribbean was their first experience of a tropical environment with
all its hazards and novelties. It exerted a powerful fascination. The

English physician and botanist Sir Hans Sloane (1660–1753) began his career there as medical adviser to the governor of Jamaica (a short appointment as the governor succumbed quickly). Sloane's huge collection of plants and other specimens, laboriously catalogued, and his description of Jamaica in two massive volumes, established his reputation as one of the great scientist-collectors of the day and a leading figure in the Royal Society. Other English visitors showed a similar urge to collect and record the products of Jamaica's exotic environment, no doubt reflecting contemporary interest in England.[8] The aspect that affected them most directly, however, was the threat that it posed to their health. For the English who went there, the Caribbean was a new frontier of disease and mortality. Malaria, yellow fever and dengue fever, all mosquito-borne, vied with typhoid and typhus to lay them low. The 'white' or 'bloody' flux – two forms of dysentery – killed them just as efficiently. There was also the 'dry belly ache' which led to paralysis. But that was self-inflicted: the result of drinking rum distilled in lead pots.

Against these terrible scourges the English had little recourse. The learned Dr Trapham published his *Discourse of the State of Health in the Island of Jamaica* in 1679. But Trapham, like many contemporary doctors, clung to the humoral theory of medicine which explained the breakdown of health as an imbalance of the four humors – melancholy, phlegm, choler and blood. Blistering, bleeding and purging were the sovereign remedies, but if they cured the disease it was by killing the patient. The English came in droves, drawn by the prospect of riches, and died like flies: of the up to 50,000 Europeans who arrived in Jamaica between 1700 and 1750, only 10,000 were living there by 1752.[9] They gradually adapted their houses to moderate the impact of heat and humidity, and in some cases altered their diet and dress. But the major adaptation (by those who could afford it) was to limit their stay: by long vacations in Europe, by restorative holidays on the more northerly mainland, and most of all by retiring to England as quickly as possible, leaving their interests in the hands of agents or kinsmen.

For the English (soon reinforced by Scots, Irish and Jews) the Caribbean was also a technological frontier. In the mid seventeenth century, when they grasped the rewards that sugar production would bring, they had to learn the mechanics of its demanding regime – usually, it is said, from Dutch pioneers in Brazil. The sugar mill, or engine house, was the plantation's mainspring, imposing its remorseless demands for cane, labour and fuel. Sugar helped to determine that the English Caribbean would be a rich man's frontier, since the capital costs of buying or financing a sugar plantation (with its heavy dependence on credit) excluded those without means. The rapid conversion from white indentured labour to black slavery that coincided with the adoption of sugar as the staple crop of the islands (in Barbados especially) had another critical consequence. It made the English Caribbean a frontier of civility where English (later British) ideas about race and slave labour were ruthlessly adapted to local self-interest. African slaves were defined as a species of property, entitling their owners to the fruits of their labour. The slave who absconded was thus guilty of theft in a peculiar form. Insofar as slaves were deemed by the law to possess human powers of volition (a necessary concession since slaves did rebel) these were assumed to be latently criminal. Indeed, the root justification for the system of slavery and the savage apparatus of coercion on which its preservation depended was the ineradicable barbarism of the slave population, a product, it was argued, of its African origins.[10] The Barbados slave code of 1688 described blacks as 'of a barbarous, wild and savage nature . . . [and] wholly unqualified to be governed by the laws, customs and practices of the [white] nation'.[11] Not the least of the issues that slavery raised was the regulation (or not) of the slave-owners' rights over female slaves and their bodies, and the social and legal status of their offspring. A powerful case has been made that the sexual exploitation of slave women (in one case with more than 130 different slaves) was a deliberate expression of white men's physical dominance over the slave population.[12]

Fear of slave unrest and rebellion as slave numbers grew (slaves outnumbered whites by 1660 in Barbados, by 1670 in Jamaica, and by the 1680s in the Leeward Islands)[13] was the 'internal frontier' of these island societies. But it was only one of the reasons why they remained tense and uneasy. A volatile climate, a threatening morbidity, the burden of debt, the sense of dependence on distant markets and prices, the quarrels and lawsuits over boundaries and land rights (aggravated by sudden and frequent mortality) helped to keep the islands in the anxious and insecure state of a social experiment. Visitors from Britain contemptuously noted that after more than a century white society was still crassly materialist in tone, a measure perhaps (if we discount the metropolitan snobbery of home-grown Britons) of the fact that those who had leisure preferred to spend it in England. To the physical and psychological insecurity of the internal frontier could be added an external frontier within English Jamaica, beyond which lay the refuge of runaway slaves, the so-called 'Maroons', the target of expeditions and wars. Looming over all was the risk of foreign invasion. The English Caribbean formed part of a geopolitical fault-line where the rival interests and ambitions of Spain, France and Britain (not to mention the Dutch and the Danes) were rarely at rest. Cheek by jowl with each other, the colonists could expect little warning if a crisis at home or in their Caribbean backyard brought a shipborne incursion that damaged their commerce and might even displace them. Although the diplomatic requirements of Europe's own balance of power discouraged a major reshuffle of Caribbean possessions (thus the British captured Havana at huge physical cost in 1762, but handed it back), the Caribbean was the setting for conquest, predation and violence between Europeans from the 1560s, when the English freebooters arrived, until 1815: a melancholy tradition.

The English Caribbean was tied by an umbilical cord to another Atlantic frontier: the coast of West Africa. Here too the English were latecomers. The Portuguese had arrived first, followed by the Dutch. The English sea captain Hawkins visited the coast in the 1560s and bought a number of slaves. In the inaptly named *Jesus* he sailed to the West Indies, hoping to sell them to the Spanish. For the moment, however, the English took little part in the slave trade: 'we were a people who did not deale in any such commodities, neither did we buy or sell one another,' said Richard Jobson, an English merchant on the Gambia river, when offered slaves in 1620.[14] It was gold and other tropical produce such as ivory, beeswax, dyewoods and pepper that attracted their interest and continued to do so. The real change came with the great shift in Barbados to sugar and slaves. By 1672 the Royal African Company, a chartered monopoly, was building a series of factories to handle the export of slaves from the coast. Even so, much of its business remained in other commodities and the main point of its castles – such as the famous Cape Coast Castle in modern Ghana – was to protect the gold trade from European pirates.[15]

West Africa was a mercantile and maritime frontier for the English: it showed no signs of becoming a plantation or colony on the Caribbean model. There were several reasons for this. Although the sea passage to and from West Africa was comparatively easy, the Caribbean remained the crossroads of Atlantic navigation and trade – a result of the wind-system and of Spain's mainland empire of silver. Secondly, although it supplied tropical produce and the infamous pool of slave labour, West Africa lacked the conditions that had enabled the English and other Europeans to create a plantation system in the Caribbean (and elsewhere in the Americas). First and foremost, that system required an ample supply of cultivable land within easy reach of the sea. Secondly, and this was just as important, it had to be land on which Europeans (in this case the English) could fasten their peculiar notions of property. A title to property was the passport to the labyrinth of commercial credit and debt. It allowed the owner to borrow the means to buy or clear land, buy or pay labour, and subsist while his crop was carried for sale in a faraway market. It sucked in investment and promoted expansion. In the Caribbean, it had been relatively easy (Carib resistance notwithstanding) to seize hold of the land and impose a system of property. West Africa was different.

West African societies had a long history of trade across the Sahara with the Middle East and North Africa, also the source of Islamic influence and religion. Partly as a result, the Europeans who came there entered a world not of scattered and primitive tribes but of highly organized states, including Ashanti (in modern Ghana), Allada, Dahomey, Benin and Oyo (in modern Nigeria).[16] There was no question of their tamely submitting to European mastery or caving in to invasion; indeed quite the contrary. The Caribbean planters might have derided their African slaves as barbarous and savage, the English in West Africa were much more respectful. They had reason to be, since their commercial activities depended upon the goodwill of the ruler and could be halted abruptly if they incurred his displeasure.

African power thus set the terms for West African contact. It was reinforced by West African geography. With few exceptions, the coast was extremely unfriendly to seaborne intrusion. The combination of sandbars and surf kept the European ships out to sea: reaching the land meant relying on the local boat-people. Even where their forts and factories were easily reached from the sea (as at Cape Coast Castle), the English had no means of exerting domination over the nearby interior against local rulers – and little incentive to try. Indeed, the number of English to be found in the forts was pitifully small: a result partly of climate and disease, partly of the limited gains that West Africa offered an English incomer. In the port of Ouidah (sometimes Whydah) in modern Benin, the main centre of the slave trade, this pattern was particularly clear. Ouidah lay back from the sea, behind the coastal lagoon. To reach it, English traders had to land on the seashore and then traverse the lagoon before approaching the city. They had to recruit canoemen from further west on the Gold Coast to help with their landfall. In Ouidah itself, their 'fort' was confined to the fringe of the city. It had mud walls, earthworks and cannon and even a moat (no doubt the mosquitoes were happy), but these were aimed at their French neighbours and rivals, not at their African hosts. Indeed, without the command of a landing place (they were prevented from building a seaside establishment) the twenty white men and their one hundred slave helpers could easily be starved into surrender. It was really a barracks where the slaves that they purchased at the inland capital at Savi were kept until the next slave ship arrived: between 600 and 800 were usually lodged there.[17]

Up until the late eighteenth century there was little sign that this modest physical presence and the deference it required to African authority would change very much. As late as 1714, the head of the English fort at Ouidah was expelled by the ruler after a fracas with the French. On the African side, the English were tolerable because they provided a commercial convenience but without posing a political threat. Perhaps the key reason for this was rooted in the slave trade itself. A different pattern of commerce might have encouraged the rise of a local mercantile class. Their English connections and mercantile interests might, sooner or later, have aroused the resentment of the ruling elite. But the slave trade, by contrast, strengthened the power of those with the means to acquire fresh slave captives by warfare or coercion: that is, it aided the rise of strong West African states and reinforced their ability to resist external intrusion. Indeed, it was only after the trade's abolition (in 1807 for the British) that the British discovered the motive and (somewhat later) the means to extend their control over the West African hinterland. In 1750, such a future would have seemed to the handful of 'coasters' the wildest of dreams.

It was on the North American mainland that the English (and British) found themselves engaged in the most intense and protracted encounter with indigenous peoples and a native environment. The expedition to Roanoke in 1585 had been a false start: the English left there had all disappeared when the relief ships returned in 1590. Their fate remains a mystery to this day. The second attempt at Jamestown in 1607 came close to disaster. This was despite the fact that it was carefully planned, drew consciously upon previous experience in the Caribbean and at Roanoke, and – as the archaeological evidence suggests – was exceptionally well equipped with masses of tools and medical apparatus. Its leader, Captain John Smith, was a well-travelled soldier and his instructions from home were carefully thought out. Go upriver, they said, to be safe from Spanish attack, but keep a lookout on the coast. Don't offend the native inhabitants but never let them carry your firearms nor see how many sick you have. Make sure the streets of the new settlement are straight to allow a clear line of fire. Avoid heavily wooded areas, and choose a good place to trade. In fact, Smith's instructions make clear that the Virginia Company, which had funded the venture, did not expect the new colony to be an agricultural community. They hoped that Smith would find minerals (the dream of gold and silver died hard) and engage in trade with the Indians. But they also directed him to look for a passage 'to the other sea'. For, like many contemporaries, they were convinced that 'America' was a narrow strip of a continent (perhaps reasoning from what they knew of Central America), and that, once over the watershed, there would be a rapid descent to the opposite coast. Virginia would be a staging post to the destinations that mattered: the Indies and China.[18] It may have been this prospect that explains why so large a proportion of the first Jamestown contingent (around half, it seems) were neither labourers nor artisans but soft-handed gentlemen. It may also explain why no women came with them.

But despite their meticulous planning, very little went right in the first decades of the colony. The site of Jamestown was chosen to be close to deep water (and safe for the ships), to be easily defended, and provide ample drinking water. The English also expected to catch plenty of fish to add to the food that they would buy from the Indians. But Jamestown turned out to be an ecological death-trap. Half of those who landed died in a matter of months. The main reason, it seems, was that it lay at the meeting of fresh and salt water, so that what was thrown in the river was not flushed away. The English drank their own waste, with fatal results. Fish turned out to be surprisingly scarce. Even the game proved hard to hunt. 'Virginia' was in the grip of a five-year drought (1607–12), which reduced food supply and fresh water, and in the midst of the 'little ice age' that produced fiercely cold weather in 1607–8. It was also malarial. In the starvation winter of 1609–10, the colony was almost wiped out.[19]

These were not the best circumstances in which to come to terms with the Indians. Here too, the English had planned carefully. They expected the Indians to be in highly organized groups and to be eager to trade. They knew that copper was prized and brought a large supply with them.[20] They assumed that they would soon fall out with their immediate neighbours and hoped to cultivate friendship with more distant communities who might be useful as allies. As a series of hunches about the colony's progress, these were not unrealistic. The political units that the English encountered around the Chesapeake Bay were 'prestige-goods chiefdoms'.[21] The chief of the Powhatan Confederacy, to whom Smith gave a suit of red cloth, a greyhound and a hat, derived his authority from distributing prestige goods to his followers. He may have intended to use his English connection to reinforce his position as a middleman: trading the copper they brought for food, and selling it on to inland communities. But any hope that this prospect of mutual advantage would create a stable relationship vanished almost immediately.

One source of friction was the English reaction to petty thefts by the Indians. They themselves came from a fiercely hierarchical society where property was sacrosanct, and disputes over ownership were settled in the stylized rituals of the law and its courts. The pettiest theft could be punished with unremitting ferocity. Since they were subjected to this savage regime, and constantly told (by their priests among others) that it formed the foundation of a godly and ordered community, the colonists found it hard to accept a less rigid view of what property meant. They were unlikely to see that from an Indian point of view their behaviour was aggressive or even immoral. They failed to reciprocate the gifts they received. These tensions were sharpened by their constant dependence on the Indians for food. The attempt to extract food 'tribute' from the Powhatans at a time of a general food shortage was bound to cause trouble, especially in a period of regional drought and dearth. To make matters worse, their trade with the Indians lost much of its use as a source of goodwill. By flooding the market with their imports, the colonists quickly lowered their value in the eyes of the Indians. They had 'glutted the savages with their commodities', complained Smith.[22] And by allowing private trade, they denied the Powhatan chief the right to control distribution of the prestige goods they offered.[23]

The effect was to bring to a head the latent antipathy between the English arrivals and their involuntary hosts. The Powhatan chief had expected (or so we might reason) that the English would remain in a state of dependence indefinitely, if only for food, and that their payment in goods would nourish his power. He meant them to be a useful auxiliary. But the English were also determined to make *him* their dependent. Their numbers kept growing. They had begun to send women. They showed little desire to intermarry with Indians (perhaps in part because marriage gave them no rights over Indian labour or land).[24] They were no longer a small enclave of traders, but instead began to grow their own crops. They were conspiring against him with neighbouring tribes. In 1622, fifteen years after the foundation of Jamestown, he resolved to erase this gathering nuisance. In what later accounts strangely describe as an 'uprising' (as if against some lawful authority), the Powhatans made war on the English, killing more than a quarter of the 1,200 settlers. But they had left it too late. The English survived to take a savage revenge. Indeed, the war marked a turning point in Virginia's transition into a settlement colony. It ended the fiction that the land could be shared. The governor, Francis Wyatt, left nothing to doubt. 'Our first work,' he declared, 'is the expulsion of the savages to gain the free range of the country for increase of Cattle, Swine etc . . . it is infinitely better to have no heathen among us, who were at best as but thorns in our side, than to be at peace and league with them . . .'[25] Separation and exclusion would in future define the English approach. Meanwhile, the colony had begun its career as a tobacco plantation (using plants brought from Trinidad): the first consignment was sold in 1614. In 1619, the first slaves arrived. The passage from contact to colony had taken little more than a decade.

Yet this was merely a beachhead: a vast interior lay ahead. The Indians were pushed back. But from New England in the north, where the first English arrived in 1620, to the Carolinas in the south, first settled in the 1670s, an 'Indian frontier' survived barely 100 miles from the sea. In South Carolina, where there were no more than 5,000 English in 1700, most lived within a few miles of Charleston, the capital.[26] Although their numbers grew steadily, the English (now reinforced by Welsh, Irish and Scots as well as by Germans – the Pennsylvania 'Dutch' or *Deutsch*) still lacked the weight to force the Indians back over the mountains. And the Indians' resilience was not simply a question of manpower. By the late 1600s, they had learned to exploit the growing geopolitical rivalry of the British and French: the arrival in force of the French on the lower Mississippi in the 1690s signalled a crucial new phase in France's drive to close the continental interior against British intrusion.[27] By 1717, the French advance guard was in Alabama.[28] 'To preserve the balance between us and the French is the great ruling principle of modern Indian politics,' grumbled a British official.[29] The pressure of British expansion had also encouraged the formation of more Indian confederacies on the Iroquois model – among the Creeks for example – and perhaps even a sense of an Indian identity: 'We are the Red People met together,' declared one Indian gathering in 1726.[30] These were not their only defences. As suppliers of furs and deerskins (Augusta, Georgia, on the Savannah river, best known today for the US Masters' golf championship, was the great centre of the deerskin trade), the Indians were valuable partners. And their forest habitation was a powerful safeguard. For all its romantic allure, the American woods were a brutal environment. Without expert guides, the traveller soon lost his way. His path was constantly barred by bogs and creeks. For most of the year, he had to carry all his food with him, and risked near-fatal delay from inclement weather. After one gruelling trip in March 1737, Conrad Weiser, an experienced frontiersman, felt at the end of the journey 'as if we had escaped from hell'.[31]

As a result, for almost a century after they had fastened their grip on the 'tidewater' regions close to the sea, the settlers were forced to accept Indians and the 'Indian country' as a permanent fact of colonial life. Settlement proceeded spasmodically into the so-called 'Back Parts': most rapidly in Pennsylvania, where the white population grew from some 20,000 in 1701 to five times that number only forty years later;[32] scarcely at all in New York whose riverine hinterland was dominated by the powerful Iroquois confederacy. Frontier wars smouldered, flared up and died down; some of the most violent were in South Carolina where slave-raiding by whites wiped out the coastal tribes.[33] But along much of the frontier, both sides were at pains to soothe the inevitable frictions by negotiation or arbitration.[34] The colonists borrowed heavily from the material culture of the Indians: their hunting practices, crops (especially maize or 'Indian corn', beans and squash), birchbark canoes, snowshoes, moccasins, buckskins and tobacco pipes. They relied heavily on Indians as guides in the forest and along the trade paths. Pidgin languages such as the 'Delaware jargon' sprang up to assist with their verbal exchanges.[35] And in their dealings with the Indians, the British were forced to adopt the long-drawn-out protocols of Indian diplomacy: the great crowds in attendance (reflecting the need for consensus in a decentralized world); the exchanges of gifts; the interminable speeches; the reliance on 'wampum belts' of shell beads, rather than paper and writing (which the Indians distrusted) to record the terms of a treaty.

This was an equilibrium of sorts, but not a stable equilibrium.[36] The Europeans' invasion of North America (Spanish, Dutch and French as well as English) created a new world for the Indians as well as the colonists.[37] It brought them a massive increase in tradable goods, and allowed a huge enrichment of ritual and ceremony, including many more artefacts to bury with the dead. A crucial addition was iron-bladed weapons and tools, to be followed by firearms. By the mid seventeenth century, so archaeological data suggest, Indians depended on trade with the whites for half the tools and materials they used:[38] indeed, they insisted on custom-made goods to suit their habits and tastes – such as ultra-light muskets. But what they had to trade in return, usually deerskins and furs, were diminishing assets. Once these had gone, all they had left was the land. Their fighting manpower was subject to even more drastic contraction: smallpox is thought to have carried off half the Cherokee people in 1738. Alcohol, to which the colonists were addicted (one calculation suggests that they typically drank the equivalent of seven shots of spirits a day),[39] was a corrosive import: Indians lacked the social, biological and even dietary adaptation that lessened its impact in settler society. Despite a long period of enforced coexistence, there was also no real meeting of minds between Indian and settler society. Their visions of landscape (one material and utilitarian, one peopled with spirits and history) remained far apart. The settlers hated the forest and longed to destroy it. Beneath a veneer of cooperation, the mutual loathing ran deep. In settler society, the desire for more land either to farm or to make a speculative profit obsessed rich and poor alike; to resist this self-interest, larded with righteousness, was political death. In the last resort, therefore, the balance between Indian country and the settler populations was geopolitical. It depended on the Indians' ability to play off the rivals for mastery on the North American continent. When the British captured Quebec in September 1759, and evicted the French from the continental interior in the ensuing Treaty of Paris, they unleashed (to their own later dismay) a frontal assault on the Indians. In less than a century, this act had transformed North America into a 'white man's country' from 'sea to shining sea'.

ASIAN FRONTIERS

The world of maritime Asia was an extraordinary contrast to the mainly north Atlantic world that the British knew well by c. 1700. It was vastly greater in scale: a huge water world from Mozambique to Japan. It was much further away. With a favourable wind, a ship could sail from England to Barbados in six or seven weeks. The voyage to India rarely took less than four months and could easily take six. The Atlantic could be crossed (with variations of comfort and safety) at any time of the year. The traveller to India had to leave

England in time to catch the south-west monsoon that would blow him north-east from the Cape of Good Hope from May to October. If he wished to return, he would have to wait on the north-east monsoon: between November and April it would carry him back to the Cape. The time and expense the journey entailed discouraged frequent trips (except for the very rich and important), and sharpened the sense of distance and difference. In their Atlantic plantations, the British were able to found distinctively British communities, except in West Africa. In their Caribbean slave colonies, they might have resembled a (sickly) garrison but the constitution, the law and the property were theirs. On the American mainland and islands, they mustered some 250,000 people by 1700. But along the coasts of maritime Asia, they could be counted in dozens and only rarely in hundreds. Very few women came from Britain to join them. There is no reason to think that before 1750 the number of British in India exceeded four or five thousand, and may have been considerably less. In their minuscule enclaves, the sense of manifest destiny that developed so quickly among the colonists in America would have been merely absurd. They could not imagine that they commanded the force to threaten or frighten the native rulers around them. Indeed, quite the contrary. In the Atlantic world of the West, they were settlers or planters, colonizers and landsmen: in the East they were transients and marginals.

This marginal status was emphasized by the power of the states into whose spheres they had wandered. Across the whole breadth of maritime Asia, trade required the consent (active or tacit) of Asian courts and their agents. In the Red Sea and Persian Gulf, that meant the Ottoman Empire and the Safavid rulers of Persia (Iran). In Western India and Bengal, it meant the Mughal emperor in Delhi – although it was also expedient to be on good terms with the rebellious Maratha confederacy inland from Bombay (Mumbai) by the late seventeenth century. In South East India, it was the Sultanate of Golkonda until it was overthrown by a Mughal invasion. Across the Bay of Bengal, the Thai kingdom of Siam, with its capital at Ayudhya, upriver from modern Bangkok, dominated the mainland of Southeast Asia from the late sixteenth century until the mid eighteenth:[40] it was wise to solicit its ruler's goodwill. In East Asia proper, the dynastic transition from Ming to Qing brought a prolonged phase of disturbance, especially in South

China. But no European would have dared to trade on the mainland without the approval of local officialdom. Japan's 'open century' came to an abrupt end in the 1640s. Thereafter, only the Dutch were permitted to retain a factory on the tiny islet of Deshima in Nagasaki harbour.

For the English, it was not simply a question of angling for favours from Asian monarchs and ministers whose contempt for these rude hairy barbarians was barely concealed (the arrogance the British were to display later in Asia may have been sharpened by the embarrassing memory of their earlier subservience). They also faced fierce competition from a host of mercantile rivals. They followed the Portuguese into India. Their hopes of exploiting the pepper and spice trade of the Indonesian archipelago were thwarted by the Dutch East India Company: better armed, better organized and better financed. From the late seventeenth century, the French Compagnie des Indes, with its base at Lorient (L'Orient) in Brittany, became a major competitor at Chandernagore in Bengal from 1673 and Pondicherry in South India from 1699. The isle of Mauritius, on the sea-route to India, was taken by France in 1715. In the 'country trade' – that is the traffic within Asia – an array of indigenous merchants plied routes that predated by centuries the arrival of European shipping. Arab and Swahili merchants in East Africa, Hadramis from Southern Arabia, Indians from Surat, Bugis from the Celebes, as well as Chinese, carried much of the trade of the Indian Ocean, the Bay of Bengal and the South China Sea.[41] Of all these groups, it was the Armenians, with their headquarters at New Julfa in Safavid Isfahan, whose commercial success was most widely envied by Europeans. As we shall see, the English in Asia were anxious to link their own fortunes with those of this remarkable network.

To make their way into this world, and snatch a profit from its trades, the English merchants had banded together into a common concern. For each eastern voyage, they raised an 'investment': to purchase the merchandise, and pay for the hire of the shipping they needed. Under its charter from the Crown in December 1600, their East India Company enjoyed a monopoly on the direct trade in goods between England and the East. To conduct their dealings on the spot, the directors in London dispatched 'supercargoes' and 'factors', to trade from the ship or from the factories or trading posts they meant to set up at any promising site. These men on the spot were soon forced to pick up a mass of new knowledge. They had to learn Asia's sea-lanes and its complex coastal geography, its seasons, currents and winds. To avoid giving offence, they must learn the court rituals and diplomatic procedure of those rulers whose favour they sought. They could hardly ignore the political and geopolitical upheavals within and between the great Asian states that might settle their own fate one way or the other. They had to know something of the religions and cosmologies of the cultures that lapped round them, or risk outrage, expulsion and worse. They acquired in the process a hybrid vocabulary, drawn from the speech of the vast maritime world between Persia and China. Words such as 'topass' (a mercenary, usually Christian, perhaps a corruption of the Turkish *top-chi*, a gunner), 'bafta' (a form of calico, from the Persian word for weave), 'cooly' (a common labourer, probably from the Tamil *koli*), 'cot' (from Hindi, via Portuguese), 'curry' (originally from Portuguese), 'godown' (a warehouse, originally from Tamil), 'kedgeree' (an oily rice dish, from Hindi), 'shroff' (a money-changer, from the Arabic *sarraf*) were all current among the English in India before 1700.[42] As a microscopic minority on the edge of vast civilizations, they felt the magnet-like force of glamorous rulership, all-embracing religions and subtle philosophies. In this universe, they were more like midgets than masters.

The English knew Asia as a sequence of coasts: the Arab and Persian shores of the Persian Gulf; Gujarat in Western India; the Coromandel coast of today's Tamil Nadu; the Hooghly delta that led into Bengal; the Tenasserim coast, the shortcut to Siam; the innumerable shores of the Indonesian archipelago; the South China coast; and, all too briefly, the west coast of Japan. At first they relied heavily on the expertise of their rivals: they sailed as they traded in the wake of the Portuguese and the Dutch. The Company's first voyages were to Bantam in Java, where the English hoped to cut in on the Dutchmen's spice trade. It was only their third voyage in 1608 that took them to India. In 1613, they established a factory at Hirado, near Nagasaki, and one in Siam. Neither was to thrive: that at Hirado was given up after a decade. They created a network of outposts to tap the spice islands, the Moluccas especially. They tried several times to gain an opening in China. Their first trip to Canton in 1637 ended in gun-fire, and it was not until 1700 that they were allowed a yearly trade visit to Amoy and Canton. By then, the growing power of the Dutch VOC had all but driven them out of the Indonesian archipelago; they clung on to a toehold on the west coast of Sumatra. Little by little, more by default than design, the Company fell back on India.[43]

Surat in Gujarat was its first Indian factory. It was the main port for North India, for the Mughal capitals at Agra and Delhi, and for Indian Muslims going on pilgrimage to Mecca. The English obtained a *firman* (or decree) from the Mughal emperor that allowed them to trade, but only after defeating a Portuguese squadron at Swally Hole, Surat's deep-water anchorage. The English were permitted a factory, where they would both live and do business, but the conditions were strict. They could not buy property. Nor was their factory to be near the river. This was partly because the site that they wanted was close to a mosque and 'it offended the moores [Muslims] especially our people pissing rudely and doing other filthiness against the walls'.[44] Perhaps just as compelling was the fear that the English would make it into a fortress easily reached from their ships. The English factory was spa-cious (there was even room for a Turkish bath), and like other Europeans the English were allowed that essential convenience, a burial ground. At the Swally Hole anchorage, there were wharfs and godowns, but until after mid-century the English who stayed there lived in tents on the beach.[45] Transience, toleration and surveillance were the themes of their tenure.

Once in Surat, the Company factors soon looked further afield. In 1614, they dispatched two of their number overland via Kandahar to the court of Shah Abbas of Persia at Isfahan. Abbas offered the Eng-lish free trade, perhaps hoping for allies against the all-powerful Portuguese and their great fortress-emporium of Hormuz guarding the Gulf's entrance. The English obliged, and in 1622 a joint Anglo-Persian attack levelled Hormuz to the ground. The English reward was a factory at Bandar Abbas, the Shah's new port-city (called by the English Gombroon), and the promise of a half-share in its customs revenues. The attraction was silk, Persia's great export. But life for the English was harsh with a fierce climate, bad water, heavy mortality (perhaps 25 per cent a year 1617–52) and little diversion. 'There was but an Inch-Deal betwixt Gomberoon and Hell,' said John Fryer, who went there.[46] Dysentery, hepatitis, malaria, cholera and even the plague were in constant attendance. Drink and sex – 'toddy, rack and women' in the Company's phrase – were the main leisure pursuits of the English (the town prostitutes lived in open thatched huts) and, in the Company's view, the main cause of ill-health. The Company had its own country house and a garden away from the port, where conditions were cooler. But relations with the *shahbandar* – the chief port official – were frequently strained. In one violent fracas, six English were killed.[47] And in the Gulf, as almost everywhere else in the East, the English struggled to keep pace with the ubiquitous Dutch.

Company men and their ships combed India's coastline looking for markets and goods to exchange. In the 1640s they arrived in Bengal. By that time, however, the Coromandel coast, facing the Bay of Bengal, had become their main field of commercial activity: in Company parlance, this was 'the Coast' and 'the Bay'. They had set up a factory at its mercantile hub at Masulipatam by 1617. Then in 1639, seeking better terms from the ruler, they shifted their headquarters 200 miles further south, to Madraspatnam, soon shortened to Madras (and now called Chennai). From then until the late 1750s, when Clive set on foot the British conquest of Bengal, Fort St George at Madras was the Company's main stronghold on the Indian subcontinent.

Arriving from Britain after a voyage of four months (Robert Clive's voyage out in 1743 took more than a year, with an enforced stay in Brazil where his ship ran aground),[48] the traveller caught a first sight of Madras: 'You would see to port a long, low line of land rising above the sullen, troubled blue of the sea.' Soon the spire of St Mary's could be seen. 'Then the Fort itself would emerge into view, with its close built houses, with a dark, low muddled mass of buildings lying close to it on the north . . .'[49] There was no dock or pier: the ship stood out as much as two miles from the shore and passengers and cargo were carried through the heavy and dangerous surf in special surf-boats or *maselas* and left on the beach. Walking up from the strand the new arrival would see the walled White Town to his left with its close-packed flat-roofed brick houses, moat and drawbridge – this was Fort St George – and in front of him Black Town, the Indian quarter, where the properties and businesses ('houses of entertainment') of Portuguese and Armenians could also be found.[50] The territory the Company leased for around £400 a year stretched five miles along the coast and one mile inland; and leaving it needed the governor's permission. Its neighbour to the south was the old Portuguese settlement of São Tomé, reputedly the place where St Thomas was martyred. It had been partly the welcome the Portuguese offered that had attracted the Madras 'founder', Francis Day, to the spot.

Within fifty years of its founding, some 300,000 people had crowded into the Company's fiefdom.[51] The number of English was minute. After sixty years, the civilian population was estimated at 114: twenty-seven Company men, twenty-nine 'freemen' permitted by the Company to settle there, thirty-nine sailors, eleven widows and eight 'maidens'. The garrison swelled the total to around 400.[52] However exclusive their instincts, the Company men (an elaborate hierarchy, from the governor and council, through 'senior' and 'junior' merchants to the newly arrived 'writers') welcomed the presence of English private traders, confined theoretically to the country trade within Asia. The capital they brought out from London enlarged the available credit. Since they tended to settle, they gave the population of White Town a more permanent aspect. Indeed, Madras was more like a colony (if on the smallest of scales) than an outpost of expats longing for home; some Madras English stayed for generations.[53] But (quite apart from its Indians) Madras was not wholly or even mainly British. Among its leading families were Portuguese from São Tomé (Carvalhos, Madeiros), with whom the English intermarried. There were also Jews – Da Paiva, Rodrigues, Do Porto, Fonseca – drawn to Madras by the diamond trade with nearby Golkonda. Far from being outcasts, they enjoyed high social status: their funerals were attended by governor and council. The Company had been eager to attract Armenians to its settlements. A formal agreement in 1688 promised them equal rights with the English on Company territory, the right to travel on Company ships, and to hold civil office. It would build churches for them at its own expense. 'They are an innocent, harmless people ... sober, frugal and very wise in all the commodities and places of India,' declared the Company's all-powerful chairman, Sir Josiah Child.[54]

How did this cosmopolitan European society adapt to life in South

India? A major effort was made to preserve an English lifestyle. Hams, tongue, cheese and butter were brought out from England, unwisely packed in lead caskets. There was a heavy expenditure on English clothes and imported wine ('Shiraz' wine was imported from Persia via Bandar Abbas).[55] Religion remained the hallmark of Englishness, reinforced by the presence of an Anglican clergyman, prayers twice a day and the building of St Mary's. But in other respects, the English compromised with the climate and country. They used rattan blinds, not glass, in their windows. They washed far more than at home, less to be clean than to be cool. It became customary to spend at least part of the day in what was called 'moors dress': the loose jacket, trousers and slippers favoured by Muslims (a practice later banned for the Company's employees) – although European dress was required for church services. The shortage of marriageable women made concubinage commonplace. Meanwhile, the combination of boredom, anxiety and heat sharpened other proclivities. Both men and women smoked heavily (preferring the hookah to the pipe after *c.* 1700)[56] and chewed betel nut (staining their teeth and requiring spittoons). The consumption of drink (more than half a pint of brandy at a sitting was officially discouraged) was heroic and with inevitable consequences. Quarrels were endemic. Births and marriages were hugely outnumbered by burials. Indeed, funerals must have been one of the commonest social activities.

In other ways too the English could hardly forget the isolation and vulnerability of their enclave in South India. To conciliate their Portuguese subjects, they tolerated Catholicism in a way then unimaginable at home. They had to manage the large Indian population that had flocked into Black Town. That meant using local 'law men' (*adhikari*) to dispense justice and order, and, in deference to local belief, avoiding the death sentence even when its imposition would have been commonplace in England. In its own court in Madras, Hindu forms of oath were permitted.[57] In 1688, the Company went further. To make it easier to tax its Indian residents, it created a municipal council with thirteen aldermen: three English, three Portuguese and seven 'moors and gentoos' (i.e. Muslims and Hindus).[58] Looming over all was the threat of interference or worse by the Indian rulers nearby. The English were careful to keep on good terms with the Sultanate of

Golkonda, the great inland state, and ward off the periodic threat of blockade. In 1688, the prospect of a Maratha attack threw them into a panic. When the Mughal emperor Aurangzeb conquered Golkonda, they staged an obsequious public celebration in Madras and transferred their deference to his vassal, the Nizam of Hyderabad, and *his* vassal, the Nawab of the Carnatic, for whom a palace was built in the city. But the fortification even of Black Town in the late seventeenth century revealed the constant fear of a sudden attack by their turbulent neighbours.

It may have been this that lent an air of frenzy to money-making. Whatever the Company rules, both its servants and the private traders sent goods back to Britain as well as trading within Asia on their own account. In reality, the Company tolerated this practice despite spasmodic attempts at enforcement. Two of its governors made colossal fortunes in Madras by exactly these means. Elihu Yale was born in Boston, Massachusetts, and came out to Madras in 1672. By 1687 he was governor. He took as a mistress the widow of the Jewish diamond merchant Da Paiva: they went into business together. Yale's own private trade extended as far as the Philippines. By the time he went home in 1699, he could live in grand style and indulge in philanthropy – towards the Society for the Propagation of the Gospel (the Anglican mission which sent missionaries to Madras) as well as a then obscure college in New Haven, Connecticut, now named after him.[59] Thomas 'Diamond' Pitt was still more notorious. The son of the rector of Blandford in Dorset, he had come out to India in 1673 as an 'interloper' defying the Company's monopoly. When he went home ten years later, he was rich enough to buy land and become an MP. By the mid 1690s, having made peace with the Company, he came back in glory as governor. 'My leisure time I generally spend in Gardening and planting,' he told a correspondent at home.[60] In 1702, he bought the famous Pitt diamond for the enormous sum of £20,000: its eventual sale in 1717 to the regent of France for £125,000 helped seal the family fortune. Thomas's grandson was William Pitt, Earl of Chatham, the great war minister of 1757–60; his great grandson, 'Pitt the Younger', was to be prime minister.[61]

In the 1740s the pattern of English activity in Madras (and in India) was violently and unexpectedly transformed. In little more than a decade, the Company ceased to be primarily a trading concern. Instead its business became the conduct of war and diplomacy. It raised and dispatched armies. It competed for allies among the sub-continent's rulers at a time when the Mughal emperor in Delhi had been reduced to a symbol. It began to acquire revenue rights over wide districts, sometimes as reward for its military help. The path to the top in Company service became success on the battlefield (like Clive) or skill in financing its military and administrative needs. What had happened to cause this astounding transition?

The fuse had been lit by a conflict in Europe. When Britain and France went to war in 1744 over the future of Austria (and thus the power balance in Europe), hostilities quickly spread to the Americas and India. Exploiting the weakness of British sea power in the Bay of Bengal, the French launched an attack from their enclave at Pondi-cherry and captured Madras in 1746. The British clung on at nearby Fort St David, while Dupleix, the French governor, was hampered by the anger and resentment of the Nawab of Arcot, ally and patron of British Madras. With the coming of peace in 1748, the British recov-ered Madras. But an undeclared war in South India continued. Both sides recruited more troops from home. The Company sent out nearly 2,000 men, including 500 Swiss mercenaries, ten times the strength of its pre-war Madras garrison. By bribing and threatening and promis-ing military help to its allies, it struggled to choke off the rise of French influence over the greatest state in South India, the Hyderabad Niza-mate. But just as this effort was reaching its climax, the Company faced an appalling new crisis in its interests in Bengal.[62]

The expulsion of the Company from its fort and factory at Calcutta by the Nawab of Bengal in 1756, and the death and imprisonment of some of its servants, was a disaster that threatened the whole British position in India. Losing its trade on the Hooghly was a devastating blow to the Company. Bengal had already become its most valuable source of the fine cotton fabrics whose resale in Europe earned it most of its profits. But the Company's riposte to this outrage revealed how much it had changed in the decade since the temporary loss of Madras. It now had an army to send, and, in Clive, a commander already well versed not just in military tactics but in the trickier skills of finding and keeping the Indian allies and troops that were essential for victory. The remaking of Madras into a country power under British control, with an army, a revenue and diplomatic expertise, was the key precondition for the return to Bengal. The sequel was even more startling. Within less than ten years of Clive's scattering of the Nawab's army at Plassey (carefully preceded by the seduction of his chief men),[63] the Company took control of the province's revenues. With this second grand bridgehead, the richest region of India fell into its hands. Forty years later, its men ruled in Delhi. The merchants' frontier, their precarious perch on the coast, had turned into an empire.

FROM CONTACT TO POSSESSION

Of course, the events of the 1750s and 1760s in North America and South Asia were only the prelude to the ultimate triumph of a settler empire in one and the Company empire in the other. No one could then have foreseen the astonishing twists of fortune and war which created the American republic and then allowed it to seize the vast continental interior in 1803 (the so-called 'Louisiana Purchase');[64] or which allowed the East India Company to become the paramount of South Asia by 1818. Meanwhile, wide 'contact zones' – the American 'frontier', the Indian 'mofussil' (strictly 'the provinces') – lapped round the edges of these expanding bridgeheads of power. Indeed such zones could be found wherever British (or other European) merchants, migrants and missionaries moved into new regions: in Southern Africa, Australia, New Zealand and even, from the 1840s, in China. In these 'middle grounds'[65] where sovereignty claims were still lacking (as in pre-1840 New Zealand) or at best merely nominal, what counted as law was the custom of the country, amended by force or by private agreement. No one group had the power (or often the motive) to drive out the others and impose its own rules. Here the hard face of empire – conquest, domination, exclusion, separation – was not yet in place.

To some at least of the incomers, it was an era of freedom, to be recalled with nostalgia. 'Ah! Those good old times, when I first came to New Zealand, we shall never see their like again,' wrote Frederick Maning, grandson of a Dublin professor, who came to the North

Island from Tasmania in 1833. 'Those were the times – before governors were invented, and law and justice and all that.'[66] Maning relished the era when a handful of *pakeha* traders were prized by the Maori and enjoyed a scarcity value 'say about twenty times his own weight in muskets';[67] and regretted the changes that followed annexation and white settlement. Those Europeans who took service under rulers in India in the late eighteenth century, such as Michel Raymond in Hyderabad or Claude Martin in Awadh, were similarly valued as soldiers or 'brokers' and richly rewarded.[68] The gradual – sometimes very gradual – incorporation of these middle grounds reflected the scale and the speed at which empire-builders could move out from their bridgeheads, drawing reinforcements of men and money from home, or (usually *and*) conscripting local resources and manpower for the task.

Contact zones left a legacy, sometimes a large one, to the age of empire that followed. They had created hybrid cultures and mixed populations. These survived in the patois, jargon and dialects of colonial societies. They survived also in place-names. From a glance at the map of New Zealand, where Maori names are as numerous as British, it could hardly be guessed that Maori were scarcely 5 per cent of the population by 1914. They also survived physically in the 'mulattoes', 'Black English', 'Eurasians', 'métis', 'Cape Coloureds' and 'half-breeds' – the descendants of unions contracted before the colonial separation of races came into effect.[69] And perhaps they survived also as a memory of how life could be lived and fortunes acquired before the convenience of contact gave way to the fact of possession.

3
Taking Possession

On 6 August 1861, the island of Lagos, now part of the largest city in Nigeria, became a British possession. 'Yesterday,' reported the British consul the following day,

> an immense crowd had collected about the Consulate to witness the proceedings, and at 1 pm the King [of Lagos] landed under a salute of seven guns from the *Prometheus* anchored close by. After signing the treaty with four of his principal Chiefs, they were conducted to the flag-staff that had been erected outside; the Proclamation [of cession] was read, and the British flag unfurled, and saluted with twenty-one guns; the National Anthem sung by a band of children from the Missionary Schools ... and concluded with dinner on board the *Prometheus* to which Docemo [the king] and some of his principal men, and nearly all the Europeans in the place, were invited.[1]

The first article of the treaty of cession was brief and to the point. 'I, Docemo,' it read,

> do, with the consent and advice of my Council, give, transfer ... grant and confirm unto the Queen of Great Britain, her heirs and successors for ever, the port and Island of Lagos, with all the rights, profits, territories and appurtenances ... as the direct, full, and absolute dominion and sovereignty ... freely, fully, entirely, and absolutely ...

Docemo himself retained the title of king and was promised a pension. But there was little pretence that his mark on the treaty had been made voluntarily. 'The Commander [of the *Prometheus*] imposed on me to sign it,' he complained the next day, 'and if I do not he is ready to fire on the Island of Lagos and destroy it in the twinkling of an eye ...'[2]

Some ninety years earlier, a very different scene had been enacted on an island near Cape York, at the north-east tip of Australia. 'The pinnace and yawl, with the captain and gentlemen, went on shore to examine the country and view the coast from one of the hills,' wrote Captain Cook in his log for 22 August 1770. 'At 6 possession was taken of this country in His Majesty's name and under his colours; fired several volleys of small arms on the occasion, and cheered three times, which was answered from the ship.'[3] Apart from Cook and his party, there was no one to witness this historic occasion (except perhaps for some unseen 'Indians' – Cook's word for aborigines – whose 'smoaks' had been seen earlier that day), and no one to contest Cook's claim 'to the whole Eastern Coast . . . by the name of New South Wales, together with all the Bays, Harbours and Rivers situate upon the said coast . . .'[4] Confident that no other European power had discovered this side of Australia, and equally confident (with momentous consequences) that there were no chiefs or kings whose local authority he might have to respect, Cook sailed blithely away. Eastern Australia (all unknowing) was now a British possession.

Still more picturesque was the ritual the British conducted when they annexed the Kowloon peninsula, across the harbour from their island colony of Hong Kong, in 1860. The British governor, Harry Parkes, handed the Chinese officials a piece of earth wrapped in paper. They handed it back as a symbol of transfer. The proclamation of cession was then read aloud, the royal standard was raised and a volley was fired. With three cheers for 'Old England', three more for 'the Queen', and a fresh blast of gunfire, the transaction was over: Kowloon was British (except for a fortified enclosure, the 'Kowloon walled city', which the negotiators unaccountably forgot in their haste).[5]

Crude ceremonies such as these symbolized the decisive act of imperial expansion: the annexation of territory. Annexation converted vague zones of influence and interest into formal possessions of the British Crown. Henceforth, they could not be lightly abandoned, however troublesome or unprofitable they proved. London also had to prescribe (sometimes in intricate detail) how its new acquisitions should be governed. It had to decide what status to grant to new 'subject peoples' and those who had ruled them. It had to make up its mind on what forms of law they should have and whether or not to respect their ideas about property, punishment and the practice of religion. It was soon pressed to lay down the conditions on which incomers and immigrants could buy land from the locals, and if they should be subject to the same regime as the natives. There was no standardized formula. Although there were certain broad categories of colonial rule, almost every acquisition brought its own special history, and demanded customized features. Both time and place mattered. Sometimes no local ruler appeared to chase the intruders away or disrupt their mumbo-jumbo proclamations. Sometimes, like King Docemo, he could be pushed brusquely aside with a pension. Sometimes, like the Zulu king Cetswayo, he was imprisoned and exiled. And behind each annexation usually lay some special interest at home, private or public, which had lobbied vociferously for this new province of empire: any new regime on the spot would have to satisfy them. The terms of annexation were just as important as the act of annexation itself.

The dramas played out by Consul McCroskey and Captain Cook show the huge range of meanings that annexation could hold. The cession of Lagos had a definite purpose laid down by London: to suppress the slave trade by gaining closer control over the West African ports where – so the British believed – slave traders still lurked with impunity despite the ruler's promise to expel them. The cession was limited to the island of Lagos: the mainland interior was not London's objective. McCroskey's instructions were to extract a treaty from Docemo so that Lagos would be ceded voluntarily, not taken by force. Docemo's status as king and his royal authority over the native population would be (at least outwardly) preserved. Cook's proceedings were utterly different. His instructions were vague. They encouraged him to claim territory thus far unvisited by other European powers which might be useful for Britain's future maritime interests in the South Pacific. Cook was supposed to seek the locals' consent before annexing their lands. In fact, by the time he went ashore at what became Possession Island, Cook was already convinced that the aboriginal population was so scattered and sparse, and so lacking in permanent settlements, that it had no rulers with whom to make treaties – and so had no claim to the land he proposed to annex. Of course, it could hardly be said that an occasional landing on the beaches of a huge continent was much of a basis for such a sweeping conclusion. Indeed Cook could have had no more than the vaguest idea of the nature of the land he was claiming for King George. There is something almost comical about the little ritual he staged. One imagines a storm-tossed crew of West African fishermen landing on Iceland and, seeing no one about, annexing Europe to Dahomey. Yet Cook's conviction that no settled population existed had immense implications. It became a fixed doctrine. New South Wales (Cook's name), said the British Law Officers in 1819, had not 'been acquired by conquest or cession but taken possession of . . . as *desert and uninhabited*, and subsequently colonized from this country'.[6] Australia was – in the eyes of British law – an empty land. Its aboriginal population had no legal existence. The consequences and complications of this we shall see later on.

There was one other great difference that these two cases highlight. Since the fifteenth century, the European states had recognized two distinct ways in which they could legitimately add to their territory – apart, that is, from dynastic inheritance. The first was by what was called 'discovery'. Overseas countries (outside Europe and Asia) to which no 'Christian prince' had laid a previous claim and which no European had properly visited or on which he had not left the mark of his presence, could be justly acquired. In practice that might mean reaching some form of agreement with other Christian princes to avoid a dispute. This left on one side how original inhabitants and their rulers should be dealt with. The second, which applied to Europe, most of Asia and those parts of Africa where Europeans found what they regarded as recognizable states, was quite different. Where states did exist, they could be made subject only in one of two ways: by cession or conquest. Cession was usually set down in a treaty – like that with Docemo – that specified what rights were transferred to the new sovereign power. The often dubious means by which agreement was gained did not appear in the treaty or affect its 'legality' – its claim to acceptance by other European states. Conquest was more arduous and usually much more expensive. By and large, the British, like other European empires, preferred a coerced form of cession to the hazardous enterprise of seeking outright military victory in a faraway place. In theory, however, conquest was best. It obliterated all local rights and left the conquered population entirely dependent on the goodwill of the conqueror, who held their lives in his hands. Far-fetched as they may seem as the basis on which whole peoples might be treated, discovery, cession and conquest were not simply legal fictions. As we shall see, they shaped the terms of possession and all that followed from them.

Yet the act of taking possession was in the end the work of individuals or groups and reflected the influence of their prejudices, hopes and ambitions. The motives of those who wanted the lawful possession that annexation secured and the reasons why governments were willing to indulge their desires are crucial to understanding how the British Empire was made. It is not always clear what possession actually meant, both for those who rushed to exploit its promise and those on whom possession was imposed – sometimes, as we have seen, without their knowledge, let alone their consent. The results of taking possession – so often presented as creating order from chaos – were often extremely untidy, a mass of loose ends, contradictions and unfinished projects. Empire-building was always a work in progress, like a house extension in which the design, the builders and even the building materials were constantly changing.

MOTIVES

The first puzzle to solve is why British expansion should require the formal extension of sovereignty that annexation embodied. It is easily forgotten that to a huge extent British empire-building was the work of private entrepreneurs, not of the state or the 'Crown' (the usual term for executive authority in the British case). The earliest attempts to found an English colony on the North American continent at Roanoke Island in 1585 was the private venture of Sir Walter Ralegh and his associates. Roanoke was a disaster: the party of men left behind to guard the settlement after food had run short disappeared without trace, presumably murdered by the Indians who resented their presence. The next venture, at Jamestown, was a precarious success. It was founded by the Virginia Company, whose backers included the Earl of Salisbury and a City grandee, Sir Thomas Smythe, as well as other merchants and aristocrats. The Company was wound up in 1624, but colonizing enterprises continued to be organized by companies or individual 'proprietors' for the rest of the century. The Plymouth Company (1620) and the New England Company (that became the Massachusetts Company in 1630) promoted the settlement of the 'northern colonies'. Maryland in the Chesapeake was founded by Sir George Calvert, Lord Baltimore, a Catholic aristocrat, in 1634. Pennsylvania was the project of William Penn, the son of an admiral and a convert to Quakerism. The Carolinas were colonized in 1670 by a group of eight proprietors, including Lord Shaftesbury, the patron of John Locke, and Lord Clarendon, Charles II's closest adviser.

This pattern was not peculiar to the American mainland or to the seventeenth century. In what became the British West Indies, the 'Caribbees' – Barbados, St Kitts, Nevis and Montserrat – were targeted by rival English combines led by the Earl of Carlisle and Sir William Courteen, another City businessman with commercial interests in the Near East and later in India. The Guinea Company of 1588 was the first attempt to exploit West African trade. It would turn eventually into the Royal African Company of 1672, whose main business was the slave trade, and whose forts on the Gambia river and at Cape Coast in modern Ghana were the germ of Britain's West African empire. Two centuries later, the Royal Niger Company, the Imperial British East African Company and Cecil Rhodes's British South Africa Company were the vehicles of a private imperialism dragging behind them with varying degrees of reluctance the government in London. New Zealand was the site of British colonization (by the New Zealand Company) before London's grudging annexation in 1840. What was to become Britain's grandest colony of all, the British Empire in India, began as the Company of Merchants ... Trading into the East Indies. After 1757 and the sharp skirmish at Plassey in Bengal, the Company was abruptly transformed into a colonial state. But it was a century later, in 1858, and only after the catastrophe of the Great Rebellion in North India, the 'Indian Mutiny', that India ceased to be a Company Raj.

Private empire-building had to be funded (if only at first) by wealthy backers in Britain. It was invariably speculative, a mixture of risk, which can be calculated, and uncertainty, which can not.[7] The investors hoped for spectacular profits by surviving the risks and containing the uncertainties. They aimed to do this by cornering the market in some high-value commodity, or by acquiring land cheaply (perhaps even for nothing) and selling it on to the emigrants they recruited. There were other motives as well. Plymouth and Massachusetts were meant to be refuges for oppressed English Puritans, as Maryland for Catholics. Georgia, a later foundation, was to provide for the indigent poor with no prospects at home. In nineteenth-century East Africa, the commercial designs of the British East Africa Company were mixed with the aim of achieving Christian conversion: its Scottish promoters were inspired by David Livingstone's formula of 'Christianity, commerce and civilization'. Rhodes's company was meant to surround the Boer republics to the south and squeeze them into an all-British South Africa. In all these cases, some form of possession was needed. Even trading companies, like those in India or West Africa, wanted a secure base where goods and personnel would be safe from local predation or attack by European rivals. The East India Company negotiated the right (in the form of a *firman* from the Mughal emperor) to set up its fortified factories at Madras and Calcutta, and before that at Surat where the merchants shared a house and dined and slept together (as in an old-style Oxford college, the inmates needed permission to be out overnight). Where a settlement was the aim, companies and proprietors had to buy or seize land, to exclude local people and provide a secure title to incomers. Politically, too, a clear right of possession to a definite tract could be a useful weapon against native rulers, as long as they lacked the will or the means to drive the foreigner out. It signalled the intent to be a permanent fixture, not a transient visitor. It made it much easier to attract local labour and skills – like the Indian merchants and artisans drawn into the Company's enclaves, the 'Black Towns' of Madras and Calcutta. It might even allow a small army to be raised. And it enabled the British to apply their own laws when they dealt with each other.[8]

But why did these private imperialists ask for 'charters' and 'patents' from the government in London? After all, they had little reason to wish for any outside control and loathed interference from Whitehall. They regarded themselves as much the best judges of the local political scene: their men on the spot would know how to deal with any difficulty there. But in their charters and patents they had to acknowledge the ultimate authority of the government at home over their local activities. They might have been private imperialists, but they also became in law the agents of empire: over what they possessed on the ground was extended like an umbrella the sovereignty of Great Britain. Thus when James I granted a patent to plant a colony in Newfoundland in 1623 (not, it turned out, a very promising venture), the grantee, Sir George Calvert, acknowledged royal authority as if he were in England, symbolized by the promise to provide a white horse in the unlikely event that the king should set foot in his colony.[9] The Virginia charter of 1606 reserved the king's right to lay down the form of the colony's government and appoint a council in London with supervisory powers. Any settlers who went there would remain his subjects.[10] Even the independent-minded Massachusetts Company acknowledged its dependence on the Crown and the obligation to conform its laws to those current in England.[11]

The willingness to accept this subordinate status rather than strike out on their own and found independent 'republics' sprang from four powerful constraints that retained their force into the late nineteenth century. The first was the need for diplomatic (and perhaps military) help. Among the European states territorial claims had to be made by governments: private empire-builders needed their endorsement to exclude foreign rivals. When Rhodes's 'Pioneer Column' marched into what is now Zimbabwe, it took an ultimatum from Lord Salisbury – the threat to break off relations (and perhaps use naval coercion) – to deter the rival Portuguese from contesting his claim. British merchants in Asia (in India and China especially) also liked the support of a royal emissary when dealing with rulers who showed little respect for mere men of trade. Second, and just as important, was the need to protect their interests against an interloper from home. The main point of obtaining a charter or patent was to secure the monopoly rights to a tract of land or a particular trade link. 'No other of my subjects,' said the Virginia Company's charter from James I, 'shall be permitted . . . to plant or inhabit behind or in the Backside of them . . .'[12] Monopoly was the key to hopes of a profit in such speculative ventures: no wise investor would have settled for less. Proprietors and partners spent much of their time fighting off other claimants. They had to do this by invoking official support, if need be in the courts, against any challenger – a task that required almost constant attention to the balance of influence at court or in government circles. A change in the political wind might cancel their patent and expose them to ruin.

This need to protect their position at home is a reminder of how much the success of trading and colonizing efforts relied on domestic resources of money and men. But there were other motives as well. Thirdly, colonial promoters, like the chief merchants in India, needed authority over the settlers and servants they recruited once out of England. Without a mandate from home, they had no jurisdiction: no right to enforce the contracts they made; no lawful means of preventing those they brought out from claiming the land as their own – or decamping completely; no legal power to lay down local rules or punish those who broke them.[13] Without some form of extra-territorial authority, all the bonds, obligations or contractual undertakings that bound men together in England were simply dissolved by stepping into no man's land. In theory, of course, they might be imposed by brute force, but that was a clumsy, expensive, and probably futile recourse. It would also deter the respectable people whom promoters were most anxious to attract. So the fourth reason was the fact that it would have been much harder to recruit settlers and servants without some guarantee that they would keep the civil rights that they already enjoyed – especially to property and personal freedom. 'All and every the Person . . . who shall dwell and inhabit within . . . any of the said colonies,' said the Virginia charter, 'and every of their children . . . shall have and enjoy all Liberties, Franchises and immunities of free denizens and natural subjects . . . as if they had been abiding and born within this our Realm of England . . .'[14]

But we should turn the argument round. Why should the Crown and later British governments assume the burden and risk of extending British sovereignty over faraway regions? After all, there was always the chance that it would lead them into conflict with a rival power, endangering their prestige abroad and their safety at home. This was a more or less constant anxiety from the time of Elizabeth I up to and after the end of empire. Still worse was the problem that if the men on the spot got themselves into trouble, it was hard to disown them however reckless their actions, or leave them to destruction by indigenous peoples, however deserved. One advantage of sovereignty was, in theory at least, that it might make it easier to control these headstrong adventurers before they became a serious nuisance. This was how London tended to view many if not all of its settler offspring from the seventeenth through to the twentieth centuries. The clear assertion of sovereignty over the East India Company's empire in India was made eventually in 1858 – after the Company government had had a close shave with catastrophe in 1857. But sovereignty, as we shall see, was not the same as control.

One motive early on was the hope of a windfall. Tudor and Stuart monarchs were careful to write into their charters and patents that if any precious metals were found, one fifth would be theirs.[15] The huge stream of silver that poured into Spain from its American empire made this a plausible hope. But this mercenary aim was mixed soon enough with a shrewder view of the government's interest. Behind Elizabeth's grant of a charter to the East India merchants was the fear (no doubt encouraged by them) that the highly profitable trade with the 'East Indies' (today's Indonesia) would be monopolized by the Dutch. Why should this matter to the queen and her ministers? Because by this time, it was already a cliché that trade nourished the realm and supplied much of its revenue. The taxes on trade as it passed through the customs houses were the easiest to collect. It was also becoming the conventional wisdom that trade was vital to the power of the state in a broader sense. Contemporary thinkers insisted that a surplus of exports was the key object of commerce, for a surplus ensured that the balance was paid over in silver or gold – bullion or treasure (the only alternative being to find silver mines of your own, as the Spanish had done). A large stock of bullion kept the state prosperous and safe. It meant that there was plenty of coin in circulation, and coin was essential for most normal transactions: without it trade froze. Bullion also provided a war-chest, the means to buy weapons or hire mercenaries quickly in a pre-industrial world where 'war economies' could not be imagined. But how to build up such a surplus of exports? The most promising strategy, most observers maintained, was to find exotic commodities which could be resold at great profit to consumers in Europe: spices, Indian fabrics, Chinese porcelain and silk, as well as furs, tobacco and sugar from the western plantations.[16]

The state's interest in commerce was thus a key motive for the assertion of sovereignty – or as much as was needed to 'regulate' trade. Colonial adventurers could not be allowed to carry their produce wherever they liked. From the 1650s, a series of laws – the Navigation Acts – forced them to send any valuable ('enumerated') product to a British port first (where it would pay duty) before being re-exported. It would have to be carried in a British ship, manned by a British crew, since ships and crew were a national asset in time of war, and a large merchant fleet was the key to naval success. This was meant to ensure that the profits of trade flowed mainly to Britain and that colonial producers would have little choice but to buy what they needed from British suppliers. By the mid eighteenth century, government, trade and the exertion of sovereign power were laced together in a huge vested interest. For its part, the London government expected that an East India Company grown fat on its monopoly trade would supply it with loans. The fear of its failing, and bringing down the rest of the City, became a critical factor in ministers' Indian policy by the 1770s.

Alongside this equation of profit and power ran two older almost visceral instincts. Firstly, governments in Britain, whether royal or parliamentary, were extremely reluctant to give up their claim on their subjects' allegiance. This may have reflected the age-old assumption that a ruler's strength and authority sprang from command over men: manpower not land was the true source of power. Withdrawing one's labour and productive potential from the reach of the ruler to whom allegiance was owed was therefore an act of betrayal, perhaps even of treason. The expansion of sovereignty was thus in part a device to preserve the state's claim to its most valuable asset, the muscle and skill of its people. Secondly, in pre-modern times especially, rulers were deeply suspicious of any attempt by their wealthier subjects to establish bases abroad in case they became a refuge for rebels and a launch-pad for invasion. The English connection with Ireland derived from the time when a great Marcher lord, Strongbow, Earl of Pembroke, was invited to lead one of the sides in the Irish factional wars. No king of England could allow so powerful a figure to build up a lordship spanning Ireland and Wales. In 1171, Henry II staged an invasion, and the following year claimed the Lordship of Ireland, with the support of the Pope.[17] The 'Strongbow rule' – that allegiance could not be shrugged off by going abroad – was enforced by English governments whenever they could. Hence the provision we have noticed already, that those taken abroad as migrants and settlers remained the king's subjects. Hence, too, the rule laid down in the 'Case of the Indian Chief' in 1801, that the British (and other Europeans) who lived in India, even in places where the Mughal emperor was technically sovereign, remained British subjects. 'Wherever even a mere factory is founded in the eastern parts of the world,' ran the judgment, 'European persons trading under the shelter and protection of those establishments are conceived to take their national character from the association under which they live and carry on their commerce.'[18] When discontented Boers trekked out of Cape Colony in the 1830s, the British insisted that nothing had changed: they remained British subjects, like it or not. The Cape of Good Hope Punishment Act of 1836 extended the authority of British magistrates over 'British subjects' as far as 25 degrees south, approximately fifty miles north of modern Pretoria. As one historian remarked caustically, 'It was an act that needed a regiment to give it effect.'[19] What governments at home disliked most of all was the idea of private individuals acquiring land directly from native peoples in newfound lands. From almost the very beginnings of colonization in America, they tried to insist that this should be done only through an authorized body with the legal power to grant 'title'. Anything else, so their reasoning went, was bound to cause trouble. In a system of government that regarded the lawful regulation of property as the touchstone of order, a less prim point of view would have been very surprising.

Lastly, of course, governments did not invariably leave it to private imperialists to take the lead in expansion. Indeed, a substantial part of the empire was acquired directly by the state, including Jamaica (1655), New York (1664), much of Canada (1763), Eastern Australia (1770–88), Trinidad (1797), Cape Colony, Sri Lanka and Mauritius (1815), Hong Kong (1842) and Kenya (1895). A mixture of impulses was at work in these cases. Some of them might be seen as the booty of wars fought for quite different reasons. With their advantage at sea, British governments were tempted to punish their enemies by seizing their colonies and disrupting their trade. The 'mercantilist' logic that we have noticed already implied that this would increase the national wealth. Even after 'free trade' had supplanted mercantilism as the ruling commercial ideology, a well-placed port such as Hong Kong helped to enforce an open economy on troublesome foreigners and their recalcitrant rulers. But as often as not, the prevailing concern was chiefly strategic. London decided that it must have Canada (and not sugar-rich Guadeloupe) because French control of Quebec and its riverine hinterland was too great a threat to British America. The same argument applied at the Cape, which guarded the sea-route to India and the East. Here it was fear that the Dutch would give it away to the colossus Napoleon (or a no less dangerous successor) that decided the British not to return it when peace finally came in 1815. By keeping Mauritius and Sri Lanka as well, they turned the Indian Ocean into a 'British lake' for more than a century. These were colonies by cession or conquest, not settlement. How to govern them, transforming possession into rule, became an immediate question.

GOVERNANCE

The earliest charters and patents granted by the Crown to the founders of plantations in America and the West Indies showed little interest in the question of how their local government should be organized. Nevertheless, it was quickly established that settler populations should enjoy a form of representative government. As early as 1619, twelve years after the first landing at Jamestown, elections were held for a Virginia assembly: male settlers over sixteen could cast a vote. The royal instructions to the governor in 1641 explicitly told him to convene an assembly of 'burgesses'.[20] The Barbados settlers took advantage of the conflicts between rival proprietors to assert their assembly's right to virtual self-government in 1668. The revised charter for Massachusetts issued in 1691 (after the Glorious Revolution of 1688) prescribed what had become the standard model for the settlement colonies: government by an elected assembly, an appointive 'council', and a governor sent from Britain and answerable to the king and his ministers.[21] By 1700, in fact, the effort to impose a more direct form of rule – for example by demanding that laws passed by the assemblies should be initiated by the Crown – had petered out in frustration: settler resistance was much too determined. In 1722, the Privy Council in London, as the supervisory body for colonial affairs, summed up the constitutional position as follows: '. . . If there be a new and uninhabited country found out by English subjects as the law is the birthright of every subject so, wherever they go, they carry their laws with them, and therefore such newfound country is to be governed by the laws of England.'[22] The sting in the tail was the doctrine of 'repugnancy' – the principle that colonial laws should not be incompatible with English law. However, in practical terms it was hard to know what the current state of English common law was (without the circulation of authoritative 'law reports'). Nor was it obvious which parliamentary statutes were meant to apply to the colonies. The Privy Council took a pragmatic view: 'After any such country is inhabited by the English, Acts of Parliament, without naming the foreign plantations, will not bind them.'[23] Indeed from then until the great crisis that burst out eventually in the American revolution, London interfered very little with the governance of its colonies, except in matters of trade. It was this that concerned the interests represented in Parliament.

Things were more complicated where possession was not the result of occupations by chartered private imperialists and their followers, but had occurred through conquest or cession. Theoretically distinct, both conquest and cession were usually formalized by some form of agreement: the 'terms of surrender' that were later inserted into the text of a treaty. The effect was to limit (sometimes quite drastically) the power to impose a new system of rule on the conquered population. In the case of Quebec, captured by the British in 1759–60, and ceded by France in the 1763 Treaty of Paris, this produced doubt and confusion at a dangerous time. The British bound themselves to respect the French-Canadians' right to retain their Catholic religion. But the first governor's instructions required him to introduce 'the laws of England' and set up an assembly on the standard British American model. However, Catholics in England could not sit on juries nor sit in assemblies, and the law of England, especially on property, was very different from the version of French law that prevailed in Quebec. If the instruction were followed, the tiny Protestant Anglophone minority in the province (perhaps 200 incomers) would have astonishing power: the subject majority (some 60,000 *Canadiens*) might be driven into revolt. By the time that London had fully understood the problem, the prospect of rebellion in Quebec on top of the seething unrest in the Thirteen Colonies to the south made a new solution seem urgent. The Quebec Act of 1774 grasped the nettle. It rejected the claim of the British minority to English law and institutions. Instead, it permitted the governor to choose the members of the colony's law-making body (the legislative council) without regard to religion, and to maintain local property law. In constitutional terms, it was a revolutionary change, setting the pattern for the flood of possessions to come where there were no British settlers or at best very few. In a crucial judgment made in the same year (the case of Campbell *v.* Hall, 1774), the rule was laid down that in such cases an 'Englishman ... has no privilege distinct from the natives while he continues there'.[24] When the British captured Cape Colony from the Dutch in 1795, the governor was simply directed to maintain 'the laws and institutions that subsisted under the antient government of the said settlement'.[25]

In practice, therefore, across a huge swathe of empire, possession was no guarantee that British forms of governance would be introduced or imposed. Whether circumscribed by treaties or the pragmatic desire to avoid too much local resistance, the British accepted the need to keep the apparatus of administration and law much as they found it – although often only after a period of conflict and uncertainty as they muddled their way on to the local political stage. In Sri Lanka, for example, that meant first trying and then scrapping the administrative system used in nearby Madras; conceding virtual self-rule to the interior kingdom of Kandy, and then reuniting it with the 'maritime' provinces where Dutch influence had been strongest. In 1840, nearly fifty years after its conquest (in 1796), a British official on the island remarked rather ruefully: 'It is very difficult indeed to say what the law is upon any question or where it is to be looked for: there is the Roman Dutch law – old Custom – Local laws – separate codes for the Hindoo and Mussulman population, and in the interior

Kandian law. Many of these the Judges of the Supreme Court have no means of knowing.'[26] Similar complaints could have been made all over what came to be called the 'Crown colony' empire. Here possession was at best a work in progress.

Nowhere perhaps was the question of what possession amounted to more baffling and complex than in Ireland and India. English kings may have acquired the Lordship of Ireland before 1200, but there had been little prospect of enforcing English law and custom except in the main ports or within Dublin's near hinterland. It was hard enough to dissuade the English who came over from intermarrying and 'going native'.[27] The Elizabethan conquest in the sixteenth century was intended to make the Crown supreme once and for all so that no Irish magnate or chief could deny it his allegiance.[28] But the conquest stalled and in the following century civil war and revolution in England allowed two great rebellions to spring up against Protestant English rule. William III's victory at the Boyne on 1 July 1690 seemed to settle the matter. So it did up to a point. Catholics were denied the franchise and excluded from public office, while many of those who had fought for James II suffered the confiscation of their lands.[29] Yet what was still unresolved was whether Ireland was a separate kingdom sharing a common Crown with Great Britain, or whether it was a British possession, subject to the will and whim of the English (later British) Parliament. The declaratory act passed at Westminster in 1719 laid down the law: 'The . . . Kingdom of Ireland hath been, is, and by Right ought to be subordinate unto and dependent upon the Imperial Crown of Great Britain, as being inseparably united and annexed thereunto . . . and that the King's Majesty by and with the consent of the Lords . . . and Commons . . . in Parliament assembled [had] full power and authority to make Laws and Statutes . . . to bind the Kingdom of Ireland.'[30] The population of Ireland, said the ministry's spokesman, were either 'native Irish' and thus a conquered people, or colonists from Britain.[31] In either case they were subject to the British Parliament. The Protestant garrison in Ireland dared not complain, although its leaders worked hard to minimize interference from London. But sixty years later, when the British Empire was plunged into crisis by the rebellion in America, they forced the Westminster Parliament to renounce its supremacy and acknowledge

Ireland's separate status as a sister kingdom under the Crown. It took the trauma of war (Catholic) rebellion and an invasion from France, as well as a heroic campaign of corruption, to induce a parliament of Irish Protestant landowners to abolish itself in 1800 and accept union with Britain. And that, as we know, was not the end of the story.

Although by 1757 the East India Company held their forts at Bombay (modern Mumbai) and Madras (modern Chennai) by right and not by a grant from an Indian ruler (the Company leased Madras for 1,200 gold pagodas a year, about £400), it was the victory at Plassey in Bengal that marked the real onset of its change into a territorial power. In 1765 the Company assumed the *diwani* of Bengal – the right to collect the revenue in return for a fixed payment to the Mughal emperor in Delhi. For all practical purposes, it became the ruler of much of eastern India. Aggressive diplomacy backed by military power pushed its control up the Ganges valley, and inland from Madras, where it fought a series of wars against the rising state of Mysore. This great change in its role on the Indian subcontinent raised a series of questions about its constitutional status. The government in London, the Company's guarantor against other great powers, demanded more control over the men on the spot and feared that over-expansion would wreck its finances. Like a modern-day bank, the Company was too big to fail: the effect of its bankruptcy on British finance would have been catastrophic. So a series of measures led to the India Act of 1784, by which the Company's Indian budgets for its three 'presidencies' in Bombay, Madras and Bengal, its external and military policy and its choice of governor-general would be supervised by a Board of Control and a cabinet minister. This system survived until the Company's abolition in 1858, when its London head office and the Board of Control were merged into the India Office under a secretary of state.

But when did India become 'British' and what was implied by possession? There is no simple answer. It was laid down as early as 1757 that territory conquered by the Company automatically became part of the king's dominions. But most of the Company's territory was a feudal grant from the Mughal emperor, for which tribute was paid. The tribute was stopped in 1772, but it was only after 1800 that the

Company asserted the claim to be sovereign over the zones that it ruled. Even so, much of its power in the subcontinent depended upon treaties concluded with Indian rulers. Were they allies or subjects? It was convenient to be vague. Then there was the question of law. In a notorious case in 1774, Nanda Kumar was executed for the crime of making counterfeit money. But should he have been subject to the law of England which prescribed this savage penalty, or to local laws whose view was much milder? Loud voices were raised among Company officials against the injustice (and danger) of imposing rules and punishments that local society could not comprehend. The laws must be codified, but they had to respect local custom and usage, and also difference of practice between Muslims and Hindus. The same issue arose over taxation and property and also religion. British opinion was fiercely opposed to feudal type tenures where all land was held from the ruler on payment of service or money, and fiercely in favour of individualized property. This, it was argued, was the secret of 'improvement'. But such a radical change was completely impracticable and risked a vast rural revolt. So while they experimented with a limited reform in Bengal, over much of India the British preserved the existing system of landholding. The Company also decided early on to avoid any appearance of championing the Christian religion or of promoting conversion. It took a furious campaign at the time of its charter's renewal in 1813 to force it even to let Christian missionaries into its territories. It was undoubtedly true that there was strong Evangelical feeling among some British officials (one reason perhaps why the Company reluctantly banned the practice of suttee). But some of the most powerful and influential of the Company's servants in India denounced interference with Indian political practice and the denial to Indians of real authority. 'The ruling vice of our government,' said Sir Thomas Munro in 1824, 'is innovation.'[32] 'I fear that some downright Englishman . . . will insist on making Anglo-Saxons of the Hindoos.'[33]

India's vast size, the different imperatives that ruled Company policy in different parts of the subcontinent, as well as variations in indigenous practice, meant that there was no uniform pattern in the way British rule was imposed, and considerable uncertainty as late as the Great Rebellion of 1857 over whom it extended. The result was more than a little confusion. 'There is,' complained the Chief Justice of Bengal in 1830,

> no uniform, no definite opinion, either as to the true character . . . of the sovereignty of the Crown, nor of the dependence of the laws on Parliament, nor as to the rights either of political power or of property of the East India Company, nor even of the relations in which the many millions of natives stand to the political authorities by which they are entirely governed . . . There are English Acts of Parliament specially provided for India, and others of which it is doubtful if they apply to India wholly or in part, or not at all. There is the English common law and constitution, of which the application is . . . still more obscure and perplexed; Mahamedan law and usage; Hindoo law, usage and Scripture; charters and letters patent of the Crown; regulations of the Governments . . . treaties of the Crown; treaties of the Indian governments; besides inference drawn from . . . the law of nations of Europe . . .[34]

India, in short, was a world of its own. But what difference did it make?

What mattered most to the British was that possession excluded all other powers and denied Indian rulers any external connections except with Britain alone. What they came to realize, as we shall see in subsequent chapters, is that there were strict limitations on the positive power that possession conferred. Indians could be taxed to maintain a large army for Britain's convenience. Indian textile producers could be denied tariff protection against British exports. But Indians had to be governed without affronting local opinion – a lesson relearned in 1857. The cautious construction of a hybrid political system became unavoidable. The tension between what it meant to be British and what was implied by British possession would never disappear.

POSSESSING THE LAND

Sovereignty and possession are abstract concepts, and, as we have just seen, it was possible for British rule to occupy, conquer, tax, and make war and peace despite legal uncertainties that drove lawyers to distraction (perhaps the normal state of the real world). Whether a colony was conquered or settled, and exactly when cession had happened, did indeed affect individual rights and titles – the reason why the issue burst into the law courts (and thus into our histories). But much more important for much larger numbers of people was what possession was to mean in terms of their livelihood, their personal property, and above all their land rights. This was not a trivial issue in India, Burma and other dependencies, where British rule introduced new legal ways in which land could be bought and sold, or its occupiers dispossessed for debts and defaults: the results of this could be profoundly disturbing.[35] But with relatively few exceptions (such as European-owned plantations for tea and indigo in India and Sri Lanka and later rubber in Malaya), there was no large-scale transfer of land from the native population to settlers in Britain's Asian dependencies, nor was there in West Africa. But in much of the rest of the empire – in North America, Australia, New Zealand and in British-ruled South, Central and East Africa – the reverse was the case and dispossession occurred on a massive scale. Here British possession became very real indeed and its effects very visible. But what had happened, and how had this come about? What was the connection between sovereignty (what the lawyers called '*imperium*') and the acquisition of the land (so-called '*dominium*')?

'The best right of possession in America,' said Oliver Cromwell in 1655, 'is that which is founded on one's having planted colonies there, and settled in such places as had either no inhabitants, or by the consent of the inhabitants, if there were any; or at least in some of the wild and uncultivated places of their country, which they were not numerous enough to replenish and improve; since God has created the earth for the use of men and ordered them to replenish it throughout . . .'[36] In fact, governments in London during the first century of the colonization of North America showed a perhaps surprising indifference to the meaning of their charters and patents for the indigenous peoples and their rights to the land. Although some early charters apparently granted the right to dispose of the land, as Cromwell's words suggested, this did not give authority to seize it by force from the original inhabitants. The presumption seems to have been that Indians should be dealt with as separate communities, although how far they remained 'sovereign' was left rather vague.[37] As far as the question of indigenous property rights was concerned, there was no dominant view. Cromwell's dictum neatly embraced three contradictory views: that it was best to move in where no one else lived; that otherwise 'consent' (implying purchase) was the right course of action; but that there was biblical authority to occupy land whose inhabitants lacked the will or the means to improve it. Indeed, some influential observers held to the view that land that was not actively cultivated was there for the taking, an idea famously expressed by the philosopher John Locke who argued that property came into existence only when men's labour was mixed with the land – a condition that did not apply if the inhabitants were shifting, nomadic or lived by hunting and gathering.

Between the sixteenth century and the twentieth, the English (later British) resorted to five different ways of taking the land from its original inhabitants. The immediate precedent for the colonization of America was the Tudors' colonization of Ireland. The motive here was plainly political: to restore royal (and English) authority over Irish clans and rebellious magnates. The method was to 'plant' English settlers and impose English-style counties in troublesome districts. The Irish accused of rebellion forfeited their land. If they submitted, one third was returned (for a payment), but the rest was granted to 'undertakers', on their promise to bring over settlers from England (in the case of Ulster, from Scotland) who would improve the soil and serve as a garrison and who were strictly forbidden to intermarry with the Irish.[38] Among those favoured with such land grants was Sir Walter Raleigh, who obtained some 40,000 acres in Counties Waterford, Cork and Tipperary – a princely estate. Of course, not all went according to plan. In the face of this onslaught, Irish resistance was fierce and the sense of grievance tenacious. Their wholesale removal was often imposed at the point of the sword. Some of the settlers fell far short of ideal: 'There were out of England . . . traitors, murderers, thieves, coseners [fraudsters], cony-catchers [cheats] . . . runners away with other men's wives . . . persons divorced, living loosely, bankrupts . . . papists, Puritans . . .' ran a contemporary lament.[39] Here acquiring the land was part of a bloody (and expensive) war of conquest, the real purpose of which was to prevent Ireland's becoming the base for the invasion of Protestant England. For that reason alone, the government was willing to pay for the force that was needed. In the American colonies, things were very different.

Although the sparseness of the Indian population (sharply accentuated by the die-off from the diseases that Europeans brought) meant that many areas in what became the Thirteen Colonies could be quietly fenced off without confrontation, in much of the settlement zone Indian tribes were in clear occupation as both cultivators (with the fields of corn and beans depicted in early travel accounts) and hunters. But though some settlers and their supporters at home talked tough about their 'right' to the soil that the Indians neglected, little force was available to make this right 'good' and the colonists found it easier and safer to buy land rather than grab it. 'From Maine to Georgia,' remarks a recent scholarly study, 'the ordinary way to acquire Indian land was to buy it.'[40] It helped of course that Indians were often very happy to sell. They were eager for the goods, including firearms and alcohol, that the proceeds would buy. Land was sometimes the price for the settlers' support against enemy tribes. Once settlers moved in, their activity spoilt Indian hunting grounds nearby, and their value was lost. And as the number of settlers expanded, swiftly surpassing that of Indian communities decimated by disease, the pressure to sell became greater and greater. Doubtless force and fraud played a not inconsiderable part, but while the balance of power on the North American continent hung in the balance between the British and French, treaty-making and purchase were the principal means by which the colonists expanded their holdings.

Thus the British acknowledged that the Indians were, in the phrase of the time, 'native proprietors'. Individual settlers could and did buy directly. But to be sure of their title (against other would-be buyers) it had to be registered with the colony's government. In most of the colonies, laws were introduced to prevent direct purchase without a government licence and the authorities sometimes demanded that the sale take place in the presence of an official surveyor as well as of the Indians who were selling. Under this system huge tracts of land had changed hands east of the Appalachian mountains by 1750, and land speculators with political influence pressed for licences to buy further west, or did so surreptitiously. But then the crash came. During the

Seven Years' War (1756–63), the scale of the Indians' hostility and their support for the French showed how deep was their fear of further Anglo-settler advance. Already it had pushed the dispossessed nations into the lands of their neighbours. When the war ended, and the British government took possession of the vast Midwest to the Mississippi, it was determined not to be drawn into a new set of frontier wars, a resolve reinforced by the outbreak of Pontiac's rebellion in the north and the Cherokee War in the south. The Royal Proclamation of 1763 was meant to cut the knot. 'Great frauds and abuses have been committed in the purchasing lands of the Indians,' it declared, 'to the great prejudice of our interests and to the great dissatisfaction of the Indians.'[41] The solution was drastic. No licences were to be given to buy land west of the mountains. All private transactions, whether by settlers or individual Indians, were banned. Henceforth, the only way in which land could be bought was by government purchase and by treaties with the Indian nations.

This sudden prohibition enraged settler opinion – Washington and Jefferson were among those with a stake in speculative land-buying. It marked a highly significant shift in the way land changed hands between incomers and the indigenous population. After 1783, the British government could no longer control the purchase of land in what became the United States. The federal government upheld the principle of no private purchase, but became the willing instrument of settler (and speculator) land hunger. In the British Empire, the Proclamation cast a long legal shadow. It became the orthodox doctrine for settler land purchase. But the British also took notice of a key legal judgment in the United States. In Johnson v M'Intosh (1823) the case turned on the legality of a purchase made privately. The Supreme Court reaffirmed the principle of the Proclamation but in a famous judicial assertion, Chief Justice John Marshall imposed three vital conditions. The Americans, he said, had inherited Britain's right of 'discovery' – their claim to the continent. That right did not confer ownership of the Indians' land, but it did deny them the right to sell it to anyone else. Secondly, Marshall corrected the notion that the Indians were proprietors: they had instead a right of 'occupancy'. Thirdly, their right to dispose of their land to whomever they wished (the right exercised by the settlers) was denied by their lack of civilization. The Indians 'lived by the chase'. 'The game fled into the thicker and more unbroken forest, and the Indians followed.'[42] Marshall had endorsed an old and highly contentious view of Indian society. But then, said a British official cuttingly, he was after all an American.[43]

The Proclamation and Marshall's dicta set the scene for the white colonization of New Zealand. By the 1830s, Sydney-based merchants and missionaries had begun to buy land from Maori tribes and chiefs, and towards the end of the decade the London government was confronted with a major settlement scheme by the New Zealand Company. It invoked the new model. Private land purchase would not be recognized. Immigrant British could only purchase land previously bought by the government from Maori communities, i.e. not individuals. But the British rejected the relevance of one of Marshall's key findings. They would not claim New Zealand by right of discovery: the Maori did not live by the chase but were a civilized, cultivating, people. They were 'the owners and sovereigns of the soil'.[44] The implications were huge. New Zealand became British not by discovery or conquest but by cession, in the treaty of Waitangi (in 1840). Maori were guaranteed 'full use and undisturbed possession' of their lands, forests and fisheries, as *proprietors* not occupants, although if they wished to sell it must be to the Crown.[45] What happened in practice somewhat belied this ideal. Maori eager to sell, British eager to buy, mixed with some fraud, speculation and racial antagonism, triggered a series of wars and by the end of the century a native population seemingly doomed to die out retained only a fraction of its pre-treaty land.[46] But as New Zealand's recent history has shown, the rules for possession laid down in 1840 turned out (perhaps surprisingly) to matter a great deal. They laid the foundation for an astonishing revival of Maori self-consciousness based on the rights that the treaty guaranteed and on which huge claims for compensation have been successfully made. Invoking the terms of Waitangi has remade modern New Zealand.

Two other cases tell a different story. In the parts of Africa to which white settlers came, there was little pretence of respecting the property rights of indigenous peoples. The earliest white settlements spreading north from the Cape (then under Dutch rule) occupied land whose original inhabitants, the Khoikhoi, were a small and declining population, and fought a vicious running battle with the

San (or Bushmen) hunter-gatherers.[47] From the 1830s, when the British encountered denser Xhosa nations on the eastern frontier, their usual practice at the close of a conflict was to seek the chiefs' agreement to the allocation of land between whites and blacks to reduce the risk of further armed struggle. Thus while treaties were made, unlike that at Waitangi, they did not recognize the Africans as proprietors. Instead the British authorities claimed effective control of the land by conquest or cession and parcelled it out as 'locations' for blacks and 'land grants' for whites.[48] The Afrikaner trekkers followed a similar practice: their commandos seized land by force, sharing it out among themselves, and turning the indigenous population into a servile labour force.[49] Cecil Rhodes's chartered company, which occupied modern Zimbabwe in 1890, upheld this tradition. Vast tracts of land were distributed to the members of the 'pioneer column' and to the company's shareholders. When Ndebele resistance was broken after the war of 1893, legal doubts were extinguished by the claim that 'conquest' had conveyed to the Crown all rights over land (since conquest must always be in the Crown's name). The Crown's land commissioners confirmed the grants Rhodes had made,[50] although the company was subsequently forced to increase the amount of land set aside for Africans. At much the same time, in the new East African Protectorate (modern Kenya), Maasai pastoralists were ejected from what became the White Highlands, a region scheduled for land grants to incoming white settlers.

But it was the Australian case that was the most astonishing. In Africa, what amounted to forcible seizure created white settler property, but there was no disputing the presence of the original inhabitants, or their rights of occupancy. It was mainly a question of what land they should have (the barest minimum in South Africa by 1913) and whether African land should remain collectively owned by the tribe or lineage or become individual property. In Australia, however, Cook's legacy was decisive. As we saw earlier, his sweeping pronouncement that he had seen no one with any claim to the land was taken at face value. Australia was empty, deserted, uninhabited, a no man's land, *terra nullius*. It followed that when occupation began in 1788, land could be apportioned as the British officials saw fit. The real disagreements arose from their effort to limit the inland extent of the settlement, and to make the sheep-farmers who squatted on the land rather than buying it, pay more for this privilege. Aboriginal resistance, which was strong in some places, created a legal conundrum. There were powerful arguments for declaring that Aborigines were subject to British law, and therefore to punishment for violence or theft. But the objections were huge. Enforcing British law on Aborigine peoples spread over a vast interior far beyond the limits of white settlement was all but impossible. And if Aborigines could be tried in British courts, would it not follow that they could also bring suits in them? That they had the right to hold property? And that they could sue those who had stolen it from them? If that were to happen, the legal basis of white settlement might begin to dissolve. Exactly this point was made in 1841 by the governor of Western Australia. It would be 'in strange opposition', he remarked, 'to the hold which the Crown assumes to possess over the lands of the Country'.[51] A similar issue arose when a group of whites from Tasmania bought land round modern Melbourne from the local Aborigine tribe. It was quickly disallowed on the grounds that private purchase was forbidden. A deeper point lay behind this. If Aborigines could sell land, it must have been theirs. If that were conceded, many others might come forward. The thin legal ice on which the colony rested would crack up completely. The real strength of *terra nullius*, like that of most legal doctrines, was that it conformed with the interests of the dominant group in Australian society: its white settler invaders.[52]

POSSESSION AND EMPIRE

Not all forms of empire needed possession in the sense of '*imperium*'. Most empires in history combined spheres of formal control with zones of influence or informal domination and 'alliances' (a polite term) with client states. In the nineteenth century, the British practised this form of empire in many parts of the world: in Latin America, the Middle East, West Africa (for a time), Southeast Asia and China. The method varied widely. In Egypt, British influence was guaranteed by the presence of a garrison and by the Royal Navy's command of both the Eastern Mediterranean and the Red Sea, the two marine gateways to the Delta and Cairo. In maritime China, 'unequal treaties' imposed by force exempted British merchants (and most other Westerners) from Chinese authority in special enclaves, the so-called 'treaty ports', while the coasts and waterways were patrolled by ubiquitous British gunboats. Strictly speaking, Britain had only one possession in China, the two parts of Hong Kong (Victoria and Kowloon) ceded in perpetuity in 1842 and 1861 (the rest of today's Hong Kong was merely leased to the British government). But in Latin America, the picture was very different. Here the British had possessions aplenty. But they were mostly in the form of businesses (such as banks), commercial property including farms and ranches, and utilities, such as tramways or waterworks.[53] Above all, by 1900, the British owned railways, from the grand Oeste in Argentina, or the highly profitable San Paulo, to the humbler Bolivar in Venezuela. These British possessions were managed in the City, not from Whitehall. By 1913, they made up nearly one quarter of Britain's huge fund of overseas wealth, part of the secret of imperial survival in two world wars.

But why not turn such valuable property into a 'real' possession? The answer was twofold. It seemed unnecessary if the object was profit, since, in Latin America at least, the local politicians welcomed the growth of trade that resulted from their British connection. But it was also unappealing. Annexation was easy where there was little local resistance and no major rival to fear. It might be the only safe course if the alternative was chronic and costly warfare: the argument for seizing New France in America. It might come as a bonus after victory in war. But by the mid nineteenth century, the British preferred if possible to 'annex by agreement' – the pattern in tropical Africa. With a limited stock of naval and military power, conquering Latin America would have been out of the question: the very idea would have been thought absurd and outrageous, not least in the City. In China (and Japan) the strength of local resistance made it futile and dangerous. The apparent exception was Egypt, occupied by the British in 1882. But, significantly, the British did *not* annex Egypt despite its huge geostrategic importance, and for years they feared the backlash of great power resentment against their dominant role in the country. Publicly they maintained the embarrassing fiction that it was only a 'temporary occupation'.

The conclusion this leads to is that those grandiose maps in which British possessions were shaded in red were (and are) a poor guide to the *substance* of empire. Much of that red on a Mercator map was desert or waste: the zones of real value were crowded into corridors along rivers, sea-lanes and (later) railways. Some of the most vital, as we have just seen, were not red at all. Possession is said to be 'nine-tenths of the law'. But by the late nineteenth century, it was, in real terms, much less than nine-tenths of empire.

4

Settling In

'When Englishmen speak or think of the British Empire,' complained Lord Curzon in 1909, 'they are apt to leave India out of sight, and to think only of the colonies that were founded and largely peopled by the men and women of our own race.'[1] As a former Viceroy of India, Curzon was convinced that the 'struggle for Asia' would decide Britain's future as an imperial power, and that the possession of India would be the key to its outcome. But he was all too aware that to British opinion at home the empire that mattered was the settlement empire of what was to become the four white dominions: Canada, Australia, New Zealand and (more ambiguously) South Africa. It was from them, so many 'imperialists' argued, that Britain could draw the additional strength that was needed to compete with the emerging world powers (Germany, Russia and the United States) in manpower and resources. It was hopes of this kind that had helped to inspire the campaign for tariff reform and 'imperial unity' with which Joseph Chamberlain had galvanized – and divided – the Conservative Party after 1903. While his grand scheme for drawing the settlement colonies into an 'imperial federation' with a shared parliament and executive made little headway, the dream of closer union between the 'British nations' (a term used by Canadians, Australians and New Zealanders as well as by Chamberlainites) remained a key theme of the 'imperial idea' deep into the twentieth century.

Twenty-five years or so before Curzon's address, his claim would have appeared strange. Then British opinion had seemed to regard the results of British migration with crushing indifference. When John Robert Seeley, a professor of history at Cambridge, published *The Expansion of England* in 1883, he denounced the failure to grasp its importance as a damning indictment of the introverted insularity of contemporary attitudes. What he called 'the great English Exodus' (Seeley used 'England' and 'English' when he meant 'Britain' and 'British') was, he insisted, 'the great fact of modern English history'.[2] Yet, if noticed at all, it was dismissed as a simple and inevitable fact: the 'unopposed occupation of empty countries by the nation that happened to have the greatest surplus population and the greatest maritime power'.[3] How and why it had happened aroused no curiosity. His urgent message, that the British at home should acknowledge their ties with the British abroad in a shared 'Greater Britain', was the text that inspired the imperial unity movement and Chamberlain's programme. And although 'imperial federation' soon proved a lost cause, Seeley's influence endured in the pervasive assumption found across the whole spectrum of political opinion that 'expansion' overseas had been Britain's 'manifest destiny' and that an indissoluble bond linked the mother country to its former settlement colonies.

There is no need to subscribe to Seeley's missionary doctrine to acknowledge the importance of British migration in the making of empire or of the 'British world' at its core. More than 22 million people left the British Isles for an overseas destination between 1815 and 1914, more than left any other European or Asian country in the period. We must be careful, of course. Two-thirds of those who migrated after 1815 went to the United States, not to British Empire countries. Perhaps a third of the total came back, some to set off again later or to adopt a routine of 'serial migration' – a pattern of movement that historians have only just begun to explore. And the British (a category that usually includes migrants from Ireland) were not the only settlers in 'British' countries. Other Europeans, from Germany and Scandinavia especially, also took passage from Britain. In the late nineteenth century, Dalmatians from the coastlands of modern Croatia could be found digging gum (the buried resin of the kauri pine) in New Zealand's North Island. Ukrainians were recruited to settle the Canadian prairie, perhaps in the belief that they would be inured to its cold. Before 1800 some 10 million Africans were dragged across the Atlantic to work in the slave gangs of the Americas. A substantial proportion went to British colonies until their importation was banned there in 1807. Migrants from India, usually travelling under strict labour contracts (the so-called 'indentures'), made their way to Britain's tropical colonies such as Fiji, Malaya, Burma or Trinidad as plantation labour, or as railway 'navvies' on the Uganda railway through Kenya. But they also arrived in 'white men's countries' (usually a political claim not a demographic description) where, like the Chinese, their presence, however modest in size, evoked paranoid fears of a stealth occupation and demands for exclusion.

Thus migration and settlement, and the physical occupation of so-called 'empty countries', formed an essential part of British empire-building. This was colonization in its most durable and often most brutal form. Yet, as Seeley implied, there was nothing 'simple' or 'inevitable' about it. Indeed, the closer we look the more puzzling and complex it seems – even if we limit ourselves just to British migration. Migrants did not move by instinct. Unless they were criminals sentenced to transportation, they had (at some level) to choose to go. They also had to choose a destination, or have it chosen by those who were paying their passage. Indeed it required motivation, calculation and organization of an intricate kind to carry the migrant to the promised land of his or her or somebody's choice. Nor was that the end of the story. It was only on arrival that the settling began. Migrants had to find land, or some other occupation, to feed themselves and their families. They entered a world where the first comer took all, or as much as he could. They had to adapt to crude frontier societies and their ruling elites. They had to learn to manipulate a natural environment, at best superficially similar, with the simplest of tools. They had to produce the cash crops, such as grain, wool or gold, to lift them out of subsistence and turn their work camps in the wilderness into dynamic economies, and destinations attractive enough to draw in ever more migrants. As we shall see, success was not guaranteed.

DECIDING TO GO

Long before the great movement after 1815, overseas migration from the mainland of Britain was an established habit. The first destination was Ireland. From the 1550s onwards, governments in London encouraged settlers from England to take up the land confiscated from rebellious Irish lords and clans. By the end of the century, there were more than 4,000 in Munster in the south, and perhaps a similar number in the province of Leinster round Dublin.[4] After 1600, migrants from England and Scotland poured into Ulster. By the 1640s, perhaps 100,000 people from the mainland had settled in Ireland, far more than had crossed the Atlantic by then.[5] Up to 80,000 more moved into Ulster after the Battle of the Boyne in July 1690 and William of Orange's reconquest of Ireland.[6] By that date, of course, trans-Atlantic migration had more than caught up. Nearly 400,000 people had crossed to America by 1700,[7] much the larger share going not to the temperate mainland colonies but to the hot humid plantations of the Caribbean (where of course their death-rate was far higher). The toll of mortality left perhaps 230,000 settlers, some 50,000 of whom had survived the Caribbean's tropical climate. In fact, by some estimates, perhaps 1 million people (70 per cent of them English) left the British Isles during the seventeenth century: this was a larger proportion of the home population than the great emigration of two centuries later.[8]

Why did they go? Part of the answer may lie in the extreme instability that affected every part of the British Isles over the course of the century, an age of civil war, rebellion and brutal repression. For both Puritans and Catholics, migration was an escape. Emigrants to New England were recruited by sympathetic merchants and gentry, or through the network of clergymen, some of whom migrated at the head of their congregations. But for the largest number, it was surely economic opportunity that exerted most influence. Unemployment, inflation, depression and the poor harvests associated with the climatic downturn of the 'little ice age' may have sharpened the urge. Many of those who went may not have intended to stay very long; this was certainly the case with the first settlers to go to Virginia, which was planned as a trading not an agricultural colony. Most of those who crossed the Atlantic went as single men to 'boom' destinations in the Caribbean where tobacco, sugar and gold promised quick fortunes or high wages. Significantly, the flow of migrants eased off after 1700 when British conditions improved, and African slaves squeezed white labour out of sugar production.[9] It picked up again after 1760 when depressed conditions in Britain and the pressure on land in Ulster coincided with the enormous publicity that the Seven Years' War had given to the American colonies. Between then and 1775 (when the American revolution brought the traffic to a shuddering halt) 125,000 emigrants, mostly Scots and Protestant Irish, crossed the Atlantic, on average three times as many as in previous decades.[10]

The great outflow revived after 1815 at the end of more than twenty years of world war. In 1832, for the first time, the number who left in one year exceeded 100,000. In the 1840s and 1850s the terrible calamity of famine in Ireland drove up the figure to astonishing heights: 1.7 million people left between 1841 and 1850; a further 1.6 million between 1853 and 1860; and just under 2 million between 1861 and 1870.[11] In each of the years 1853 and 1854, more than 1 per cent of the population departed. In the 1850s and 1860s, migrants from Ireland were still the largest body of leavers: after 1870, the English took over.[12] The total fell back a little in the late 1870s, but from 1880 until the end of the century, it usually exceeded 200,000 a year and never fell below 140,000. Then in a huge burst up to 1914, more than 3 million people left the British Isles, just under 400,000 in 1913 alone. Just as striking, perhaps, was the shift in their target. In the 1890s most British migrants still went to the United States; after 1900 they chose empire destinations. Over 1 million migrants from Britain went to Canada in these years.[13]

A whole set of impulses was pushing and pulling this vast mass of people. Most were economic in some form or another. The Great Hunger in Ireland was a symptom of the huge pressure of people on land, much of it marginal, whose effects had been hidden by the amazing productiveness of potato cultivation – until the catastrophic onset of blight. Even before the famine set in, Irish emigration had been rising steeply with 1.5 million people leaving the island between 1815 and 1845. In the Highlands and Islands of Scotland, the so-called 'removals' ('clearances' was a later coinage)[14] afflicted a peasant population subsisting on marginal land. They faced large landowners (such as the Duke of Sutherland) who were desperate to turn their 'territorial empires' into going concerns. After 1815, and in the 1830s and 1840s, the British economy lurched into depression.

For many skilled workers – weavers especially – the unemployment this brought turned out to be 'structural': weaving machines for cotton and wool threw their skills on the scrapheap. The gradual industrialization of many skilled trades through the rest of the century pushed men and women out of work or threatened a sharp decline in their wages (and thus of their status). As Britain imported more and more of its food, and especially its grain, many rural districts, not just in Scotland and Ireland, began to seem 'marginal'. Harsh weather, thin soil or poor roads sharpened rural poverty in North Devon and the Chilterns (among many regions); the collapse of wheat prices against American competition impoverished rural labour in the old 'corn countries' – the great grain producers of south and east England.

These economic pressures did not act alone, nor could they have done. In other parts of the world, even in Europe, where population pressure on land was as high if not higher, migration began later or was lower in volume. What made the British (and Irish) so prone to migrate was in part ideology. From the late eighteenth century, most influential British opinion converted to free trade. There was nothing new in the eagerness of the landed and commercial elite to make money quickly, nor in their willingness to try every possible method: the Elizabethan aristocracy had invested in piracy, colonization and exotic new trades, as well as mining and draining for land reclamation. But until the late eighteenth century, it was widely assumed that manufacture and farming in Britain should be protected against competition from abroad. In fact, it took more than seventy years before the programme spelt out in Adam Smith's *The Wealth of Nations* (1776) was implemented in full with free trade in corn (1846) and the end of the Navigation Laws (in 1851). Long before that, manufacturers had been free to impose new conditions of work, while the state outlawed 'combination' (i.e. trade union organization) or cleared the way for the huge railway projects that, in London at least, removed thousands of people from the path of the line. A 'progress' ideology regarded economic 'improvement' as an imperative goal and almost any social cost as a necessary evil. Any interference with the laws of economics came to be seen as futile or worse. It became the conventional view among English economists that the problem of Irish

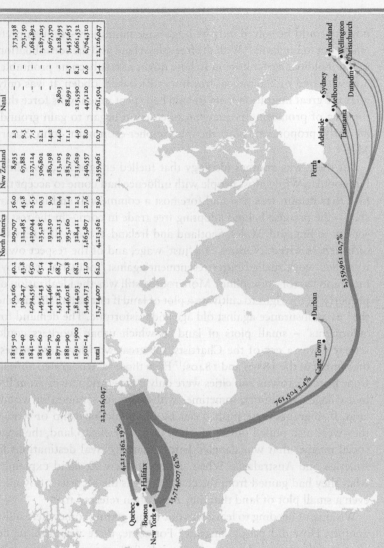

emigration from Britain, 1815–1914

	United States	%	British North America	%	Australia and New Zealand	%	Cape and Natal	%	total
1815–30	150,160	40.2	209,707	56.0	8,935	2.3	–	–	373,338
1831–40	308,247	43.8	312,485	45.8	67,882	9.5	–	–	703,150
1841–50	1,094,556	65.0	429,044	25.5	127,124	7.5	–	–	1,684,892
1851–60	1,495,243	65.4	235,285	10.3	506,802	22.1	–	–	2,287,205
1861–70	1,424,466	72.4	192,250	9.9	280,198	14.2	–	–	1,967,570
1871–80	1,531,851	68.7	232,213	10.4	313,105	14.0	9,803	–	2,128,395
1881–90	2,446,018	70.8	395,160	11.4	383,729	11.1	88,991	2.5	3,455,655
1891–1900	1,814,293	68.2	328,411	12.3	131,629	4.9	215,590	8.1	2,661,532
1901–14	3,449,173	51.0	1,865,807	27.6	540,557	8.0	447,120	6.6	6,764,310
total	13,714,007	62.0	4,213,362	19.0	2,359,961	10.7	761,504	3.4	22,126,047

22,126,047

4,213,362 19%

761,504 3.4%

2,359,961 10.7%

13,714,007 62%

Quebec
Boston
Halifax
New York

Durban

Cape Town

Perth
Adelaide
Sydney
Melbourne
Tasmania
Dunedin
Auckland
Wellington
Christchurch

poverty could be solved only by large-scale migration – though preferably not to England.[15] With the free sale of land and the consolidation of landholding, agriculture in Ireland might at last become profitable, a view shared by the radical free trader Richard Cobden. It was only after the great migration from Ireland had spent much of its force that the idea of promoting peasant proprietorship began to gain ground, an early proponent being the philosopher-economist John Stuart Mill.[16]

But there was another ideology that fuelled emigration, not elitist but popular. While most people with influence had come to accept the idea that Britain was first and foremost a commercial and industrial state – the premise behind adopting free trade in corn – in the rest of society in England, Wales, Scotland and Ireland, a quite different set of beliefs survived. Notions of a 'just' wage, and of the respect owed to skilled work fuelled bitter resentment against 'industrial' employment and 'factory discipline'. More rooted still was the idealization of property, of the right to cultivate a plot of land if not as a main income then as an insurance against old age and misfortune. The demand for 'allotments' – small plots of land to which urban workers could retreat – was a cry of the Chartists, the great working-class protest movement of the 1830s and 1840s.[17] Even those who migrated abroad from Britain's towns and cities were only a generation away from life in a village community, sometimes with rights to common or woodland. If migrants were pushed out by economic hardship or worse, they were also pulled out by the lure of free or cheap land, the huge social magnet that was dangled before them by rival destinations in America and Australasia. When settlers in New Zealand explained what they had gained from the change, it was the security of owning even a small plot of land that they most often referred to.[18]

Wishing or needing to leave was one thing, getting somewhere quite another. How did people migrate? For some, there was little or no choice in the matter. Between 1783 and 1868, around 160,000 convicts were transported, almost all to Australia and usually for fixed terms before being freed as 'emancipists'.[19] In parts of Ireland and Scotland, landlords 'assisted' the migration of those that they wanted to clear from the land.[20] The geologist Archibald Geikie watched one small community on Skye being herded on to ships bound for Canada in a mood of helpless passivity.[21] But the numbers involved were small: even during the Famine, when many more might have been willing to accept passage from their landlord, less than 4 per cent of departures were paid for like this.[22] More important were government schemes to recruit potential migrants and dispatch them to approved destinations. In 1749, London advertised for settlers to go to what became Halifax Nova Scotia, a key forward base against the French. Free land, no taxes and twelve months of rations were promised: 2,500 rushed to take up the offer.[23] After 1815, the military budget paid to bring migrants from Scotland to Canada to hold the strategic triangle between the St Lawrence and Ottawa rivers against the threat of an American invasion.[24] In 1819, fear of social disturbance as depression bit deeper brought a sudden decision to fund settlement in South Africa; 80,000 applied, 5,000 were chosen.[25] A more long-term arrangement was the Colonial Land and Emigration Commission, which funded assisted passages from the proceeds of land sales in Australia. Between 1840 and 1872 it paid for 340,000 to migrate – more than a quarter of those who settled in empire countries.[26]

But most of those emigrating to Britain's settlement colonies were not sent there by the government. Three other 'agents' played a critical role. The first was the 'land company'. These had been active in the American colonies and more sprang up after 1815. The Canada Company, the British American Company, the South Australian Company, the New Zealand Company, and many more, aimed to buy land cheaply, or receive it as a grant, from colonial governments. It would then be resold to investors in Britain and to would-be emigrants, usually on terms that required occupation and some cultivation. For their part, the companies engaged in vigorous advertisement of the prospects of their undeveloped estates with planted accounts of their charms and fertility by enthusiastic settlers and travellers. Secondly, emigration was a business with an obvious appeal to merchants and shipowners. In 1830, the Bideford businessman Thomas Chanter advertised four of his ships as 'conveniently fitted for Families and will take out passengers on moderate terms to Prince Edward Island, Cape Breton, Nova Scotia and New Brunswick'. Seventy-four passengers, 'farmers, labourers and mechanics' from North Devon and Cornwall and their families sailed on the first ship.[27] It made excellent sense to ship people out and bring lumber home from Quebec or the Maritimes. Thirdly, emigrants were not always recruited by somebody else. Emigration societies sprang up to advise and inform, and sometimes to organize the actual move.[28] In 1773 the Scots American Company of Farmers was formed in the lower Clyde valley. Its 105 subscribers, a mixture of small farmers and artisans, paid a modest membership fee to cover the cost of buying land in America, and the expenses of an advance party who would select the site.[29]

For many would-be migrants, the key question was cost. In the mid nineteenth century, an Atlantic passage cost three or four pounds, multiplied by the size of the emigrant's family. For Irish migrants the total often exceeded a family's annual income. The commonest way of meeting the cost, for single men in particular, had once been by an indenture. The intending migrant sold his labour for a period of four or five years to a merchant or ship's captain who agreed to transport him to an American port, a practice widespread by the mid 1600s.[30] A contract ('indenture') was drawn up. When the ship arrived in America, the captain would auction his indentures to the highest bidder. The migrants, male and female, stood on the dockside while the price on their muscle was haggled over and settled. Indenture for white migrants faded out after 1800. An alternative system enabled migrants to travel as a part of 'proprietary parties', under a 'leader'. Leaders usually bid for large parcels of land on highly favourable terms on condition of bringing out so many 'heads' to settle their lands. They advertised for recruits and paid for their passage and might also arrange for 'their' settlers to reach the promised location. But by far the most popular way of financing migration in the nineteenth century was by family self-help. Family members clubbed together to send an advance guard of the strongest and fittest. Once settled and earning, they remitted the cost of bringing over their kin, or bought them a ticket from a nearby shipowner. Thus one Mary Duggan could write to her sister enclosing four pounds for her passage from Ireland. When she arrived in Quebec, Mary instructed, she should tell the emigration agent that she had no money to reach her sister in Kingston; he would give her a ticket and also some rations.[31]

The 'business' of migration could hardly have thrived except in a climate of intense public awareness and interest. British society was deluged with 'news' about immigrant prospects. By as early as the 1620s and 1630s a flood of chapbooks, plays and pamphlets extolled the virtues and profits of overseas settlement. Clerics were hired to preach apposite sermons: John Donne gave one for the Virginia Company.[32] By the mid eighteenth century, the promotional literature included plausible maps: the one for Halifax carefully thinned out the forests, omitted wild animals and excluded the Indians.[33] In the nineteenth century, there were huge numbers of 'emigrant guides', warning, cajoling, steering, misinforming. The migrants had to make the best sense they could: hence, perhaps their reliance on the letters sent home – although even these could be doctored by a vigilant company. But perhaps most important of all was the fact that by the time the era of mass migration arrived in the 1840s and 1850s, the British at home were already a nation of movers and settlers: from region to region, from village to town, from all over Britain to the metropolis in London. Migration, like charity, began at home.

ARRIVING

For most emigrant families, it was the arrival not the journey that mattered. They might have been lucky and enjoyed a smooth voyage. But until the 1860s most of those who crossed the Atlantic did so under sail; the cost of coal at a great distance from Europe and the convenience of a southerly route delayed the change from sail to steam still further in the case of Australia and New Zealand. A typical passage westward across the Atlantic took six weeks under sail. To Australia and New Zealand it might take four months or more. The North Atlantic was notoriously fretful in winter. The main access to Canada by the St Lawrence river was closed off by ice from late November to April. Through the Roaring Forties – the sea-lane due east from the Cape of Good Hope to the southern tip of Australia where westerlies could drive ships at enormous speeds – the howling winds and mountainous seas could make the voyage traumatic even without misadventure to mast or sails.[34] 'Blowing tremendous heavy with a high sea,' recorded a surgeon sailing to New Zealand in 1842. 'Ship rolling and labouring heavily and shipping immense quantities of water . . .' A few days later, 'parted with main topsail; 2 am split the mainsail'.[35] When they disembarked, it was often at ports that were little more than a cluster of houses and stores, like Wellington or Melbourne in the 1840s or Dunedin in the 1850s or any of the small harbours in Nova Scotia or New Brunswick to which many Scots went. The emigrants sent to the Cape in 1820 had to land through the surf at Algoa Bay, the later Port Elizabeth. Arrival at a major port town like Quebec, the main terminus for those travelling on to modern Ontario, or Sydney, was only the first step towards the final destination. Yet many lingered there. The cost of onward travel, the urgent need for work and pay, or perhaps the wish to bring over the rest of the family sooner rather than later, conspired to make wage labour in the city a better prospect than pioneering inland. The rapid growth of many port towns (by 1850 the combined population of Quebec City and Montreal had reached 100,000) encouraged this trend. It was even more marked in Australia where the high cost of inland transport, the low labour requirement of the rural interior, and the need to process and pack the bulk export of wool meant that the colonies' capital cities grew out of all proportion to their thinly settled hinterlands.[36]

For those migrants who pressed on, what mattered most was access to the land: the right to buy a farm on easy terms. Here they might hope to scratch their subsistence until little by little they built up a surplus to be sold for cash. Indeed, land was *the* question in all the settlement colonies: all politics was land politics in one form or another. This was hardly surprising since land was the most valuable asset in the colony, the source of its revenues and the fastest means to make a private fortune. The political struggle over the acquisition of land, its allocation among claimants, and (eventually) its redistribution, was bound to be bitter.

In theory, at least, the colonial authorities in all the settlement colonies were eager to fill up their territories as quickly as possible with migrants from Britain. The reason was obvious. Clearing the land of forest or bush to bring it under cultivation would enable the colony to feed itself. This could not be taken for granted. The early American colonies had faced the risk of starvation. Twenty years after its foundation at Botany Bay in 1788, New South Wales was far from the haven of 'food security'. The wheat harvest had been very poor, Governor Bligh (sometime of the *Bounty*) told his patron Sir Joseph Banks in 1806.[37] A shipload of rice was expected, and he had sent for another from China, but nothing else would arrive in time. Rations would be tight. The hope in new settlements was to produce foodstuffs for export, or to support a colonial workforce producing saleable exports such as timber or wool. Such export commodities, sometimes called 'staples', were vital to the effort to escape from stagnation or worse. They would attract investment from home, the attention (perhaps even the presence) of those who controlled capital, and increase the circulation of money. Profitable trade would suck in more migrants, to clear more land and produce larger crops. Land sales would boost the government's income and enable it to borrow more deeply to dig canals (as in Canada), improve roads or build railways. A virtuous circle of ever-increasing prosperity would be the reward. For the settler population, economic well-being and financial independence would strengthen their case for 'responsible government': removing London's control over their internal affairs.

It was not, of course, quite as simple as this. The acquisition of land from indigenous peoples was the first hurdle to clear. As was discussed in chapter 3, in the American colonies this was achieved mainly by purchase. In what became Canada (strictly 'British North America' until 1867), purchase, or cession by native first peoples, was the typical pattern. In modern Ontario and the Atlantic provinces of Nova Scotia and New Brunswick, the pre-colonial population was small, and then thinned out by disease or internecine warfare. In Australia, indigenous claims were disregarded completely, although the slow pace of settlement, the relatively small numbers of Aborigines (a very rough estimate suggests 1 million at 'contact' in the 1770s) and the vast scale of the landscape partly hid this from view except in Tasmania until the 1830s and 1840s. In South Africa, where the scale of migration from Britain was tiny until the golden 1890s, conquest and cession were the norm in both the British-ruled zone in Cape Colony and Natal, and in the trekker republics north of the Orange. The real exception was New Zealand, where, in the North Island especially (perhaps only 5,000 Maori lived in the South Island, 5 per cent of the total at the time of British annexation), Maori land rights were bought out, or erased by chicanery, in a long-drawn-out process that was still incomplete at the end of the century.

But who got the land? The answer was often the well-connected few. When Prince Edward Island (today one of Canada's Atlantic provinces) became a British possession after 1763, it was divided up between sixty-seven absentee proprietors who had applied for a grant: it was not until 1895 that the last absentee landlord was bought out. In Upper Canada (today's Ontario), where many Loyalists took refuge at the end of the American War, free grants were made to ordinary settlers, but much larger grants to high-status Loyalists, army officers and officials, who received as much as 5,000 acres apiece. In 1820, in a township not far from the colony's capital, some 60 per cent of the available land was owned by such absentee landlords, including the surveyor (who got 5 per cent for making the survey), while nearly 30 per cent was set aside as the Crown and clergy reserves, to support the cost of the government and the established Anglican Church. Only 12 per cent (in the least desirable sections) was scheduled for sale to incoming settlers. Fifty years later, much of the absentee property remained uncleared forest.[38] In another part of the colony, an Anglo-Irish army officer, Colonel Talbot, amassed an enormous estate of some 65,000 acres in return for recruiting some hundreds of settlers from Britain. By the late 1830s, with little supervision from government, he controlled the settlement of some half-million acres.[39] The colony's government sold off much of its reserve to a huge land company, the Canada Company, in return for an annual revenue conveniently free from the scrutiny of the elected assembly.[40] But vast tracts of land sold off or granted away remained unoccupied.[41] It was only gradually that the system of grants was abandoned in favour of auctioning land in family-sized lots with a reserve or 'upset' price and by then much was locked up in absentee ownership. As a result, although thousands of settlers did obtain their own family farms, thousands of others (perhaps 43 per cent of farmers) were tenants as late as 1848,[42] and many thousands more remained as landless labourers.

The Australian case showed some similarities. New South Wales was a gaol with a government farm that was meant to provide food. But from the beginning, there was a small 'free' population including officials, the officers of the New South Wales Corps (the small colony garrison), and a handful of merchants and settlers. The governors were empowered to make land grants for services rendered – a convenient device since money was scarce. The settlers were expected to grow food for the colony. But they soon adopted the habit of letting their livestock roam freely on available land, granted or not. For the governors in Sydney this was doubly annoying. They wanted grantees to show proof that they were improving the soil by regular cultivation; and they were also determined to prevent the habit of squatting – using the land but paying no charge – from enlarging the colony and imposing new burdens on its shoestring finances. A spate of new rules led to the replacement of grants by a system of auctions with a set minimum price. London's objective was a neat compact colony with a zone of close cultivation by skilled farmer settlers. This was not what it got.

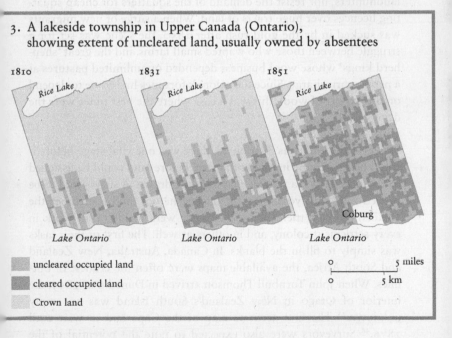

3. A lakeside township in Upper Canada (Ontario), showing extent of uncleared land, usually owned by absentees

1810   1831   1851

Rice Lake   Rice Lake   Rice Lake

Coburg

Lake Ontario   Lake Ontario   Lake Ontario

■ uncleared occupied land
■ cleared occupied land
□ Crown land

0   5 miles
0   5 km

The real problem it faced was that controlling the squatters was beyond the governor's power. The squatters, remarked one, 'are only following in the steps of all the most influential and unexceptionable Colonists whose cattle and sheep stations are everywhere to be found side by side with the obnoxious squatters and held by no better title'.[43] In other words, he was saying, everyone's at it. Against this tide of self-interest, there was little hope of restraint. The governor would have liked to prevent the sudden occupation of the Port Phillip district (modern Victoria) by a group from Tasmania. But, as ruefully noted in London, 'the power of the law is unavoidably feeble when opposed by the predominant inclination of any large body of people'.[44] The best London could do was to use the proceeds from land sales to subsidize free immigration and replace convict labour – transportation to Eastern Australia was to be stopped in 1840. But it could not prevent land being sold in large blocks to speculative landhunters, nor resist the demand of the squatters for cheap squatting licences over huge tracts of land. When a surge of new migrants was sucked in by the gold rush after 1850, the scene was set for a struggle between those who wanted small farms and the great 'shepherd kings' whose wool business depended on unlimited pastures at a peppercorn charge. Since the colony's fortunes had come to depend on the export of wool, this was a case where the best tunes were the devil's.

However the land was distributed, there was one vital stage before it could be sold to the immigrant farmer. Before land could be assigned to any new owner, a reliable map must be drawn. A survey had to be carried out. Surveyors were the unsung heroes (and sometimes the villains) of the settlement process. They were maids of all work in every settlement colony, and in others as well. The first of their tasks was simply to fill in the blanks. In Canada, Australia, New Zealand and South Africa, the available maps were often the crudest of outlines. When John Turnbull Thomson arrived in Dunedin in 1855, the interior of Otago in New Zealand's South Island was an empty unknown.[45] The first accurate map of the Cape had to wait until 1876.[46] Surveyors were also expected to note the potential of the tracts they traversed, to search for passes through mountains, and recommend the best routes for roads. They encountered 'first peoples', sometimes with fatal results since surveyors were seen with good reason as heralds of white occupation. Some were enthusiastic botanizers or ethnographers; some recorded their journeys with sketches or paintings or wrote up their notes as a travel memoir.[47] It was usually rough work. 'The Colonial Surveyor,' said John Turnbull Thomson, 'is clothed in fustian trousers and blue shirt, Panama hat and hob-nailed boots ... he has a hundred things about him, knives, needles, telescopes, matches, paper, ink, thread, buttons' and his indispensable notebook. He walked through bogs and creeks at a steady three miles an hour. He lived on 'damper' (a kind of flour cake), 'salt junk' and 'oceans of tea'.[48]

While the best surveyors were professionals, some adeptness in mathematics was the basic requirement. For many young men, it offered a well-paid adventure, and also the chance to make a speculative killing. The equipment was simple.[49] The theodolite, a combined compass and telescope that could be flipped backwards and forwards, allowed the surveyor to draw a straight line between two visible points whose exact position he could fix. With a small crew of chain men, he used a surveying chain of sixty-six feet to measure the line: a laborious process that would often require hacking through bush, cutting down trees and marking each length on the ground. With his base line completed and duly drawn on his map, the surveyor could begin to record other topographical features and divide up the landscape into administrative units: townships, land blocks and lots. The surveyor was the true maker of the settlement landscape. The lines he drew on his map and the ground became roads and boundaries. They formed the 'rectangular quilt' that imposed a gridiron-like order on the forest and bush – an astonishing contrast with the far more disorderly landscape created by the medieval colonization of Britain. The surveyor was also the planner of towns, imposing his vision of identical lots and streets that were straight. He chose the names that the landscape would bear, sometimes discarding the old for new and more dignified versions, or drawing on memories of rivers and hills in the Old Country at home.

It is easy to see why colonial governments were under great pressure to survey their territories: unless it was done land sales would

stall, since would-be buyers were deterred by the cost of arranging
their own. Yet however efficient the survey (and many were not) it
gave no assurance of the migrant's success. Having purchased his
lot, the incoming settler might find it located far from the road and
back in the woods, so that hauling his goods there was an arduous
toil.[50] The land he had bought might be swampy and acid, or rocky
and thin-soiled; in eastern Ontario that was often the case. The settlers brought out to the Cape in 1820 mostly abandoned their farms
in disgust as soon as they could. If progress was slow in clearing the
ground and expenses were high, the farmer might be forced to seek
work as a labourer building roads or canals. The townships laid out
with a flourish of trumpets might wither and fail if trade passed
them by. If his harvest was poor, the farmer might sink into debt and
perhaps even gaol; many in Canada did so in the depressed 1830s.[51]
His neighbours might be very uncongenial. The huge consumption
of alcohol, the gender imbalance, the rough living conditions and
the competition for work were a volatile mixture. When this was
combined with ethnic and religious antagonism – between Catholics
and Protestants, French, Irish and Scots – violence was not far
away.[52]

Just how much could go wrong can be seen in the early history of
New Plymouth, today a comfortable town (with a superb museum)
on the west coast of the North Island of New Zealand. New Plymouth was the project of the Plymouth Company, founded by a group
of West Country landowners and merchants in 1840. Their motives
were mixed. Some had connections with the New Zealand Company
set up several years earlier to found a colony in the islands by purchasing land from the Maori. The New Zealand Company owed its
inspiration to the charismatic (and perhaps pathological – he was
imprisoned for three years for abducting a fifteen-year old heiress)
personality of Edward Gibbon Wakefield.[53] Wakefield had argued
that colonization was essential to British prosperity (as a market, supplier and consumer of capital) and that the British themselves were
'natural' colonists. But he also believed that colonies must be planned
to ensure that they did not regress into subsistence societies that produced nothing for export. The great danger they faced was that if land
was too cheap, no one would work for anyone else, preferring instead

to carve out a smallholding to feed themselves and their families. No one with capital would come to such a stagnant 'peasant' society. Without social leaders it would lapse into squalor. The solution was planning and price. The colony must be carefully laid out with towns and amenities that would attract the well-off. Above all, the land must be sold at a 'sufficient' (i.e. high enough) price. Those who bought it would have to make it pay: they would have a powerful incentive to hire the labour needed to make it productive. The emigrant without capital would have to work for some years before buying his farm. Driven together by mutual dependence labour and capital would make profits and progress.[54]

Wakefield's ideas appealed strongly to several interested parties. They promised the creation of an orderly world whose tone would be set by those with education and leisure. They attracted those who believed that only planned colonies could protect indigenous peoples from the avarice and brutality of European settlers – a major public concern in the late 1830s. Land would be kept for the native inhabitants; their conversion to Christianity and commerce could be carefully regulated. Nor would altruism be its own reward. The Wakefield scheme allowed those who bought land but stayed home to lease it or sell it at considerable profit. By buying land cheaply from Maori and selling it on, the company could also afford to pay for the passage of the labouring migrants, the settlement workforce.

The Plymouth Company's founders favoured Wakefield's ideas. They seemed a solution to the hardship and poverty in parts of Devon and Cornwall. Among the first party of settlers were labourers recruited by a leading Cornish landowner, Sir William Molesworth, one of the Company's directors and an active proponent of 'colonial reform'.[55] A ship was chartered and sailed for New Zealand in November 1840. Where the settlers would actually go was still undecided. With no land of its own, the Plymouth Company had bought a claim to some 50,000 acres from the parent New Zealand Company. Frederick Carrington, an experienced surveyor, was sent out ahead to choose the best site and prepare for the settlers. Carrington arrived at the tiny township of Port Nicholson (now Wellington) in December 1840 and presented his claim to the Company's agent. With no time to lose he cruised the neighbouring coast in search of a harbour and a cultivable plain. New Plymouth was a compromise. It had many attractions. Around the great cone-like peak Cook had christened Mount Egmont (now called Mount Taranaki) stretched a wide level plain. Near the Sugar Loaf rocks, where Carrington landed, the forest was thinner. There were few Maori about, and those he saw were 'in the greatest state of wretchedness'.[56] The New Zealand Company claimed to have bought the land. There was no sheltered landing, but the alternative sites offered too little cultivable land. Carrington made up his mind.

There was plenty to do. With his small group of workmen, he began clearing the land by setting fire to the fern. Crops had to be sown and the township laid out. Carrington gathered the Maori inhabitants and explained that their land was now his. 'I then drew squares upon the ground,' he wrote in his journal, 'and made them understand the value of their reserves with which they were very much pleased.'[57] He gazed at the forest and dreamed of the profits their lumber would yield. Then on 30 March the first migrants arrived. New Plymouth was founded.

Things soon began to go wrong. On his arrival at Port Nicholson, Carrington had hired the services of a beachcomber called Barrett. Barrett, originally from Rotherhithe, had lived in Australia before crossing the Tasman Sea: New Zealand was then New South Wales's maritime frontier. He took to whaling, acquired a family in Taranaki and then made himself useful as factotum and interpreter to the New Zealand Company. Carrington wanted Barrett to be his intermediary with the Maori of New Plymouth. But Barrett suddenly claimed that much of the Company's land was actually his and that of his (Maori) children.[58] Perhaps at his instigation, other Maori began to complain that the land had never been sold to the New Zealand Company (from whom he had bought it), a claim that Carrington later concluded was almost certainly just.[59] Meanwhile the little colony's prospects soon began to cloud over. The lack of a harbour proved a serious disadvantage. Everything had to be brought on shore in the Company's whaleboat, a slow and costly procedure. Few ships called in. 'We have not the slightest communication with any part of the world except by chance,' grumbled the Company's New Plymouth agent.[60] Carrington, who was very sensitive on this issue, claimed that Taranaki was the 'garden of this country', a 'great granary'.[61] Whatever the truth, there was no rapid path to agricultural success. Worse still, Taranaki's bush was unsuited to the rearing of sheep, the economic salvation of Australia and other parts of New Zealand. With little hope of transforming the land they had cleared into profitable farmland, or even feeding themselves, the colonists were a drain on the Company's straitened resources. And before the first year was out the Plymouth Company's bankers collapsed and it was forced into merger with the New Zealand Company whose commitment to New Plymouth's survival was uncertain at best.

Things got no better. The British government had annexed New Zealand in 1840, but it regarded the white colonists as little more than a nuisance. They would stir up the Maori and incite a costly colonial war. London's solution was to impose close limits on settler land purchase. The New Zealand Company's land claims were scrutinized with suspicion and in some cases rejected. To the land-hungry settlers this was a sentence of death. Without a supply of fresh land, said Carrington grimly, no one would come to New Zealand and those there would leave. To make matters worse, the best land in New Plymouth along the Waitara river was fiercely disputed, and the numbers of Maori began to grow quickly. The settlers discovered that the marked absence of natives was a temporary consequence of the Maori 'musket wars' of the 1820s and 1830s, when the arrival of guns had given some tribes a brief but crucial advantage over neighbours and rivals. Once they were over the locals returned from captivity to reclaim their land.[62] Before long there were armed confrontations between settlers and Maori. Interest in New Plymouth at home began to decline. How could they hope to attract more recruits, wailed the directors in Plymouth, if no letters came back extolling the colony's charms (a volume was published of suspiciously cheerful accounts but by then it was too late).[63] Unless men of capital came, warned the Company's agent, it would have to bear the cost of employing all the immigrant labourers. Unless they were paid well, they would abandon New Plymouth for better wages elsewhere. All work would cease – on surveying the land and everything else.

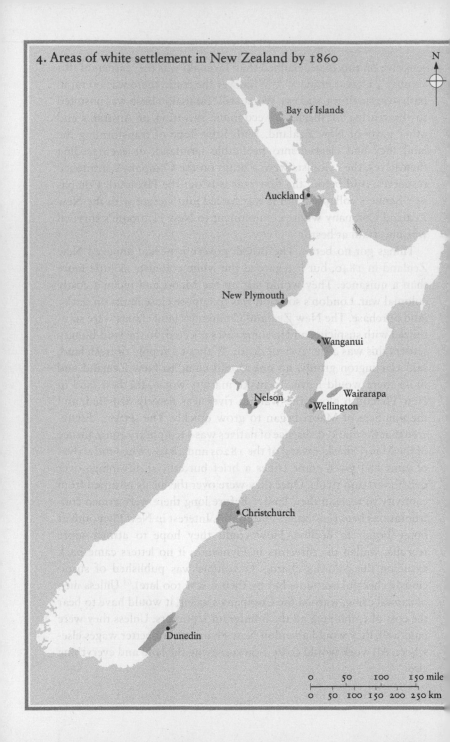

4. Areas of white settlement in New Zealand by 1860

N

Bay of Islands

Auckland •

New Plymouth •

• Wanganui

Wairarapa

Nelson • • Wellington

• Christchurch

• Dunedin

| 0 | 50 | 100 | 150 mile |
| 0 | 50 | 100 | 150 | 200 | 250 km |

But by the third year of the settlement that was ceasing to matter. Maori pressure increased. 'The Maori are bringing matters to a crisis,' raged the agent. They should be dealt with as in 'other countries where the aborigines and settlers have had quarrels'. Someone should 'pick off' Te Rauparaha, the Maori chief; no jury would convict.[64] Meanwhile, the unemployed artisans in the colony came to demand work from the Company and threatened to pull down the agent's verandah and break up his fences. A few months later there were reports that the Maori were building a *pa* – a fortress. Even those settlers who bought land were refusing to pay for it, fearing that Maori resistance would make it unusable. The Company gave up the effort to make New Plymouth pay. The settlement lapsed into uneasy subsistence while Taranaki slid deeper towards a white–Maori conflict. By the mid 1850s, the settlers needed a garrison and a blockhouse to defend them.[65] By March 1860, the first Taranaki War had begun. Stunted by war and depression, New Plymouth and Taranaki had to wait until the mid 1880s before the prosperous future that the first arrivals had dreamed of began to unfold.[66] It was railways and refrigeration that saved the day. Like other parts of New Zealand, Taranaki became a land of small farmers who prospered by sending dairy produce and meat to the British consumer at home.

ADAPTING

Wherever they went, settlers had to adapt their patterns of life to the worlds they had entered. North America, Australia, New Zealand and the Cape might have been temperate lands, but they imposed, nonetheless, a real physical challenge to Europeans used to the distinctive agricultural environment of north-western Europe. The dense forest of eastern North America was a threatening wilderness full of bears, panthers and wolves. The settlers faced it with an assortment of hand tools: axes, saws, hammers, guns and knives. Trees were their enemy. Indeed, it was widely believed into the mid nineteenth century that removing the tree cover would warm up the climate and reduce the savagery of the North American winter. But clearing the woodlands was very laborious work. Contemporary accounts suggest that it could take one man the best part of a year to clear little more than an acre.[67] A settler on his own would need most of a working life to carve out a viable farm. There were no power saws to cut down the trees, no machinery to drag them away or 'square' them as lumber for sale. In Australia, the first arrivals from Europe found themselves in a landscape of extraordinary strangeness: trees that shed their bark not their leaves; stingless bees; mammals with pockets; black swans and white eagles.[68] It was also a harsh and demanding environment. Australian soils were impoverished and infertile. They did not retain water and lacked plant nutrients and trace minerals. The climate was subject to huge variations in rainfall.[69] The great inland sea which the early colonists expected to find proved a chimera: there was no vast interior to be filled up with farms as in the American Midwest, just an arid and empty 'dead heart'. In New Zealand, much of the North Island was covered with dense forest and its hilly terrain made overland travel a poor second best to travel by sea, which became the usual way of moving between the coastal enclaves where white settlement clustered. In South Africa, the vast arid expanse of the Karoo lay like a wedge across the 'road to the north', pushing the advancing trekboers towards the eastern frontier and their clash with the Xhosa.

Of course, the lands that the settlers invaded were not pristine or virgin. In eastern North America, the Native Americans had shaped the woodland environment to their agrarian needs. Where the trees were open and park-like this was because of regular burning to clear spaces for crops or to encourage large game.[70] Early settlers moved on to the croplands vacated by native peoples and adopted part of their diet. In early New Zealand, the settlers throve best where they found grasslands for sheep (the lack of which was New Plymouth's misfortune). The evidence suggests that much of this was first cleared of its forest by the Maori who had arrived in New Zealand c. AD 1000.[71] Most dramatic of all was the case of Australia. What the first white settlers inherited was a natural environment modified by perhaps 60,000 years of human habitation. When they settled Australia, the Aborigine colonists (crossing the sea from Southeast Asia) thinned out the woodlands and practised the regular burning of grassland to encourage young growth and the small game that this attracted. 'But for this simple process,' remarked an early explorer, 'the Australian woods had probably contained as thick a jungle as those of New Zealand or North America.'[72] Like the Maori in New Zealand, they hunted large fauna to extinction. The result was the enormous expanses of pasture that delighted the squatters, and a vast grassy world which the Europeans' sheep could roam without fear of predators or rival grass-eaters.

But the settlers' adaptation to their newfound surroundings was only part of the story. Settlers had no intention of adopting an indigenous lifestyle: they intended to impose as much of their own as they could. The native ecosystem was usually the victim and the results were often unhappy. The Europeans' cattle and pigs were let loose to graze in the American forests, an aggressive advance-guard that invaded the croplands and hunting grounds of native communities.[73] Because land was cheap and labour was dear, there was little incentive to husband the land. Rather than clear the forest completely, it was common to 'girdle' the trees (burning their trunks) and sow between the stumps. Farmers drew off as many crops as they could and then abandoned the land for somewhere else further on, bequeathing an exhausted soil and eroded landscape.[74] In Australia, the arrival of European livestock quickly compacted the loose friable topsoil, crushing the native grass species and baring the ground. The natural grassland at which the first European travellers had marvelled survived scarcely six years before the flocks were forced to move on. In New Zealand, settler impatience produced startling results. A box of matches, it was said, was the settler's prime tool. The forest was set on fire and grass seed thrown into the ashes to make the new pasture. Sheep were swiftly brought on to keep down the scrub, a practice called 'fern-grinding'. Sheep's feet, loose soil, hilly terrain, strong winds and heavy rain produced massive erosion. Diagnosis and repair had to wait till the twentieth century. The settlers were also determined to reshape the landscape and make it familiar. By the nineteenth century, they had begun to do this on an almost industrial scale. A vast acreage of New Zealand was sown with European grasses. In Australia, the settlers were quickly convinced that native plants and animals were useless relics that needed replacement by those from a richer environment. 'Acclimatization societies' sprang up to introduce songbirds, garden flowers, ornamental shrubs and trees, as well as a huge range of supposedly 'useful' additions including rabbits and camels; both became plagues.[75] Europe's plants and animals (not to mention its weeds and pests) proved to be even more successful colonizers than the human variety, especially where the growing season was year-round and natural rivals were lacking.[76] A British traveller in modern New Zealand might encounter a strange sign: 'Danger: blackberries'.[77] The warning is real. The plant is so rampant that sheep become trapped and die in its terrible thickets. The blackberry, said a pioneer naturalist, was 'the terrible pedestrian' that had followed the roads.[78]

Much of the damage was hidden from contemporaries or revealed only when the strain was too great. In settler societies there was a strong disposition to ignore the downsides of the settlement process – the breakneck occupation of sometimes fragile environments. To attract money and men – more migrants and investment – it was vital to be 'positive'. *Australia Unlimited* was a characteristically exuberant publication in 1906. Those who questioned the evidence, or, like the geographer Griffith Taylor, pointed to the hard facts of Australian aridity, were made very unwelcome: Taylor soon left the country for Canada.[79] The other side of the coin was the gradual emergence in settler societies of a sense of their permanence and their distinctive characteristics. By the 1870s, it was becoming intellectually fashionable to describe Canada as a 'Northern country inhabited by the descendants of Northern races . . . a healthy, hardy virtuous race'.[80] Australians and New Zealanders invented similar myths of themselves as 'better Britons', fitter, hardier and healthier than the metropolitan version. As settlement became denser, a feeling for place and locality replaced the vision of dreary sameness of which earlier settlers complained. The local landscape acquired 'character' and became 'picturesque'.[81] The Australian bush, like the Canadian North, became romantic, a subject of artists such as the Canadian 'Group of Seven', a symbol of a national identity.[82]

EXCLUDING

There was an uglier side to forging a local identity in a new country. The British settler societies were open on one side (the side that faced Home) but closed on the other. Where they encountered indigenous peoples who challenged their claim on the land, their instinct was to buy out or drive out, and if need be, wipe out. In these white men's countries there was no place for natives: or at best a marginal place while they took time to die out (the common expectation of their cultural and physical fate).[83] In Canada, Australia and New Zealand, despite great variation in treatment, indigenous peoples were forced to give way. By 1914 they appeared as a footnote to the story of white occupation – except in New Zealand where dogged resistance had preserved a large Maori zone in the North Island uplands and key political rights: four seats in the parliament were reserved for Maori representatives. South Africa was different. There exclusion (by wipe out) was practised against the San (or Bushmen) hunter-gatherers. But against the Xhosa, the Zulus and other pastoralist peoples (who also grew foodgrains), these tactics were useless. They were too numerous, too rooted, and in white eyes too useful, to be driven away. In a country too poor (before the finding of gold) to attract mass immigration from Europe (the British were always fewer in number than the local-born 'Dutch'), black land and black labour were equally valuable. So the mode of exclusion was varied. South Africa's blacks were (largely) dispossessed of their land and transformed into serfs. Penned into 'locations' and forced to earn their living by labour, they were excluded by rule from the white man's South Africa. Physically omnipresent, they were culturally and morally invisible – an imagined exclusion of astonishing power.[84]

The settlers were also obsessed by an external threat – an invasion by stealth of migrants from Asia. Chinese came to Australia at the time of its gold rush in the early 1850s, and some moved on to New Zealand when gold was found there a decade or so later. Others crossed the Pacific (or came up from California) to British Columbia, first to its gold fields and then, in the 1880s, to work on constructing the Canadian Pacific – the transcontinental railway that was built from both ends and met in the Rockies. Indians were brought to Natal to work in its cane fields as indentured labour. Chinese were brought to the Rand to restart the gold mines after the Anglo–Boer War of 1899–1902. In each of these cases, white settler communities grew more and more hostile. White workers suspected that cheap 'coloured' labour would drive down their wages and steal their employment: in times of depression, as in 1890s Australia, this fear rose in a crescendo. White shopowners loathed the competition of Indians. This naked self-interest was fuelled by a more complex emotion. By the late nineteenth century white settler nation-building in Australia, New Zealand and Canada had come to stress the importance of moral and religious reform, intense social discipline and democratic equality. Outsiders and 'deviants', miscreants and ne'er-do-wells, the flotsam and jetsam of pioneering life, were no longer welcome. A modern society required order and progress. It was easy to think that in this new social stage Chinese, or Indians, were illicit intruders, a threat to moral cohesion, an unwelcome reminder of the crude and coarse past.[85] So by 1914, laws had been passed to exclude Chinese and Indians from White Australia, White New Zealand, White Canada and (not without irony) White South Africa.[86]

Settling in was a fraught and uncomfortable process racked with doubt and uncertainty. The sometimes traumatic experience of migration was only a start. Claiming the land, exploiting the soil, remaking the landscape, putting down roots, excluding all rivals were all stressful endeavours: scruples were costly and doubts might be fatal. The hard racist edge of settler society was the product of fear and anxiety as well as of arrogance. It reflected the pressure, all but relentless, to move restlessly forward in case stagnation set in and the experiment failed. 'Populate or perish' became a political cry in one settler society. As a populist motto, it fitted them all.

5
Resorting to War

COLONIAL WARS

In December 1902 the War Office in London (which administered the army) drew up a list of the 'principal British wars of 1857–1899' – the period between the two great wars of the second half of the century – the Crimean War of 1854–6 and the South African War of 1899–1902. The tally was fifteen, although some extended over several campaigns, and, as the title implied, lesser conflicts (for example in Kenya, Uganda, Nigeria, the Eastern Cape in South Africa and the Canadian West in 1870), where less than three or four thousand British troops were employed, were omitted entirely.[1] Even so, the list revealed the astonishing scope of British military action in those forty odd years: in Persia 1856–7; India (the Great Rebellion of 1857–9); China (the second Opium War of 1858–60); New Zealand 1860–66; Ethiopia 1867–8; West Africa (the Ashanti War of 1873–4); Afghanistan (the second Afghan War of 1878–80); Zululand 1879; the Transvaal (the 'first Boer War' of 1880–81); Egypt 1882; the Sudan 1884–5; Burma 1885–6; Chitral (on the Northwest frontier of India, 1895); 'Matabili' (the Mashona War in modern Zimbabwe, 1896); Tirah (the Northwest frontier again, 1897–8); and the second Sudan War of 1896–8. If we extended the list to include all the colonial wars in which the British engaged after 1600 in Ireland, North America, the Caribbean, South America, the Middle East, South and West Africa, India, Sri Lanka and South East Asia, it might be hard to resist the impression that the British had bought imperial power chiefly with blood, some of it their own.

As we shall see, that view will need qualifying. But the essential truth remains that more or less organized violence played a huge part in British expansion. On the North American continent, the growth of settlement colonies required the steady attrition of the Native American peoples, partly by the direct use of force against them, partly by conflict with France and Spain, culminating in the conquest of New France in 1759–60.[2] The British Caribbean was enlarged by wars against colonial rivals, against the scattered indigenous peoples and rebel or runaway slaves. In Australia and New Zealand, against very different opponents, the British resorted to force to extend the settlement zone and discourage resistance.[3] In South Africa, they fought a hundred years war against the Nguni communities of the Eastern Cape and Natal, and built a conquest state in modern Zimbabwe.[4] The South African War of 1899–1902 was meant to break the power of Afrikanerdom and indeed largely contained it until c.1950.[5] In Africa, British colonial authority drew on the dividend of military victories: over the Ashanti and the Yoruba in the west,[6] and over the Kikuyu, the Luo and the smaller kingdoms of lacustrine Uganda in the east.[7] The extensive privileges that the British enjoyed in China and their stronghold at Hong Kong were the prize of two wars in 1839–42 and 1856–60. Their command of Egypt and its vital canal, which lasted from 1882 to 1956, was won in September 1882 at Tel el-Kebir, the battle that laid the foundation of Britain's Middle East power in the twentieth century. Nor was India different. At Plassey (1757) and Buxar (1764) in Bengal, at Seringapatam (1799) and Assaye (1803) in South India, at Aliwal and Sobraon (1846) in Punjab, the British built up their Raj on the assertion of military force and the ruthless (but far from effortless) demolition of any competitor.[8] Even before 1800, the British in India, with more than 150,000 men, commanded one of the largest regular armies in the world.[9]

Of course, some of the violence behind British expansion took place outside the control of the imperial state or against the will of its political masters. Settlers and traders, explorers and adventurers, native allies and clients exploited the weakness of colonial authority or preempted the decisions of colonial officials. Forceful governors such as Bartle Frere in South Africa and George Grey in New Zealand engineered frontier wars while trying to convince London that their sole concern was defence. Much of the violence occurred not in battle but in skirmishes, raids, reprisals and police actions – a relentless, continuous low-intensity warfare that lasted until the indigenous population was driven away or enserfed. It was sometimes a matter of 'whites' fighting 'blacks'. But more often the conflict involved non-Europeans on both sides. The British in North America used Native American allies to fight both the French (who did the same) and other Native American peoples. British armies in Africa were usually small forces of white soldiers with a large contingent of black allies and camp followers. The great exception was the South African War of 1899–1902, but even then both sides recruited Africans for combatant and non-combatant roles including spying and message-carrying.[10] The armies with which the East India Company conquered India were largely composed of native Indian sepoys, for whom service under the Company was as honourable as fighting for an Indian ruler.[11] An essential component of the *pakeha* onslaught on Maori resistance were the so-called *kupapa*, Maori tribes loyal to the government and in receipt of its favours.[12]

Colonial wars were not all of one type. The costliest form for the British at home were those they fought against European rivals, sometimes as a sideshow to a main war in Europe. But the commonest variety of colonial war was the more localized conflict, like those that appeared in the War Office list. These localized conflicts also varied considerably. Some might be classified as straightforward wars of conquest, against indigenous states like Zululand or Burma or Mahdist Sudan, or stateless peoples such as the Kikuyu or Maori. But usually the context was much more ambiguous. Violence often broke out long after the moment of conquest, revealing its partial or incomplete nature. It was when nominal sovereignty turned into real interference, or the settler occupation of land, that subject populations rose in revolt. Colonial wars were thus as likely to be wars of resistance (or 'pacification') as wars about conquest. The Great Rebellion in India of 1857–9 was a war of this kind.[13] These were wars fought by the British to control, contain or fix the location of half-conquered peoples, and by them to preserve as much political, cultural or economic autonomy as could be salvaged from the wreck of lost independence. At the extreme, this form of conflict could approach a war of extermination, the result, if not the intention, in early nineteenth-century Tasmania. But colonial wars were not only fought against Asians and Africans and Native Americans. From the British point of view, the most dangerous conflicts of all were those with white settlers, who were usually well armed, well organized and well informed – not least about Britain's own military weaknesses. Though the American settler revolt of 1775–83 received critical help from Britain's European rivals, the staying-power of the rebels and their fighting capacity had made them more than a match for the British troops sent against them. It took 10,000 regulars and a loyal militia of British Canadians to suppress the French Canadian revolt of 1837–8. The struggle to defeat the two small Afrikaner republics in South Africa between 1899 and 1902 tested British military power to its limit – and provoked widespread anxiety about the army's all-too-visible shortcomings.

Wars, however local, require two (or more) sides to take up arms rather than seek peace, cave in or abandon their war aims. As a rule, we might say, such organized violence seems an acceptable risk under two broad conditions: when the outcome is uncertain enough to offer both sides a chance of success; or when the 'peaceful' alternative looks even more threatening. Of course, the choice between peace and war is never so simple. It is invariably complicated by all sorts of contingencies. One of the most critical is the supply of information, the basis on which the judgement of risk must be made. The information available to one or both sides may be sparse, misleading or outdated. It may derive from informants whose motives are tainted by self-interest or whose understanding is poor. It will always be biased by both source and transmission. Just as important are the expert advisers to whom rulers and generals, or humbler participants, have to turn to interpret the knowledge they have. But advice and assessment will also be skewed by unspoken assumptions, private objectives, ignorance or prejudice. Thirdly, much will depend on *where* the decision is actually made. Where no strong centre exists, or if it lacks real control, unauthorized action in a particular place might ignite a much larger conflict. A trivial mêlée (what Kipling called 'a scrimmage at a border station'), a case of 'hot pursuit', a provocative gesture, could set off an explosion. Even the most sophisticated governments were (and are) prone to these dangers. In colonial conditions, the risks that they posed were bound to be high.

UNDIPLOMATIC RELATIONS

Part of the problem was that the rules of diplomatic behaviour and the thinking behind them were not the same in different parts of the world – why should they have been? Diplomatically speaking, Europe was a rarefied world with peculiar habits. Firstly, since the Renaissance or earlier, the European states had exchanged resident ambassadors, 'men sent to lie abroad for their country', as the Renaissance quip had it. The most efficient of these sent back a stream of reports: the detailed accounts of English affairs by Venetian ambassadors have been a valuable source for later historians. Secondly, the shared protocols of diplomatic procedure (including minute variations of language and etiquette) supplied a range of delicate signals by which changes in the temperature of the relations between two states could be constantly monitored. Thirdly, from the mid seventeenth century onwards, the European states had acknowledged that full members of their state-system enjoyed the status of sovereignty: freedom from interference in their domestic affairs and the right to exist as separate self-ruling units.[14]

Of course, none of this was enough to restrain the ambitions of dynasts and despots, prevent the murder of Poland (one of Europe's largest states) by three successive partitions (1772–95), or keep the European peace. The main advantage of the European system lay in the ceaseless flow of intelligence, in the conventions that regulated the treatment of foreigners in peacetime, and in the strict central control that most states maintained over their external relations. By the mid eighteenth century, if not earlier, Europeans increasingly regarded this regional pattern as the ideal against which other (non-European) behaviour was judged and found wanting. Having clear recognized borders, imposing effective control over this bounded terrain, protecting foreign persons and property, and using 'civilized' methods for policing and punishment became the criteria of a civilized state if it was to be treated as equal with the states of Europe. As might be predicted, many of the world's rulers fell into the 'barbarous' category.[15] This did not preclude making treaties with them for mutual advantage, or, as happened across Africa after 1815, to get local support to outlaw the slave trade. But it did mean that respect for their boundaries, independence and even their property was conditional on their 'good behaviour' or their willing acceptance of trade. 'It may be true in one sense,' said Lord Palmerston, musing on West Africa, 'that Trade ought not to be enforced by Cannon Balls, but on the other hand Trade cannot flourish without security, and that security may be unattainable without the Protection of physical force. The occupation of Lagos,' he went on, 'may be a very useful and important step for the suppression of Slave Trade and for the promotion of Legitimate Commerce.'[16] Lagos, as we saw, was duly annexed. Convenience not right was the basis on which the Victorians acknowledged the sovereignty of African rulers.

However, the barbarous category was of limited use in other parts of the world. The image of China in eighteenth-century Europe was quite the reverse. Since China manufactured the luxury goods that Europeans valued so much, it could hardly be otherwise, and some commentators contrasted the orderly rule of its rational 'scholar-mandarins' favourably with that of Europe's aristocracies. The problem with China was that the status allotted to Britain (and Europe) in its rulers' world-view was disconcertingly humble. In 1793, London sent Lord Macartney, a highly experienced diplomat, to persuade the Qing emperor to accept a permanent embassy. Macartney was appalled to discover on arrival in Beijing that when meeting the emperor he was expected to fall on both knees and perform 'nine prostrations', touching his forehead to the ground – the famous 'kow tow'.[17] After tetchy discussion, the Chinese officials accepted a compromise: Macartney would fall on *one* knee, and, so far as we know, he escaped the prostrations. But the difference of view went well beyond knees. Macartney pressed the case for a permanent embassy. 'I told him [a senior Chinese official] that the sovereigns of Europe usually kept ambassadors constantly resident at each other's Courts for the purpose of cultivating reciprocal friendships, and preventing misunderstandings.'[18] But, he was told, 'it was otherwise in China which never sends ambassadors to foreign countries' and allowed those that came to Beijing only forty days' stay. This dismiss-ive response was part of a well-ordered view of the world. The Chinese knew enough about Europe to be alarmed at reports of what was then happening in France. But they regarded Europeans as 'outer barbari-ans', faraway peoples of whom they knew little and cared even less. Their civilized world (in practice East Asia) was made up of tributary states who acknowledged the primacy of the Chinese Middle King-dom, and of the 'Son of Heaven' as its ruler.[19] Far from cultivating reciprocal friendship, the Chinese preferred to keep their commercial dealings with Europe under strict supervision. The system in force since the early eighteenth century required all foreign merchants to visit only one port (Canton), to deal with the *Hong*, an approved clique of merchants, to keep to their factories on an island in the river, and to leave the city altogether when the trading season ended.[20]

Macartney himself warned against attacking China, which he lik-ened to 'an old, crazy . . . man-of-war'. If China broke up '(no very improbable event)', Britain's interests in Asia might suffer great dam-age, not least from the expansion of tsarist Russia.[21] But some forty years later, the precarious stability of Anglo-Chinese relations began to break down. As the China trade opened up (the East India Com-pany lost its official monopoly on trade with China in 1833), more and more British merchants crowded in to sell opium, the one foreign commodity for which demand was assured. When the Chinese authorities imposed their ban on the import of opium, and then seized and destroyed the stocks held by the merchants in April 1839, the British riposted with an attack on their war-junks. But it was as much the unbridgeable gulf between two views of the world as the lobbying of merchants against the ban on opium imports which trig-gered the British invasion in the first Opium War of 1839–42.[22] 'We have given the Chinese a most exemplary drubbing,' wrote Lord Palmerston several years later. 'But we must stop on the very thresh-old any attempt on their part to treat us otherwise than as their equals.'[23] The pursuit of equality led, ironically, to the 'unequal trea-ties', of which the Nanjing treaty of 1842 was the first of many. It exempted British merchants from Chinese jurisdiction in a set of treaty port enclaves, annexed Hong Kong island to Britain, and restricted Chinese duties on British goods to a minimal 5 per cent.[24]

For the rest of the century, the presence of the British (and other Europeans) and the restless attempts to expand their mercantile and missionary activity were a source of chronic if usually localized friction, and the underlying cause of two further wars.[25] Yet the British resisted the lure of partitioning China or attempting its conquest. 'One India is enough,' was the view in London. But perhaps there was also a feeling that China's sheer longevity as a unified state ruled out a colonial-type conquest, the opinion of the famous international lawyer F. F. Martens.[26] Instead, the British pinned their hopes on reforming China's systems of law and finance and pushing open the door for more railways and trade. China's sovereign status might have been battered and bruised, but it was meant to survive, even if under tutelage. India had been different.

The British had gone to India after 1600 as merchants not conquerors. To ply their business as traders, they had needed the goodwill of the local authorities, and most of all that of the Mughal emperor in Delhi. Whatever private feelings they had, the East India Company's officials were careful to show proper deference to the emperor. When his delegates called, they dressed up in the styles that his courtiers wore to show they were 'his' men.[27] The one attempt to defy him before 1700 had ended in disaster. When the Company had waged war in 1688–9, sending a military force to strengthen its position in India, its Surat factory was closed down and Bombay blockaded. Peace had to be sought on the emperor's terms.[28] The war in Bengal that Clive won at Plassey in 1757 arose from the decay of Mughal authority and the bid for power by the Muslim viceroy of the province. Yet even after his victory, and the further triumph at Buxar, Clive was very reluctant to change the Company's subordinate status and deny Mughal overlordship. To do so, he argued, would arouse the suspicions of other European powers. Fear that the Company would bankrupt itself by over-expansion (with huge knock-on effects in the City of London) also unnerved the politicians at home. In the India Act of 1784, drawn up to control the Company's government in India, it was roundly stated that 'to pursue schemes of conquest and extension of dominion in India are measures repugnant to the wish, the honour and the policy of this nation'.[29] Faced with other powerful 'successor states' such as Hyderabad, Mysore and the Maratha confederacy, the Company's policy was to maintain a 'balance of power'.[30] But everything changed with the rise of Napoleon, his invasion of Egypt in 1798 and the prospect of French help for Tipu Sultan, the dynamic ruler of Mysore and an inveterate enemy of the British. The British were determined to form a coalition against him. The governor-general, Lord Wellesley (elder brother of Arthur, later Duke of Wellington), denied any suggestion that the Company meant to expand, insisting instead that its aim was solely to prevent the intrusion of a foreign power (perhaps a case of pot calling kettle black). Mysore was invaded and Tipu was killed in the battle for his capital in 1799. The French threat receded (they were chased out of Egypt). But there was no peace in India.

Instead, the defeat of Mysore sharpened the mutual animosity between the Maratha states and the Company. Both vied for control over the puppet Mughal emperor in Delhi still venerated 'by all classes of people in India, and especially by . . . Mussulmans'.[31] The British feared a new Indian coalition against *them*, between Marathas and Sikhs (the Punjab was another successor state), and other militant peoples in North India. The result was a ragged series of wars that raged across central and northern India until the final Maratha defeat in 1818 (the Punjab Sikhs' independence survived until 1849). Only then could the British begin to think of themselves as the 'paramount power' in India, with the right to make and unmake princely rulers.[32] But they remained circumspect. There was no public denial that Britain's position in India derived from a grant by the Mughals to the Company. It was a considerable embarrassment when 'the king of Delhi', as the British now called him, sent an emissary to London, the great intellectual Ram Mohan Roy, to complain about the Company. Until 1835 the Company's money was issued with the emperor's head on its coins. It was the trauma of rebellion in 1857 that finally forced the issue. The last emperor, Bahadur Shah, was implicated in the revolt, tried for rebellion and exiled to Burma, where he died in 1862.[33] The 1858 Government of India Act that abolished the Company swept away all ambiguity. 'India,' it said, 'shall be governed by and in the name of her Majesty.' The British queen was now the sovereign of India.

The British in India thus displayed a jumble of attitudes. For reasons

of prudence, they maintained most of the old apparatus of government, even if they exploited its revenue system more severely. They
consulted Hindu and Muslim scholars in their effort to codify laws.
Despite strong evangelical feeling among many British officials, the
Company raj observed a careful neutrality towards all religious
belief. In their wars of conquest, they tried to present themselves as
one of the subcontinent's country powers, not as foreign intruders,
and were anxious to claim the Mughal emperor's goodwill. In all
these ways, they were careful to treat India as a different world, not
as a zone of barbarity. But there was another side to their thinking.
As their dominance grew, they were inclined more and more to see
British rule as having rescued India from chaos. They tended increasingly to harp on those features of Indian society that Europeans
found least appealing. Neither had the motives behind their expansion been as entirely defensive as the Company liked to pretend.
The Company's servants had a great deal to gain from its wars of
expansion. The officers of its army gathered prizes and plunder. Its
officials invested their incomes in 'agency houses' whose profits often
depended upon enlisting official support against their Indian creditors.[34] On one celebrated occasion, Company officials in Madras
were so enraged by the governor's refusal to send the army to collect
the debts privately owed them by the ruler of Arcot that they staged
a coup and threw him in gaol (where he later died). On this frontier
of empire, it was often hard to distinguish the private interest from
the public.

The dangers to peace posed by 'unofficial' expansion were much
harder to tame when and where settlers were numerous. In both
China and India, the British were relatively few, official control was
quite strong, and local resistance was considerable. But there were
plenty of places where conditions were different. The first settlers in
New England were a law unto themselves. When the Pilgrim Fathers
went ashore in a group led by a professional soldier, Myles Standish,
they helped themselves to an Indian grain store (a 'providential discovery'), returning some weeks later to take some more, as well as
ransacking Indian graves and huts.[35] Fear and hunger created a paranoid mood that saw conspiracy everywhere. With little understanding
of the Indian peoples around them, they were easily duped into savage

reprisals against those who had done them no harm. Few settlers had the time or inclination to study their indigenous neighbours: their values, beliefs, interests and fears remained a closed book, except to a handful of intermediaries (usually traders or missionaries) whose opinions were often mistrusted. Short of a major upset to their view of the world, settler communities had little reason to shed the racial, religious and cultural preconceptions that informed their attitude to indigenous peoples. They had, on the contrary, strong motives of self-interest to cherish their prejudices and, if necessary, express them in violence. For in most settler societies the main source of new wealth lay in access to land. Crude methods of agriculture, the addiction of wealthier settlers to speculation in land, and population pressure created an insatiable demand for expansion at all costs. Fear of land shortage would drive away capital and condemn the colony to stagnation. Because the stakes seemed so high, the buying (or taking) of land from first peoples was often accompanied by coercive, aggressive or threatening behaviour. The absence or inadequacy of frontier tribunals to resolve disputes to the satisfaction of both sides meant that trivial infractions (such as theft or trespass) were easily inflated into local and perhaps regional violence. Revenge and reprisal kept alive the tradition of mutual antipathy until (sometimes long after) all resistance collapsed.

The result was a rash of 'frontier wars' in most of the regions where settlers confronted indigenous peoples from the seventeenth century to the early years of the twentieth. In 'King Philip's (or Metacom's) War' in 1675–6, the whites in New England broke the resistance of the Algonquin peoples of the region, although French support from Quebec for the Abenaki tribes kept their northern frontier in turmoil until 1760. The Yamasee War in South Carolina in 1715–16 (where the whites had encouraged Indian tribes to enslave each other) and the war against the Tuscaroras in North Carolina in 1712–13 cleared vast areas of land for white occupation and killed or enslaved large numbers of Indians.[36] In South Africa, the British inherited two long-running frontier wars against the San (or Bushmen) in the arid northern interior of the Cape, and against the Xhosa to the east. For the hunter-gatherer San, the arrival of Boers with their firearms, cattle and sheep meant the loss of the wildlife on which they depended, and

of the scarce sources of water. Their resistance was fierce and frequently deadly.[37] With the Xhosa communities, the source of conflict
was different. Boers and Xhosa competed for pasture, since both lived
from cattle. Once their paths had crossed in the late 1770s, there were
constant disputes over rights to grazing, accusations of cattle stealing
and the reprisals that followed. The lack of effective authority on
both sides of the 'frontier' (a zone of mutual intrusion, not an agreed
boundary) made local agreements very hard to police. The frontier
Boers briefly declared themselves independent in rage against the lack
of support from the colony's government in Cape Town.[38] Nor was
London willing to find the resources (financial or military) to impose
a fully fledged conquest until almost a century after the opening shots
in the struggle.

Much the same pattern could be found far away in Australia. Here,
as we saw, the British intruders had simply denied that the Aborigines
had rights to the land. But for the first fifty years or so, the invasion of
Australia was one largely of beachheads, comparatively small areas
usually close to the sea.[39] The Aborigines retreated and racial conflict
was limited. But by the end of this period, the rapid growth of sheep
farming and the search for new pastures brought a surge of white
movement into the deeper interior. Faced, like other hunter-gatherers,
with the flight or destruction of wildlife and the loss of scarce water,
Aborigines staged a guerrilla resistance: stealing and killing sheep,
chasing away or murdering shepherds. The whites responded with
unrestrained ferocity. At Myall Creek in New South Wales, some
twenty-five Aborigines were murdered in cold blood in 1837, a crime
for which several whites were hanged by the colonial authorities.
Partly as a result, much frontier violence went unreported thereafter.
In the late 1830s, whites began to move into Gippsland, a wooded
and beautiful district in south-east Victoria. They soon came to blows
with the Kurnai Aborigines, with tit-for-tat killings. This quickly gave
way to something much darker. At Warrigal Creek in 1843, whites
surrounded and murdered up to 150 Kurnai men, women and children. Between then and 1860, the Kurnai population was all but
erased in a series of group murders the evidence for which has only
quite recently been pieced together.[40]

But it would be a mistake to suppose that settlers had it all their own way and defeated first peoples at will. It was not always true that their firepower was greater: the Aborigines were unlucky that there was no time to trade (and very little to trade with) before the whites arrived in force. There was no time to get guns before the whites were upon them. In the Americas, New Zealand and in much of Black Africa, guns could be bought and gun tactics tried out before the whites became strong. Settler militias drawn from farmers or traders were unlikely to fight well in the forest or bush. They often lacked discipline, were unwilling to take losses, and reluctant to leave home for more than the minimum time. Even Boer commandos, trained to the gun and the saddle, had a very mixed record against Xhosa and San. Neither the arid northern interior, nor the dense bush of the Cape eastern frontier, favoured the warfare in which they came to excel. It was only on the great open grasslands of the South African Highveld that their firepower, mobility and the defensive 'laager' of trek-wagons proved decisive. Against the Zulus, or the Pedi of the eastern Transvaal with its mountains and bush, they were much less successful.[41] Of course, settlers were helped by the effects of disease, their invisible ally, and the internal divisions among indigenous peoples. But it may have been the frustrations of conflict against tenacious opponents that helped make frontier warfare so violent. For victory seemed to be earned not by success on the battlefield, but by the elimination or removal of the other side altogether, or – in the South African setting – by its complete subjugation as a servile workforce. Terror, atrocity and the 'total war' methods later grimly familiar in twentieth-century Europe were the gruesome results.

THE 'SMALL WARS' OF THE EMPIRE

The British at home could not ignore these colonial wars, tiresome and squalid as they sometimes appeared to high-minded contemporaries. Indeed, before 1815 British expansion and prosperity seemed to much influential opinion to depend overwhelmingly upon the use of military force on land and sea. In the age of intense competition between rival mercantile powers – the French, the Spanish, the Dutch and the British – the connection between 'power' and 'plenty' was unusually close. Mercantilist doctrine recommended not free trade but the deliberate exclusion of foreigners from the metropole's trade with its colonies. The British were eager to break into the commercial empires of their rivals, especially that of Spain with its vast American realm stretching from Florida to Cape Horn (Spanish colonization of California was delayed to the 1770s). They were also afraid that their own spheres of trade would be hemmed in and suffocated unless they followed a policy of aggressive expansion, or perhaps lost altogether. It was thus an almost irresistible temptation, whenever hostilities broke out in Europe, to look for booty abroad. Here the British could exploit their usual advantage at sea, already established by 1700, compensate for their relative weakness on land, and (especially valuable for a government that depended upon parliamentary support) appeal to patriotic or jingoistic emotion.

For these kinds of reasons, British troops were dispatched to many far-off locations. The Caribbean was a cockpit since the 'sugar islands' were the single greatest source of colonial wealth. Cromwell sent an army there to capture Jamaica from Spain in 1655. An expedition was sent in 1741 to capture the key Spanish base at Cartagena, a débâcle in which 80 per cent of the force of 10,000 men quickly died of disease. To safeguard their North American colonies, the British were eager to capture Quebec, the impregnable fortress set on a high cliff, from which the French commanded the St Lawrence and the riverine entry to the North American interior. In 1711, a large expedition of over 12,000 men was sent to seize this grand prize. It was an embarrassing failure. After the loss of some ships in a storm near the mouth of the river, the commanders lost their nerve and the expedition was abandoned. The British had better success during the War of Austrian Succession when Louisbourg, the great fortress that guarded the Gulf of St Lawrence, was taken by a force of 4,000 colonial militia from New England in June 1745 – only to be handed back at the peace of Aix-la-Chapelle. In India, meanwhile, where the British and French East India Companies competed for allies and tried to disrupt each other's trade, the French seized Madras in 1746. The British regained it, but peace was elusive and the first British troops were sent to India in 1754 (the Company had until then relied on its own local force, supplemented in 1748 by 'independent companies' raised in Britain and marines from the naval squadron London had sent to support it).[42]

The outbreak of the Seven Years' War in 1756 was a turning point. For the next fifty years colonial campaigns in North America, the Caribbean and India were no longer side-shows but part of the world wars fought by the British for their imperial survival. Indeed, in the American War of 1775–83 and even more in the wars fought between 1793 and 1815, the struggles in the Caribbean and India could be realistically seen as vital to the defence of Britain itself, so often embattled both economically and strategically against a hostile Europe. As we will see in a later chapter, the long war of attrition against Napoleon produced two remarkable triumphs: on the sea at Trafalgar in 1805 and on land in the great allied victory of 1815. Together these yielded a huge geopolitical dividend. Naval supremacy and the postwar balance of power in Europe conferred an extraordinary freedom from the mercantilist rivalries of the previous century. Of course, the British remained nervous of French and Russian intentions in the Eastern Mediterranean especially, fearing their grip on the overland route to India. They were also on constant alert against a Russian move towards India, once the Tsar's armies advanced east of the Caspian in the 1860s and 1870s. But across a huge swathe of the world, they could act militarily as if, in the words of a much-travelled Victorian, 'the ocean was a British possession'.[43] Much of their army was dispersed in 'penny-packets' – small colonial garrisons weeks if not months from home. They sent expeditionary forces to China, Ethiopia, West Africa and Egypt, confident that they would face only local opposition. For most of the century they could be reasonably sure that only small armies were needed for the wars outside Europe, and that their campaigns would be short and relatively cheap.

The great exception was India. Militarily, India was a strange combination of liability and asset. By 1840 the Company had an army of 250,000 men, the largest and most modern in Asia. But it also paid to keep on the spot some 20,000 men from the British army at home (over 30,000 in 1847) – as an ultimate safeguard.[44] The sepoy Mutiny – the core of the Great Rebellion of 1857 – changed all that: 90,000 British soldiers had to be sent to restore British control. When the dust had settled, the decision was made to shrink the Indian army to half its size, while the British garrison was increased to over three times its pre-Mutiny strength. Henceforth there would be one British soldier to every two Indian: any hint of mutiny would be stopped in its tracks. The main advantage of this was to keep nearly half the British army as a strategic reserve for Britain's empire east of Suez at the Indian taxpayer's expense, for India met all its ordinary costs. The great disadvantage was the need to provide a constant stream of fresh men to make up for the wastage, since the death-rate in India remained appallingly high. The strain on the rest of the army was a chronic complaint.

In principle, then, the British disposed after 1860 of an army of more than 300,000 regular soldiers, two-thirds of them Indians or stationed in India. They liked to keep around half the remainder at home to be trained, to watch over Ireland or in case of tension in Europe. The rest were scattered in colonial posts. The workhorse of the British army was the 'line battalion', each with thirty officers and some 900 men. They manned the garrisons, and made up the forces that were sent overseas. There was no general staff. When an expeditionary force was assembled, its commander recruited his staff from his circle of protégés or career-minded applicants. Since he expected to fight outside Europe and in frontier conditions, his immediate concern was transport and logistics: to get his force to the war zone and keep it supplied. Before 1850, most senior officers had fought as young men in what was then called the 'Great War' of 1793–1815. After that date, few lacked experience in either Asia or Africa or against the Maori in New Zealand. The greatest challenge they faced, having arrived on the scene, was deciding what goal to aim for and what tactics to use. In European warfare the rules of the game were straightforward. When its army was beaten, the sovereign state would surrender and a new treaty was made. Against non-European foes, nothing could be taken for granted.

In his classic study *Small Wars: Their Principles and Practice*, published in 1896, Colonel Charles Callwell identified three different kinds: campaigns to suppress insurrection, campaigns of conquest and annexation and campaigns 'to wipe out an insult, to avenge a wrong or overthrow a dangerous enemy'.[45] The difficulty with small wars, as Callwell admitted, was that conditions varied so much. Generalizations were chancy, but certain maxims stood out. What he called 'moral effect' was 'often far more important than material success' and 'operations are sometimes limited to committing havoc which the laws of regular warfare do not sanction' – a delicate phrase to cover the destruction of houses and crops and the looting of palaces as in China, Ashanti and Burma.[46] The lack of reliable knowledge, the problem of transport where roads and railways were absent, and the threat posed by disease were what gave small wars their peculiar nature. Unlike the warfare between modern regular armies, 'they are in the main campaigns against nature'.[47] Logistics, intelligence and an eye to moral effect (what a cynic might call terror) were the keys to success.

In fact, long before Callwell British troops had applied his nostrums in their colonial campaigns. Military operations were dictated by the 'leash' – the line of communications that led back to their main base, the source of supplies and the haven in case of disaster. The 'LoC' had to be protected at all costs. British forces sometimes severed the link to gain greater mobility, but the price could be high. Dragging food, water and munitions behind them in a long baggage train slowed a force to a crawl and diverted much of its firepower in the event of a battle. One of the worst British defeats, at Maiwand near the Helmand valley in Afghanistan in July 1880 when a British and Indian brigade was routed with the loss of over 1,700 killed, can be attributed to this distraction. The logic of the supply problem was to bring the enemy to battle as soon as possible, to inflict a knock-out blow. The thinking behind this was as much psychological as military. 'Dash at the first fellows that make their appearance and the campaign will be our own' was Wellington's prescription.[48] 'That is the way to deal with Asiatics,' opined Callwell, 'to go for them and cow them by sheer force of will.'[49] One decisive defeat would destroy the will to fight on. If their opponents declined to stand and fight, the aim was to inflict the maximum damage on prestige and possessions: to chase a ruler away, demolish his capital and seize any movable property.[50]

But (as we will see) it was not quite as easy as that. At the tactical level, the question was how to bring superior firepower (the usual

British advantage) to bear. The favoured method was to advance towards the enemy in a column to maximize impact and speed, but then deploy in a line to deliver the heaviest volley of fire. The risk that this ran was that if the line was broken by the sheer weight of the enemy, disaster would follow, as at Isandhlwana in January 1879. The alternative tactic, forming a square, was often preferred. But it was not a perfect solution. If the force's supplies and transport were kept safely inside, the square might swell to an indefensible size, with a herd of terrified oxen penned up in its midst. Left out, they might be an easy prize for the enemy, destroying the column's future mobility. By definition a square reduced available firepower on any one side, making it vulnerable to a heavyweight punch. A cool-headed opponent might aim at its corners where its cohesion was weakest. It was dangerous to use against serious enemy firepower or guns. A campaign commander had to weigh up the odds: the terrain, what he knew of the enemy's strength and equipment, and the effect of his tactics on the loyalty and morale of the local auxiliaries – whether white settlers or native contingents – on whom he relied not least for intelligence, scouting and skirmishing. His usual concern was to husband his handful of British battalions as the shock troops whose disciplined fire and bayonet charge was expected to break any foe.

What was it like on the other side of the hill? Those who resisted a British invasion needed time on their side. British commanders were always in a hurry: they knew London's patience was short and their careers in the balance. The best tactic against them was irregular warfare, to wear down their resolve and drive up their costs. But few local rulers found this easy. They feared its effects on their political power, since irregular war was by nature decentralized. Most indigenous states in Asia and Africa were also dangerously vulnerable to the hardships of war. The loss of a harvest and the diversion of manpower from the production of food might be economically fatal: without a supply system resistance would simply collapse. In a small population, any losses in battle were hard to make up: without medical care the wounded soon turned into the dead. Guns were often available, but typically they were old-fashioned, inefficient and inexpertly used. Once the British made use of rapid-firing rifles in the 1870s and after, once the clumsy and unreliable Gatling ('the Gatling's jammed and the colonel dead')[51] had been replaced by the Maxim machine gun, and when they were able to deploy light field guns (a particularly devastating weapon against most African armies), the disparity in firepower was often overwhelming, producing a staggering disproportion in casualties. At Omdurman in September 1898, Kitchener's mixed force of British and Egyptians lost forty-eight killed: his Mahdist opponents at least 10,000.

There was, perhaps, no 'typical' colonial war, and we should not assume that the British could always exploit the advantages of discipline and technology. In America in the 1750s, they learned the hard way that a column of redcoats could be destroyed in the forest by a 'primitive' foe. In July 1755, the attempt under Braddock to capture Fort Duquesne (modern Pittsburgh) suffered a catastrophic defeat when ambushed by Indians: two-thirds of his 1,200 men were killed (the fate of Braddock himself) or wounded. Braddock had failed to use scouts, his troops were too close together, and he had neglected to occupy the high ground around his line of march.[52] In India, they often faced armies whose training and firepower was as good as their own. It was careful attention to the problem of supply (Wellington's great skill later put to good use in Europe) which allowed the Company's armies to stay in the field and outlast their enemies. It was the Company's revenues that helped it to buy up the supply of professional soldiers, squeezing the so-called 'military labour market' on which all armies in India had come to depend by the late eighteenth century.[53] But there were critical limits to British success. In the American War of Independence, the British were beaten by the sheer scale of support that the rebels enjoyed from the population around them. Their local loyalist allies were crushed by a murderous war of dispossession and terror.[54] In the second South African War (1899–1902), the British struggled against mobile Boer commandos who 'swam' in the veld, where every farm might be used as a temporary base. Only the ruthless clearing and concentration of the civilian community, and the minuscule size of the Boer fighting force, secured an ambiguous victory in May 1902. Nor was it just against European enemies that their military power faltered. The Northwest frontier of India, with its vast Afghan backdrop, soaked up the military power of the Raj like a sponge. Two British invasions of Afghanistan (1838–42 and 1878–80) had led first to disasters, then to secondary onslaughts to inflict retribution, and then withdrawal. Against the tribes of the frontier, who could muster perhaps a half million fighting men, and a savage landscape of mountain, ravine and dark defile, they fell back on containment: a variable mixture of bribery (or 'subsidy'), diplomacy, periodic forward movements and punitive warfare – 'when punishment has been meted out operations cease' remarked an army handbook in the 1930s.[55] The art of colonial war lay, partly at least, in the wise choice of foe.

GENERAL WOLSELEY'S WARS

A closer look at three Late Victorian campaigns will allow us to see the British way of colonial warfare – and the tactics their enemies tried against them – in a little more detail. Each of the three was in Africa, although on quite different terrain: dense forest, open veld, desert and delta. Each revealed above all the key role of supply and communications: two by design and one by default. It was not accidental that in the third case – the Anglo-Zulu War of 1879 – Wolseley, the grandmaster of small wars, arrived too late on the scene to insist on his methods. The war, he remarked caustically, had been 'commenced in madness and continued in folly'. Instead Wolseley's main role was to impose the punitive peace that ended for ever the military power of the Zulu state.

Wolseley's fame was assured by the Ashanti War of 1873–4. Ashanti (or Asante) was a West African state in what is now the central portion of Ghana. It had a well-organized army ('disciplined, under command and well in hand' observed one British officer during the war),[56] well supplied with firearms. Its rulers (the Asantehene) resented the foreign presence at the coast (where the British occupied a handful of decrepit forts) and periodically asserted their claims over the Fante tribes who enjoyed British protection. In the bloodiest of these conflicts, the then British governor had marched out against the Ashanti only to be abandoned by his allies: he and his twenty-five white officers were cut down and beheaded. So when a new Ashanti invasion began in March 1873, London watched nervously. The Ashanti routed the Fante resistance. So London sent a black battalion from Barbados, the West India regiment, and 100 Royal Marines, most of whom fell sick. Its man on the spot urged an attack on Kumasi, the Ashanti capital. But London prevaricated. Instead it dispatched Major-General Garnet Wolseley who took with him thirty 'special service officers'.

Wolseley was the model of Victorian professionalism. He was a Protestant Irishman whose father, also an army officer, had died when he was seven. He served in the war against Burma (1852), in the Crimea (1854–6), in India during the Mutiny, in China (during the second Opium War of 1858–60), and in Canada during the American war scare of the early 1860s. His *Soldier's Pocket Book* (1869) was a widely used manual of practical warfare and showed his close grasp of logistics. His organizational talents were shown to advantage in the expedition sent to disperse the *Métis* resistance to the Canadians' takeover of Manitoba in 1870–71.[57] He was the obvious choice to deal with the inconvenient emergency that now arose on the Gold Coast.

It was not entirely clear what he was meant to do. Wolseley himself almost certainly thought that to defeat the Ashanti would require British troops to be sent from home. He drew up an elaborate plan to select a crack force drawn from the best line battalions. But ministers made no promises. Wolseley should seek an 'honourable peace', the Colonial Secretary Lord Kimberley told him. On his way out, Wolseley had arranged to hire some martial assistance from Muslim fighters in Sierra Leone ('Kossoos') and Hausas brought from Lagos. His cadre of special service officers (among them the best and brightest of the Late Victorian British army) were expected to recruit a large local army from the coastal tribes and then lead them in battle. 'The utmost good temper, affability and patience, mingled with fixity of purpose and determination, are of the greatest importance,' Wolseley instructed them. When he arrived in early October 1873, his first task was to arrange the defence of Cape Coast Castle, the British headquarters, against an Ashanti host scarcely a few miles away. But it soon became clear, in the confused struggle at Abrakampa, that Wolseley's Fante army, driven into battle by their British officers with blows from sticks and umbrellas, were no match for the Ashanti.[58] To the cynical eye of the *Times* correspondent, Winwood Reade, Wolseley presented the 'ludicrous spectacle' of a major-general with no troops, the attack on the Ashanti had been a fiasco, and (so he claimed) he found Wolseley lost in the bush and facing the wrong way.[59]

Wolseley meanwhile had sent London a message that it dared not ignore. It threatened in effect a shameful disaster if British troops were not sent. Wolseley's reputation (and the attendant publicity) meant that his views could not be dismissed. On the day his message arrived, the two battalions he asked for received orders to go, and a third was made ready. But the conditions were stringent. Wolseley was only to use them if it was of 'paramount importance', and if conditions ensured the swift execution of their military task. They were not even to be landed 'until the time for decisive action has arrived'.[60] Part of this extreme caution reflected the strain on the army that we have noted already: a product of its huge commitment in India. But it mainly reflected the fear of disease in a region often referred to as 'the white man's grave'. Malaria, yellow fever and dysentery could wipe out an army with appalling efficiency. Wolseley had to defeat the Ashanti with the utmost speed and at minimum cost.

He had already decided that the 'moral effects of a great victory' to 'destroy forever [Ashanti's] military prestige' would best be achieved by destroying its capital, Kumasi.[61] Wolseley's hallmark was planning. He laid down precisely what his white troops should wear: grey tweed jackets and trousers (to guard against fever and chills) and helmets (against the sun). To fight in thick forest they should have short rifles. Lime juice was to be issued four times a week; fires to be lit to keep 'miasma' at bay; and cocoa, biscuits and quinine to be served before marching. 'If any irregularity of the bowels is experienced,' Wolseley ordered, 'go at once to the doctor for a dose.'[62] The immediate task was to prepare the advance base for the attack on Kumasi: an inland depot for stores and equipment linked by a road to the coast. A large labour force would have to be found to build the road, carry the stores and help transport the army: one porter was needed for every three soldiers and one each for the officers. Only when the build-up was ready would the white soldiers land and the expedition begin.

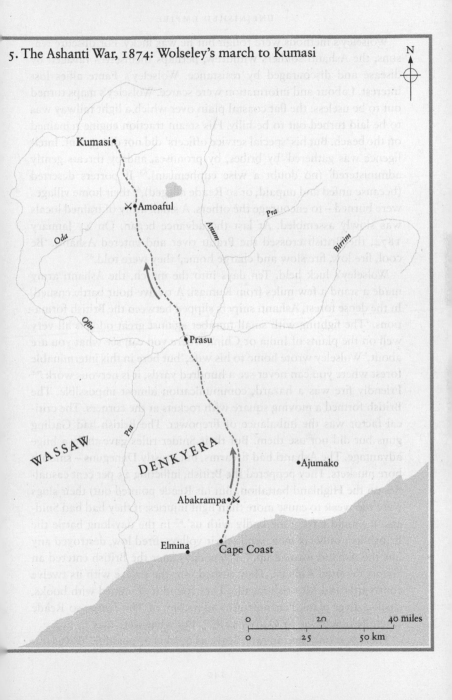

5. The Ashanti War, 1874: Wolseley's march to Kumasi

N

Kumasi

Amoaful

Oda

Pra

Anum

Birrim

Offin

Prasu

Pra

WASSAW

DENKYERA

Ajumako

Abakrampa

Elmina

Cape Coast

| 0 | | 20 | | 40 miles |

| 0 | 25 | | 50 km |

Wolseley's methods were rough but he was lucky. For obscure reasons, the Ashanti soldiers withdrew, perhaps themselves ravaged by disease and discouraged by resistance. Wolseley's Fante allies lost interest. Labour and information were scarce. Wolseley's maps turned out to be useless: the flat coastal plain over which a light railway was to be laid turned out to be hilly. His steam traction engine remained on the beach. But his 'special service officers' did not disappoint. Intelligence was gathered 'by bribes, by promises, and by threats gently administered' (no doubt a wise euphemism).[63] If porters deserted (because unfed and unpaid, or so Reade alleged),[64] their home villages were burned – to encourage the others. A small army of trained locals was slowly assembled. At last the advance began. On 21 January 1874, the British crossed the Prahu river and entered Ashanti. 'Be cool, fire low, fire slow and charge home,' they were told.[65]

Wolseley's luck held. Ten days into the march, the Ashanti army made a stand a few miles from Kumasi. A twelve-hour battle ensued. In the dense forest, Ashanti snipers slipped between the British formations. 'The fighting with small number against great odds is all very well on the plains of India or China where you can see what you are about,' Wolseley wrote home to his wife, 'but here in this interminable forest where you can never see a hundred yards, it is nervous work.'[66] Friendly fire was a hazard, communication almost impossible. The British formed a moving square with rockets at the corners. The critical factor was the imbalance of firepower. The British had Gatling guns but did not use them. But their Snider rifles gave them a huge advantage. The Ashanti had firearms, but mostly Daneguns – smooth bore muskets. They peppered the British, inflicting 25 per cent casualties on the Highland battalion. But (as Reade pointed out) their slugs were too weak to cause more than light injuries: if they had had Sniders, 'it would have gone badly with us'.[67] In the day-long battle the British lost only six men, while their volleys, fired low, destroyed any line the Ashanti formed up.[68] A few days later the British entered an almost deserted Kumasi. They rushed into the palace with its twelve courtyards and Moorish façade. They found it crammed with books, clocks, silver plate, Persian rugs and a copy of *The Times*, so Reade carefully noted, for 17 October 1843. But what were they to do?

There was only one answer: leave as quickly as possible. 'It was out of the question,' remarked Brackenbury, Wolseley's chief of staff, 'to undertake any operation which might involve another battle' or to hunt the king down.[69] Sickness was mounting and supplies running low. Wolseley feared that lengthening his line of retreat to the coast would make it impossible to bring out his wounded and sick. At first light on 6 February, after barely a day in the city, the British marched out, loaded with plunder and setting numerous fires. A fortnight later, Wolseley was back at the coast; by 4 March he was at sea. On 14 March, the Ashanti king signed a treaty renouncing his claims on the coast. He promised free trade and to keep open the road to Kumasi, and paid an indemnity in gold dust. Wolseley had triumphed (the greatest triumph of all was to have kept the mortality in his white troops to 1 per cent – an unprecedented achievement). But the margin of victory had been strikingly narrow. The Ashanti lived to fight another day.

The Zulu War was a different story. The British had lived nervously in the shadow of the Zulu state since they annexed Natal in 1843. The whites on the spot lacked the power to defeat it. London showed no interest in sending an army to do so. But in the late 1870s the situation suddenly changed. The crude Boer state in the Transvaal was on the brink of collapse: a disastrous war against the Pedi in the mountain and bush along its eastern frontier pushed it into bankruptcy. When the British sent a mission to impose annexation there was little resistance. To the British governor at the Cape, egged on by London and his key local adviser, the Natal official Sir Theophilus Shepstone, now was the moment to impose a single political system on the whole of South Africa, uniting its jumble of quarrelling white and black states.[70] The Zulu kingdom seemed the last major obstacle. Its military power was based on the *amabutho* service owed by adult males to the king. They were formed into regiments (organized by age) and carefully trained in the complex manoeuvres the Zulu rulers had evolved: the so-called 'horns' in which the enemy was first drawn into battle and then enveloped from the wings and the rear. Success also depended on expert reconnaissance and, at the critical moment, on the disciplined ferocity of the assegai charge – the equivalent of Wolseley's 'fire low . . . charge home'.[71] Until Zulu power was demolished, the British now reasoned, the peaceful development of the whole region would be held up indefinitely – a view which white land speculators endorsed with enthusiasm.

The Cape governor, Sir Bartle Frere, decided to strike while the iron was hot. A small British army was already on the spot, since another frontier war had erupted in the Eastern Cape. At its conclusion, it was rushed north to Natal. From a minor provocation, an ultimatum was framed to Cetshwayo, the Zulu king, to dismantle his *amabutho* army. When he refused, the invasion began. Frere and his commander Lord Chelmsford were anxious to win quickly, not least because London had not approved of their plan and a *fait accompli* was needed. So Chelmsford rushed his fences.[72] Instead of the patient build-up on which Wolseley always insisted, three British columns marched into Zululand. One got stuck in a siege from which it was too weak to break out. The second in the north was mauled by a Zulu *impi*[73] that arrived unexpectedly. The third crossed the Tugela and then split into two. One part, under Chelmsford, pressed forward to reconnoitre. The rest camped at Isandhlwana.

What followed there on 22 January 1879 was a massacre: of the 1,700 men in the force, British regulars, white colonials and blacks, barely a hundred escaped. It was a classic demonstration of how a colonial battle could go badly wrong for the British. They had too large a camp to be safely defended. Their intelligence was poor: until the last moment they had little idea that a large Zulu army was close. With little time to prepare and too much to defend, they formed a line and not a square, relying on firepower to break the Zulu advance. But their line was too long and too thin, was easily broken by the disciplined weight of the Zulu assault, and then attacked from the side. Once that had happened, the British force broke up into groups which had to fight at close quarters. Only those with luck (or a horse) escaped the slaughter since the Zulus took no prisoners. Under its brooding lion-like mountain, the battle-site retains to this day an eerie suggestion of the terror and horror.

Isandhlwana was a shocking defeat, the largest loss of life in a single day the Victorian army was to suffer in any colonial war.[74] But it was not decisive. Two months later, further north at Khambula, Evelyn Wood, a veteran of Ashanti, commanding a mixed army of whites

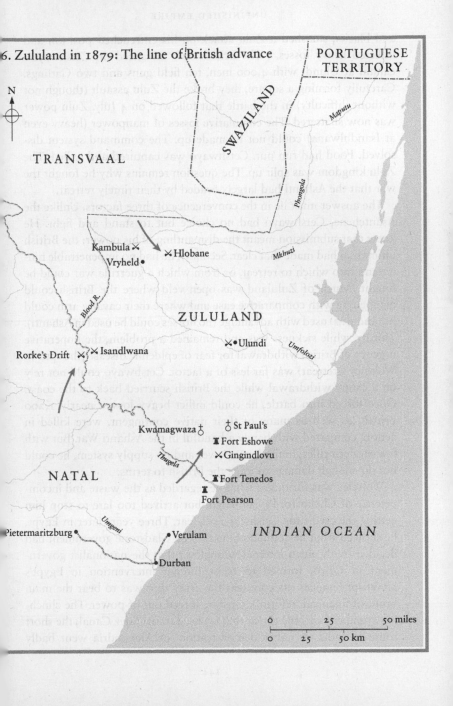

6. Zululand in 1879: The line of British advance

PORTUGUESE TERRITORY

N

TRANSVAAL

SWAZILAND

Maputu

Phongola

Kambula ✕
Vryheld ●

✕ Hlobane

Mkhuzi

Blood R.

ZULULAND

Rorke's Drift ✕
✕ Isandlwana

✕ ● Ulundi

Umfolozi

Kwamagwaza ✞

☿ St Paul's

☿ Fort Eshowe
✕ Gingindlovu

Thugela

NATAL

☿ Fort Tenedos

☿
Fort Pearson

Umgeni

Pietermaritzburg ●

● Verulam

● Durban

INDIAN OCEAN

0   25   50 miles

0   25   50 km

and blacks, smashed a Zulu attack on his entrenched position and inflicted heavy losses.[75] The British now advanced on Cetshwayo's capital at Ulundi with 4,000 men, ten field guns and two Gatlings. Carefully forming a square, they broke the Zulu assault (though not without difficulty) in the battle that followed on 4 July. Zulu power was now shattered. The cumulative losses of manpower (heavy even at Isandhlwana) could not be made up. The command system dissolved. Food had run out. Cetshwayo was captured and exiled. The Zulu kingdom was split up. The question remains why he fought the war that the Ashanti had largely evaded by their timely retreat.

The answer must lie in the convergence of three factors. Unlike the Asantehene, Cetshwayo had no choice but to stand and fight. He knew that submission meant the dismantling of his power: the British ultimatum had made that clear. Secondly, he had no impenetrable hinterland into which to retreat, or from which a guerrilla war could be fought. Much of Zululand was open veld where the British could manoeuvre with comparative ease and where their cavalry arm could be (and was) used with advantage (no horses could be used in Ashanti). Thirdly, while sickness was and remained a problem, the imperative urgency of British withdrawal for fear of epidemic disease (the spur to Wolseley's retreat) was far less of a factor. Cetshwayo could not rely on a canny withdrawal while the British scurried back to the coast. Once forced into battle, he could inflict heavy losses: nearly 1,200 British, as well as many of their native contingent, were killed in action, compared with barely a handful in the Ashanti War. But with few modern rifles, limited manpower and no supply system, he could not do enough damage to force the British to terms.

Wolseley was furious at what he regarded as the waste and incompetence of Chelmsford's campaign, but arrived too late to stop him getting the credit for Cetshwayo's defeat. Three years later in Egypt, he showed what he could do himself. The Gladstone government had decided (with much internal wrangling) that the nationalist government in Cairo, formed to resist foreign intervention in Egypt's bankrupt finances (its core was the army that was to bear the main brunt of financial 'reform'), must be forced out of power. The clinching argument was the threat that it posed to the Suez Canal, the short route to India. A naval 'demonstration' at Alexandria went badly wrong. Far from inducing an Egyptian collapse, the bombardment provoked a furious mob into killing a number of Europeans. Plans had already been laid for a potential invasion and in early July 1882 the orders were sent out. Not without trouble, 25,000 men (by colonial standards a large army) were scraped together from battalions at home and the Mediterranean bases. Some 7,000 men (British and Indian) were ordered from India. No one expected a walkover. Egyptian terrain posed a formidable challenge; the Egyptian army was a professional force and well armed; and the nationalist leader Colonel Arabi was thought to command wide popular backing. A military setback to the British invaders might be politically fatal: Arabi's prestige would soar and the British might come under international pressure to give way.

It was the kind of conundrum that Wolseley excelled at solving. He had to decide where to invade and how to win quickly and decisively. The terrain was the key. Between Alexandria (the obvious gateway to Egypt) and Cairo lay the Nile Delta. During the High Nile from August to October much of it was submerged, and much was easily flooded. It would be hard to manoeuvre and to move quickly. Instead Wolseley chose to land at Ismailia, halfway down the Suez Canal, where the contingent from India could join him. The main advantage of this, apart from being closer to Cairo (only some seventy-five miles away), was that his army could march along the edge of the desert where the going was firm, not least for his cavalry (if you travel today from Cairo to Ismailia the white sand of the desert can be seen from the main road). There was also a railway that he hoped to exploit and a freshwater canal – a precious resource. But Wolseley had to get his army ashore and ready to move before Arabi could disrupt him. He had to prevent damage to the freshwater canal or the railway. And he had to inflict a crushing defeat as soon as they met.[76]

Wolseley adopted his 'Ashanti' technique: an advance supply base to which the main army would move when its stocks were sufficient. Arabi, meanwhile, prepared his defences at Tel el-kebir, barring the road to Cairo. From the end of August into early September, the British held off the attacks on their forward position, before moving in strength. But they faced a much larger army (perhaps three times as large but with many 'irregulars') dug in behind earthworks. There

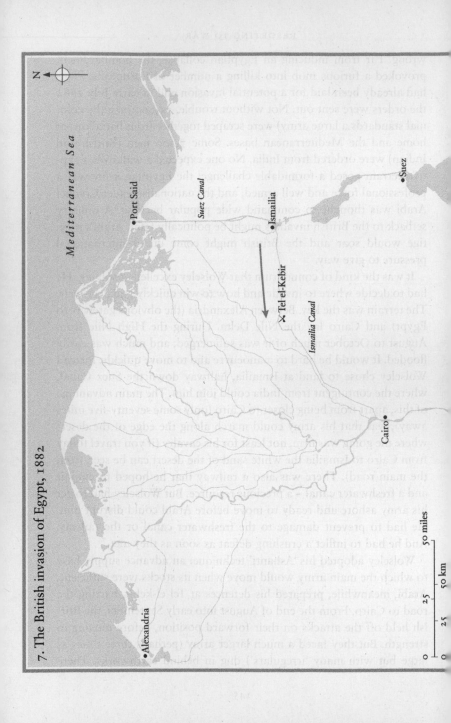

7. The British invasion of Egypt, 1882

N

Mediterranean Sea

Port Said •

• Suez

Suez Canal

Ismailia •

✕ Tel el-Kebir

Ismailia Canal

• Cairo

Alexandria •

0   25   50 km
0   25   50 miles

would be no superiority in firepower and a frontal assault might mean heavy losses. Wolseley's advantage mainly lay in the discipline and morale of his army. The British moved into position by night and in silence – a considerable feat. At dawn on 13 September, the Highland brigade stormed the Egyptian defences. Despite fierce resistance, Arabi's army was soon dislocated; it was said that by the time he was roused from sleep, his men were already in flight. The British cavalry raced forward to Cairo before Arabi could organize its resistance or – as Wolseley feared – set it on fire. Its governor was persuaded to march the garrison out and lay down its arms. By the morning of the 15th, the British were in control of the city. Within a few weeks much of their army had left. The battle for Egypt had cost them 57 men and officers killed in action, 30 missing and some 400 wounded.[77] It was an astonishing triumph. The key was supply: the means to assemble an adequate force and deliver its blow.

CONSEQUENCES

For all its limitations and setbacks, the British army proved a highly effective instrument for the defence and enlargement of empire for most of the nineteenth century until brought up short by the protracted struggle with the Boers in 1899–1902. Much of its success derived from the close attention to logistics of which Wellington, Wolseley and his 'successor' Lord Kitchener (who displayed the same combination of planning and caution) were past masters, and to the remarkable speed with which troops could be equipped and dispatched from India or home. After c. 1870, much could be attributed to the superiority of its firepower over less advanced armies – although (as we have seen) this was not always decisive. Where wheeled transport was lacking and a machine gun and its ammunition had to be carried by porters (five men were needed to carry a Maxim), it had to be used very sparingly. In two battles in Northern Nigeria in 1897, each lasting two days, machine guns were fired for no more than three minutes to conserve ammunition.[78] A good deal of that firepower was probably wasted: one expert has reckoned that at the famous siege of Rorke's Drift soon after Isandhlwana the British defenders fired some

20,000 rounds and killed 650 Zulus – more than 30 shots to claim an enemy life.[79] Discipline, morale and the cult of reckless exposure in the officer corps imbued ferocious aggression. Skill in improvisation – invariably necessary in unfamiliar terrain – was the reward for almost constant activity. And some battlegrounds became wearily familiar: the Northwest frontier of India and South Africa most of all.

But the British army did not fight alone. In the huge arc around India, a good deal of the burden fell on the 'sepoy' army: they bore the brunt of the Afghan disasters. Wherever they could (as in the Ashanti and Zulu Wars), the British conscripted large numbers of natives, as irregular battalions or native contingents. Part of their role was to clear the path for the white British battalions. 'When a body of Natives is attached,' ran the official instruction, 'it should invariably be employed in examining bush or rugged ground offering concealment to the enemy before any European body is ordered to advance ...'[80] Local auxiliaries were also conscripted to provide the labour that logistics required. Where white settlers were present, their local knowledge was used. Above all, perhaps, the army relied on an invisible ally. It was the screen provided by the navy's command of the ocean, and the assurance that gave of ready reinforcement from home, that permitted the amazing dispersal of British military power. There were few parts of Asia or even of Africa where a British brigade might not arrive on your doorstep. Who would have guessed that, when he took a few British hostage in 1867, the emperor of Ethiopia would find an army of 12,000 men invading his mountain fastness at Magdala 250 miles from the sea? Surrender and suicide were his desperate response.[81]

But there is another side to this story less often told. Much of the violence of British expansion was local, obscure and grimly banal. Even where British troops were engaged much went unnoticed or escaped official record. Civilian casualties, direct or indirect, attracted little attention. But some idea of their impact can be gauged from what happened in the kingdom of Bunyoro in what is now Western Uganda.[82] The British invaded Bunyoro in 1894, perhaps to strengthen their political influence in neighbouring Buganda: alliance with Buganda became the key to their position in the Great Lakes region of East-Central Africa. The force was a scratch one: a handful of British officers attracted by adventure or the hope of paying their debts from special service pay; some Sudanese mercenaries; a mass of Waganda led by their chiefs; and the indispensable Maxim and Hotchkiss guns. The Bunyoro warriors were outgunned; their stockades were shelled from long distance; their cattle were taken; their villages burned. A blind British eye was turned to beatings and murder. But their king Kabarega eluded capture and resistance continued. A decade of desultory war had catastrophic results. The violent disruption of the rural economy caused famine. Cultivation receded. The frequent forced movement of people led to the breakdown of the sanitary practices by which disease was controlled: here as elsewhere, war was a vector of sickness. The effects were long-lasting. Bunyoro was impoverished and suffered a demographic collapse from which its recovery was painfully slow.[83] In such a fragile ecology, the long arm of empire could inflict a terrible wound without seeing or knowing whom or what it had struck.

6

Traffic and Trade

'I conceive,' wrote the economist-courtier Samuel Fortrey in 1663, 'no foreign Plantation should be undertaken . . . but in such countreys that may increase the wealth and trade of this nation . . .'[1] It seems a simple enough point. Colonies were costly to found, could be expensive to rule, and cost even more to defend. There was no point engaging in empire unless it increased British trade. A profitless empire was a contradiction in terms.

In fact, this commonsense view was only the start of the argument. From the beginning (c. 1600) to the end (c. 1970) of Britain's overseas empire, contemporaries rarely agreed on how much it was worth. There was general agreement that plenty and power were closely related: that trade created wealth; that wealth produced power; and that power was the guardian, and should be the promoter, of trade. After that point consensus broke down. The most basic of questions asked whether colonies had any special value commercially. Was it really good business, as Adam Smith asked,[2] to give artificial encouragement to the 'colony trade' at the expense of markets nearby where the turnover of shipping and credit was faster and the employment they gave greater? Did having colonies *add* to Britain's commercial activity or merely divert it in a particular direction? Was it wise to restrict the economic life of a colony to producing certain commodities and selling them only to Britain (the rule in Smith's day)? If that made it less prosperous than it might have been otherwise (a reasonable presumption), it would surely buy less from Britain than if it were richer and freer. And if controlling the trade of its colonies was at best counterproductive, what was the point of Britain's *imperial* power, with all the costs and risks that came with the attempt to maintain it – a very pertinent question in 1776, the year *The Wealth of Nations* was published?

Nor was it obvious (at least not to everybody) that all trade was good trade. Some seventeenth-century observers (including James I) were deeply suspicious of the moral effects of smoking tobacco (the export on which Virginia's economic survival depended). It would loosen inhibitions and encourage licentious behaviour (indeed the sign of the pipe once indicated what we would call a 'red-light district'). In the eighteenth century, there were worries that the import of luxury fabrics from India would debase British taste and promote 'oriental' sensuality. The flood of Chinese ceramics and silks roused fears of a culture of excessive consumption that would vindicate greed and erode social cohesion. By the late eighteenth century, the scale of British involvement in the West African slave trade had provoked a moral revolt. Some of this spilled over into a ferocious assault on what was seen as the predatory methods of the British East India Company in India. The actions of British business abroad, especially in an imperial or quasi-imperial setting where coercion or force lurked in the background, came under fierce scrutiny in the nineteenth century and after. Selling opium in China, guns in Africa, cheap alcohol everywhere; buying land or mineral rights suspiciously cheaply (as Cecil Rhodes's British South Africa Company did in what is now Zimbabwe); resorting to forced labour to build railways or roads: all roused the anger not just of humanitarians but of those who believed that if commerce was to bring peace and civilization it must be conducted by peaceful and civilized methods.

Lurking behind these debates about trade was a set of deeper anxieties about the impact on Britain itself. Wherever trade was seen to depend upon state action – by asserting imperial rule, annexing new lands, granting preferences and subsidies, or using military power to force open a market – the question was bound to arise: who stood to gain most? Was it the case, as Adam Smith argued, that the trade rules that forced colonies to sell their produce in Britain benefited nobody except the mercantile interests that had lobbied ardently for them? If so, then the mercantile system on which the empire was built was simply a means of enriching the few at the expense of the many. In the mid nineteenth century, the great free trader Richard

Cobden denounced British expansion in India as a plot to enrich a redundant aristocracy at the risk of world peace – the real guarantee of British prosperity.[3] A similar cry was raised at the end of the century. The radical J. A. Hobson saw the growth of Britain's 'tropical' empire (in Africa, Southeast Asia and elsewhere) as a financiers' conspiracy. Cowed by a (corrupt) press and the 'jingo' attitudes it promoted in an ill-informed public, pliant governments in London had spent millions of taxpayers' money on annexing new regions the sole purpose of which was to yield windfall profits to financial interests in the City.[4] Here, once again, the economics of empire were a fraud: the few made a profit while the many were cheated of both social reform (lost in the wave of patriotic emotion) and the genuine prosperity of peaceful free trade.

How accurate or otherwise such criticisms were is beside the point. What they reflected was the widespread suspicion (not just among radicals) that empire and trade were *not* natural partners, and that the use of political power for commercial objectives was always the handiwork of well-connected insiders. This was bound to give rise to a further concern: that the profits of empire would allow favoured groups to increase their power or entrench it more deeply, shifting the social and political balance and remaking the moral and ideological climate in their image. The attack upon nabobs in the late eighteenth century grew out of the fear that those returning from India with huge ill-gotten gains and an oriental morality (by definition unchristian) would buy their way into the landed aristocracy and become the new ruling class. So-called 'West Indians' – absentee planters and merchants grown fat on the profits of sugar and slavery – evoked similar antipathy. J. A. Hobson's polemic (and those of other radical writers) exploited contemporary fears that a class of cosmopolitan plutocrats was now pulling the strings. The extraordinary wealth of Johannesburg's gold mines (and the profits to be made by speculation in gold shares) was the visible proof. It was easy to claim that South African 'Randlords' (Rhodes chief among them) and their friends in the City were behind the attack on the Boers, and the costly, humiliating and over-long war it provoked. It was a short step to argue that protectionism, conscription, an aggressive foreign policy and the apparatus of militarism would follow quickly behind, sealing the fate of democratic reform. Against the radical anti-imperialists were ranged those who insisted that dogmatic attachment to free trade (the ruling doctrine in Britain between c. 1850 and 1931) made Britain dangerously vulnerable to unforeseen shifts in the global economy. Indeed, much of the passion that informed the debate about empire and trade long before Adam Smith and long after his death sprang from awareness of how much the economic security of all social classes was tied to overseas commerce.

For British merchants and traders, however, it was the practical aspects of commercial success that they thought about most. Like all businessmen, their first concern was to find (and keep) their market. This was not just a matter of beating the competition. Gaining access to markets was the merchant's first task, and often his hardest. In the mercantilist age before c. 1830, he faced straightforward prohibitions against buying and selling in overseas empires other than Britain's. Spain, like Britain, applied an exclusionist policy in its American empire for as long as it could – a constant grievance among British merchants. It was Portugal's dependence on British help against France in the Peninsular War that forced open its colony trade to British exporters. In other parts of the world the prohibitions were different, but just as effective. Japan was closed to the British until the late 1850s. Apart from a handful of privileged Dutch, few Europeans risked defying the rule of seclusion – or lived to tell the tale. Until the 1840s, the only lawful trade with China was conducted through the port of Canton. Under the Canton system, official merchants (*hong*) dealt with the agents of the British East India Company, and all foreign traders were required to leave the city once the trading season was over (they usually retreated to the nearby Portuguese colony of Macao). There was no question of dealing direct with Chinese customers, or selling 'unapproved' goods.[5] The selling of opium by British merchants cruising up and down the coast was a double affront to the Chinese trade rules – and the cause of a war. Even where they did not have to face such bureaucratic regulation, British merchants could be deeply unwelcome. Existing middlemen interests, used to their cut from the flow of exports and imports, regarded their presence as an obvious threat. African merchants in the port-towns of the Niger Delta such as Bonny and Calabar, used their fleet of war-canoes (some armed with cannon) to prevent foreigners from sailing upriver and trading direct for slaves and (later) palm-oil. They killed the explorer Richard Lander (partner of the great Birkenhead entrepreneur Macgregor Laird) in 1832 and largely maintained their grip until the 1880s.[6]

Apart from these human-devised barriers, merchants faced plenty of obstacles, not least of a physical kind. In the age before steam power was applied to shipping (after 1830 in the Western world; after 1860 east of Suez) and land transport (the time difference was similar), they were largely the slaves of wind and water. Winds and sea-currents determined where they could go and when, and thus, indirectly, what it was profitable to carry. The ease with which river systems could be entered was another key factor: famously the mighty Congo basin was largely sealed off from outside by the falls and rapids that choked its final headlong rush to the sea. It was a gruelling nineteen-day trek of over 200 miles from Matadi to Stanley Pool (modern Kinshasa) where the Congo once again became navigable – a journey Joseph Conrad made in July 1890.[7] Without railways or all-weather roads, only luxury goods could bear the cost of overland transport for more than a few miles – unless, like slaves or Australian sheep, they could be driven to market on their own feet. But even when he had pushed his way into a market, no merchant could assume that he could sell his goods easily. The shrewder among them paid very careful attention to the wants and tastes of clients. If their main line was cloth, it was vital to know the designs and (especially) the colours that enjoyed social and religious approval, as well as what kinds of cloth suited local climate and fashion. 'Every tribe,' wrote the East African explorer Joseph Thomson a touch irritably, 'must have its own particular class of cotton, and its own tint size and colour among beads.'[8] Nothing else would do. The huge variation in markets that were often small-scale and in the cultural traditions that influenced their tastes obliged merchants to know them in intricate detail: not for them the high-volume, mass-market approach of modern world trade.

The merchant could not concern himself solely with selling the goods he had shipped out from Britain. Commercial success depended on two-way trade: finding return cargoes to fill up the hold and help his customers pay for their purchases. Trade with Latin America languished in the first half of the nineteenth century for lack of returns.[9] Adventurous merchants scouted for produce to buy. The lure of gold dust and ivory led two ex-naval officers, Farewell and King, to the coast of Natal in the 1820s. From the site of modern-day Durban they dispatched a nervous trade mission to the Zulu king Shaka.[10] Merchants might have to wait for a harvest, or until some desirable product could be dragged to the sea from a distant interior. They had to weigh up the costs of demurrage (hanging about in harbour) against the profits from collecting a full load to take home. Once back in Britain, they had to dispose of their purchases to major wholesalers like the great 'sugar factors', through the organized markets (or 'exchanges') that had grown up in London or through auctions and fairs. They hoped to promote the consumption of exotics such as gamboge (a vegetable dye), gum Arabic, gutta percha (used in making telegraph cables), ivory (of which 500 tons a year were imported into Britain in the late nineteenth century – hippo ivory was best), isinglass (a gelatine drawn from the bladders of warm-water fish) and shellac, alongside the familiar bulk goods that poured into Britain: sugar, coffee, tea, timber, raw cotton, wool and grain.

But as all merchants knew, breaking into new markets and making profits in old ones really depended on the invisible factor in overseas trade. What gave them their edge (and Britain its edge over most trading nations) was the supply of cheap credit. Credit was the lubricant of all their transactions. It was the astonishing abundance of credit in London (as the banking system mobilized provincial savings after c. 1800 for use in the City) that made it so cheap and available. Long credit was vital for far-distant markets. It paid for goods to be shipped out and waited for the proceeds to be sent home or remitted in goods sold later in Britain – the whole transaction might take up to two years. Increasingly it allowed British merchants to make advances to farmers, planters, pastoralists, lumbermen, wild-rubber collectors and palm-oil growers whose incomes were seasonal and who supplied the vital returns. Credit was the magnet that drew this highly diverse group of producers into the network of trade and helped to swell its volume (globally by some twenty times over the long nineteenth century to 1913). But credit (or its failure) was also one of the riskiest parts of the merchant's business. A whole series of dangers threatened his profit – and even his solvency. He had to judge credit-worthiness in places where commercial information was absent or sparse: even at home the struggle for prompt payment – or any payment at all – took up much of his time.[11] He had to deal in multiple currencies whose exchange value was uncertain and might fluctuate wildly. In 1860s Calcutta, the cowry shell was still current: 256 were worth a single rupee.[12] In Burma, before 1852, no coins were used: transactions were paid for in gold, silver and lead, which had to be weighed and assayed.[13] His creditors at home might fail in a crisis and drag him down with them. His own agents and partners might speculate unwisely (a constant temptation when prices were volatile), and destroy him without warning. In the long century of wars that ended in 1815, his most profitable ventures might end in disaster if his assets were seized by enemy action and his market suddenly closed – the fate of James Crisp, unlucky husband of the more famous Elizabeth.[14] Even after 1815, more local disorders could threaten his business and even his life.

In all times and places, merchants and traders face two constant problems that distance and delay make much more acute. The first is the difficulty of obtaining accurate information – about markets, about prices, and about the honesty and credit-worthiness of those with whom they do business. In the age of sail before c. 1840, as much as in the steam age that followed, merchants were desperately thirsty for news. They demanded regular letters from their men on the spot and impatiently looked for the mails. Maintaining a wide correspondence was commercially vital: the business partner of John Gladstone (the prime minister's father) thought nothing of sending off twenty letters or more after a long day in the saddle.[15] John Gladstone himself covered 14,000 miles in 1791–2 speculating in American corn.[16] At home and abroad, merchants clustered together to listen and gossip, count the ships in the harbour, tremble at rumours and watch each other's activity. They formed chambers of commerce to pool the information that they were willing to share, and established 'exchanges' where produce prices were listed. From the 1850s the spreading network of telegraphs and submarine cables allowed vital price information to be gathered with revolutionary speed: a transatlantic cable was laid in 1866; by the 1870s India, Southeast Asia and even

Australia were connected to London. Even so, in the City of London as everywhere else, much commercial intelligence spread by word of mouth, as it had always done.

The second great problem was trust – what economists call the 'principal-agent problem'. Most commercial transactions required a long chain of contacts between producer and consumer. A merchant in London needed reliable overseas agents just to make sure that his goods arrived safely, were sold at a fair price, the payment collected and the return goods dispatched. His men on the spot had to deal with another long chain of debtors and creditors, suppliers and salesmen, often in places where legal enforcement was the wildest of dreams and the language barrier Himalayan.[17] They often had little choice but to find local-born intermediaries – compradors in China (the name reflects the older Portuguese presence), *dubashes* (i.e. 'double-speakers') in India – important men in their own right with the contacts and authority to promote their trade, extract payments due and placate local potentates. Against fraud and theft and the misuse of his funds, the faraway merchant had little recourse. His main defence was the careful selection of his partners and agents. He chose family members if he could, or those connected by marriage. Outside the family he preferred those who shared his religious denomination, its ethical rules and (ideally) the same congregation and minister. A shared ethnic or regional background was a further assurance; hence the high number of Scots trading partnerships found all over the world. Right up to 1914, the trading houses through which a huge proportion of British trade was conducted continued to recruit employees on these time-honoured principles. As late as 1936, the head of the famous firm of Jardine Matheson, the great China trader, could say

> With all due deference to the 'east coast of England' [a reference to Cambridge] I do feel that men from north of the border are the most suitable for our routine business ... I am very keen on keeping the Scottish entity of the Firm.
>
> But, I hope I have not conveyed that I have swung against the University man ... I merely consider that he must be aided and abetted by the solid, plodding type from Scotland.[18]

Oxbridge for brains, but Scotland for trust, Keswick, a Scotsman, seemed to be saying.

THE VIEW FROM JAMAICA

[We] 'cannot but point out to the House,' remarked a committee of the Jamaica assembly in 1792,

> the extraordinary advantages resulting to the parent state from the cul-
> ture of canes in the West Indies . . . The productions of the British West
> India islands are as much a part of the national wealth as if the same
> had come to the port of London from any part of Great Britain . . .
> every acre of land turned into a state of cultivation by the colonists, is
> an increase of wealth to the parent state.[19]

The planters and merchants of Jamaica, who sat in the assembly, could be forgiven for thinking that the British Caribbean islands, and Jamaica especially, were the indispensable hub of British world trade. In the later eighteenth century, their exports to Britain (mainly of sugar) made up a third of all imports. Caribbean produce was then re-exported to Europe: by 1805, its coffee ranked first. As the com-mittee observed, sugar paid a high duty on entry, worth £1.4 million a year – around one third of the total yield from the Customs, and perhaps one twelfth of government revenue.[20] The Caribbean also consumed more British exports than anywhere else outside Europe. In 1775, it took more than mainland North America, much more than Asia and twice as much as Africa.[21] Part of the reason was the aston-ishing wealth of its (white) population. In 1770–75, the average net worth of free Europeans in Jamaica was £1,200, nearly ten times that of the richest part of the mainland (Virginia and the Carolinas) and nearly forty times that of New England.[22]

Caribbean prosperity was built on the insatiable appetite for sugar in Europe, especially in Britain, which consumed more than anywhere else, not least in its tea. The value of sugar imported into Britain rose by four times between 1700 and 1790. In the next fifty years it tripled again. Sugar, added to tea or turned into treacle and jam, was soon to become the first 'convenience food' for a time-poor industrial population.[23] But the British West Indies were also the pivot for Britain's Atlantic trade as a whole. Their voracious demand for imports of slave labour (some for re-export to nearby Spanish America) drove Britain's trade with West Africa (until the ban in 1807). Dozens of Guineamen, specially designed for the transport of slaves, left Britain each year, picking up trade goods for barter in Europe or the Americas before arriving on the slave coasts where they might spend up to a year. They were usually accompanied by smaller ships ('tenders') which shuttled across the Atlantic with successive consignments of slaves until the barter goods were exhausted.[24] By the 1780s and 1790s, some 15 per cent of British shipping was employed in the trade.[25] From the other direction, the Caribbean bought North American foodstuffs and used New England shipping; what it paid for these helped the mainland colonies to buy much more from Britain than they otherwise could have. The Caribbean, and especially Jamaica, was also the base for British contraband exports into the theoretically closed markets of the Spanish American empire. Perhaps half the goods sent there from Britain in 1813 were re-exported to Spanish America.[26] Much of it was paid for in bullion. 'I am inclined to think,' wrote the merchant Thomas Irving in 1786, 'that in the exchange we received not less than a million dollars annually which not only furnished our Islands in the West Indies and our Colonies on the Continent with a medium of circulation, but also afforded a considerable object of remittance in specie to England.'[27] Once sent back to London, the bullion was a vital reinforcement to Britain's money supply in an age when the shortage of coin could stop trade in its tracks.[28]

By the late eighteenth century, Jamaica was the most dynamic of the British sugar islands, as well as the largest. The number of its sugar estates had soared from 429 in 1739 to nearly 800 forty years later. Its slave population shot up from under 100,000 in the 1730s to nearly 350,000 by 1810, almost half the total for the British Caribbean.[29] As late as 1817, more than a third were still Africa-born.[30] Its white population (at 25,000) was also the largest. Its planter class exuded a confidence, not to say arrogance, born of commercial success. It furiously rebutted what it saw as the unconstitutional interference of the British Parliament in its local affairs – including the institution of slavery. The House of Commons resolution against slavery in 1823 (ten

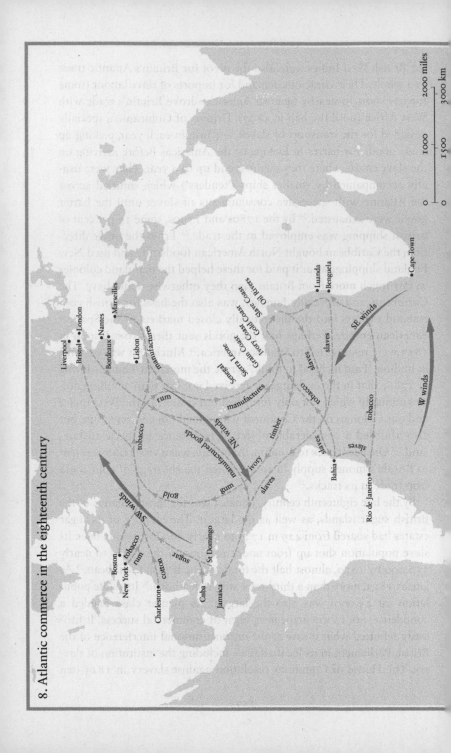

8. Atlantic commerce in the eighteenth century

Liverpool
Bristol • London
Nantes
Marseilles
Bordeaux
• Lisbon

Senegal
Sierra Leone
Grain Coast
Ivory Coast
Gold Coast
Slave Coast
Oil Rivers

Luanda
Benguela

Cape Town

manufactures

rum
manufactures
tobacco
slaves
slaves
slaves

ivory
timber
gum
NE winds
manufactured goods

SE winds
W winds

Boston
New York • tobacco
rum
Charleston • cotton
sugar
St Domingo
Cuba
Jamaica

tobacco
gold
SW winds
slaves
ivory

Bahia
Rio de Janeiro •
slaves
slaves
tobacco

0   1000   2000 miles
0   1500 3000 km

years before the act to abolish it) was denounced by the Jamaica assembly as a 'work of destruction . . . whereby the inhabitants of this once valuable colony (hitherto esteemed the brightest jewel in the British Crown) are destined to be offered a propitiatory sacrifice at the altar of fanaticism'.[31] The slave rising of 1831–2 was blamed on the 'evil excitement' this interference had caused.[32]

Two weeks' sail to the east (a difficult voyage against the wind) lay Barbados and the Leeward Islands (St Kitts, Antigua, Nevis and Montserrat) where English colonization had begun between 1624 (on St Kitts) and 1632 (on Montserrat). Barbados (1627) had been the first great English sugar colony. The technique of cane sugar production (the cane had to be crushed at a mill as soon as possible after cutting to maximize the yield of juice, and the juice then heated in a boiling house to separate the sugar crystals from the residue of molasses) was probably borrowed from the Dutch in Brazil. It was the arduous labour involved in planting, weeding and cutting the cane in a tropical climate, as well as working the mills (if not as dark then perhaps even more satanic and deadly than their British counterparts), that led to the rapid substitution of indentured labour from Britain by African slaves in the late seventeenth century.[33] Barbados had developed with exceptional rapidity to be the 'jewel' of the empire, long before Jamaica claimed the title. By the early eighteenth century it enjoyed (by contemporary standards) rapid and regular links with Britain. Although beating up the Channel from the Thames was often a laborious business against the prevailing westerlies, ships sailing from Plymouth or Falmouth could expect to reach Bridgetown, the colony's capital, in just over eight weeks, which meant that Barbados was closer than Turkey or what was then called the 'Levant' (modern Syria and Lebanon). Once the ship reached Madeira, a favourite stop to buy the fortified wine ('madeira') of which the planters were fond, it could pick up the reliable trade winds and be in Barbados in less than six weeks. By 1700, a hundred ships a year left Britain for the island while the pattern of winds allowed a return voyage (of some eight to nine weeks) throughout the year, unlike the voyage to and from India which was governed by the alternating monsoons in the Indian Ocean.[34] It had been this ease of access, and their control of Barbados and the Leewards, that had allowed the

British to seize Jamaica from Spain in 1655, and to accumulate a long list of Caribbean conquests by 1815: Dominica, St Vincent, Grenada and Tobago (1763); Trinidad (1797); St Lucia and Demerara – part of modern Guyana – (1803).

More than anywhere else, the British West Indies seemed proof that commercial success and the wealth it brought depended on empire – the assertion of rule. The sugar plantations created large profits but they required a steady supply of credit and capital for their mills and machinery, to buy their slave labour, and cover their running costs from season to season. That meant close and regular contact between the planters and their agents in London (such as the ex-planter William Freeman who retired to the splendour of Fawley Court in the Thames valley)[35] and between wealthy absentee owners and their men on the spot, sometimes, like Simon Taylor, a major planter in their own right.[36] It meant having ready recourse to the English system of law, since a planter's success and his credit often turned on the outcome of disputes over property. Most of all, perhaps, the continued prosperity of the sugar plantations depended on the security that only the mother country could offer. With the overwhelming disparity between the islands' white populations and their huge force of slaves (in Jamaica most of all), the imperial garrison and expected reinforcement from home was the best guarantee that recurrent unrest among slaves would not get out of control. How quickly this could happen if the imperial power dropped its guard was (to the planters) the terrible lesson of Haiti after 1791 where revolutionary politics uprooted the colonial order and ignited revolts on the British islands as well.[37] It was no coincidence that the British West Indian planters refused to follow the mainland slave colonies (whose white populations were far larger) into revolt in 1776. Nor was it only a question of repressing the slaves. From their earliest foundation until 1805, when Trafalgar secured Britain's naval supremacy in the West, the British islands were exposed to disruption and conquest by rival great powers who practised the same rules of commercial exclusion that the British applied. During the Seven Years' War of 1756–63, some 1,400 British merchantmen were seized in West Indian waters by cruisers from the French base on Martinique.[38] In 1778, British Dominica was captured by a French expedition. Without the will and the power to protect their most valuable overseas assets, the British would have faced a drastic contraction in their share of the lucrative trades of the Atlantic economy.

Before the 1780s, and for a long time thereafter, few contemporaries would have challenged what seemed an obvious truth: that prosperity required the exertion of power. It was those states that had acquired an overseas empire and exploited it properly that had become the most prosperous. To neglect the supervision of the colonial economies, worse still to allow them to fall into another power's hands, were acts of betrayal or folly. This view was not as naïve as later free traders made out, when they invoked Adam Smith's *Wealth of Nations* (1776) with biblical (and often ill-informed) fervour. It was based on what seemed merely hard-headed realism about the limits of opportunity in a pre-industrial world, where the vagaries of the weather and the consequent yield of the grain harvest held the whip hand over wages and living standards and the prospects of growth.

Historians long ago demolished the idea that a coherent theory of mercantilism ruled economic doctrine and policy from the 1650s to the 1780s. The hundreds of writers who published essays, discourses, considerations, tracts and dialogues on commerce, improvement and treasure offered different prescriptions, highlighted different priorities, and (as often as not) were lobbying for rival interests and pressure groups. But behind the wrangling and acrimony we can see several powerful assumptions that proved very hard to shake off. The first was an essentially pessimistic understanding of the global economy. Of course, contemporaries were well aware of the expansion of European commercial activity from the time of Columbus and Vasco da Gama. The rise of the Spanish American empire and the growth of Dutch trade in Asia were regarded with envy, not to say bitter resentment, by English mercantile interests. They responded enthusiastically to the commercial possibilities of their own Atlantic settlements.[39] Trade with the Levant and with India assumed a growing importance from the mid seventeenth century, and after the mid eighteenth century, Pacific exploration and the gradual opening of China held out the glittering prospect of a new world of trade. But contemporaries in general had little idea that the *total* volume of trade, let alone of production, would or could grow indefinitely.[40] They also assumed that any increase in consumer demand was bound to be limited, soon to reach saturation point.

The logic behind this was simple. Until the application of steam power to overland transport and the production of textiles and metal goods, the scope for productivity gains in most manufacturing activity seemed very moderate at best. Producing more goods meant employing more artisans. If their wages remained level, or rose in response to the increased demand for their skills, then the price of their products was unlikely to fall. What mattered then was how much consumers could afford. If they were to buy more, their real wages or buying power had to increase. Before that could happen, their costs of subsistence – food above all – would have to come down, leaving more room for additional purchases. But could the cost of food fall? In modern times, the agrochemical revolution and a range of intensive technologies have increased the crop yields of foodstuffs by massive proportions with comparable gains in the rearing of animals. In the mid eighteenth century, while improved methods of cultivation and animal-breeding were widely adopted (and English farmers did indeed achieve productivity gains)[41] it seemed very unlikely that the supply of foodstuffs would ever outstrip the number of mouths to be fed – the key point made by the economist Thomas Robert Malthus. Indeed, the opposite seemed more likely as increasingly marginal land had to be brought under the plough. Least certain of all was the effect of the weather on the size of the harvest. It was not entirely surprising that those who lived through the 'little ice age' of the seventeenth century took a gloomy view, and although famine as a threat had receded in Britain, it hovered like a ghost over the mainland of Europe. That reliance could be placed on cheap imports of grain from farmlands in Europe, especially in a century of warfare – Britain was at war with one or more of its European neighbours for forty-one years between 1700 and 1800 – would have seemed absurdly optimistic.

The larger implication of this was that the total amount of production that was available to trade could not grow very much, and that the overall size of the market (globally as well as in Britain) was fixed by what might be called environmental constraints. Even Adam Smith, who insisted that the division of labour, specialization and wide commercial freedom would allow efficiency gains and stimulate trade, acknowledged that sooner or later (he preferred to think later), every country would acquire 'that full complement of riches which the nature of its soil and climate, and its situation with respect to other countries, allowed it to acquire [and] could therefore advance no further', adding optimistically, 'perhaps no country has ever yet arrived at this degree of opulence'.[42] If trade was a more or less fixed quantity (barring windfall additions from newly opened countries), one country's gain was another's loss. It made sense to keep as much as possible in the hands of its own merchants and shippers, using regulation where commercial incentives were lacking. Indeed, there was an obvious danger that without vigorous enforcement, even a temporary setback might prove lasting and fatal. This siege-like mentality was sustained by two further assumptions of exceptional force.

The first stressed the dangers of an imbalance of trade. This was partly because an excess of imports was thought to mean the loss of employment at home, threatening impoverishment and social unrest. But it was also expected to lead to an outflow of bullion, to pay for the gap. The export of silver by the East India Company to pay for its import of luxury textiles from India (where British woollens sold poorly) had been highly controversial. A positive trade balance, by contrast, sucked bullion into the country. Later writers poked fun at the notion that bullion was true wealth as the 'bullionist' fallacy. But contemporaries understood that an outflow of bullion would reduce the amount of coin in circulation and were obsessed by this danger. If coin became scarce, its real value would rise, wages would shrink, employment would fall and domestic trade dwindle. These fears were even more acute in the colonies.[43] In periods of crisis or war, a shortage of bullion became even more serious. In an age before 'war production' by industry was remotely conceivable, governments needed cash to buy foreign supplies, hire foreign mercenaries and subsidize allies. Hence trade that yielded an income of bullion was prized: one of the main aims of the trade treaty with Portugal was to earn its Brazilian gold.[44]

The second obsession concerned shipping as much as trade. Every English and British government since medieval times had stressed the importance of a large merchant fleet, partly to act as an auxiliary force against the threat of invasion, partly to act (in the popular phrase) as a 'nursery for seamen' – the experienced mariners who could be press-ganged in wartime. It was partly on these grounds that London had blocked Newfoundland's development as a settlement colony, arguing that the cod fisheries (in which up to a third of British shipping was employed) must remain a deep sea not a coastal activity. 'Your Majesty's subjects . . . in Newfoundland,' declared an official report, 'ought never be allowed to form themselves into a colony, and . . . possess . . . any landed property there.'[45] It lay behind the insistence since the great Navigation Act of 1660 that goods shipped to Britain from British possessions should use British ships manned by British sailors. 'Remember,' said Lord Liverpool, one of the most commercially minded ministers, 'that it has been the great policy of this country during the course of many centuries to prefer the interest of our navigation even at the expense of our trade.'[46]

It followed from this that colonies were exceptionally valuable – but only under certain conditions. Colonies (like New England) whose produce was similar to Britain's, were of indirect value if they helped to prop up those of first-rate importance. The really desirable colonies were those that produced the tropical goods for which an insatiable demand existed in Europe – tobacco, sugar, coffee, indigo, rice – and which took in return the manufactures that were less easy to sell there. They must not be allowed to produce their own manufactures, nor sell their produce direct to foreign buyers, nor buy foreign manufactures, nor use foreign ships. If these rules were kept, then the colonies became a virtual extension of Britain's own landmass (as the Jamaica assembly observed), a windfall enlargement of its productive capacity, an invaluable means to improve the balance of trade. But without the apparatus of commercial control – the real meaning of empire – plantations like Jamaica, Barbados or Virginia were as likely to profit the shipping and trade of Britain's great rivals, the French and the Dutch, as the British themselves. And though the separation in 1783 from the Thirteen Colonies that became the United States did nothing to stop the rapid expansion of Anglo-American trade (despite apocalyptic predictions), the case for freer trade could make little political headway until the new era of peace and apparent stability after 1815.

FREE TRADE AND EMPIRE

What Adam Smith had lambasted as the 'mercantile system' was really a complex of protections and privileges acquired over decades by both producers and merchants, and given legitimacy by the 'national safety' argument. By the 1820s and 1830s, it was falling apart. The great West Indian sugar interest was tainted by slavery, and challenged by planters elsewhere in the empire with much lower costs and using 'free' labour (a relative term). The British slave trade had gone – outlawed in 1807; slavery itself was abolished from 1834. A third great pillar of the old commercial establishment had been the East India Company which had held a monopoly on trade between Britain and India. Its notorious abuses and the anger of merchants driven out of Europe by Napoleon's 'continental system', had forced the abolition of its commercial monopoly in India in 1813. Twenty years later, the Company lost its monopoly on the import of tea from Canton – its most profitable line.

Behind these great changes was a merchants' revolt. The world war of 1793–1815 had demolished the empires of Britain's main rivals and opened the markets of previously closed colonies. After 1815, British merchants traded more widely and freely than ever before. The lobby against the protection of imperial trade (goods imported into Britain from one of its colonies) and against the high level of duties that kept all prices up, grew louder and louder. After 1815, it was much harder to claim that British safety and prosperity depended on special treatment for the colony trade and the close regulation of shipping and crews. A much greater danger to Britain's stability in the postwar depression was the high price of food, causing mass discontent, reducing consumption and therefore employment, and throwing large numbers on the overstrained system of 'poor relief'. Leading figures in government accepted much of the logic of free trade but faced a solid phalanx of protectionism.[47] Free traders denounced the so-called 'corn laws' (preventing the import of wheat until the price rose to a high level) as an abuse of power by the landed aristocracy (the politically dominant class) that stood to gain most. Worse still, restricting the import of cheap food was seen as a double imposition on the fast-growing manufacturing interest: it prevented manufacturers from reducing their costs by lowering wages in line with food prices, and discouraged potential foreign customers, who might sell grain in return, from buying British goods. The great champion of this view was the economist David Ricardo, the inventor of 'comparative advantage'.[48] It was wisest, said Ricardo, to buy what you needed from those who made it most cheaply, and concentrate your resources of labour and capital on what you did best. That would maximize trade and also 'utility' – meaning enjoyment and welfare.

Thus a combination of geopolitics – the break-up of mercantilist empires – and industrialization gradually destroyed the old rules and the beliefs they were built on. It took nevertheless a huge political crisis to clear the way for free trade. Industrial methods – especially the use of steam power for the spinning of yarn and the weaving of cloth – might have given British manufacturers a huge cost advantage, but in the depressed conditions of the 1830s and 1840s it also seemed likely to saturate their markets and reduce them to bankruptcy. Cutting their costs and finding new buyers were more urgent than ever. Even Robert Peel, the Conservative prime minister of 1841–6, who had defended the corn laws in the 1841 election, acknowledged the need to 're-balance' the interests of farm and factory.[49] But it was the catastrophe of famine in Ireland in 1845 that destroyed the old guard, broke the back of protection, swept the corn laws away and opened the road to the almost complete abolition of commercial restrictions in the 1850s. That this coincided (fortuitously) with the great expansion of world trade was the proof to most British opinion that free trade was the secret of British prosperity.

Had the conversion to free trade made empire redundant? In the Western world, the answer might have been 'nearly, but not quite'. By the mid nineteenth century, the British West Indies had become a commercial backwater, left behind by lower-cost sugar producers such as Brazil, Cuba and Java. The United States had become Britain's greatest trade partner (in the nineteenth century Britain's *imports* from the US usually exceeded in value its whole trade with Asia). Its slave South produced the raw cotton that fed Lancashire's mills, the source of Britain's largest and most valuable export up to 1914, cotton cloth. Americans bought British textiles and metal goods, but they resisted the pressure to adopt free trade. Instead, the Old Northeast (the commercial and manufacturing district between Philadelphia and Boston with New York at its centre) was both rival and partner, with close links to London and Liverpool. Indeed Liverpool lived by American trade. The largest firm in the cotton trade with 75 per cent of the business was American – Brown Brothers, founded by an Ulster expatriate, Alexander Brown.[50] By 1810, it had a Liverpool branch, run by Brown's British relatives, to manage its shipments of cotton and sell the bills of exchange that these earned. By 1863, the financial side of its business was important enough to establish Brown Shipley as a merchant bank in the City, one of the largest in the financing of American trade, and a rival to Barings. Barings too drew much of its business from across the Atlantic. It arranged the loan for Jefferson's Louisiana Purchase – when Napoleon sold France's claim to the vast western interior in 1803. It was a Baring (Lord Ashburton) who was sent to smooth over the crisis when both sides laid claim to the 'Oregon country' in 1846. From the merchants' point of view, the ill-feeling aroused by the relics of imperial power in North America, American resentment of the anti-slavery crusade headquartered in Britain, and the lingering rivalry in the Caribbean and Central America (ironically the Americans suspected the British of designs on Cuba),[51] made empire an encumbrance to commerce, not an aid.

In South America, the picture was different but not completely. With the opening of Brazil and the former Spanish American colonies, British merchants had rushed in. But it took time to organize a return trade and overcome the suspicions of local politicians and businessmen. When British sea power was used to put pressure on the Argentinian government in the late 1840s, British merchants petitioned against it: the effects had been ruinous. It was local self-interest, not British insistence, that persuaded the South American states to open their trade: powerful landowners in search of a market and the promise of a customs revenue to bolster the state.[52] Where they could tap local produce and ship it to Europe, British merchants dug in. In Peru, the firm of Anthony Gibbs secured a hugely profitable concession to ship guano – the dung of seabirds – to fertilize British fields. In Brazil (still a slave state), they moved into the sugar trade in Bahia and Pernambuco. When the coffee trade boomed in the 1860s and 1870s, much of it was handled by the firm of Johnstons, based in Rio de Janeiro,[53] while the British-owned São Paulo Railway linked the coast to the coffee zone. In Argentina and Uruguay, British merchant houses in Buenos Aires and Montevideo controlled much of the export trade in hides and salt meat.[54] When the regional economy took off in the 1870s and 1880s (on the back of frozen meat and grain), the British were perfectly placed to provide the banks, insurance companies and railway investments that trade growth required.

British sea power – the main arm of empire – was not entirely irrelevant. It had helped to make sure that European schemes for reviving Spain's empire remained just that.[55] By and large, however, the South American states had the legal institutions (from their colonial past) and the political will to promote market capitalism and support an open economy. What gave British merchants their special position was the shortage of credit and capital in local economies and the lack of commercial intelligence – the information about prices, markets and credit ratings so vital to merchant success. It was access to overseas funds and networks of knowledge that made them much more robust than their local competitors, better placed to ride out the crashes and crises of the commodity trades.

In our third case, Canada, empire was much more important. As the disjointed remains of Britain's American empire, British North America depended on the imperial connection. The merchants who created its separate northern economy (mostly Scottish-born or of Scottish descent) needed Britain's help to escape commercial annexation (or straightforward conquest) by their wealthier neighbour to the south. They enjoyed imperial preference in the British market for their timber and grain – until the British adopted free trade. Because London worried about reinforcing its garrison if the Americans attacked (a recurrent fear until the late 1860s), it was willing to guarantee the investment in an inter-regional railway, priming the pump for the railway spine that helped to make Canada an economic as well as a political reality after confederation was agreed in 1867–73.[56] London also held the keys to the vast hinterland to which merchants in Montreal – the local metropolis – looked for economic salvation: the huge and (largely) empty North West beyond the Great Lakes.[57] Until 1869, this was the domain of the Hudson's Bay Company whose charter from the British Crown went back to 1660, and whose claims successive British governments had defended against American pressure.[58] It was the knock-down sale of this colossal inheritance and the addition of the separate British colony of British Columbia that turned Canada into a true transcontinental dominion after 1867.

The result was to create a powerful nexus of commercial and financial interests centred in St James Street (today rue St Jacques) in Montreal, the local headquarters of the Canadian economy. The Bank of Montreal relied on its London connections to suck in the credit and capital it advanced to its clients.[59] It was closely allied with the Canadian partners of the Hudson's Bay Company (which retained its commercial interests in the North West as well as some of its property), among them the erstwhile fur trader Donald Smith, later Lord Strathcona and the richest man in the country. Grandest of all by the mid 1880s was the Montreal-based Canadian Pacific Railway, whose completion in 1885 had marked the physical unification of Canada. The CPR was the kingpin. It was largely financed by British investors. It turned the Canadian West into an economic colony of Montreal. It was the prime guarantee that Canada would remain a separate North American economy. Its profits depended on an effective monopoly of transcontinental traffic, especially the wheat from the prairies that was exported to Britain. Its managers dreamed of its being part of an all-empire route from Britain to East Asia. They understood very well that its fate was bound up with Canada's place in the empire, Canadian loyalty to the Crown (against American republicanism) and the flow of British migrants and capital to fill up its spaces. It was hardly surprising that deep into the interwar years, the business elite of Montreal asserted its Britishness and remained vociferously loyal to 'British connection' – the pole of its universe.[60]

'Few places are more interesting to a traveller from Europe', wrote the naturalist Alfred Russel Wallace,

> than the town and island of Singapore ... The government, the garrison and the chief merchants are English but the great mass of the population is Chinese, including some of the wealthiest merchants, the agriculturists of the interior, and most of the mechanics and labourers.

The native Malays are usually fishermen and boatmen, and they form the main body of the police. The Portuguese of Malacca supply a large number of clerks and smaller merchants. The Klings of Western India are a numerous body of Mohammedans, and, with many Arabs, are petty merchants and shopkeepers. The grooms and washermen are all Bengalese, and there is a small but highly respectable class of Parsee merchants. Besides these there are numbers of Javanese sailors and domestic servants, as well as traders from Celebes, Bali, and many other islands of the Archipelago. The harbour is crowded with men-of-war and trading vessels of many European nations, and hundreds of Malay praus and Chinese junks . . . little fishing-boats and passenger sampans; and the town comprises handsome public buildings and churches, Mohammedan mosques, Hindoo temples, Chinese joss-houses, good European houses, massive warehouses, queer old Kling and Chinese bazaars, and long suburbs of Chinese and Malay cottages.[61]

This was the world evoked in the novels of Joseph Conrad. Its commercial life, like that of much of the world south and east of the Isthmus of Suez, was very different indeed from that of the Atlantic economy. The eastern economy was much further from Europe: the voyage to India round the Cape took about three times as long as that to Barbados. Traffic to and from India was governed by the monsoon, blowing ships north from the Cape between March and October and then blowing them south in the rest of the year. Before the cutting of the Suez Canal, it was possible to send mail and even some passengers (always in fear of the plague) via Egypt and the Red Sea or down the Euphrates to Basra and the Gulf.[62] But the speed, regularity, convenience and cheapness of transatlantic travel and shipment did not apply east of Suez. There were no slave economies to produce the great staples that crossed the Atlantic in bulk – cotton, sugar and coffee – and no large settler societies. (The settler economies of Australia and New Zealand where around 1 million whites were producing wool and gold in the 1860s are better thought of as detached portions of the Atlantic economy. Their trade and communications, while not entirely unconnected with Asia, became focused more and more on direct exchanges with Britain.[63]) Everywhere Europeans faced stiff competition from Asian, Arab and African merchants who controlled the trade of the coasts and interior and whose junks, praus and dhows[64] could carry goods for a tithe of the cost of a European ship. This was a world in which the mechanics of trade were much more demanding. The huge variety of weights and measures (Indian 'ruttees', 'mashas', 'tolas', 'seers' and 'maunds' – the Bengal maund weighed nearly four times the Bombay one – Chinese 'catties', 'piculs' and 'taels') and currencies, as well as the means of exchange (silver bullion from China was sold in shoe-shaped ingots called 'sycee'), reflected an old and intricate trading world with a dense network of mercantile links and an immense range of specialized produce. This was a far cry from the simplicity of Atlantic commerce. The British, like other outsiders, had to adapt to it.

They were able to do so in large part because of India. The English had originally opened for business in India as the anxious licensees of its imperial regime, the Mughals in Delhi. They had had to compete with Portuguese, Dutch and French as well as Asian merchants. Without its monopoly on the trade back to Britain, the risks and overheads would have wrecked the Company – perhaps several times over. But by the mid eighteenth century, the scale of its trade (partly a consequence of Britain's own prosperity), its stealthy entrenchment in maritime India, a small private army and the growing dependence of the local regimes that it dealt with on the profits of overseas trade, had made it the strongest of the European East India companies. When its position in Bengal came under attack from an insecure ruler in 1756, its men on the spot began its transformation into a military and administrative power, first in Bengal (from 1765) and then, by 1820, over much of the subcontinent. The annexation of Awadh in 1856 was the Company's high tide. Two years later, after the unexpected catastrophe of the Great Rebellion, it was summarily dissolved and sovereignty over India (till then a legal fog) was explicitly vested in the British Crown.

India's colonial remaking in the century after Plassey (1757) had major commercial implications. When the Company took over the revenues of the nawab of Bengal, it diverted part of them to financing its purchases of the Indian cotton goods for which there was so much demand in Europe. No longer did it have to ship bullion to India. This proved a bonanza for the Company's servants, growing rich (some enormously so) on the salaries, perks and side deals that the Company's new power permitted. This nefarious activity (denounced in Britain by the high-minded and envious) ironically laid the foundations of wider British commerce in Asia. The Company's charter had always allowed private British merchants to engage in the country trade, i.e. the local trade within Asia. The Company's new wealth affected this in three ways. First of all, it attracted a swarm of new players drawn east by new opportunities, not least those created by supplying the Company's needs in its successive wars of expansion. Secondly, the funds available for the country trade were hugely increased by the earnings – licit and otherwise – of Company servants in search of local investment. Thirdly, the task of investing those funds, overseeing their use, and arranging for their eventual remittance to Britain when the investor 'retired' was taken up by what became known as 'managing agencies' – the commercial partnerships through which most British trade in Asia was organized up to and even after the Second World War.[65]

Managing agencies were maids of all work. They were a classic expression of the British advantage in access to credit, long-distance partners and commercial intelligence. They advanced cash and credit, acted as travel agents, supervised plantations and other British-owned business ventures, arranged the purchase and sale of produce and the import of European 'necessaries', provided insurance, owned or chartered ships, and took savers' deposits – often at eye-watering rates of return. They were far from risk-free: in the crash of 1829–34, almost all were wiped out by excessive speculation. But in 1861, there were some seventy in Calcutta alone.[66] They were the vanguard of British commercial expansion, setting up branches wherever they could fasten a limpet-like grip on the local pattern of trade: in Burma, Malaya, Singapore, the Persian Gulf and East Africa. In Burma, for example, managing agents in Rangoon assumed command over the export of the country's highly prized timber: they were the 'teak wallahs'. In Singapore, they bought pepper, spices, camphor (for mothballs), beeswax, coffee, ebony, tortoise-shell, gold dust and sandalwood.[67] Their branches were staffed by young men from Britain, discouraged from marrying, living in 'chummeries' (bachelor quarters) and relieving boredom with concubines, drink and the slaughter of animals. But they also relied on a host of local intermediaries, usually Arab, Armenian, Indian (often Parsi) or Chinese merchants and money-men. It was they who knew at first hand what the customers wanted, and who could do deals with the long chain of middlemen. Catties and piculs, mashas and maunds were no mystery to them. They understood local currencies, raised local credit, and advanced loans to producers that no foreign bank would have touched.

India was the pivot, the indispensable engine-room, for Britain's part in this eastern economy. The constant flow of funds between Britain and India (much of it arising from payments by the Indian government to investors and pensioners at home) was the financial ballast for a vast business network. India's naval and military power – or the manpower and resources that the British conscripted there – was the battering ram for expansion, both commercial and political. It was the Bombay Marine (later the Indian navy) that turned the Persian Gulf into a British lake and guarded the sea-lane from Basra to Karachi and Bombay. Bombay became the emporium for much of Iran's foreign trade.[68] 'British' influence in East Africa was really 'British Indian' influence, so much so that in early colonial Kenya and Uganda the rupee was the currency. Singapore and Malaya were the fruit of the Company's attack (with London's approval) on the Dutch East Indies during the Napoleonic Wars – although the Company's directors at first resisted the idea of keeping Singapore as pointless and provocative (what is now Indonesia was handed back to the Dutch in 1815). Above all, there was China.

The East India Company had traded with China throughout the eighteenth century to buy the silks and ceramics fashionable in the West. It was hindered by the lack of Chinese demand for British manufactures and the need to pay for its purchases in American silver – for which Chinese demand was relentless. At first sight, the fast-growing British thirst for tea (China was the prime source) after 1760 made this problem much worse. In fact, the Company's new role in India supplied a solution. It could use its Indian revenues to buy Indian goods, such as raw cotton and indigo, which the Chinese would buy. Then it discovered opium, grown in both western and eastern India, whose sale was quickly turned into a government monopoly and the source of nearly a fifth of its revenues. Closely watched at Canton, the Company dared not sell opium under the nose of the Chinese authorities. But it could sell it in India to the country traders who would ship it to China and arrange for its sale. A great commercial operation now cranked into action. Company servants wanting to remit their Indian earnings to Britain placed them with agents in Calcutta or Bombay. These funds were then used to buy opium for export to China. India-based British traders (this was how the firm of Jardine Matheson began) sold the opium in China in exchange for tea (or a claim on tea), and then sold the tea to the Company in exchange for a bill that the Company's headquarters in London would redeem in sterling. In this roundabout way, Indian receipts made their way back to Britain (sometimes bills on London were bought from American merchants coming to buy tea)[69] and the China trade was opened up. The sequel is well known. When the Company lost its China monopoly, the free traders took over, and the opium trade led to a war. By winning the war, the British forced open China's coast, extended the market for opium, and allowed British merchants to settle in treaty ports exempt from Chinese control. An exotic commercial society in miniature sprang up on the treaty port bunds – the grand riverside wharfs with their godowns (warehouses), shipping agents, banks, telegraph offices, custom-houses, clubs, chummeries and verandah-shaded residences.[70] Some 10,000 Chinese compradors managed the interior trade with the treaty ports while Chinese money-shops, offering short-term 'chop' loans, were as vital to treaty port commerce as the foreign-owned banks.[71] But the initial victory had been won by troops and ships sent from India, and it was to India (as well as the navy's China squadron based in Hong Kong) that the tiny population of treaty port British looked for rescue during China's time of troubles between 1850 and 1911.

The long arm of India and its British rulers in the eastern economy can be seen most vividly in the career of William Mackinnon.[72] Mackinnon was a Scot, born in Campbeltown, at the maritime entrance to the Firth of Clyde. At an early age he sought his fortune in Glasgow. But his crucial step was to go to Calcutta in 1846, initially as representative of a firm in which his elder brother was a partner. Within a year or two he had formed the partnership that became Mackinnon Mackenzie and Co. in Calcutta. In 1852 he established his own firm in Glasgow to manage the export of cotton goods and, in alliance with Hall, Mackinnon in Liverpool (his elder brother's firm), became both

9. Principal British trade routes and commodities, 1923

PACIFIC OCEAN

JAPAN
8
16

N CHINA & JAPANESE PORTS

CHINA
TEA
SILKS

Calcutta
TEA
PETROLEUM
Rangoon
40

INDIA
COTTON
Bombay

Ceylon
TIN RUBBER PETROLEUM
Singapore
9

INDIAN OCEAN

AUSTRALIAN PORTS
WOOL
MUTTON
MEAT

NEW ZEALAND
WOOL
MUTTON
MEAT
MUTTON

Aden
48
10
28
29
32

COAL
COTTON
MAIZE
COTTON

WOOL
WHEAT
GOLD
DIAMONDS

S. AFRICAN PORTS

SOUTHERN OCEAN

Suez
COTTON

Malta 43

Gibraltar

London

British Isles
COAL STEEL
MACHINERY
COTTON GOODS
ROME PORTS

1140
197
41
199
164

ATLANTIC OCEAN

PALM OIL
W COAST PORTS
20
38

PETROLEUM
17
19

W COAST PORTS
NITRATES RIVER PLATE
BEEF
6

PANAMA CANAL
& W INDIES

Falkland Is

Cape Horn

Halifax
38

DOMINION OF CANADA
LUMBER WHEAT
NICKEL

Vancouver
WHEAT
PETROLEUM

UNITED STATES
COTTON
PETROLEUM
33
26

San Francisco

PACIFIC OCEAN
8
16
8
5

The figures indicate the number of British vessels of 3000 tons and over in the routes on 1 April 1923 shipper and shipowner. In the early 1850s, as the second Burma War of 1852–3 threw open the port of Rangoon and the Irrawaddy river trade, he started the Calcutta and Burmah Steam Navigation Company, the seed of great things to come. A few years later, another steamship company was formed to bid for the mail contract along India's east coast. The mail contract and subsidy were the key to steamship success: it was where seaborne commerce and empire clasped hands. When Mackinnon met Bartle Frere in January 1862, his triumph was assured. Frere was one of the most powerful officials in India, and about to become the governor of Bombay. He was determined to strengthen Bombay (and India's) influence on the Persian Gulf and promote the trade of Karachi. He saw Mackinnon's steamships as the ideal means for this purpose, and with his support, Mackinnon won the mail contract to the Gulf. With this in his pocket (the £55,000 annual subsidy equated to a capital sum of over £1 million), he turned his patchwork of steamers and contracts into a grandly named enterprise: the British India Steam Navigation Company. It became the government's official carrier (of troops as well as mail). By the 1870s, every fifth ship at Calcutta was a British India steamship.[73] Much of the rest of Mackinnon's career was spent in the restless search for ways of extending this maritime empire, especially in East Africa, where, as a pious Scot, he was drawn by Livingstone's grand project for promoting 'Christianity, commerce and civilization' to destroy paganism, slavery (and Muslim overrule). The sad end of this venture – the inglorious failure of his Imperial British East Africa Company – probably hastened his death.

THE GOLDEN EMPORIUM

Of course, the eastern economy was not just the handiwork of the India-based British. Around a vast arc of the southern oceans, from Natal to Fiji, Indian emigrant labour (some of it indentured and short-term) was vital to the growth of plantation economies. Indian merchants and money-lenders, like the Madras *chettiars* who followed the British into Burma,[74] were indispensable commercial auxiliaries who were willing to work for much lower margins than their British counterparts. They reached into parts of Asia and Africa that European merchants overlooked or disdained. With the opening of the Suez Canal in 1869, the linkages between the eastern and western economy became much stronger. By the 1870s, it becomes possible to speak of a global economy in which improvements in transport and communication by telegraph had encouraged the integration of markets and the convergence of prices in ordinary foodstuffs – perhaps the best indicator that the world was becoming a single economic space. And it was not just an increased flow of goods. After 1870, the flows of money from Europe – long-term investment as well as speculative 'rushes' – also rose very sharply. So did the numbers of long-distance migrants, mainly from Europe, but also from China and India.

For the British, however, the rapid extension of the global economy was also a warning. It signalled the rise of new rivals both industrial and imperial, the Germans above all. Unlike the globalization of the late twentieth century, it took place in a world already partly partitioned between colonial empires, and in which the annexation of territories without 'civilized' governments was regarded (in Europe) as entirely legitimate. It also seemed likely that the increase of commercial activity, and the heightened dependence on outside agents and markets that it tended to bring with it, would speed up the decline of pre-modern regimes in Asia and Africa, creating new zones of geostrategic instability. To add to this cauldron of potential antagonism, any downturn in world trade – however shortlived – would prompt powerful voices in the world's strongest states to demand exclusion zones where their exports would be safe from the competition of rivals. It was from precisely these kinds of anxieties that the movement grew up that challenged free trade and favoured imperial protection: to seclude the British Empire behind a wall made of tariffs. It would protect British industry from 'dumping' by low-cost manufacturers abroad. It would guard British jobs and improve living standards – Britain's slums were the product of unrelenting free trade, argued an ardent tariff reformer.[75] And (by reducing the pressure for access to overseas markets outside the empire) it would ease the geopolitical friction between Britain and its global rivals: Germany, Russia and France.

But tariffs were rejected by the British electorate before 1914. A large part of the reason was that the global economy, whatever tariff reformers might say, had created a vast hoard of new British wealth. The growth of world trade, especially the bulk shipment of commodities in exchange for manufactures (British imports of grain increased by three times between 1870 and 1912)[76] was a great opportunity. It created an ever-growing demand for the long-distance transport systems in which the British had invested so heavily and in which their expertise was unrivalled: steamships and railways. Indeed, it was the large fall in transport costs that steam power achieved that sustained the expansion of trade. British-owned cable systems, such as the great Eastern Telegraph Company created by John Pender, a former Manchester cotton merchant, dominated the supply of commercial information. As more and more regions were drawn into the commercial economy, specializing in the export of staples (in which their market advantage was greatest) and buying more imports, their need for exchange banks, insurance companies, shippers and shipbrokers, as well as the hardware of railways, harbours, ships and cables, rose astronomically. These were all services in which the British enjoyed a long lead, and through which they could levy a large rent on the new streams of trade. Above all, the new world economy required the mobilization of additional capital: to build new railways, equip the new cities (from Buenos Aires to Shanghai), and exploit the natural resources (rubber, tin, copper, gold) for which there now seemed an insatiable demand.

This was the setting in which London asserted its global supremacy. This was not the London of Whitehall, but the City, the square mile of commerce at the other end of the Strand. Lining its handful of streets, by-ways and alleys were the offices of clearing or high street banks, merchant banks, overseas banks, insurance companies, Indian and South American railway companies, shipping companies and shipbrokers, the famous China firm of Jardine Matheson, traders in the mundane (sugar) and the exotic (human hair), great imperial corporations (such as Cecil Rhodes's British South Africa Company on London Wall) as well as a host of highly prized experts like mining engineers.[77] The City's two poles were the Bank of England and the Stock Exchange. Lying nearby were the Docks – the London, Surrey,

10. British submarine cable system, 1929

cables

Limehouse, West India, East India, Millwall and Victoria. Together they symbolized the huge range of its global activities as the centre of world trade, the supplier of credit and the source of foreign investment. London was the marketplace to which a great mass of produce was sent, partly because Britain imported so much food and raw materials for its industry, partly because of free trade, which attracted goods that would later be re-exported to other markets in Europe. A throng of specialist dealers and merchants examined, repackaged, auctioned off and sold on the goods that arrived. But many commercial transactions in London concerned goods that never reached it or any other British port.

This was because an enormous share of world trade used what was known as the 'bill on London' to reduce the inconvenience, cost and delay inseparable from purely bilateral trade. If a merchant in country A wished to buy goods from country B, he might find it difficult to strike an acceptable bargain. Unless the balance of imports and exports between the two countries was more or less equal, he would not be able to pay in either money or goods. The same problem arose for merchants in country B. What both parties needed was a common token of payment, acceptable anywhere. The bill on London answered this need. Those who received it were confident that it could be cashed in London for any world currency, or exchanged for a consignment of goods that they wanted.[78] The sheer scale of transactions that took place in the City was the real guarantee that cash or consignments were always available. A complex commercial machinery ensured (for a price) that this would be so. It depended in turn on the reservoir of deposits, filling and refilling the tanks of short-, medium- and long-term credit extended by merchant banks and 'accepting houses' to facilitate trade. Presiding over this seeming chaos of dealing was the grand controller of credit, the Bank of England, whose 'bank rate' determined the cost of advances and thus the price of doing business. The Bank was the guardian of the City's reputation, and, above all, of the value of the bill on London which depended on faith that it would always be met. Since (by 1913) some 60 per cent of those bills involved goods exchanged between third parties outside Britain that faith could not be taken for granted.

11. British foreign investment to 1914

Japan £78m

Russia £139m

China £73m

India £317m

Egypt £66m

South Africa £262m

Australia £339m

New Zealand £84m

Canada £412m

USA £836m

Mexico £81m

Brazil £172m

Argentina £349m

London was a city of paper, but its foundations were golden. The ultimate guarantee of good faith was London's (and Britain's) adherence to the 'gold standard'. That meant accepting three obligations. First, the pound sterling had a fixed value in gold, and could be exchanged for gold (a gold sovereign) on demand. Second, in practice that meant that the issue of banknotes had to be limited to a ratio of the gold reserve kept in the Bank's vaults: approximately three pounds in paper for one pound in gold. Hence, devaluing the currency by printing more banknotes, or 'quantitative easing', was ruled out completely – an important reassurance to foreign holders of sterling who supplied a good deal of the City's liquidity. Third, a deficit in the balance of payments had to be met by supplying gold in lieu – leading automatically to a reduction in available money and a rise in the bank rate to attract foreign depositors. In fact, London was able to meet these exacting requirements with relative ease, partly because the world supply of gold increased rapidly after 1890 with the huge discoveries on the South African Rand, in Western Australia, on the Yukon and elsewhere. More to the point, it was able to persuade most of its trade partners in the world outside Europe to accept the same discipline – painful for them as it was at some times. The reason was simple. They were desperate not to miss out on the great boom in world trade that set in strongly from the mid 1890s. In the furious competition between rival producers of wheat, maize, sugar, cotton and a mass of other commodities, credit-worthiness was all. To reject the gold standard was to be a third-class risk. Indeed by 1913, some twenty-eight countries were on the gold standard, and eleven more claimed to be – around 900 million people.[79]

The City could dangle another powerful inducement. If the 'developing' economies of the world beyond Europe were thirsty for credit they were also hungry for capital to build the infrastructure that would bring their products to market. By 1913 perhaps half the world's total of foreign investment had been raised in London. Whether constructing a railway, sinking a mine, or laying out a plantation, the first step was to write the prospectus for a share issue in London. With a fair wind (and a favourable puff in London's not over-scrupulous financial press), the shares could be launched on the Stock Exchange and business would begin. With so many unknowns and so little hard information (one favoured tactic was to recruit 'guinea pig' peers on to the board of directors to create the illusion of solidity), cautious investors preferred familiar technologies and 'hard' convertible, gold-backed currencies. Going off gold, or not getting on it, threatened an investment famine just when new capital promised the richest rewards for the borrowing country. The assurance of gold helped to persuade British investors to keep more than a third of Britain's total assets abroad – an astonishing figure.[80]

The results of all this activity focused on London were spectacular. Of course, Britain remained a manufacturing economy, exporting one quarter of all it produced. Cotton textiles (around a quarter of exports) still lay at its heart. But the real surge of wealth sprang from its role as the world's greatest emporium. The invisible income from commercial services (shipping, insurance, etc.) increased by some 70 per cent between the mid 1880s and 1913. It earned at its peak the equivalent of nearly one third of the income from exports. British investment abroad doubled from £2 billion to £4 billion between 1900 and 1913, producing an equally spectacular rise in overseas earnings. The two put together ensured a large surplus on the balance of payments, and a growing fund available for re-investment abroad. Just before 1914, there were signs that the boom was petering out, but little to hint that the British were losing their privileged place in the global economy. It seemed as if they had made themselves indispensable to the commercial prosperity not just of their empire but of most of the rest of the non-European world. To the empire coloured red on the map, the City had added an empire glued together by debt and defended by gold.

BUSINESS AND EMPIRE

The British had built a worldwide empire of commerce, containing within it a vast property empire of railways and telegraphs, tramways and waterworks, banks, warehouses and docks, mines and plantations. But how far did their business depend on the *apparatus* of empire: its projection of force by gunboats and garrisons; its assertion of rule; its insertion of outsiders to commandeer local resources? The answer, of course, varied widely with place. The British lent much to the South American states. But when a default seemed likely, as happened in Peru in the early 1890s, even full-blooded imperialists dismissed the idea of armed intervention, 'British squadrons, Johnny Atkins, and all that fustian'.[81] Financial discipline was imposed not by orders from Downing Street, but by a quiet word in New Court, the Rothschilds' London headquarters. In the 'white dominions', which enjoyed full internal self-government, it was less their sense of subservience to empire than their wish for full partnership in it (as well as familiar institutions and tastes) that made them attractive destinations for British investment and exports.[82] But in the rest of the world outside Europe and the Americas, a strong case could be made that British trade needed empire or gained much from its presence.

In China, for example, it could hardly be doubted that British and other foreign businessmen existed on sufferance. Their access to China's ports and then its interior had been extracted by force and upheld by displays of naval and military power: the ubiquitous British gunboats that policed China's main rivers and coasts. Few Britons in China believed that their business would last without their treaty port status (exemption from Chinese taxes and law courts, and the right to own property), the unequal treaties that held down Chinese tariffs, and the largely British-staffed Chinese Maritime Customs Service that administered the ports and provided the lighthouses.[83] For the British at least, colonial Hong Kong was a Chinese Gibraltar, a rock of assurance if things went amiss. The great Boxer rebellion of 1899–1901 confirmed all the fears of the 'Old China hands'.[84] A motley expedition of Russian, French, German, Austrian, Japanese and British troops rushed to relieve the 'siege of Peking' where a small group of Westerners had been trapped by the rebels. The Boxers were crushed but in London a gloomy conclusion was drawn. The arrival in force of other great powers whose armies and navies could also threaten Beijing meant that British commerce in China would need the levers of empire for an indefinite time.[85]

In Africa, the uses of empire were different. In West Africa, the British had resorted to force on occasion to open the pathways of trade and imposed their protectorates to pre-empt the loss of potentially valuable markets behind the French empire's tariff walls. In

East, Central and South Africa, the commercial meaning of empire was much more direct. For all the myths that were peddled about African wealth, Europeans quickly discovered the limits imposed by a harsh physical environment, sparse populations and the hardships of travel: to go from Zanzibar to Uganda in the mid 1890s meant a *walk* of two months.[86] The brutal corollary was that coercion was needed to accumulate wealth – at least on the scale that outsiders demanded. Coercion permitted the seizure of land and the conscription of labour, often both simultaneously. Colonial rule thus became, for a white master-class, the means of economic control: dividing the land between a large settler zone and reserves for the natives; and imposing the taxes that forced African males to seek work on the farms or on the diamond, coal and gold fields of South Central Africa with their insatiable demand for cheap migrant labour. In barely one generation, tens of thousands of African men were hurled into an industrial world of arduous physical labour, prison-like compounds (where they ate and slept) and a brutal work-discipline in which beatings were commonplace.[87] On the mining frontier of Southern Rhodesia, to take one example, labour conditions were appallingly harsh. Accidents, disease and malnutrition produced a death-rate of 76 per 1,000 men employed in 1906 (the rate in England for adult males was 16.5).[88] And when, as happened not infrequently, Africans were kicked or beaten to death by whites, (white) juries preferred to attribute death to an 'enlarged spleen' – a strangely common condition – and acquit the accused.[89] Yet by 1914, it was an almost universal assumption that only white *rule* could ensure economic advance.

But the critical case was surely India. As we have seen, India was the platform from which British business had advanced across Asia. Indian merchants and manpower had been its auxiliary motor, and sometimes the main engine. But India's importance went well beyond that. It absorbed the largest share of Britain's main export – cotton cloth. It did so partly because British rule wedged open its borders and forbade the imposition of tariffs to protect India's own textile producers; and partly because the British insisted on building more and more railways (at India's expense) to open its markets. There was no reason to think that a self-governing India would have followed this course: quite the reverse. The economic plot thickens. India's large British garrison, the pensions of British officials and the money it borrowed in London to build more railway miles – sometimes for reasons that had less to do with economic or strategic utility than with the profits from lending[90] – made India in fact a debtor to Britain. These debts it paid every year from the foreign exchange earned in non-British markets. The so-called 'Home Charges' brought India's dollars and marks (the indirect dividend of imperial rule) to London and helped to make up its deficit with other parts of the world – a valuable prop to British financial supremacy.[91] Just to make sure, at the turn of the century, the rupee's value was carefully pegged to the value of sterling. For practical purposes, the British had annexed the parts of the Indian economy that could strengthen their place in the global economy.

But there is one missing link in this story of empire and wealth. To some of the shrewdest observers of Britain's place in the world, the real secret was coal. What one writer called Britain's 'Black Indies'[92] and another its 'Power Belt'[93] were some hundreds of coal fields , the source of abundant cheap energy and the one great advantage that Britain enjoyed over all other rich countries – except the United States. And it was not merely an internal resource. By 1913 coal had become Britain's third-largest export. The export of coal as far away as Argentina helped keep British shipping profitable. But the reign of King Coal (as the pessimists warned)[94] would not last for ever. It was growing more expensive to dig and its place would soon be threatened by oil. After 1914, an empire founded on coal and dependent on trade would enter a world in which its principal assets began to dwindle away.

7
Ruling Methods

'AN EXTENSIVE AND DETACHED EMPIRE'

In his wartime tract *Mitteleuropa* published in 1915, the German imperialist Friedrich Naumann (1860–1919) remarked (a touch enviously) on the 'unsystematic character of English Imperialism'.[1] Britain's 'sea and colonial empire', he wrote, 'scattered over all parts of the world, is organized quite without system, just as the history of each world province and the chance process of its acquisition has brought it about ... the English elasticity consists in this: that what we call principles, it regards as working methods, an instinctive calm adaptability among its leading men, combined with an unshakeable self-confidence ...'[2]

It was a flattering but also insightful description. By contrast, the conventional image of imperial rule, in which mustachioed titans in shorts impose their authority on resentful populations by sheer assertion of will, is an agreeable (or disagreeable) fiction, but one still found lamentably often in what purports to be 'history'. It creates the illusion of a standardized apparatus of power whose command and control were centred in London. But it could never have been so. The first stumbling block was the astonishing scale and diversity of British possessions. By 1913, more than one hundred separate political units (even excluding the 600 or so princely states of 'Native State' India) owed allegiance to the British Crown. They had been acquired over centuries. They displayed almost every variety of human community, and their internal diversity was sometimes extreme. Desert peoples and nomads; hill peoples and tribals; mining, forest-dwelling and fishing communities (such as Newfoundland); farmers bound to the gruelling regime of wet-rice cultivation (as in the Burma delta) and yeoman-farmers in the temperate Dominions; slave-owners and slaves (until the 1830s); workers and masters in plantation economies; industrial societies with 'proletarians' and 'capitalists' – all these and more could be found in an empire that contained some of the world's largest cities as well as some of its poorest and emptiest landscapes. If imperial rule (or perhaps overrule) was to achieve even a minimal level of cohesion and order, its practitioners would need not a head full of rules but a Machiavellian pragmatism to match the Florentine master himself.

And that was not all. For in every society over which they claimed some authority, the British encountered a political 'tradition': sometimes deeply disguised as religious allegiance, sometimes fiercely contested. This tradition prescribed what forms of power were legitimate in the eyes of the local elite, the criteria of good rulership, and usually the limits of intervention in the private or sacred. Breaking these rules, by intention or not, could be risky or worse. In some cases, this meant giving a very wide berth to all those concerns over which religious teachers or hierarchs claimed a sole dispensation. In others, it meant conceding the right of expatriates and settlers to representative government or exemption from laws that applied to native inhabitants. In yet others, it required the careful observance of rights laid down in a treaty of cession or conquest – the pattern in Quebec or ex-Dutch Guiana.

It followed from this that to try to impose any single pattern of rule would have met fierce resistance. It could hardly succeed without a programme of conquest to remake the political landscape completely. The British were not averse to large-scale coercion, but they were reluctant to pay for it. Where it could not be funded from local resources (as it could be in India), they showed little appetite for its systematic application. Indeed (as we have seen), across much of their empire, they had preferred to expand by treaties of cession, usually extracted by *some* measure of force, or through the 'demographic imperialism' of settler migrations. The logic of both was the devolution of power. In the first case, they were bound to come to terms with enough local power-brokers to uphold their authority and reduce the military bill as quickly as possible. In the second, they were forced soon enough to concede internal autonomy to colonial communities who claimed self-rule as a birthright, proclaimed their allegiance to the 'British connection', and whose violent repression (not least in the shadow of the American revolution) was almost unthinkable.

If caution and pragmatism had been guarantees of success, then ruling a world empire would have been easy enough and its lifespan much longer. But like most large-scale endeavours, imperial rule had more than one object. An imperial policy – consensual, coherent and focused – was always a pipe-dream. This was partly because there was no single helmsman to steer the great ship. Instead, because rule depended on so many agents and allies, a whole mass of hands tugged the wheel this way and that in a series of zigzags or even U-turns. But it was also because the quest for imperial authority was always shot through with contradiction and paradox. It was obvious, for example, that an effective system of rule required a strong revenue base, the *sine qua non* of all modern states. But from the Stamp Tax revolt in the American colonies in the late 1760s to the Hut Tax revolt in Sierra Leone in the late 1890s, the British had learned and relearned that imposing new taxes could provoke opposition with dizzying speed. The enjoyment of power forced strict limits on ambition: the colonial state must not do too much in case it broke down completely. The same kind of brake restrained its promotion of social and economic reform. From one point of view, it was perfectly obvious that if the colonial economy was to be useful to Britain, or cover the administrative costs that British rule had imposed, it should be made more dynamic. Wherever they went the British made gingerly efforts to encourage free trade and stimulate capitalist habits. Here and there (as in Burma and Kenya) they licensed immigrant traders and farmers to encourage a cash-crop economy. But imposing Western ideas of property rights, enforcing a free market in land, or giving free rein to foreign settlers, planters and merchants to create a 'modern' economy was rejected again and again by British officials who were afraid of enraging the local elites on whose support they depended. They were equally nervous of offending local religious belief or lending open support to Christian missions despite their suspicion that Islam (for example) was intellectually bankrupt and Hinduism a medley of superstition and ignorance.

Hence the trend of British 'policy' – so far as such a thing existed in London – was to accept wide local variations and leave much to the discretion of its men on the spot. To do anything else would have been very difficult given the inadequate means to superintend events on the ground. This was partly a matter of snail-like communications. 'Seas roll, and months pass, between the order and the execution,' said Edmund Burke in 1774 at a time when the voyage 'uphill' to the American colonies could take thirteen weeks and was never less than four.[3] 'In large bodies,' he warned his countrymen, 'the circulation of power must be less vigorous at the extremities . . . This is the immutable condition, the eternal law of extensive and detached empire.'[4] Until the advent of steamships, months could elapse between sending or seeking instructions and receiving an answer. Mail-steamers (and railways) gradually reduced this to weeks (Calcutta was nineteen days away by 1911, Cape Town twenty, Singapore twenty-three, Sydney thirty-four and Wellington forty-seven) and even to hours when telegrams (although often discouraged on grounds of expense) were commoner. But it was also because there was no single command centre for imperial affairs as a whole. From the mid nineteenth century, supervision in London was divided between half a dozen departments. Most colonies (but not all) fell under the Colonial Office. The African protectorates of the 1880s and after were at first placed under the Foreign Office, which also took charge of Egypt (all but a colony from 1882) and the Sudan, as well as the treaty port enclaves in China (but not Hong Kong). Britain's grandest colony, the Indian empire, had its own department, the India Office, to which the Viceroy of India reported. But since the Viceroy (who had his own foreign office) managed British interests in the Persian Gulf, southern Iran, Afghanistan and Tibet, and administered both Aden and Burma, much of the eastern empire was also part of its remit. Other departments had fingers in the imperial pie. External defence was the sphere of the Admiralty and its reluctant collaborator the War Office, where the exiguous stock of British infantry battalions – the vital reserve currency of imperial power – was watched over jealously. All fell under the baleful gaze of the ogre of Whitehall. By the mid nineteenth century, the relentless struggle to reduce public debt had brought the Victorian Treasury to its pinnacle.

The 'Treasury knights' regarded overseas spending as the next thing to vice. They treated its supplicants with open contempt: missives to the War Office were sometimes dispatched in words of one syllable: the implication was obvious. When, as happened in the first years of British rule in northern Nigeria, a grant-in-aid was required to meet administrative costs, the Treasury took its revenge with 'Treasury control': every item of spending down to the last penny needed sanction in Whitehall, a procedure that often took months if not years and drove the luckless British officials, sweating in tents over sodden columns of figures, to madness or drink.

Taking the initiative in London was not impossible under these conditions, but it was extremely difficult. The overlapping spheres of authority between different departments made their cooperation essential. When it was lacking, disputes had to be settled in cabinet which, in summer, might not convene for weeks. The worst that could happen, for the departments concerned, was that the affairs of a colony should attract public attention. It was a fact of life, of course, that for every colony there existed vested interests in Britain, usually composed of businessmen, missionaries, humanitarians, former officials ('Old India hands'), or the agents of settler communities. They lobbied vociferously although often contrarily. For the most part they attracted little public attention in Britain since their squabbles and grievances were remote and obscure. But two things could make their grumbling more dangerous. If they were united enough to raise a cry that the colony was in danger, or if they discovered a cause that touched the nerve of Victorian morality – slavery, forced labour, financial irregularity or licensed prostitution were best for this purpose – they could then spark off an uproar. The press became active, questions in Parliament soon followed, and the minister could be called to account. Still worse was the case if disorder or rebellion broke out in a colony, or a military mishap occurred. Then the press storm might rage on for weeks, while ministers promised vainly that prompt action had taken the situation in hand. This was the moment of maximum danger for the colonial official concerned. If his failings embarrassed a minister, his fate would be sealed. He might be informed in an open dispatch that the minister had lost confidence in him (a career-wrecking reproof), removing his name from those in line for promotion – exactly this happened to an outstanding official in Northern Nigeria.[5] Or he might be dismissed.

It is easy to see why the Colonial Office, whose empire included the settler colonies like Canada and Australia, a turbulent South Africa, the old West Indian colonies, the new acquisitions in tropical Africa (after 1880), Gibraltar, Malta, Cyprus, Ceylon (now Sri Lanka), Malaya, Singapore and Hong Kong, as well as a long tail of lesser possessions, preferred reaction to action. Its resources were tiny: some thirty senior staff by 1914. Its finest hour had come and gone with the abolition of slavery in the 1830s – the one great policy that it had had to impose on disgruntled settlers and planters. With the onset of free trade it abandoned any attempt to control the colonial economies. Its prime concern lay with the selection of governors for all its varied dependencies, drawing up their instructions (to discourage too much initiative), and watching them carefully in case of infringements. Governors could be rebuked, or even dismissed, if they exceeded their powers or (for example) tolerated slave-trading or slavery. Their requests for new laws, more money, fresh troops or a frontier advance could be approved or (more likely) rejected. But a governor with friends in high places, who had an eye to the press, and who knew how to exploit the officials' reliance on the information he sent, was hard to control and still harder to remove.

In administrative terms, then, the British presided over a ramshackle empire, full of contradictions and quirks, and with a control apparatus that was spasmodic at best. It had grown Topsy-like with much improvisation. But by the mid nineteenth century, three different patterns of rule (a term defined broadly) were at work in three different empires: the settler empire, the Indian empire, and the vast residual category to which most were consigned, the Crown colony empire.

SETTLER POLITICS

Of all colonial peoples, it was white settlers who were hardest to rule and who gave London most trouble. 'There is no longer a man to be found who dissents from the opinion . . . that the intervention of the British Government in the affairs of a colony is an inconvenience to be avoided by every concession and arrangement which would not ... induce some still greater mischief ...' advised James Stephen, the tough intellectual lawyer who had served as the head official at the Colonial Office from 1836 to 1848.[6] Stephen, whose arrogant nickname – 'Mr Over-Secretary Stephen' – belied his insight, insisted that interference from London usually ended in tears: 'we are almost always worsted'.[7] He was mainly thinking of the settlement colonies and there was much in Britain's imperial past to back up his claim.

As we saw earlier, those who migrated to the American colonies after 1607 believed that they took their rights as free-born Englishmen with them, including the right to representative government. Far from denying this claim, the London government had acknowledged it in a series of charters, and representative bodies had sprung up in all the plantations. In theory, of course, executive power remained in the hands of the governors, usually appointed in London, and the hand-picked advisers on their executive council. In reality, the balance had tilted decisively against them because the elected assemblies gained control over spending and governors lacked the patronage to reward their supporters.[8] By the 1690s, the imperial government at home had adopted a policy of 'salutary neglect' towards these tiresome colonials, leaving them to stew in their own political juice. The colossal expense of the Seven Years' War (1756–63), largely fought in America, created a new situation. Yet when London pressed for an American contribution towards its imperial expenses (especially its huge war debt), and tried to collect it, it met a storm of ideological polemic, accusations of tyranny and then violent resistance. By the mid 1770s imperial authority had collapsed except where a garrison stood by to enforce it.[9] When Cornwallis's army surrendered at Yorktown in October 1781, it vanished altogether.

The shock of losing the Thirteen Colonies forced a major rethink. In the rump of its American empire, today's eastern Canada, London tried to shore up its governors by using land grants to create a loyal 'aristocracy' and fund the Anglican Church, its spiritual ally. By the 1820s this was wearing thin. English-speaking settlers resented what they saw as a corrupt oligarchy and (since few were Anglicans) the unfair distribution of clerical land. In French and Catholic Lower

Canada (modern Quebec), religious animosity made these grievances sharper. In 1837, as economic depression bit deep, both colonies broke out in rebellion: short and sharp in English Upper Canada; longer and more bitter to the east in French Canada. It was a major crisis. The French lower province controlled access to the continental interior and suppressing rebellion required a large force of troops.[10] It coincided with a crisis in the eastern Mediterranean, the threat of war with Russia, and the diplomatic campaign over the future of Belgium. Worrying comparisons with Ireland (rebellious and Catholic) were drawn. An urgent solution was needed.

It took some time to emerge. In 1839, a commission under Lord Durham produced its report. The best answer, said Durham, was to swamp the troublesome French with the mass emigration of British people and neuter them politically. His more famous pronouncement was to denounce the form of representative government as futile and unworkable. It was as useless, he said, to have an assembly that could not replace the executive as to have an executive that could not control the assembly. Both led to weak government. Since the elected politicians were never in office, they had little incentive to show moderation and sense. Far from offering the voter a practical programme, they became irresponsible demagogues, whipping up passions and undermining political order. A way had to be found to harness their energy to orderly government. Durham's conclusion was simple: the elected politicians should form the executive (as they did at home) and the assembly should have the power to dismiss them from office. This was the germ of 'responsible government' – from that moment on the constitutional talisman of all British settler societies. The corollary was obvious. The settler politicians would enjoy almost total autonomy in their local affairs. The imperial government would control only what was truly imperial: external affairs and defence and the constitutional rulebook. Left to themselves, the settler leaders would get on with what mattered most – the rapid development of the colonial economy.[11]

It was nearly a decade before Durham's prescription was followed. London rejected the division of powers he envisaged as a dangerous abdication. Governors tried hard to build local support and become party leaders. But by the late 1840s, they faced a strong coalition of

'English' and 'French' politicians determined to wrest real executive power. London waved the white flag. Henceforth, it said, only politicians who enjoyed the assembly's support should serve in the governor's executive, and be removed when they lost it. But this new system was barely in place in the new province of Canada – a quasi-federation of English Upper Canada and French Lower Canada – before it faced a huge crisis. The governor's new ministers proposed compensation for those who had suffered losses in the rebellion of 1837–8 including (the controversial part) the rebellion's supporters. A storm now arose. Loyalists raged that the governor must veto a disloyal bill. There was riot and arson and a brutal campaign in the press. But the governor, Elgin, stood firm. If he vetoed the bill, he told the government at home, his ministers would resign and denounce him as partisan. Precisely the danger that responsible government was meant to avoid would return with a vengeance. If he was to preserve the British connection – the link with empire and Crown – as a thing above party, he must be seen to act only on the advice of his ministers, so long as they had an elected majority. 'If I am unable to recover that position of dignified neutrality between the contending parties which it has been my unremitting study to maintain,' he told the Colonial Office in April 1849, 'it may be a question whether I should be removed from my high office . . .'[12] It was a critical turning point. Soon after, in 1850 and 1852, London conceded the principle that the Australian colonies and New Zealand should have responsible government as well.

It may seem surprising that migrants from Britain should have been so insistent on ruling themselves and quite so aggressive in pressing their claim. It was certainly true that, as Stephen had said, they were extremely hard to control. But neither peculiarity is really so puzzling. Settler societies were hard to bully. They were usually much better organized than non-settler communities, using familiar institutions imported from home: associations, parties and above all the press. Secondly, the tradition of maintaining a local militia meant that many settlers had arms: London never enjoyed a monopoly of firepower. Thirdly, even had they done so, it was of limited use. The hallmark of settler societies was their wide range of contacts with opinion at home, where they had religious and business connections as well as friends and relations. Violence against them (on the pattern of 1776–83) was thus almost out of the question. The other side of the argument was that settler politicians dismissed as absurd the idea that officials in Whitehall could manage the business of British expansion. It was the settler on the spot, they said, who understood Britain's real interests in North America, Australia or on the New Zealand frontier and how to promote them. It was they who embodied the real virtues of Britishness, who displayed a real British patriotism, who championed Britain's 'manifest destiny'. Slowly but surely this settler vision of empire made progress at home until, by the mid 1880s, it enjoyed growing acceptance.

Yet responsible government was not a universal solution even where a colony had a settler community. There were numerous complications that could make it too dangerous or simply out of the question. It might be the case that the settlers or planters were too few in number and faced too big a native, slave or free black population. London ruled out any form of representative government for Trinidad, Ceylon and Hong Kong on these kinds of grounds. What made matters worse was the well-founded suspicion that, as one governor put it, 'the Agricultural, Commercial interests of the Higher Race must clash with those of the Inferior'.[13] This was code for saying that left to themselves the settlers would steal the land of first peoples, reduce them to serfs, or even try to obliterate them. Quite apart from the risk that humanitarians at home might raise the cry of 'slave labour', there was always the danger that settler oppression would ignite a massive rebellion to which, like a fire brigade, British troops would be summoned in haste. A third complication arose where the colony's borders were still undefined or the scene of disorder and violence. If the scale was too great for a local settler militia to cope, and British troops were involved, settler politicians could not be allowed the last word on internal security lest they waste or abuse the precious resource of British military power. Lastly, where a settler colony was only part of a complex of colonial authority which included a native protectorate or zones of indirect rule, permitting settler home rule might weaken the governor's position in the non-settler parts of his administrative sphere.

These problems did not only arise where the white settler presence was small. In Australia, there was an obvious clash between the interests of aborigines and whites, and a violent frontier to boot. But the imbalance of physical power was too much in the whites' favour and London itself had decreed under the *terra nullius* doctrine that there were no native land rights. In the 1830s British troops were withdrawn and little effort was made to restrain white expansion and its encroachment on Aborigine land. New Zealand was different. Here the Maori had land rights assured by the treaty of cession at Waitangi. They were also well armed and in places more than a match for the small settler bridgeheads they faced. Official thinking in London regarded the settler presence as a nuisance and resented its efforts to enlist London's aid in expanding the colony. The best solution, thought the Colonial Office, was to keep the settlers or *pakeha* penned up in a series of enclaves and rule the rest of the country (especially the North Island since most Maori were there) as a 'native protectorate' through magistrates who would answer not to settler politicians but to the governor alone. Hence responsible government was granted but relations with Maori withheld. It was an unstable solution. The white population grew fast and much Maori land was sold. When, in the mid 1860s, an aggressive and self-confident governor, George Grey, went to war with the Maori to assert his authority, deploying an army of 10,000 British soldiers, the settlers joined in with glee.[14] And although some shadow of Maori rights did survive, the *pakeha* victory ensured that by 1870 New Zealand had become a white man's country where settler power was no longer constrained by supervision from London.

The hardest case was South Africa where each complication appeared in the most acute form. When the British seized Cape Colony from the Dutch to safeguard their sea-lane to India, they blundered unknowingly into a strife-ridden subcontinent. They refused representative government to the local whites partly because they were Dutch (and thus doubtfully loyal), partly because enforcing new rules on the treatment of black labour and then abolishing slavery met stiff opposition from them. But they quickly discovered still more compelling objections to conceding self-government to the settler minority. The Cape's eastern border was a brutal war zone where raid and retaliation by Afrikaner (Boer) and Xhosa cattle-herders were punctuated by outbreaks of larger-scale conflict – what the whites called 'kaffir wars'. Once British troops were committed to guarding the frontier (the first major fort was built at Grahamstown in 1812), there was no question of giving the settlers a predominant say in the colony's relations with its African neighbours. The problem grew worse. In the late 1830s, in the notorious 'Great Trek', discontented Boer farmers outflanked the Xhosa-held lands, moving north and east first to Natal and then, when the British annexed this region as well, back on to the great grassy Highveld interior. Their institutions were crude (two independent republics emerged from the ruck of competing Boer factions), but their firepower decisive. Fast mobile 'commandos' of horse-mounted riflemen made good their claim to the Highveld, pushing its black population into so-called 'locations' and conscripting their labour. The effect was to turn the South African subcontinent into a vast turbulent frontier whose black populations milled hither and thither, crashing into each other as well as the whites. From their faraway lookout at the tip of the continent, British governors were oppressed most of all by their impotence. Of one thing they were sure: handing over control to the whites – old Dutch or (a small number of) new British – would lead to disaster.[15]

But standing still was no longer an option after mid century. The whites at the Cape demanded self-government like other settler communities. In 1853, they were allowed an assembly but not executive power. London's tactics were blunt. 'If the colonists will not allow themselves to be governed ... it follows that they must accept the responsibility of governing,' remarked one colonial secretary wearily.[16] But if they did so, the British troops would go home, and the defence of the frontier would fall on the settlers. In fact this was a bluff. London's real aim was to make the colony pay for policing the African districts (including modern Ciskei, Transkei and Lesotho) that it had gradually brought under imperial protection, while preserving the governor's special authority as 'high commissioner' over these borderland regions. Once diamonds were found in 1867, and the colonial economy began to pick up, Whitehall dreamed of the perfect solution: a South African federation under the Cape; a carefully harmonized policy towards all the African peoples to ensure frontier peace; a progressive, reliable, self-funding British state on the Canadian model. Boer resistance in the two northern republics aborted this plan and the doughty Boer warrior Paul Kruger restored the Transvaal's independence after a brief British takeover in 1877–81.[17] When gold was found on the Rand in the mid 1880s, the newly rich Transvaal looked safe: indeed it soon seemed set to become the dominant state in the Southern African region, threatening the primacy that London regarded as vital to its sea links with India and its Asian possessions. But by the strangest of twists, the longstanding claim of expatriate Britons to representative government blew up Kruger's state and set off a war.[18]

These were the 'uitlanders' or foreigners, mainly British, who rushed to the gold fields and supplied the skilled labour and commercial expertise that Johannesburg needed. Encouraged from outside by Cecil Rhodes and his friends (eager for a Cape-led British South Africa), and by the new British High Commissioner at the Cape, Sir Alfred Milner, they demanded London's help to win the political rights that Kruger denied them as foreigners. A reluctant British cabinet found itself jerked into confrontation with the Boer republics who then declared war to pre-empt a military squeeze by the British. A bitter three-year war followed in October 1899. On a peace of mutual exhaustion, an uneasy bargain was built. The Boer leaders abandoned their quest for an independent republic. They supported the union of South Africa's four settler states (Cape Colony, Natal, the Orange Free State and Transvaal) in a self-governing 'dominion' modelled on Canada, Australia and New Zealand inside the empire and under the Crown. Their motives are not very puzzling. The English in South Africa were a minority among whites, but they were a substantial minority and their part in the conflict (alongside British troops) had made it, as the ablest Boer general, Jan Smuts, admitted, a white civil war.[19] To try to impose a republic on them was to risk a new struggle and, perhaps in the process, the future of *baaskap* – white supremacy – in the subcontinent. What the Boers got in exchange shaped South African history for the next eighty years. With responsible government, political union and dominion status, the white settler minority, Afrikaner and English, acquired full control of the fate of South Africa's blacks, now a subject population. By the grimmest of ironies, settler self-government and its language of liberty had opened the road to apartheid.

Did the British still *rule* their settlement colonies? A jesting proconsul might have asked: 'What is rule?' London had conceded self-government. It had encouraged settler communities to become more self-reliant by federation or union. Using armed force to prevent their leaving the empire (taking the 'American exit') was not a conceivable option. Instead the British relied on three different kinds of British connection to preserve their attachment. The first was the sense of 'Britannic' identity among Canadians, Australians, New Zealanders and the English in South Africa and a conception of empire as a shared enterprise, a white ethnic commonwealth. The second was awareness of mutual dependence – financial, commercial and strategic – that made real separation unattractive, even dangerous. The third was more subtle. In all the dominions, and especially South Africa, the settler state derived its legitimacy from a web of constitutional rules whose ultimate source was an almost mystic allegiance to the faraway British Crown. To renounce that allegiance by becoming a republic or leaving the empire would unravel the fabric of political unity, risking fragmentation or worse. Perhaps this was rule in its most acceptable – and most insidious – form.

'UN-BRITISH RULE'? GOVERNING INDIA

The contrast between India and the world of settler self-government could not have been greater. In India, British officials appointed from home exercised executive power, unrestrained (before 1909) by any real element of representative government. At their head was a viceroy, usually a British politician of the 'second eleven' (perhaps on his way to the 'first') and usually also a peer. The right to local self-rule, successfully claimed by settler societies, was explicitly denied. Instead, the so-called 'Civilians' of the Indian Civil Service formed an administrative oligarchy, what Edmund Burke had called 'a kingdom of magistrates', with a keen sense of common interest – 'a common interest separated both from the country that sent them out and from the country in which they are . . .'[20] Their warrant to rule depended not on Indian opinion but on managing the sometimes conflicting demands of their political masters at home and their colonial subjects in India. They had to present India as a source of honour and profit to Britain. They were bound to insist that their regime was secure, but also indispensable. But they had to show Indians, whose acquiescence was vital, that their alien authority was both just and immovable: that resistance was futile but also redundant.

Such a dramatic departure from an older conception of empire as the planting of free British communities under Britain's commercial and strategic umbrella was a deep source of unease. The wealth and power enjoyed by the East India Company's 'servants' after its effective annexation of Bengal in 1765 alarmed and astonished opinion at home. Clive and Warren Hastings were not like the settlers, planters and merchants of British America. They resembled conquistadors: flamboyant, all-powerful and rich beyond dreams. In Burke's famous assault on Hastings's administrative record (Hastings's trial before Parliament from 1788 to 1795), he denounced the corruption of power as an 'oriental' autocracy that answered to no one. 'The English nation in India,' he declaimed, '. . . are a nation of place-men. They are a republic, a commonwealth, without a people.'[21] It was a short step to suggest that the multiple vices acquired in the East would return to pollute the British at home.

This tradition survived in radical politics. In its polemics, rule over India was the road to British ruin. Soldiers in search of promotion and plunder, indigent aristocrats in search of a salary: both had an interest in expanding the Company Raj, courting new wars in the East, and perhaps even with Russia. The risk of an Indian revolt, frighteningly real after 1857, required an army-in-waiting at home, perhaps even conscription.[22] It would be a happy day, said Richard Cobden, when Britain ceased to rule any part of India. An ideology of 'liberal imperialism' sprang up to rebut these jeremiads. Its inventors included the politician-historian T. B. (later Lord) Macaulay and the philosopher of Victorian liberalism, John Stuart Mill. Both took the Company's shilling: Macaulay as Law Member of the government of India in Calcutta, Mill as a bureaucrat in the Company's

London headquarters at India House in the City. In a famous speech in 1833 and his two widely read essays on Clive and Warren Hastings, Macaulay rejected Burke's orientalist nightmare. The conquest of India became a heroic endeavour where British valour and virtue had triumphed. British rule was a rescue mission since under the Mughals Indian 'society was a chaos'. Far from engaging in an orgy of plunder, the Company had begun 'the reconstruction of a decomposed body'.[23] Macaulay's grand theme of order and progress was taken up by Mill in his *Representative Government* (1861). Representative government, argued Mill, was a means not an end. Its premature extension to India would wreck its ultimate aim: progress and good government. Enlightened British rule, not a hasty abdication, was the liberal's true path. The shock of the Mutiny added weight to the claim that the liberal mission in India must be defended by force if need be.[24]

In fact, the post-Mutiny charter of the new British regime was much more ambivalent. Firstly, the Queen's Proclamation of 1858 promised an end to the Company's practice of annexing princely states at every opportunity – one of the prime causes of the revolt. The princes would be left in peace. Secondly, in recruiting its administrative servants, the Raj would ignore both race and religion – a promise observed only in the breach until the interwar years despite much local complaint. Thirdly, the enforcement of 'progress' would be tactfully adapted to Indian opinion. There was to be no question of pressing Christianity upon the Indian people, nor of any interference with their religious beliefs. Most striking of all was the promise that 'in framing and administering the law, due regard [would] be paid to the ancient rights, usages and customs of India'.[25] Burke and Mill had been reconciled.

But how did the British actually govern India? It is a familiar tale that the British were few and that their Raj was a case of 'hundreds ruling millions'. There is some substance to this. The Indian Civil Service, the ruling bureaucracy created in the 1790s, numbered fewer than 1,000. Its 'covenanted' members (so called from the covenant they signed not to trade or receive presents) – almost all white British and recruited by the late nineteenth century largely from Oxbridge – filled almost all the most senior appointments in India, reserved for them like parking spaces. Of course, they were not the only official Europeans in India ('European' was the generic term for whites). Several hundred others served in the Indian Imperial Police (like the writer George Orwell in 1920s Burma). In the post-1860 Indian army, reduced from 250,000 to some 140,000 men, there were by 1887 around 1,600 British officers,[26] a figure that rose steadily up to 1914.[27] After 1857, there was also a large all-British garrison of 70,000 officers and men stationed in India. Doctors, teachers and engineers recruited in Britain swelled the official payroll.

Yet it remained true that the political and administrative management of India was undertaken by a tiny administrative elite deeply conscious of its foreignness to those it ruled over. 'At best we are an alien, and worse than that an unbending and unsympathetic race,' wrote one official in the 1870s. 'The race we are called upon to rule is essentially an impulsive and a feeling one . . . we never thaw to them and they never open to us . . .'[28] Of course, across nearly one third of India British rule was indirect: exercised through Indian princes under a mass of treaties and 'sanads'. The princes were supervised, with varying degrees of success, by British 'residents', drawn partly from the Civil Service, partly from the officer corps of the Indian army. Here the penalty for what the British deemed misgovernment (not to mention more serious misdemeanours) was – in the worst case – removal if the resident could persuade his distant superiors to risk the upheaval involved. The usual scenario was much more prosaic: a game of intrigue and manoeuvre, official reproofs and protestations of loyalty, angry complaints and a blind eye to abuse. The resident might give tacit encouragement to the prince's opponents to check any waywardness. Official marks of distinction (titles especially, since the princes were highly competitive) could be rationed or withheld.[29] Elsewhere, on India's turbulent frontiers – the border with Afghanistan was not demarcated until the 'Durand Line' of 1893 – the British made sporadic attempts to assert continuous control over well-armed tribal communities in what they called optimistically the 'Settled Districts' west of the Indus. But they often fell back on a rough border diplomacy using cash as a carrot and the punitive patrol as the stick. In the game of raid and riposte, as Kipling pointed out, 'the odds were on the cheaper man'.[30]

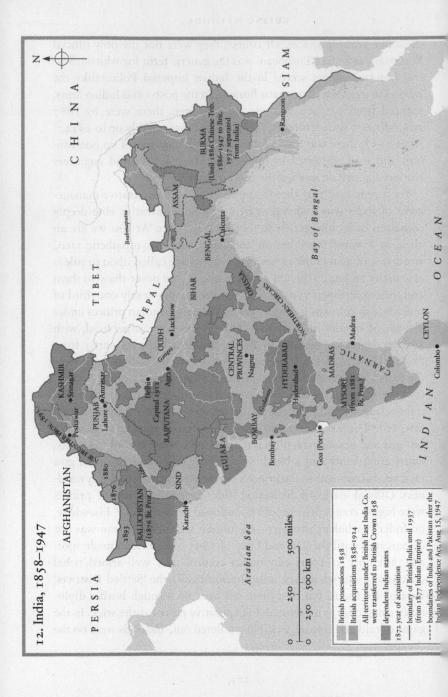

12. India, 1858–1947

N

CHINA

SIAM

BURMA
(Until 1886 Chinese Trib.
1886–1947 to Brit.,
1937 separated
from India)

● Rangoon

ASSAM

TIBET

Brahmaputra

● Calcutta

Bay of Bengal

BENGAL

NEPAL

BIHAR

ORISSA

OUDH

● Lucknow

NORTHERN CIRCARS

KASHMIR

● Srinagar

● Peshawar

PUNJAB

● Amritsar

1880

● Delhi

Capital 1912

● Agra

Ganges

RAJPUTANA

CENTRAL
PROVINCES

● Nagpur

HYDERABAD

● Hyderabad

MADRAS

● Madras

MYSORE
(from 1881
Br. Prot.)

CARNATIC

● Lahore

NW FRONTIER PROV. 1901

AFGHANISTAN

1876

1893

BALUCHISTAN
(1876 Br. Prot.)

Jhelum

SIND

GUJARA

Godavari

BOMBAY

● Bombay

● Goa (Port.)

● Karachi

PERSIA

Arabian Sea

INDIAN

OCEAN

CEYLON

● Colombo

British possessions 1858

British acquisitions 1858–1914

All territories under British East India Co.
were transferred to British Crown 1858

dependent Indian states

1872 year of acquisition

—— boundary of British India until 1937
(from 1877 Indian Empire)

---- boundaries of India and Pakistan after the
Indian Independence Act, Aug 15, 1947

0   250   500 miles

0 250 500 km

The real work of Indian government was a good deal more hum-drum. The setting was not the princely court or the dark defile but the endless plains of agricultural India, with its thousands of villages and millions of cultivators. Here the first task was to keep order in a densely layered agrarian society which piled a mountain of rent-seekers and -claimers (some absentee, some organized into powerful 'village brotherhoods') over the long-suffering, debt-ridden labourers in the field. The second was to collect the 'land revenue', the staple of Indian finance. This was the government's share of the agricultural surplus, collected in cash, and based on its rights as the land's ultimate owner. Much of the elite manpower of the Indian Civil Service, the Civilians, was stationed in the 250 or so districts (many with more than 1 million inhabitants) into which the provinces of directly ruled British India were divided. The 'collector', as he was typically known, was the head of the district. He presided over its courts and collected the revenue while maintaining a close watch for signs of political unrest that might threaten British authority. A show of disrespect towards him or other Europeans, or a sudden friendliness between usually antagonistic communities, would arouse his suspicions and occasion a warning dispatch or even a telegram. There had been 'curious instances of fraternization between Hindus and Mahommedans', reported the governor of the North-West Provinces (today's Uttar Pradesh) in July 1897, although 'I am far from saying that it has attained the dimensions of a conspiracy'.[31]

The usual explanation for the British ability to govern India with such an exiguous administrative presence (perhaps three or four ICS men in a district) is their success in attracting 'collaborators' among the rural elite whose social power was the key to political calm in the countryside. It is an explanation that begs a whole series of questions. Why should Indians have collaborated with such a minuscule force of British intruders, however self-confident? Why should they have been ready to pay over such a large part of their surplus when it was heavily spent not on Indian improvements but on maintaining the army and paying the rent on the huge British garrison, not to mention the pensions and salaries of official Europeans? Why were resistance and rebellion not much more common? And why were they not more successful? The answers can be found, partly at least, in the distinctive conditions in which the British Raj was constructed, and in the legacy it inherited from India's earlier overlords.

In their first century of rule (1757–1857), the British in India were not so much an administering as a conquering force and the East India Company a garrison state, organized mainly for war. By the end of that century, they had defeated, annexed or subjugated every significant regional power in the Indian subcontinent. Their motives for doing so were partly strategic (an insurance against Russian or French interference). The enormous Company army (more than 300,000 regular soldiers at its height) with its voracious demand for plunder and pay also created a forward momentum. Indeed, the self-funding nature of the Company's wars blunted the impact of London's objections to further expansion, based on its fear that the Company state would bankrupt itself and set off a new crisis at home like that which had raged in the 1770s and 1780s. But the men on the spot were also concerned that their straggling possessions, spread out across India in the shape of a horseshoe, could be preyed on by the heavily armed retinues that many princes maintained.[32] Whatever their motive, the Company's wars achieved a crucial result. After 1860 (and well before that in much of the subcontinent), there was no Indian state with the means to ignite political dissidence in a British-ruled district, or to coordinate opposition on a regional scale. By crushing princely ambition, the British had imposed a form of extreme localization on India's politics. This was to prove an enormous advantage in the longer-drawn-out and less glamorous campaigns of administrative conquest. Of course, in the northern interior of British India, in what was called 'Hindustan', this conquest was interrupted by a massive upheaval, the great Indian Rebellion of 1857 (to be discussed in the next chapter). But, astonishingly, much if not all of the Company Raj's fabric survived.

The main battlefield of administrative conquest was the revenue system. The crucial fact here was that the British did not have to invent or impose a new method of taxing the land: they inherited it from the rulers who preceded them. They had a powerful motive to make it work in their favour: to pay for the Company's wars, and (up to 1813) to help finance its commercial activities. Indeed, control of the revenue system was the key to the assertion of British political power district by district. Everywhere, so the Civilians insisted, they found the revenues owed to the state had been siphoned off by local magnates. The gradual eclipse of Mughal authority in the eighteenth century and the rise of regional states had created the perfect conditions in which local elites had effectively privatized their functions as collectors of revenue and custodians of order. The tribute and revenue they had once had to pay over had been diverted to build up their own local power base: their strongholds and forts and their private armies of 'enforcers'.[33] So everywhere that British rule was proclaimed, it was rapidly followed by a revenue offensive. Tax records were scrutinized, old tax demands raised and inquiries begun into abuses and shortfalls. It was laborious work that depended for success on a host of Indian auxiliaries – and on the claim that the British were merely reasserting the ruler's legitimate rights.

But it was bound to be difficult. In some districts the magnates were too powerful and well armed to be safely confronted – at least not until the British had demolished the larger regional powers such as Chait Singh in Benares or the terrible Tipu Sultan of Mysore, eventually defeated and killed in 1799. In South India they faced a mass of 'poligars' who ruled little kingdoms from their compounds and forts. The British tactic was to press their revenue claim and demand the disarming of the poligars and their retinues. Poligars who complied were rewarded with a once-for-all revenue settlement, fixing their tax obligation indefinitely. With their incomes cut down, they faced the choice between paying their retinue or the Company's collectors. The aim was to isolate the poligars who resisted, or goad them into open revolt. Revolt would be followed, though not always quickly, by armed retribution. Sooner or later, a detachment of the Company's huge sepoy army would arrive to depose the poligar, demolish his fort and install in his place a more cooperative magnate.[34]

For the British could usually find wealthy, well-born and literate Indians who would throw in their lot with the new *sarkar* or ruler, and who regarded its claims to legitimate power as greater than those of the warrior chiefs, poligars and 'zemindars' (their North Indian counterparts) who had exploited the decay of central authority. Once more or less in control of the revenue system, the British could use to the full the legal and administrative privileges of the *sarkar*. Thus estates whose heir was a minor fell under the British-controlled 'court of wards' which installed its own manager. The lower rungs of the district bureaucracy provided a large fund of patronage to reward the loyal and punish the troublesome. A cadre of honorary magistrates, who tried lesser cases, was recruited from the local elite; to be excluded or dismissed was a humiliation to be avoided at almost all costs. There were also titles and honours to be distributed (a favourite British device): the obvious implication was that their holders enjoyed the collector's goodwill, and thus that of the government. In return, the collector made clear that he expected local bigwigs to report very quickly on any unrest whether criminal or political. They knew exactly what was going on in their localities, remarked one British official, and should be held to account. If necessary, they should be watched by a system of spies.[35] In times of difficulty, they were expected to form 'loyal' associations.[36] Indeed, in such a localized system, a great deal depended on the collector's skill and energy in manipulating the multiple sources of political influence. To do his job properly, remarked the Madras government, the collector had to be very active. 'He must make himself acquainted with the languages, dispositions and circumstances of the people; the various descriptions of land tenures; the sources from which the public revenues are drawn' and the means to enlarge them.[37] From 1796 onward, proficiency in one of a province's main languages became a condition for promotion to collector. Collectors were also expected to tour their districts for up to four months a year, to show the flag and keep an eye on their Indian subordinates. In most of the provinces, there were periodic reassessments of the land tax to be paid. This required a village-by-village, field-by-field survey by a British 'settlement officer'. These settlement reports, with their mass of information about fertility, crops, land tenures and population, remain a prime source for India's social history.

Sheer bureaucratic persistence was thus a key explanation for the success of British rule in overcoming the barriers of ignorance and foreignness. Of course, the British officials were far from displaying a machine-like efficiency. In the newly conquered Punjab of the 1850s and 1860s, an austere macho ethos was deliberately cultivated. Punjab Civilians were expected to live hard and to be on the move constantly, to be seen everywhere. One was idiosyncratic (or rash) enough to bring a piano. His reward was to be moved ever more frequently. 'I'll smash his piano,' the governor was heard to declare.[38] As in any bureaucracy, the route to the top was not always straight. John Beames complained bitterly that family connection and favouritism often decided promotion.[39] He wryly recalled the occasion when he had assembled a large fleet of river boats at very short notice to transport a military force. Shortly before it arrived, he was dismissed from the scene by his official superior who proudly laid claim to this administrative feat and was duly rewarded. There were also bound to be limits to the Civilians' administrative reach, precisely because they were so dependent upon their Indian allies and auxiliaries. Where they faced a dominant faction among the notables in a district, its grip on appointments to the district bureaucracy, even in the collector's own *cutcherry* or office, might be hard to break.[40] The British had little success in controlling village-level appointments such as the *chaukidar* (constable), the *patel* (tax collector) and *karnam* (accountant).[41] Creating an efficient, reliable and uncorrupt police force proved equally difficult. To make matters worse, the strict limitations on the size of the ICS (because its pay and pensions were so costly) meant that officials were constantly transferred from district to district to cover for leave and other disruptions.

In the 1870s, once the dust of rebellion had settled, the Civilian regime faced an insidious new challenge. India was to be modernized. The British pressed ahead with the building of railways. The telegraph, the steamship and the Suez Canal drew India closer to Europe. The circulation of news, information and ideas between Europe and India and across the Indian subcontinent began to speed up. More Indians read English, and their knowledge of Britain increased, just at the time when Gladstonian Liberalism, which stressed the need for a close political bond between people and government, was transforming its politics. The claim began to be heard that British rule in India was 'un-British' and in 1885 the Indian National Congress was founded to campaign for Indian home rule. To complicate matters, as in much of the rest of the world, the pressures of economic and social development forced the Civilians to interfere more widely in Indian life and society and to spend much more money on railways, irrigation, the conservation of forests, the promotion of agricultural improvement as well as on public health and the prevention of plague. The rapid growth of many towns demanded a more systematic approach to problems of sanitation and policing. The British needed more, and different kinds of, cooperation from Indian elites. They needed to raise more in taxation.[42] And they needed to head off the claim that India's new class of Western-educated professionals (in one district of Bengal there were 403 pleaders – barristers – by 1913)[43] had a better moral claim (on Gladstonian principles) to govern India than they did.

The Civilians reacted like an oligarchy under siege, but with Machiavellian ingenuity. The substantial minority of 'scholar-mandarins' in their ranks knew how to rule by the pen. They produced a torrent of learning in censuses, gazetteers, ethnographic reports, political histories and an ever-growing list of inquiries. This was not a mere database. It presented India through their eyes as a mass of incompatible fragments, divided by race, language, religion, caste, occupation and region, and India itself as a 'geographical expression'. It poured scorn on the claims of the 'microscopic minority' of English-speaking Indians to represent a subcontinent of unimaginable diversity. It reshaped the whole conception of India as a polity – as much in Indian eyes as in British – and vindicated in so doing the Civilians' own moral authority as its progressive, enlightened and impartial custodians. In terms of opinion at home, this campaign was a dazzling success: no British minister, however liberal his views, dared criticize the ICS openly. Its selfless guardianship of India's downtrodden masses became (perhaps appropriately) a sacred cow in political discourse.

Meanwhile in India, the Civilians pursued an ever more devious strategy. They acknowledged the need to associate representative Indians with their government and soften its overly authoritarian exterior. Indians were allowed to participate on local government boards and then, in the reforms of 1892 and 1909, to serve as nominees and elected members on the provincial councils where legislation was framed.[44] These concessions were greeted with initial enthusiasm by the leaders of the Congress. But they were artfully designed to appeal much more widely than to the English-speaking elite. The Civilians made sure that they kept in their hands the decision on whom or what should be represented, and the balance between elected and nominee members. Representation should mirror the divided and 'cellular' structure of Indian society as they had defined it, so that councils were chosen not by the Indian people but by its communities of caste, occupation, religion and district. They also made sure that their executive power was left almost untouched by the procedural rules of the councils. The Civilians were coming round to the view that the decentralization of India was the best guarantee of their Raj. Above all (and revealingly) they rejected point blank the key demand of the Congress that recruitment to the ICS should be opened up properly to suitably qualified Indians. The racial solidarity of the Civilian ruling caste was to be kept intact.[45]

Before 1914, despite periodic outbreaks of unrest and (an echo of Europe) a bomb-throwing campaign in Bengal, there was little sign that the British regime was in any real danger. The idea that British rule would be swept away in little more than thirty years would have seemed absurd to any rational observer, British or Indian. That rule had its foundation, as the British admitted themselves, in its monopoly of armed force. The large British garrison, and an Indian army recruited deliberately from minority elements in the Indian population, were strong enough to destroy any armed insurrection (and India was now a disarmed society) with comparative ease. The memory of the brutal 'second conquest' of India in 1857–8, and the 'white terror' that followed, died hard: to almost all Indians, the forcible overthrow of the British was the idlest of fantasies. The second great strength of the Civilian Raj was the racial solidarity of the British in India, carefully reinforced by commemoration of the Mutiny: the danger of trusting the natives, the need for race loyalty at all times were its obvious lessons. Stick together and rule was the ICS motto. Thirdly, despite the outward appearance of an alien colonial regime, in its everyday functions the ICS Raj drew heavily upon older traditions of governance in India, not least in its revenue system and its careful respect for indigenous custom and law, now formally codified. Colonialism in India was not just a command system. It embodied a vast web of procedure, regulation and official identity, Anglo-Indian not British, within which Indians were required to conduct public life and express public views. It was expressed in a curious social and administrative jargon, neither English nor Indian.[46] Breaking out of its mindset was easier said than done. For many nationalist Indians, however deeply committed to the ideal of a free Indian nation, British rule still appeared as a providential release from the shackles of the past, and the best road to the future as long as the British could be persuaded to open the gate. They thought that British values of manliness, individuality and physical vigour must be injected into any new Indian elite if it was to govern successfully. That was why Motilal Nehru sent his son to Harrow and Cambridge, and hoped he would become not a nationalist politician but a truly Indian Civilian.

But as we know now, change was lying in wait. No system is proof against unforeseen crisis and political genius. The massive political strains set off by the First World War, and apparent failings of their government, forced the Civilians to concede the ideological claim of India's right to self-rule. Meanwhile, Gandhi, the supreme mobilizer, invoked the new doctrine of 'non-cooperation' in the great campaign of 1920–22. Almost single-handed, he transformed the Indian National Congress from an annual convention into a modern mass movement. The Civilians were down but not out. With characteristic ingenuity, they devised an arsenal of new tactics to conciliate, contain, divide and delay. But the rules of the game, long secure in their grip, had been changed for good.

THE TRIUMPH OF INDIRECT RULE: THE 'WHISPER BEHIND THE THRONE'

Since the 1790s, when they began to acquire a mass of new colonies in an age of world war, the British had used what became known as 'Crown colony government' as the default setting for their new dependencies. The formula was simple, although its precise operation varied with local conditions.[47] The basic rule was to maintain the executive power of the governor while making some provision for local opinion in a law-making body, the 'legislative council'. On grounds of prudence, if nothing else, it was thought wise to draw the leading men in the colony – hereditary notables, landowners and merchants – into visible cooperation with the alien ruler. But two vital qualifications were made. Firstly, the local representatives were usually chosen by nomination and co-option, not election. Secondly, these 'unofficial members' were almost always outnumbered by the so-called 'officials', mainly selected from the executive officers and expected to vote as the governor directed. With this there was no danger of the American problem, where the legislature had exploited control of the budget to appropriate executive power. Equally, there was no obvious path to genuinely representative, let alone responsible, government. To its champions in London this was surely the point. They regarded their non-European subjects as unsuited to either and dismissed the constitutional claims of the handfuls of white planters and merchants in tropical colonies as a transparent tactic to exploit the non-white majority. They were even willing to reverse a colony's progress under certain conditions. Thus the West Indian colonies, with their free or freed black majorities, were largely converted to Crown colony rule after the Jamaica rising of 1865 had revealed the shortcomings of representative government by small white minorities.[48]

The convenience of the Crown colony method was that it could be tailored to a very diverse set of possessions by adjusting the choice and number of unofficial members and by widening or narrowing the scope of legislative council business. A moderately skilful governor could head off discontent or find a new ally by using his powers of appointment. But it seemed to work best in relatively small-scale societies where linguistic and ethnic divisions were not too acute or where the population was one mainly of migrants – European, Asian or African. When these conditions broke down, it quickly came under strain. In the colonial enclaves of West Africa, British jurisdiction had long reached inland (in the picturesque phrase of one British minister) only as far as a gunshot from their forts on the beach. But in the 1880s and 1890s, with the partition of Africa, these small coastal enclaves acquired vast straggling hinterlands, the result of jostling and sabre-rattling among the European powers and their men on the spot. The whole question of rule was thrown up in the air. In both West and East Africa, the eventual result was to entrench a quite different notion of imperial governance, what came to be called 'indirect rule'. Its impact was profound.

Indirect rule first appeared in Nigeria.[49] Its inventor was Frederick (later Lord) Lugard, High Commissioner of Northern Nigeria 1900–1906 and Governor-General of Nigeria as a whole 1912–19. Lugard had had an exotic career.[50] Disappointed in love, he took leave from the army in India to seek death or glory (apparently preferring the former) in East Africa, in the 1880s still largely *terra incognita* to Europeans. After a brief period fighting Arab slavers in modern Malawi, Lugard was sent by the Imperial British East Africa Company to assert its claims in Uganda for which it held a charter from the British government. With his small force of Sudanese mercenaries, Lugard showed a talent for coercive diplomacy and an equal flair for publicity. His *Rise of our East African Empire* (1893) was published to win the debate on whether Uganda should be annexed to the empire. Lugard also campaigned in the press and on the platform, invoking Britain's anti-slavery mission to trump liberal unease. Uganda was duly annexed in 1894.

Lugard now had the perfect credentials for a colonial proconsul. Another ex-soldier turned trader, George Goldie, had extracted a charter from London to defend Britain's stake in the Niger valley against a commercial takeover by France. Goldie formed his Royal Niger Company in 1886. It used strong-arm methods to force open the trade routes into the Nigerian interior. By the mid 1890s, it was embroiled in all but a shooting war with French advance parties, moving south from the Sahel. Lugard's task, as commander of Goldie's private army, was to repel French influence and sign up local rulers to support the Company. When the armed struggle proved too much for the Company's finances, its assets were nationalized (in 1898) and London took over. Lugard was appointed High Commissioner to turn the Company's claims into a political fact.[51]

Indirect rule was the paradoxical by-product of Lugard's wars of conquest in Northern Nigeria between 1900 and 1906. Despite the advantage of some modern weaponry, the tiny size of his army, almost all of it African, forced Lugard to take extraordinary risks. The Fulani emirs of the North ruled from 'palaces of red mud with crenellated walls'[52] in fortified cities of which the greatest was Kano, the great slave market of inland West Africa. Their cavalry armies commanded the open savanna. Firepower and nerve, helped by the passive disloyalty of the Hausa majority towards their Fulani overlords, enabled

Lugard to win.[53] But he had few illusions. He realized from the first that he had little choice but to retain the existing system of government, demanding merely that the emirs acknowledge British supremacy. 'I swear in the name of Allah and of Mahomet his Prophet,' so ran the oath, 'to well and truly serve His Majesty King Edward VII . . . I will cherish in my heart no treachery or disloyalty.'[54] The emirs had to make it with their hands pressed on the Koran. The old order was saved, with its Islamic laws and judges, its feudal aristocracy and its direct taxation of farmers and pastoralists. There was no question of administering Northern Nigeria with a mere handful of British political officers, minimal means of coercion, and without even the money for office equipment (Lugard's officials had to buy their own typewriters). Indirect rule started life as the pragmatic acceptance of very limited power.

But to Lugard and his followers, it quickly assumed the force of a creed. Elsewhere in Nigeria, in the Yoruba states behind Lagos, or among the Ibo people east of the delta, the British, being few, had tended to leave most local affairs in the hands of the locals, only demanding protection for their travellers and trade. Lugard regarded this practice as dangerously flawed. British authority must be firmly asserted through a single chain of command. This could be done only through an African ruler strong enough to collect taxes and enforce local laws – and answerable for both to a British official, the Resident. Only in this way could British rule be effective: carefully concentrated but also discreetly concealed. Where there were rulers who lacked these powers, as in the Yoruba states where authority was dispersed among hereditary notables,[55] or among the chiefless Ibo, the British should intervene to correct this anomaly. 'Traditional' monarchs should rule in fact as well as name; where chiefs were missing, a 'big man' should be found and given a government warrant. There were obvious objections, angrily voiced by British officials in the South. It would encourage abuse, especially in hitherto chiefless societies. But after 1912, when he returned with a mandate to unify the Northern and Southern Protectorates, Lugard swept all objections aside.

Lugard's success was partly the fruit of his growing prestige, the success of his wartime proconsulship (parts of Nigeria were a war zone) and the efforts of his wife, Flora Shaw, colonial editor on *The*

Times. But his ideas also had an undeniable logic. Lugard rejected the Crown colony model as artificial and dangerous. There were two key objections. Traditional rulers, who, even if literate, were unlikely to speak English, could not play a role in its key institution, the legislative council. Instead its procedures and practice favoured the educated (often Christian) African elite of the coast, the Creoles or Krio, whose claim to represent inland Africans and the Muslims of the North Lugard dismissed as absurd. 'It is a cardinal rule of British Colonial policy,' he said, 'that the interests of a large native population shall not be subject to the will either of a small European class or of a small minority of educated and Europeanised natives who have nothing in common with them and whose interests are often opposed to theirs.'[56] Secondly, under Crown colony government, there was a separate judiciary, a presumption in favour of English legal procedure (including legal representation) and often jury trial. Lugard regarded all these with undisguised horror. A judge second-guessing the executive power, legal rules in conflict with customary or Islamic law, juries selected inevitably from a tiny Anglophone minority, fee-hunting lawyers turning demagogues in a trice: for a government spread wafer-thin over a vast hinterland, and reliant on the personal authority of a handful of Residents, such a regime threatened chaos.

Lugard's strongest card was his claim that without British support the traditional forms of authority would simply collapse, turning their new African subjects into an ungovernable rabble. Without the revenue base, bureaucratic apparatus and military power that they possessed in India, a 'rescue from chaos' on Indian lines was simply impossible. Indirect rule was thus the key to social and political stability. If this case had been harder to make before 1914, the effects of the War and of revolution in Russia had a salutary impact on imperial self-confidence. The Lugardians hammered this home with a canny appeal to a fashionable new ethos. Indirect rule, so they claimed, was the regime best designed to meet the needs of trusteeship. It was the acceptable face of colonial control: combining the safest approach to self-rule with the scientific adaptation to local custom and practice.[57] So when Lugard's successor as governor listed its defects (the failure to encourage commercial development, the abuses of 'warrant chiefs', the continued reliance on 'punitive' patrols), he got short shrift in

London. A year or so later, he deemed it wise to convert to Lugardian doctrine. 'In all that he does or leaves undone,' he told his officials, '. . . the Political Officer must be careful to lend his support to the authority of the Emir . . . The Political Officer should be the Whisper behind the Throne, but never for an instant the Throne itself'.[58]

In British East Africa, the scope for Lugardian methods was narrower. In Uganda, the British did find highly organized states. In the Uganda Agreement of 1900, they conceded autonomy to Buganda, the largest and strongest of these, on terms of which Lugard would not have approved.[59] 'Kenya' began as a footpath: the arduous portage from the sea to the lake, the great Victoria-Nyanza, where travellers embarked for landlocked Uganda. It was the prospects for trade in the rich inter-lake states, not Kenya's own prospects, that had attracted the Imperial British East Africa Company to the northerly route by-passing Germany's sphere in modern Tanzania. The trade path threaded its way through desert and forest, across the escarpment and down to the lake. It crossed the great belt where the warlike Maasai, the cattle-kings of East Africa, were the lords of the land.[60] The Company needed 'food stations' for its weary convoys of porters, where grain could be bought from the agricultural peoples of the forests and uplands, who maintained an uneasy equilibrium with the Maasai of the plains. They wanted a stable food market and safe passage for their goods. The Company men and the imperial officials (often the same individuals) who took over in 1895, formed small local armies to protect the food sellers.[61] They allied with the Maasai, who were badly affected by a huge epidemic of cattle plague, to impose their authority on resistant Kikuyu, paying the Maasai in the cattle they captured together.[62] When the Uganda Railway was built (it reached the lake at Kisumu in 1902), they were no longer reliant on vulnerable trade paths and could bring their limited firepower of some 200 Indian and 700 African soldiers to bear more quickly and heavily.

But how to govern the widely dispersed peoples of their raw new protectorate? He had seventeen stations, reported the Commissioner, Sir Charles Eliot, in 1901, usually with one European officer and up to twenty soldiers. The European officer dared not leave the station for long, and there was little control beyond its boundary fence. There was no question of levying tax. He needed more European officers who could take it in turns to go out, and more police. 'Mere touring is not sufficient. In order that savage natives may understand who a European officer is ... he should repeatedly visit them ... What is wanted is ... a continuous and steady pressure.'⁶³ Nine years later, something more like an administration had emerged. Kenya now had a cadre of provincial commissioners, district officers and assistant district officers, expected to 'tour' for three months of the year. A new governor, Girouard, a veteran of Northern Nigeria, spoke in Lugardian terms. The British field officers should record local customs and laws. In selecting chiefs, elders and headmen, they should find out the 'wishes of the people' and avoid upsetting local rules of succession. It was vital to govern through 'native institutions': 'the introduction of civilization when it has a denationalizing and demoralizing tendency should be avoided'. 'I warn those who are in favour of direct rule,' he went on, as the spirit of Lugard grew stronger, 'that if we allow the tribal authority to be ignored or broken ... we, who numerically form a small minority ... shall be obliged to deal with a rabble ...'⁶⁴

But in Kenya there was a large fly in the Lugardian ointment, indeed two flies. Kenya had been made governable by London's building a railway at the British taxpayers' expense. It had to be paid for, and so had the costs of its admittedly skeletal government. The lines had been laid not mainly by African labour, but by 'coolies' from India. Many stayed on in the country as storekeepers and traders, and by the 1920s Indians had begun to lay claim to a political voice. However, in political terms, the white fly was bigger. To make Kenya viable, so London decided, a commercial economy should be fast-tracked into life. That meant implanting white farmers to make freight for the railway and grow produce for export. Thus Kenya quickly turned into an administrative hybrid, with settlers demanding self-government on South African lines (as well as access to black labour and a large slice of the best land), while the colonial officials were supposed to uphold tribal authority and traditional customs. It was an unstable mix, the source of Kenya's volatile history up to the time of the Mau Mau Emergency (1952–60) and beyond.

'Had William the Conqueror been possessed of maxim guns, typewriters and a few modern inventions,' remarked one of Lugard's officials, 'he would have occupied Britain with diminutive force; he would have established a bureaucratic form of government with a few District Commissioners scattered over the land.'[65] Despite the obvious differences between the patterns of British rule in India and Africa, they also had a good deal in common. In both they depended on local political allies – the collaborating elites – and preferred those they saw as a conservative force. They regarded their rule as reinforcing tradition, but also improving it. By requiring Indians and Africans to act politically as members of caste, religious or tribal communities, they strengthened the grip of what had been more fluid divisions in pre-British times. With perhaps surprising success, they fashioned a web of identities which colonial peoples accepted, or at least acquiesced in. But while their rule came to depend upon indigenous allies – clerks, policemen, village headmen, chiefs, landowners and princes – their original insertion into local and regional politics had required military force, which remained its ultimate sanction. Here the British advantage lay only partly in weaponry: India was conquered without the maxim gun or the repeating rifle. It was the means to *hire* soldiers, often in distant locations, and to retain their allegiance by regular pay that was usually more vital. It reduced the need to pay for military help by concessions to local power-brokers and was the critical factor in making the collaborative bargains that underwrote their control.

There was something else. The secret of British authority was to keep their conquered peoples in more or less separate compartments, and to restrict to a minimum the horizontal connections between them. Political linkage was vertical: up to the 'capstone' – the slim British cadre poised over the top. That was not all. The political risk that all empires faced was that their administrative agents would construct their own local bargains, build local power bases to feather their nests, intermarry and 'go native'. In India and Africa, the British created a safeguard that grew stronger and stronger through the nineteenth century. This was the *racial* solidarity of their administrative steel frame: defection to the locals became culturally unthinkable. It was reinforced by the device of deliberate social distance and the strict codification of almost all social contact. Whether intended or not, it added a mystery ingredient to colonial authority. Without social access, Indians and Africans had few means of grasping the outlook, values and motives of their alien rulers. Guessing their aims and intentions was sometimes impossibly hard. It was a self-policing official secrets act. This conferred an advantage but it came at a cost. As the shrewdest of British politicians once remarked philosophically: 'Nobody ever believes in our good intentions.'[66]

8

Acts of Rebellion

'Louis Riel ... you have been found guilty of a crime the most perni-
cious and greatest that man can commit. You have been found guilty
of high treason ... It is now my painful duty to pass the sentence of
the court upon you ... that ... you be taken to the place appointed
for your execution and there be hanged by the neck until you are dead
...'.[1] So spoke the judge in the (then) small dusty town of Regina in
Western Canada on 1 August 1885. Riel's crime was to have led a
rebellion by *métis* (mixed-race Francophones) and native first peoples
against the authority of the federal government in Ottawa (and therefore the Crown): to have attempted, in the words of the charge,
'maliciously and traitorously ... by force and arms to subvert and
destroy the constitution and government of this realm by law established'.[2] Three months later Riel went to the gallows.

REBELLION AND EMPIRE

Rebellion was the dark side of rule, the threatening shadow that could
turn frighteningly real. There was always a thin line between subservience and revolt, and rebellions were far from unusual. Colonies were
raw and turbulent places. Upholding colonial authority in the Caribbean plantations had always been arduous. Governors fell out with
the planters: one who displayed megalomaniac propensities was
besieged in his house and eventually murdered, after a battle using
cannon. On the American mainland, a wealthy Virginia planter led
'Bacon's Rebellion' in 1676, and burned the colony's capital. The
unlucky Lord Pigot, the governor of Madras, was deposed by his own

British officials in 1777, and died in their custody. William Bligh of the *Bounty*, a colonial governor in 1808, enraged the free settlers in New South Wales and was seized by the garrison while hiding under his bed. After a year-long interregnum, he was allowed to leave on a ship, whose commander he urged in vain to 'blow down the town of Sydney' with his guns; the leaders of the so-called 'Rum Rebellion' in 1808 escaped very lightly.[3] These and other incidents were comparatively trivial, and some of them farcical. But there were plenty that were neither.

In fact, a realistic account would see British expansion as a zigzag progression: a series of colossal explosions diverted its course, or stopped it dead in its tracks. These were the great rebellions. Some of the most violent were closest to home: the Irish rebellions of 1641 (which helped to detonate the English Civil War), 1689 (whose failure drastically strengthened the Protestant Anglo-Irish 'Ascendancy') and 1798 (which triggered the Union of 1801); the 1880s 'Land Wars', to which 'home rule' became the 'solution'; the doomed Easter Rising of 1916; and the partially successful insurrection of 1919–21, which created the Irish Free State (and today's Irish Republic). On the American continent, Pontiac's rebellion in 1763 threatened a vast native uprising in the trans-Appalachian interior, just as the British were celebrating the defeat of the French. The concessions they made to prevent a recurrence – closing the Indian country to further white settlement – enraged a far more dangerous, better armed and organized foe, the colonists themselves. The great settler rebellion of 1775–83 in the Thirteen Colonies, later grandly retitled as the 'American Revolution', cut the British Empire in half and shaped by default the half that remained. In the post-revolutionary empire, India loomed larger, and so did London's fear of white settler revolt. In the Canadian rebellions of 1837–8, fear of American influence (and direct intervention) was a major anxiety: it was one of the factors that forced the eventual concession of full internal self-government ('responsible government') in Britain's North American colonies and made it the 'birthright' of white settler societies elsewhere. The slave rebellions of the British West Indies after 1815, especially the Jamaica rebellion at Christmas 1831, in which some 20,000 slaves joined, were the final proof that abolition could not be delayed any longer; the abolition act followed in 1833. The Great Rebellion in India in 1857 did not destroy the British Raj, but it had a seismic effect on both imperial self-confidence and British race attitudes, and made a lasting impression on the style of their rule. After 1857, the British were condemned to look constantly over their shoulders and to imagine more mutinies: the effects were pervasive. Nearly half the British army was henceforward stationed in India. In the late nineteenth century, the Afrikaner revolt derailed British advance in the South African subcontinent. Its bitter, bloody climax in the South African War of 1899–1902 triggered a major British rethink about their place in the world, while its indecisive local result served as a warrant to rivet white settler supremacy over the African peoples of South-Central Africa.

If the major rebellions made the British Empire what it was (rather than what British politicians and policymakers would have liked it to be), the same could be said on a more intimate scale of the lesser revolts that blew up in almost every colonial society. Thus the 'Glorious Revolution' of 1688, that overthrew James II, and paved the way for parliamentary supremacy in Britain, had its distant echo in the American colonies. In Massachusetts, New York and Maryland, there was open rebellion against James II's governors and the centralizing policies they had tried to impose, and effective resistance elsewhere both on the mainland and in the island colonies of the British Caribbean. The result in the main was to strengthen the colonial autonomy that seven decades later London tried in vain to restrict.[4] On the other hand, slave insurrections in the smaller colonies of the British West Indies, and the so-called 'Maroon War' of 1729–39 in Jamaica (Maroons were runaway slaves), reinforced both the climate of fear amongst the white planter minority and their sense of colonial dependence. Despite similar grievances, they dared not support the slave colonies of the mainland, where whites were more numerous, in *their* great rebellion after 1770. In nineteenth-century New Zealand, annexed in 1840 by the Treaty of Waitangi, the British faced endemic resistance by Maori communities fearful of the settler advance. The Maori Wars of 1860–72 sprang from the efforts of some Maori leaders to prevent the sale of land to the whites by other Maori landholders, and to reassert a sovereignty they denied had been lost. They went down to defeat, but their tenacious resistance, and the settlers' dependence on the help of *kupapa* ('loyal' Maori), preserved vital political rights in what had largely become a 'white man's country'.[5] In the two North-West or 'Riel' rebellions of 1869–70 and 1885, first *métis* (in 1869) and then *métis* and native first peoples together, resisted the influx of whites from Protestant British Ontario. In the first, almost bloodless, revolt, Riel's 'provisional government' quickly collapsed with the arrival of General Wolseley and his 1,000-man army, a mix of British regulars and Canadian militia. Both London and Ottawa were keen to avoid creating political martyrs. The Canadian prime minister, while loudly declaring his desire to catch Riel, privately advanced money to help him escape.[6] The second rebellion was a much more serious affair. Once again Riel declared a provisional government, this time in the north of modern Saskatchewan. But when his followers drove back a force of mounted police at Duck Lake, killing twelve men, they ignited a wider revolt of *metis* and native first peoples (the Indian nations of the Prairie West amounted to around 20,000 people) alike. Some 8,000 men were sent to contain it, dozens were killed and Riel surrendered after the fight at Batoche, to meet the fate with which this chapter began.

Riel's rebellion and death had a lasting effect in Canadian politics. His execution became symbolic of the French-Canadians' struggle against a growing Anglo-Saxon predominance in the Canadian federation. By the mid nineteenth century, the inflow of British migration had reduced French-Canadians to a demographic minority. From the late 1880s, *Canadien* nationalism became a political force with which all Canadian politicians had to come to terms. The Bambatha rebellion in colonial Natal had a quite different impact. It was a violent uprising in 1906 by mainly Zulu communities, embittered by land loss and the breakdown of customary status as white settler exactions for compulsory labour grew fiercer and fiercer.[7] Its savage local repression drew a public rebuke from the young Winston Churchill, a junior minister in the Liberal government in London. But if the Riel rebellions drove 'English' and 'French' apart, the Bambatha uprising drove English and Afrikaner together. At a critical time, as South Africa's white politicians discussed a political union of its four separate states, the shock of revolt highlighted the need for a strong central government and dissolved the resistance of the mainly English Natalians to an Afrikaner-ruled state.

This list of rebellions could be lengthened indefinitely if we included every violent disturbance that threatened to subvert colonial governments 'by law established'. Of course, we need to remember that 'rebellion' itself is a slippery term. It was both a colloquial expression that might be applied to any form of disturbance, however local and limited, and a legal description that governments used to intimidate the discontented or justify their punishment. In many uprisings, the challenge to colonial authority was more incidental than direct. Between 1836 and 1919, the *Moplahs*, or *Mappilas*, impoverished Muslim cultivators in South India, rose on more than thirty occasions to attack their Hindu landlords, usually in revenge for eviction.[8] They were invariably suppressed by military action, mainly for fear that the contagion would spread. Their aim was not to overthrow the rule of the British, but to appeal for its help against their local oppressors.[9] The British themselves often preferred to classify armed disturbance as crime or *dacoity* (banditry), and deny any political objective. Military or financial convenience might also dictate a blind eye to 'treason'. Resisting settler demands for military action against the Maori 'King' movement in 1860, the Colonial Secretary (12,000 miles away in London) remarked coolly 'if they [Maori] merely honor their King . . . and commit no breach of the Queen's peace . . . such folly should be left to the influence of time'.[10]

Yet acts of rebellion, on a large scale or small, and with or without the grander ambition of deposing the ruler, were remarkably prevalent. They tell us something about the nature of empire and the methods of rule that the British employed. The British system of empire was notoriously decentralized, strikingly so in the settler colonies. Except in a few 'fortress colonies' such as Gibraltar or Malta, it depended almost everywhere on the support of local elites, European, Asian and African. This brought a huge saving in the costs of imperialism: it averted the need for an expensive British officialdom except in very small numbers, or for large military forces to impose their diktats. But it came at a price. Devolving so much local power created a political risk and inflicted a burden. The local 'agents' and allies of empire had their own aims to pursue: part of their 'bargain' with the ruler was his implicit support for their social status and interests. Armed with this asset, it was hardly surprising that local elites (or white settlers) were tempted to exploit the peoples under their thumb to the limit and beyond – a tendency of which shrewder British observers were very aware. But without constant surveillance and administrative meddling (just what 'collaboration' was meant to avoid), it was very hard to restrain such abuses of power, or even to judge what dangers they posed to the colonial regime. Yet, if trouble broke out (like the *Mappila* revolts, or the Maori Wars in New Zealand), sooner or later (and it was usually sooner) the imperial power was bound to step in with military force.

In part, this was tacit acceptance that the power of their local agents and allies was largely dependent on force not consent. If *they* lost the means to coerce, and the prestige that that gave them, then the whole structure of rule (and taxation) would quickly crash down. Like it or not, the collaborators must be shored up. The British were bound also to fear in such cases that without a demonstration of *imperial* power their grip on their agents would weaken, their prestige would decline and the political cost of collaboration would inevitably rise. Coercion and collaboration were thus two sides of the same coin. The reliance on collaborators had a second crucial effect. Imperial authority worked best when its subjects believed in its permanence and legitimacy. Where this was complete, it conferred a form of 'hegemony': domination over the mind as well as the body of the colonial population. But authority that was filtered through local elites and bent to *their* needs was much more diffuse and much more exposed to local pressures and conflicts. For subject populations, it could have little mystique. Their quiescence reflected not willing consent but 'pragmatic submission', to be quickly withdrawn if the threat of compulsion were lifted.[11] Hence the obsession of so many colonial officials with the preserving of *izzat* (prestige) with its promise of deference and fear on the part of the governed. It was the brittle reality of colonial control that made resistance so dangerous and explains the often brutal response of its uneasy masters.

What prompted rebellion as a collective act of resistance? The case studies that follow examine the motives in close-up. Here we can note some of the commoner causes. The obvious trigger might be hardship or loss. But in most cases it seems much more complex than that. Extreme hardship was the lot of many who worked on the land, in India especially, and of the huge force of slaves (some 800,000) who worked on farms and plantations before emancipation in 1833. But revolt by the desperately poor and even by slaves was spasmodic and occasional. It was more likely to come when they feared a further attack on their living conditions, perhaps by eviction, new burdens of work or (as among Jamaican slaves in 1831) a cut in their rations.[12] The sense of injustice arising out of new impositions, or out of what might be seen as an onslaught on status and honour, was often far more compelling. If a whole occupation group, or an organized community, felt under such threat, collective resistance became much more likely. If the grievance acquired a religious dimension, the mixture could be explosive.

Religion was the glue that held most colonial societies together. The great world religions and their localized variants prescribed accepted beliefs from those governing sexual morality and gender relations to ideas about property and the shape of the cosmos. The presence of aliens was always disturbing. Any sign that they meant to upset religious observance or show disrespect for holy persons and places was bound to cause trouble. If a religion's adherents feared that such change would endanger their own hopes for an after-life, or inflict ritual pollution, the urge to resist might become overwhelming. Of course, the landscape of religion could vary enormously. Where it was controlled by the social elite (such as the emirs and ulema – 'learned ones' – in Northern Nigeria)[13] they usually preferred to damp down its explosive potential. On a frontier of conversion, where religious competition was especially acute, or in marginal zones where the social elite was not securely entrenched, ecstatic forms of religion (and perhaps a tradition of martyrdom) were likely to thrive. The appearance of 'prophets' and 'saints' promising spiritual and physical liberation could inject purpose, organization and solidarity into what might otherwise be disorganized discontent. The influence of Baptist missionaries and catechists was widely blamed by the planters for the Jamaica rebellion. The slave Sam Sharpe, its main instigator, was just such a preacher.

Hence rebellions were both commoner and more dangerous where grievance was deepened by religious solidarity and given emotional meaning by articulate spokesmen. Where a local elite was the intermediary between the colonial state and its subjects, its behaviour was crucial. It might be divided, or itself under pressure from its social inferiors. Rather than acting as the imperialists' watchdog, its reaction to revolt might be to sit on the fence as long as it dared or until the outcome was clear. In zones of recent conquest, where colonial incorporation was still incomplete, this instinct might be particularly strong. Indeed rebellion was always more probable where the routines of colonial authority were not well engrained, where a frontier outlook prevailed, or where desert, marsh, mountain and forest supplied a safe haven for rebels and runaways.

Yet the catalyst for rebellion cannot always be found in the objective conditions of those in revolt. Time and again we can see the effects of three critical triggers whose impact was sharpened by rumour, misinformation and fear. The first was the fear of pre-emptive attack or reprisal by government. In the minds of those who rebelled, their actions were often defensive, to ward off a threat or prevent retribution. Before the Jamaica slave revolt, the story went round that the planters intended to frustrate abolition by killing the male slaves and refusing to liberate women and children.[14] Slaves accused of indiscipline could expect such savage punishment that often violence seemed preferable to peaceful submission. In the 'Nat Turner revolt' in Virginia (also in 1831) this led runaway slaves to kill more than fifty whites (by contrast only two whites were harmed in the much larger uprising of that year in Jamaica). *Mappila* rebels in South India, fearing dishonourable death at the hands of the *sarkar* (government), preferred to seek martyrdom.[15] The sepoy mutineers at Meerut, knowing their fate if the British returned, erased every physical trace of *angrezi* rule – by killing the British they caught – as the best hope of surviving. The second was belief – all too often misguided – in the wider support that a rebellion might enjoy. Perhaps those who led insurrections were bound to believe their own hopeful predictions, or quell their own doubts: they rarely had access to hard information. Thirdly, what lent rebellion its 'logic' was, almost equally often, a gross underestimate of the force it would face. In semi-literate societies, or where communications were poor, visibility was all. With limited knowledge of the reach and resources of their imperialist adversary, usually hidden over the colonial horizon, rebels often had little conception of the firepower and ferocity it would level against them. Sometimes they hoped against hope that the British would just go away. In fact, sooner or later – and it was usually sooner – the British returned, having assembled the means to crush a rebellion. It took barely a week to destroy the Jamaica slave insurrection, less than six months to contain (though not end) the Great Rebellion in India and little over a year to reduce the Afrikaner bid for independence in 1899 to an unwinnable war of attrition. None of this is to argue that the impact of rebellion was in each case anything less than profound. And in one case at least, the British suffered an outright defeat. Maritime war against three European powers after 1778 on top of a settler rebellion imposed an unbearable strain. In 1783, London abandoned its thirteen rebel colonies – but not the rest of its claim on the North American continent.

But how did men rebel? A violent collision between rebels and government soldiers or police was usually the climax to a series of acts of rebellion, not the first step. Indeed, not all forms of rebellion required early confrontation with the forces of order. Exit or emigration was a tacit rejection of colonial authority. In a favourable setting, such 'stealth rebellions' might be able to win a surprising degree of autonomy. Runaway Maroons in Jamaica's hilly interior fought the planters' militia to a standstill in the late 1730s; their reward was a treaty and a good deal of freedom. Afrikaners who trekked away from Cape Colony in the late 1830s went first to Natal, and when that was annexed fanned out on the Highveld, the great grassy tableland in the South African interior. The British demanded submission, denounced the Boer leaders as rebels, and fought a bloody encounter at Boomplaats in 1848. But then they gave up and conceded an ambiguous independence that they came to regret.

Where no exit existed direct action was needed to disrupt the grip of authority and force it to terms. The immediate priority for a rebellion's first movers – transforming their personal defiance into a political act – was to mobilize wider support. It was vital to win, or at least to engage in, the war of the printed or spoken word. It was essential to create the widespread impression that government's authority was already dissolving, that its cause was lost. But this was rarely enough. Swift counter-measures by a vigilant government – gaoling conspirators, seizing key points, deploying a military presence – might destroy the illusion and scotch any uprising before it gathered momentum. Its opponents had to move fast to escape such a fate. They needed protection from the long arm of the state. Widespread disorder would distract the state's attention and divide its military power. Destroying its communications (telegraphs and railways) would slow down its response and delay its return. But something else was required. They must persuade their supporters to form up in large groups, preferably armed, to create a parallel or provisional government. Most urgent of all, they must use the power that this gave them to smash the government's hold on its local collaborators, terrorize (or worse) its network of spies and informants and wreck its remaining prestige. Unless they could do so, their chances were slim. The very best they could hope for was the catastrophic collapse of the government's military power. It was such a collapse – the result of military mutiny – that lit the fuse for the greatest rebellion the British were to face in their century of power.

SETTLER REBELLIONS

Of all the rebellions they faced, British governments had reason to fear those of settlers the most. This was partly at least because in such cases their own political and military tactics were bound to attract close and often highly critical scrutiny at home as well as overseas. It was, after all, a characteristic of most settler societies that they had many connections in Britain and many friends and supporters there. Information was readily sent by rebellious colonials to feed the government's critics. It was bound to be harder for the government or party in power to preserve a unified front in British opinion – although failing to do so would lend obvious encouragement to the rebels themselves. The contrast with non-settler rebels was obvious and sharp. *They* rarely had political allies to take up their cause, or the contacts through which to put their case in the press. It was always much easier to portray their actions and aims in the worst possible light, to highlight their 'savagery' and deny the existence of any genuine grievance. This had the added advantage that, however brutal the methods used to suppress such insurgents, they were less likely to attract much attention at home, and even less likely to evoke critical comment.

It went deeper than that. Imperial authority over settler societies was inherently fragile, from almost their very beginnings – unless (like the whites in the West Indies) they had special reasons to be loyal. It had to be based not so much on collaboration as on explicit consent, usually by some form of representative body. There was no 'right' to levy taxation of the kind the British inherited in India, and, from quite early on, a convention that colonial laws would be vetoed only in exceptional circumstances. The governor as the agent of the imperial centre commanded few local resources and saw his patronage trimmed back by jealous assemblies. If he asserted himself he would face an ideological blizzard against infringing the rights of free-born Englishmen and the unsubtle suggestion that he harboured despotic ambitions. Worse still, his settler subjects possessed a disturbing capacity to mobilize quickly for political action. Newspapers and other print forms such as pamphlets and handbills could rally opinion. The everyday institutions of colonial life – juries, township meetings, even race meetings – allowed local opinion to organize, solidify and signal its strength. Above all, and here the contrast with most non-settler peoples was particularly stark, settler societies were invariably armed and their local militias often embodied both a political and a military unit.

These were all excellent reasons for the imperial government in London to follow a policy of what Edmund Burke famously called 'salutary neglect'. But it was not always possible, let alone wise, to follow this sagacious advice. Firstly, few issues aroused more passionate feeling in settler societies than access to land, not least because its speculative purchase and re-sale were usually the main source of wealth for the settler elite. They were sure to resent any attempt to control their territorial advance. But to imperial officials this settler logic appeared both selfish and stupid. Left unchecked, its certain result was constant war on the frontier as indigenous peoples resisted the loss of their land. Restoring the peace would require imperial troops – and imperial spending. Secondly, where indigenous peoples enjoyed imperial protection, perhaps under a treaty, and settler transgressions offended religious or humanitarian opinion at home, imperial intervention might be hard to avoid. Thirdly, a settler society might pursue its economic self-interest in ways that conflicted with that of the mother-country. What in ordinary times was little more than an irritant could become a major bone of contention in a period of commercial or financial upheaval. If settler politicians had to please exacting local constituents, their imperial counterparts were no less exposed to metropolitan interests, with their own view of the world and their own axe to grind.

On the night of 26 August 1765, a large mob attacked the home of Thomas Hutchinson, then chief justice and lieutenant governor of the province of Massachusetts. Once Hutchinson and his family had fled, it spent the night systematically looting and wrecking his house, tearing down its fittings and even its walls.[16] It was the first and most violent of the mob acts which progressively terrorized those members of the colonial elite identified with the government of the province and its British-appointed governor. There seemed no way of controlling these outbursts of violence, in which their victims detected the manipulative hand of their political enemies. They signalled the fact that the colony had become almost ungovernable. 'Authority is in the populace,' Hutchinson wrote a few months later. 'No law can be carried into execution against their mind.'[17] Less than ten years later, with the scrappy exchanges of fire at Concord and Lexington, Massachusetts broke out in an open rebellion which rapidly spread to the rest of the colonies.

This accelerating slide into violence and war was not just extraordinary: it seemed perverse and paradoxical, even to many Americans. For (white) Americans already enjoyed greater political freedom than anywhere else in the world. The franchise was far wider than in Britain itself and taxation much lighter. Elected assemblies could check the executive's power to a much greater extent than the House of Commons in Britain; there was no House of Lords (whose members could be named by the king); and no fund of patronage with which to create the party of placemen on which British ministers could usually rely for their voting majorities. The relative abundance of land allowed a much more equitable distribution of wealth than existed at home – or perhaps anywhere else. Religious freedom was much wider.

The paradox, of course, was more apparent than real. The wide degree of self-government that the American colonies enjoyed had encouraged the growth of a 'country party' ideology in which all executive power was viewed with suspicion as corrupt and despotic by nature. The threat of its growth and abuse required aggressive surveillance and a tradition of forceful resistance.[18] As long as London persisted with salutary neglect, this ideology coexisted more or less happily with the theoretical recognition of the British Parliament's supremacy, and with pride in the British connection and inheritance. Fear and loathing of France, still entrenched on the continent and the principal barrier to the westward advance of the Anglo-Americans, made loyalty natural as well as prudential. Without British protection, the hope of expansion was bleak. But after 1763 – and the destruction of French power – everything changed.

The crisis began over money. To meet the cost of their ballooning debt and appease the angry taxpayer at home, British ministers decided to recoup some of the huge cost of the war from its main beneficiaries (as they saw it) – the American colonists. The result was the 1765 Stamp Act, an attempt to levy a modest American revenue on the use of the stamp that gave public authority to legal documents. The reaction was uproar. 'There is not a family between Canada and Pensacola that has not heard the name of the Stamp Act,' groaned Hutchinson, himself a fierce critic of its reckless unwisdom.[19] The Act became a popular bogey – and proof of the British design to subvert the assemblies and unravel colonial self-government. The attempt to enforce it through the authority of the colonial governors and their allies highlighted for many Americans the 'danger within' posed by those who would later be called 'loyalists' or 'tories'. And imperial assertiveness was not confined to the Act. The abrupt prohibition on settler expansion beyond the Appalachian mountains in the 1763 Proclamation (meant to forestall further uprisings like Pontiac's) enraged those for whom it had been the main goal and gain of the war. The more rigorous enforcement of imperial trade regulations to stop the evasion of duties by colonial merchants was a further source of bitter resentment, another symptom of 'tyranny'.

It is not difficult to see why so many Americans could believe themselves victims of a corrupt aristocratic elite intent on imposing its despotic authority, crushing the rights of free-born Englishmen in the colonies. If they doubted this threat, by the late 1760s there were also plenty of British radicals eager to tell them that they were part of a great Anglo-American struggle to preserve British liberties. It was, nonetheless, a long and dangerous step from resistance and protest (or even mob terror) to outright rebellion. Although there was opposition to British oppression in all the Thirteen Colonies, that step was first taken in Massachusetts, the cockpit of Anglo-American conflict from 1765 to 1775. In Massachusetts the revolt against the British connection was fiercer and the collapse of British authority more complete than anywhere else.

There were good reasons for this. Massachusetts was always likely to be a difficult province. Its pattern of self-governing townships, the custom of popular meetings and the very broad franchise (perhaps 80 per cent of adult males) meant that political power was very widely diffused. Literacy among men was near universal, creating a large market for print of all kinds. A tradition of intense localism bred a rooted suspicion of all central authority. Congregationalist Protestantism, which rejected Anglican hierarchy in favour of autonomous 'congregations', reinforced the dislike of appointed officialdom. By the mid eighteenth century, the growing shortage of new land and a reluctance to migrate were fuelling new social tensions. As land prices rose, and a class of large landowners emerged, voices were raised against the loss of yeoman equality and the rise of an unjust and impious plutocracy.[20] The religious 'Great Awakening' sharpened the feeling against display and consumption.[21] It was not hard to see the 'court circle' of office-holders like Hutchinson and his family as engaged in an amoral conspiracy to concentrate wealth and power at the expense of small farmers, artisans and the landless poor.

The intense factionalism of the colony's politics, and the grievance of those excluded from office, supplied the explosive material which the Stamp Act ignited. Thereafter the office-holding elite struggled in vain to reassert their control over the elected assembly against a storm of abuse in the press and the continuous threat of mob action. Their best chance was to persuade the imperial government in London to abandon its hope of raising a revenue and revert to the methods of salutary neglect. But London refused, partly because it needed the money, partly because to give way to Massachusetts would invite the general collapse of its imperial authority, including its control of the frontier 'Proclamation line' and the trade regulations. Instead it decided to teach Massachusetts a lesson. In September 1768 a squadron sailed into Boston harbour and levelled its guns on the city. Two battalions of infantry were landed to back up the governor. But the effect was disastrous. The propaganda of the whig opposition was handed a triumph. The troops were harassed and provoked into the infamous 'massacre' of 1770, after which they were abruptly withdrawn. But when further attempts to collect an American revenue, this time by granting the East India Company a monopoly of selling tea in the colonies, incited a dramatic act of resistance (the 'Boston tea party' of December 1773), London tried again. The result was a further catastrophe.

In effect, London imposed a form of emergency rule. The troops were sent back. The port of Boston was closed. To prevent the intimidation of juries, criminal trials were to be held in Britain. The Massachusetts constitution was altered. These were the 'coercive' or 'intolerable' acts. They sounded a general alarm. In September 1774, the first 'continental congress', attended by delegates from all Thirteen Colonies, assembled at Philadelphia to denounce the infringement of colonial rights, but without at this stage renouncing allegiance. In Massachusetts, meanwhile, an explosion was imminent. To its last royal governor, General Thomas Gage, twenty years in America and married into an American family, the most urgent task was to prevent the political furore turning into armed conflict.[22] But it was already too late. In September 1774, he sent a party of troops to seize the gunpowder at the Massachusetts Powderhouse, the main arsenal in the province. But far from cooling the political heat, this convinced his opponents that he planned a military coup and the arrest of their leaders. Their response was a huge demonstration of armed militia, vastly outnumbering the British, and further attacks on known or suspected loyalists. A few months later, Gage tried again, choosing this time the arsenal at Concord. Forewarned and forearmed, the local militia assembled. An unlucky shot turned confrontation into the calamitous firefight at Concord and Lexington. As the British struggled back to the safety of Boston through ambush after ambush, they lost sixty-five killed and over 200 wounded. By June 1775, they were besieged in the city. They reclaimed Bunker Hill, overlooking the harbour, but at such heavy loss as to end any hope of breaking the siege. The contagion of revolt spread further and further. In Virginia, the largest and oldest of the American colonies, an agrarian aristocracy who had almost nothing in common with 'democratic' Massachusetts, echoed the call. Its ideologue, Thomas Jefferson, asserted the equality of the colonial assemblies with Parliament and denounced the king's failure to prevent Parliament's unlawful intrusion.[23] When King George III told Parliament in October 1775 that the American colonies had broken out in rebellion, he was merely stating the obvious.

In a longer perspective we can see that as a settler rebellion this was an extreme case. For the British, American intransigence became a perfect storm. They were driven forward by what seemed the imperative need to meet some of the costs of empire defence in a still dangerous world of rival great powers. Their view of economic self-interest made relaxing the rules on American trade a potentially fatal concession. They regarded settler designs on the unsettled interior as greedy and reckless, bound to ignite the dirty frontier wars – for which London would have to pay dearly. The British misfortune was to lack almost all means of exerting their will. They lacked the patronage to build a stronger party of loyalists, and lacked the force to protect those that they had. They skimped on the means for a strong military presence until it was too late. Their political intelligence was poor and they paid little attention to the men on the spot. But it was more than that. America was a highly exceptional colony. Despite the recent surge of migration, it was largely composed of deep-rooted communities, notably in New England, the storm-centre of rebellion. This nourished a strenuous sense of local identity. In Massachusetts particularly, there had been little new in-migration from Britain of the kind that might have reinforced the loyalist ranks. It was partly this that explained the ideological gap between mother-country and colony. The British were never able to counter the intense American feeling, that even loyalists shared, that their actions after 1763 infringed recognized rights. In the propaganda war, they were always on the back foot against the huge flood of print – newspapers, cartoons, handbills and almanacs – that poured from American presses. To add insult to injury, it was a recent emigrant, Tom Paine, the corset-maker from Thetford, whose *Common Sense* (1776) sounded the trumpet for an independent republic, changed the terms of debate – and sold 150,000 copies.[24]

Nor was America an impoverished outpost just hacked from the bush. By the 1760s it was a highly sophisticated commercial economy with the wealth and expertise to sustain a major war effort. What perhaps mattered more in the revolutionary prelude was the existence of a wealthy highly educated elite with the intellectual self-confidence to imagine a separate national future. Not the least of the extraordinary features of this settler rebellion was the cerebral power of its principal spokesmen, John Adams and Thomas Jefferson among several. Of course, it also needs to be said that the ultimate success of rebellion depended quite crucially on help from abroad. What destroyed the last British attempt at a compromise settlement in 1778 was the Franco-American treaty and its promise of aid to the embattled revolutionaries. Indeed, from this moment on, the struggle to suppress the American rebellion was overshadowed by the far wider war in defence of Britain's interests in India, the Caribbean and the Mediterranean, and by the fear of an invasion of the Home Islands themselves.

Sixty years later, the British faced another eruption on the North American continent, this time in Canada, the rump of their former transatlantic empire. They faced in fact two simultaneous rebellions in what were then called 'the Canadas' – today's Quebec and Ontario. The target in both cases was what the rebels regarded as corrupt and over-privileged elites into whose hands the British had largely devolved the colonies' government. In both cases the matter was complicated by questions of race and nationality, and by the looming presence of the United States next door. The eventual outcome, however, was quite 'un-American': not separation but a constitutional formula that squared local autonomy with British connection. Why was this possible?

The rebellion in Upper Canada (Ontario) was briefer and less serious. Here small farmers and artisans resented the power of the 'Family Compact' – a rich oligarchy that formed a court circle surrounding the governor. Fattened by land grants, it was closely allied with the Anglican Church, whose 'clergy reserves' embraced much valuable land, and with bankers and land companies. The opposition was led by Dundee-born William Lyon Mackenzie, who arrived in Canada in 1820. After several false starts, Mackenzie found his métier as a campaigning journalist, very much in the style of smalltown America, exposing graft, corruption and privilege. He became a thorn in the side of the provincial elite and a leading 'reformer'. An admirer of the republican constitution just over the border, he successfully pressed for the vote to be given to American-born settlers who had moved into the province.[25] What tipped his radical politics over the edge into rebellion was a growing frustration that wide popular backing could not be translated into executive power, since neither the governor nor his tory advisers could be removed by the elected assembly. Mackenzie was also convinced (not without some justification) that his tory opponents were using their militant allies in the local Orange Order (many Protestant or Scots-Irish settlers had recently entered the province) to harass and threaten him.[26] In an increasingly feverish atmosphere, he planned an armed demonstration at the end of 1837 to march on the capital York (modern Toronto) and force a change of regime.

It was a fiasco. Mackenzie's advance guard was fired on by a small group of loyalists and quickly retreated. The rest of his followers were ready to stage a demonstration, but showed no stomach for full-scale rebellion. The leaders fled over the border. Meanwhile a second uprising by American-born settlers in the west of the province, angered by rumours that they faced dispossession and encouraged by false news of Mackenzie's 'success', also quickly fizzled out.[27] But this was not quite the end of the matter. The British strongly suspected an American hand behind the uprisings. There were 30–40,000 Americans engaged in conspiracy to invade British territory, complained London's man in Washington, Henry Fox. 'Vast hordes of banditti and assassins,' he said, 'are maturing their plans for the desolation and ruin of a British territory.'[28] What is now the tourist playground of Niagara Falls became the scene of cross-border skirmishes. In one famous incident, a group of (loyal) Canadians seized the steamboat *Caroline*, meant, they suspected, to transport a Yankee invasion, set it on fire and sent it over the Falls. The furore that followed threatened briefly to lead to an Anglo-American confrontation.

The rebellion in Lower Canada (Quebec) was a good deal more serious. In its two phases of violence more than 250 people were killed. One was Joseph Chartrand, a mason or carpenter, in a rural parish near Montreal. While collecting some money, perhaps from a customer, he fell in with a group of young men. Chartrand quickly made off but they soon caught him up and beat him to death by the road. In the eventual inquiry, it emerged that the young men had been on their way to a meeting and that at least some had been armed. Several witnesses claimed that a climate of fear had prevailed in the parish and that 'the loyal had no protection'. Chartrand, said another, was known as a violent man, and was considered a spy.[29] The clear implication was that Chartrand was murdered to stop him reporting on the assembly of armed men to which his killers were hurrying. But why was the countryside on the verge of revolt? Another witness declared that 'Mr Papineau had directed orders to be read at the church-door that the people were to march ... those who refused would be punished by loss of life.'[30]

Louis-Joseph Papineau was no backwoods bandit but a wealthy and well-connected lawyer, the son of a successful surveyor turned landowner. By the 1830s he was the leader of the Patriote party in the elected assembly. The Patriotes voiced the growing resentment of the French-Canadian middle class at the disproportionate share of the English-speaking minority in the province's government. Dislike of commercial domination by that same minority, and the nagging belief that migration from Britain was fast eroding the province's Catholic Francophone character, helped to widen the Patriotes' appeal. The English government, said Papineau, wanted 'to denationalize us in order to anglicize us'.[31] The Patriotes' aim was to turn their command of the assembly into control of the government.

As the struggle went on, Papineau's language suggested that a French-Canadian republic was the ultimate goal. The angry response of the loyal British minority, entrenched in Montreal, lent the political conflict an increasingly racial tone. But not completely. Among the Patriote leaders were two brothers called Nelson, the sons (curiously enough) of an ex-naval officer. Both were doctors and radicals; both were to play a more vigorous part in the impending insurrection than Papineau himself.

As the deadlock grew worse, the government in London became more assertive. To break the assembly's veto on all public expenditure (thus crippling the executive), it gave the governor authority to spend without their approval. The Patriote leaders claimed that this was the prelude to a wave of repression, a concerted attack on their political movement. They denounced London's move as an attack on their liberties. Their rural supporters began to mobilize quickly. They took full advantage of an old local tradition: the ritual humiliation of those accused of transgressing the community's norms – what was called 'charivari'.[32] Amid rumours that the English were planning a pre-emptive attack, parish assemblies warned the government men in their midst to resign their commissions and break off their contacts. In November 1837, the government issued warrants for high treason against the Patriote leaders. Their response was to summon a large gathering of armed men at the villages of St Denis and St Charles, thirty miles from Montreal. The rebellion had begun.

And then it seemed to collapse. The Patriotes had planned to declare Lower Canada's independence. Before they could do so, a British detachment arrived and shots were exchanged. But this was no Concord. The rebels scattered back into the countryside. Some of their leaders crossed the American border, about sixty miles off, but eight were arrested. The British governor, Colborne, told London that it was a storm in a teacup: he had resisted the howls of the loyal minority and released most of the prisoners. By the end of April 1838 martial law had been scrapped. The British government's Special Commissioner, Lord Durham, decided against bringing the leaders to trial (where they risked a death sentence) and exiled them to Bermuda. But there was a curious twist. To Durham's consternation, a meddlesome lawyer proved that he had exceeded his powers. The prisoners were released and quickly made their way back to the American border where a fresh rising was planned. The British began to suspect a much wider conspiracy. 'A formidable organization, bound together by secret oaths and secret signs undoubtedly exists,' Durham reported to London. 'Terrified by signs of this . . . mysterious organization and sometimes by secret menaces or warnings of murder or massacre, the loyal inhabitants of the country quit their . . . isolated habitations.'[33] Some fled the province altogether. Everything seemed to wait on the threatened invasion.

It came in early November. Alerted by the rebel network of Frères-Chasseurs ('Brotherhood of Hunters'), groups of armed *habitants* began to assemble: 3,000 met at the village of Napierville, not far from the American border to which more weapons were to be brought; others went to an Indian reservation near Montreal hoping to seize their arms and ammunition. The original plan had been intended to time the uprising with an attack at Niagara by Mackenzie's supporters. Robert Nelson crossed the border and proclaimed a 'provisional government'.[34] Nothing went right. The Americans seized the cache of weapons at the border. The Indians killed or captured their assailants. The loyal militia (including 5,000 British Canadians from nearby Upper Canada) and British troops harassed the rebel force led by Robert Nelson and another (French-Canadian) doctor called Cote, and then broke it decisively. The militia burned the houses of suspected rebels. The leaders fled once more, Robert Nelson as far as California before returning to New York, where he eventually published a treatise on cholera. Not all were so lucky. Joseph Cardinal, a lawyer who had led the attack on the Indians, was one of two men to be hanged for treason. Severe examples were needed, said the governor.[35] The others convicted escaped with their lives.

The revolt had been crushed. But it had been a terrible shock, made worse for the British by the danger of war with the United States and by the crises over Belgium and the Eastern Mediterranean (the 'route to India') which coincided with it. London dispatched some 10,000 troops to keep Canada safe, more than it had sent to Gage in 1775. A political solution was extremely urgent. It came from Lord Durham, but in a roundabout way. Durham detected a deep racial antagonism between the British and what he called the 'Canadians'. Their 'mutual dislike' meant that they did not meet socially: 'even the children when they quarrel divide themselves into French and English, like their parents'. The Canadians 'had found the British pressing upon them at every turn, in the possession of land, in commerce, in the retail trade ... in religion, in the whole administration of government'. Durham's solution was drastic. The (French-) Canadians, he said, were a 'stagnant people'.[36] If Lower Canada, with its French majority, were merged in a union with more dynamic British Upper Canada, the effects of immigration from Britain would soon act as a solvent on its backward society. The ambitious would anglicize: a distinct *Canadien* identity would gradually vanish. The union act of 1840 followed his prescription. But Durham proved wrong.

The main reason lay in his second proposal. Durham had argued in his famous report of 1839[37] that revolt was the child of political frustration. Where there was no way of making executive power respond to local opinion, and where opposition leaders were denied any prospect of office, politics were bound to descend into irresponsible demagogy, and, at worst, into rebellion. The answer was to encourage moderation. Those who enjoyed wide public support should be allowed to take office. The expectation of doing so would discourage wild promises and rein in the temptation to subvert political order. It took six years of political manoeuvring before London accepted that responsible government – a cabinet of ministers who enjoyed the support of the elected majority – was the only workable basis for governing the colony. But among those who grasped the immense possibilities of this constitutional formula was a former Patriote leader, Louis-Hippolyte La Fontaine. La Fontaine had been abroad during the period of rebellion. When he returned, he pushed aside Papineau (somewhat discredited by his disappearing act during the uprising)[38] and argued instead that cultural survival – *survivance* – required French-Canadians to accept the British connection and to work with the loyal Reform party in Upper Canada to achieve responsible government.[39] Against ferocious hostility and threats of assassination from the Montreal British (for whom he remained a closet revolutionary), but with the support of a wise British governor, La Fontaine reconciled the Patriote party to his plan. His alliance with the Upper Canada leaders created at last a stable parliamentary regime. By reconciling British and French, La Fontaine, largely forgotten today, was the architect of the modern Canadian state and of responsible government as a workable way of combining local autonomy and the connection with Britain.

The Canadian rebellions did not follow the revolutionary path of the grand settler rebellion to the south. Some of the reasons are easy to spot. There was an obvious difference of scale. In neither Canadian uprising were the rebels able to muster a large enough following to overawe the government's supporters. Neither came near to inflicting the kind of early defeat that the British suffered at Lexington, with its electrifying effect. A tradition of loyalism (several thousand loyalists had fled the United States in 1783 and settled in Canada) and the tide of recent migration from Britain smothered the localist republicanism that Mackenzie had favoured. For reasons that still puzzle historians of Quebec, French-Canadian rebelliousness was largely confined to the southern district round Montreal – within easy reach of loyal militia from British Upper Canada. The ideological convictions that fuelled the American rebellion were less intense or widespread. Nor, despite British fears, did the Canadian rebels enjoy enough American sympathy to make a critical difference: external aid was thus a negligible factor. Indeed, the Americans had actively prevented weapons crossing the border. The political climate in Britain was also quite different. The radical upsurge that had heartened the American rebels was much less apparent. The unbending assertion of parliamentary supremacy and the demand for a revenue were absent as well. The proconsuls London sent to manage the crisis – Lord Durham, Lord Sydenham, Sir Charles Bagot, Sir Charles Metcalfe (Sydenham, Bagot and Metcalfe all died prematurely) and Lord Elgin – were not of one mind. But they had more room for manoeuvre, and a good deal more skill than their 'American' predecessors. The result was to allow a much larger space for moderates and reformers to find a compromise formula, breaking the logjam. La Fontaine was able to show that a *non*-British people could use 'British' institutions to preserve their identity – a lesson later eagerly grasped by Indians and Africans. Rebellion may have made the United States; by a subtler route, it also made Canada.

THE GREAT INDIAN REBELLION

The Indian rebellion of 1857 began as a mutiny but became a political earthquake. It took six months to contain, but more than two years to suppress. It required a huge British force of more than 90,000 men, mostly rushed out from Europe. It was almost entirely a North Indian event, but it spread into Bihar and also Bundelkhand, where the Central Indian uplands dropped down to the plains. Despite early alarm, Bengal remained quiet and so did the 'presidency' of Madras in the south. Its real epicentre – where the struggle was lost and won – was in Hindustan: the wide Ganges plain between Delhi and Lucknow, including the Doab (the land between the Jumna and the Ganges), Awadh (called Oudh or Oude by the British) and Rohilkhand (the land of Rohillas or Afghans, settled there since Mughal times). This was India's agrarian hinterland (the Doab was 'one of the most fertile regions of the globe', remarked an early Viceroy, Lord Wellesley), the old Mughal heartland, the historic pivot of empire in India, and the hearth of India's Islamic and Hindu cultures. No ruler of India could afford to neglect it, or allow it to fall into enemy hands. But while the British had occupied parts of this zone since 1801, in three vital regions – Punjab, Awadh and Jhansi – their power was a novelty. And they could not forget that not far away to the north lay their frontier with Afghanistan (much closer after the annexation of Punjab), the scene of their ill-starred invasion of 1839–42, and a source of perennial anxiety.

The rebellion is best thought of as a vast uncoordinated coalition of anger, resentment and fear, blended with hope that the British might vanish and an older India return. But it could not have begun without the original mutiny at Meerut, north of Delhi, on Sunday 10 May 1857, and the train of events that it triggered. Equally, the mutiny itself, while a shocking occurrence and a formidable challenge to British authority, would have mattered far less had it not served to release the pent-up fears, frustrations and hatreds that British rule had provoked. For, in asserting their power, the British had dealt roughly, sometimes brutally, with those who stood in their way. As a conquering force possessing immense military power – their largely Indian-manned Bengal army – they were set on reshaping North India to their imperial design. Once they had defeated the remaining country power of North India, the Sikh state of Punjab, in 1849, they used the doctrine of 'lapse' (where no legitimate male heir was forthcoming)[40] to take over the important princely state of Jhansi in 1853. On the very eve of the uprising they brusquely annexed the kingdom of Awadh with its capital at Lucknow, the largest inland city in India and one of the two (the other was Delhi) great centres of India's Islamic civilization.[41] They incurred the bitter resentment of the heir of the last Peshwa (hereditary convenor of the Maratha Confederacy that had once rivalled the British as the great power of India) by removing much of his pension. This was Nana Saheb, who maintained a shadowy court at the old city of Bithur, fourteen miles from Cawnpore, and whose agents were suspected of constant plots and intrigues.[42] The Mughal emperor in Delhi, to whom the British had shown a formal – if fictional – deference as their technical sovereign (the East India Company was his vassal), was now increasingly treated as an impotent pensioner. To some of the Muslim *ulama* (or scholars), Islam itself seemed in danger from the fanatical *Faranghi* – the Protestant Christian 'Franks'. Indeed, the evangelical missionary fervour now displayed by some British officials and soldiers alarmed both Hindus and Muslims and the threat that it posed was to appear time and again in the proclamations of rebels. Above all, perhaps, it was the British attempt to standardize the system for collecting land revenue, making it easier to evict those with 'revenue rights' (the right to levy a revenue on behalf of the state and pass on a proportion to the Raj's collectors) who defaulted on payment, that widened and deepened the reservoir of rebellion. The actual effects were very uneven and defy simple causation. Some of those taxed to the hilt remained loyal or passive; some least affected by the commercialization of agriculture and the boom in sugar, opium and indigo rose in revolt. 'Dry' districts were angrier than those that were irrigated. Where the revenue right had been held and lost by so-called 'village brotherhoods' (a dominant caste group) being forced back on the land as mere cultivators was a loss of status and honour as well as of income.[43] But, as we will see, there were soon other factors to inflame rural rebellion.

How far fear of ritual pollution from the greased end of a cartridge (that the soldier had to bite off) was the real cause of unrest in the Company's Bengal army may never be known. But it was certainly used to push those on the verge into full-scale revolt. By 1857 the seventy-four regiments of the Bengal native infantry were very discontented. The level of pay, the loss of allowances, the lack of plunder and booty, the 'general enlistment order' of 1856 making all liable for overseas service (there was a ritual objection to crossing the seas for high-caste Hindus) had all contributed to this.[44] The annexation of Awadh upset the large number of those who were drawn from the kingdom and who now lost certain privileges. A deeper cause may have lain in the fact that the army had in the past been mainly recruited from high-caste Hindus, Brahmins and Rajputs. They disliked its dilution by lower-caste entrants, resented the threat to their status, and dreaded any hint of ritual disgrace. Signs of widespread unrest appeared as early as January 1857. In late March, a Brahmin sepoy, Mungul Pandy, attacked his European officers at a barracks near Calcutta while his fellows looked on. Mungul Pandy was hanged. Meanwhile the British began to disband native infantry regiments suspected of disloyalty. Whites in Calcutta became increasingly nervous. But when the storm broke, it was far away to the north, at Meerut near Delhi.

The trouble began when eighty-five men refused firing practice for fear of pollution by cartridge grease. They were sentenced to ten years' hard labour and the shackles were hammered on in front of their comrades and under the guns of the large British contingent. The next day, probably fearing that the British were coming to remove their weapons and disband their regiments, the sepoys struck first. Before the British could reach them from their side of the station, they killed forty-one whites – officers, civilians, women and children – and set off for Delhi. Within a matter of days – this is what astounded the British – their example was followed all over North India. From as far away as Peshawar (by the Khyber Pass), Indore to the south and Dinahpur in the east, reports began to pour in of murder and mutiny.

The critical fact here was the sheer scale of the mutiny. The sepoys revolted at more than forty military stations. Altogether, perhaps,

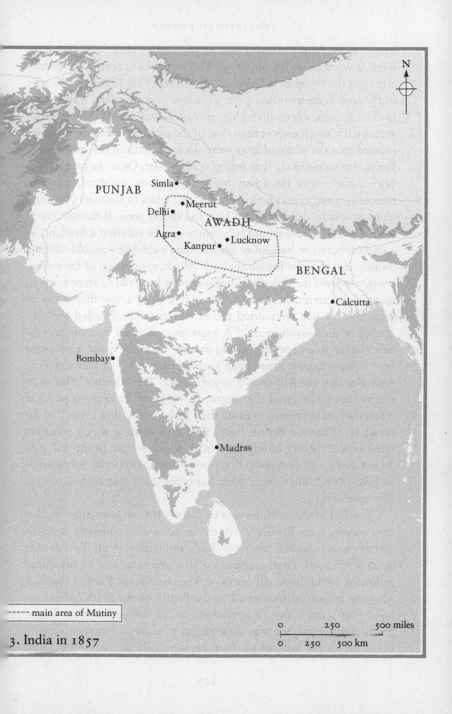

N

PUNJAB   Simla•

• Meerut
Delhi•
          AWADH
Agra•
    Kanpur•   •Lucknow

                    BENGAL

                    •Calcutta

Bombay•

                •Madras

----- main area of Mutiny

0   250   500 miles
0   250   500 km

3. India in 1857

some 70,000 mutinied and a further 30,000 deserted.[45] Several causes were at work to widen upheaval. There may have been a conspiracy although the evidence is lacking.[46] Discontent may have been greatest in the Indian under-officers, the subadars and jemadars, whose hold over their men, whom they often recruited from neighbours and kin, was usually much greater than that of the officers. It was widely complained that the white officers were slack and lacked real authority.[47] But it also seems likely that fear played its part. Once the mutiny had begun, there was no going back. Any sepoy involved, however remotely, could expect little mercy. At the whiff of suspicion, his regiment would be disbanded, and his livelihood gone. If British troops were nearby, his fate would be summary: if he survived a firefight, he could expect to be hanged or blown from a cannon – an old Mughal punishment that the British revived. 'Much, very much, of the excitement,' reported the Calcutta *Englishman* in June 1857, 'arose from an undefined fear on the part of the sepoys. They knew that many of their number had committed themselves and they dreaded the vengeance of the Government.'[48] A grim logic dictated that the sepoys' best chance to escape retribution was to kill every white who might bear witness against them. Even keeping them prisoner was a chilling reminder that the British might come back. The intuitive belief that, unless they obliterated the *angrezi* completely leaving no physical trace, they would return to exact their revenge thus drove much of the savagery. (That the British never forgot or forgave was a common rebel saying.) 'Every building . . . with which we are connected' was 'burnt down and demolished', reported the magistrate at Saharanpur in July 1857.[49] But it was what happened next that turned mutiny into rebellion.

The effect of the mutinies was to destroy the infrastructure of coercion on which the British relied: the indispensable counterpart to the co-opting of notables into the Raj's political system. Two results quickly followed. First, magnates with a grievance and an organized following could throw off restraint. The charismatic Rani of Jhansi, a Maratha princess dispossessed by the British on the death of her husband four years before, was restored to the throne when the Jhansi garrison mutinied. She may have meant to make common cause with Nana Saheb, the 'heir' of the Peshwa, to rebuild the old order. 'These

English are perverters of all men's religion' her proclamation declared.[50] The Nana's opportunity came when the British in Cawnpore asked for his help against the mutinous garrison. At first he sat on the fence. But when the sepoys marched off to Delhi, the Nana and his lieutenant, Tantia Topi, persuaded them to return and assumed command over them.[51] The great feudal landlords (or *taluqdars*) of Awadh, suspecting their fate when the British got into the saddle, rallied their retainers and took over Lucknow. The king of Awadh was hauled back to the throne. Meanwhile at Delhi, to which the Meerut sepoys had marched, the last Mughal emperor resumed his old place as the source of lawful authority – if not of real power. Across a great swathe of North India, the *ancien régime* was making a comeback. When the Nana visited Lucknow (a short ride from Cawnpore) in August 1857, he reminded his hosts that his status required a twenty-one-gun salute.[52] He made do with eleven.

The second result was much more unnerving for the British. They might have snapped their fingers at princes, but a great peasant uprising was a different matter entirely. The likeliest trigger for this peasant insurgency was the news, or the rumour, that the British were leaving and that their Raj had collapsed. Much might also depend on the role of the landlords or big men of the district, who had to decide with whom to throw in their hand. Wherever mutinous sepoys appeared, the local balance of power was transformed. If they had not done so already, the British officials quickly retreated to the nearest stronghold. The peasants marched into town, or to the district headquarters, sometimes to loot (the English word 'loot' is borrowed from Urdu), but usually to burn down the government's *cutcherry* with its tax records and claims. Like its historians a hundred years later, the British were baffled by the pattern of rural revolt. The descent overnight into violent disorder, the sudden physical threat to themselves and their families, and the nerve-jangling uncertainty as to who was loyal or not (a frequent cause of disaster) created a desperate mood. What made matters worse was the extent to which firearms were still widely available: rural society was not yet disarmed. 'The armed populace numbers ... at least three millions,' declared the *Friend of India* angrily. They were the 'armed scum of India'.[53] No less puzzling perhaps was the fact that the Great Trunk Road from Calcutta to

Peshawar – the Raj's military backbone – that ran through some of the most rebellious districts still remained open, the people nearby having preferred to decamp. Perhaps the road was a symbol of what *angrezi* power had once been, as well as the likeliest place where its revenge might strike first.

What mattered most to the British was to contain the revolt. In much of the Hindustan heartland they had little success. But in the Punjab, forewarned by telegraph, and with ruthless impatience, they had just time to act. They had the advantage that most of their white troops had been kept in the province, so recently conquered and with its threatening Afghan frontier. Even so, disarming and disbanding their Indian battalions entailed a good deal of bloodshed. At Peshawar, some forty mutineers were blown from the guns, their blackened heads falling on the crowd of spectators.[54] This ferocious display paid a huge dividend. The British were able to raise a large 'irregular' force through Punjab's tribal chiefs. This was the army (together with their remaining detachments from Meerut and elsewhere) with which they laid siege to Delhi, the head and centre – so it seemed – of the Indian rebellion.

It became a savage hand-to-hand struggle. For some of the time, it was the British themselves, perched up on the Ridge, who were the actual besieged. The turning point came with the column from the Punjab and its notorious commander, John Nicholson, the barrel-chested, charismatic (some said psychopathic) Dublin-born Evangelical. When their heavy guns were assembled in early September, the British were ready to batter their way into the fortified city. But once through the gates, they entered a warren of byways, and were faced with the urban street-fighting that armies fear most. 'For the first time in my life,' wrote the young William Hodson, 'I have lived to see English soldiers refuse repeatedly to follow their officers.'[55] It was perhaps fortunate that sepoy resistance then melted away. The sepoys abandoned the city. The last Mughal emperor was seized. His sons fled with an escort but were overtaken and shot down by their British pursuers in what seems a deliberate act to destroy the dynastic succession. Most of his courtiers were soon to be hanged.[56] The city itself was given over to killing and plunder. In one quarter alone, about 1,400 were murdered as British troops took revenge for their losses. One third of those who had launched the assault were dead by the evening: some 600 British officers and men (including John Nicholson) and nearly 500 of the loyal Indian troops.

If the British now hoped that the rebellion would subside, they were sadly disappointed. While they battled for Delhi, it had widened and deepened. The attempt to disarm the sepoys at Benares (Varanasi) went disastrously wrong. The British overcame their resistance and hanged the mutineers, but the news provoked violence at Allahabad, the key river city where the Jumna met the Ganges, and some whites were killed there. When the British arrived on 17 June, their retribution was savage. Hundreds were hanged, and thousands more killed in the purge that followed: perhaps 6,000 in all.[57] Upriver at Cawnpore the British garrison had surrendered to Nana Saheb and his sepoys. But in the confusion, its departure downstream by boat was disrupted by shooting. A massacre followed and then a much more notorious event: the killing of 200 British women and children whose bodies were thrown down a well in the city. It was a further catastrophic incitement to the black mood of vengeance that the British now felt. Meanwhile Nana Saheb (whose hand was seen in the killings) had himself proclaimed Peshwa in early July, with the apparent intention of reviving the Maratha Confederacy. The mutiny at Gwalior, a hundred miles to the west, brought a new rebel force into the field.

The British faced a dilemma. Despite the recapture of Delhi at one end of the plains and Allahabad at the other, they confronted a vast scene of revolt from Rohilkhand in the north to Bundelkhand in the south. They lacked the military strength to reimpose their control: reinforcements from Britain were still on their way on the long voyage round the Cape. But they could not abandon Upper India until these forces were ready. To do so might harden the rebel resolve and allow a new regime to emerge. For political reasons, recapturing Cawnpore and Lucknow, the main urban centres in the zone of rebellion, was urgent and crucial. They could also not leave the pockets of British resistance to an uncertain fate. In Agra, for instance, the British hung on, mounting armed sorties against rebel-held villages, but rarely in touch with their compatriots elsewhere. Thus in July 1857, a small army under General Sir Henry Havelock fought its way into

Cawnpore. But its grip on the city was fragile and the first attempt on Lucknow was thrown back by the sepoys. It was not till November that they relieved the British in the Residency (where books had been used as sandbags – 120 pages of *Lardner's Encyclopaedia* would stop a musket ball).[58] It was another four months before they regained control of the city. Meanwhile their return at half-cock pushed the bounds of revolt ever wider and wider. Six months after the recapture of Cawnpore, the governor-general in Calcutta reported to London that 'the whole of the Middle Doab [the region nearby] was more completely than ever in the hands of the enemy . . . Nothing was heard from Agra for days together.'[59] Even when they were able to beat a sepoy formation or capture a city, they lacked the resources to make their victory decisive or round up the rebels. Instead the sepoys vanished into the countryside, to return to their villages or form the 'military wing' of a magnate's local levy. What else could they do?

But it was not only the British who faced a dilemma. Where their rule disappeared (sometimes for six months or a year and in less accessible districts for much longer than that) and a party of sepoys arrived in the district, its politics were transformed. When the rebel leaders appear, reported a British official, 'their proceedings are by no means hurried, but are conducted in a most systematic way. They summon the zamindars [landlords] of village after village by letter and exact from them submission and tribute.' If they refused, armed men were then sent.[60] The local elite might hope to build a power base around them, or be cowed by their presence. In either event, they were likely to be tarred with the brush of 'disloyalty'. This was not a mere label, but a life-and-death matter. When the British returned to a district, they too called on the zamindars to reaffirm their allegiance. But no zamindar could be sure, if he gave himself up, that his affirmation of loyalty would be accepted at face value. If the British believed, if their spies had reported, or if his enemies claimed that he had been disloyal, he might find his neck in a noose before he could mount a defence.[61] The Indian deputy magistrate at Cawnpore remained in his post when the city fell to the rebels. When the British came back he was hanged in a trice. Martial law was the method and vengeance the mood; hanging the default mode of summary justice. It was hardly surprising that many who feared and disliked the 'sepoy Raj' in their district feared even more the dishonourable fate that the Company Raj might inflict. Yet ignoring its summons was (in British eyes) a clear confession of guilt. They would punish it when they could.

This tragic dilemma shaped the whole course of the uprising once the fall of Delhi, Cawnpore and Lucknow had ended all prospect (faint at best) of a coherent rebel regime. This was not a police operation surrounding and suppressing a defined rebel area. It was more like a war. In practice, the British assumed that every man's hand was against them. 'In consequence of the general nature of the rebellion and the impossibility of identifying the majority of the rebels, or of bringing their crime home to them, the Magistrate recommended the wholesale burning and destruction of all villages from which rebels had come.'[62] 'All men able to carry arms were shot down or put to the sword and their residences burnt,' recalled one member of the 'Khaki Ressala', a troop of British irregulars. Prisoners were executed.[63] The result was often to drive the rural population together against the threat of indiscriminate killing and burning and to prolong rural resistance long after the main towns were retaken. Indeed, the sight of hundreds of Indians hanged by the roadside as the British armies advanced, alarmed and disgusted even many British observers.

With the turn of the year, the British made steady progress in re covering the rebel-held cities: Farrukhabad in January 1858, Lucknow in March, Jhansi in April (where 5,000 were killed in the city), Bareilly in May, Gwalior in June. The Rani of Jhansi died at Gwalior; but the Nana Saheb and Tantia Topi retreated into the countryside. There the struggle continued. Driven out of Lucknow, the sepoys dispersed into Awadh to rally support – and save their necks. As the British pursued them, they and the *taluqdars* (whose forts were surrounded with impenetrable stands of bamboo) staged a fierce rearguard struggle. By October 1858, complained one British officer, only one quarter of Awadh had submitted and the British police posts were still being overrun.[64] On the southern edge of the plains in Etawah, and in the Bundelkhand uplands, fighting persisted to the end of the year and beyond. 'Hundreds of rebels are still in arms . . .' reported the magistrate at Hamirpur in July 1859.[65] The Nana Saheb vanished into the Nepal *Terai*, a region of jungle and marsh at the foot of the Himalayas, and is thought to have died there. Tantia Topi was less lucky: he was caught by the British and hanged. A 'state of peace' was declared by the Viceroy in July 1859. The rebellion slowly subsided. By the time it had ended the British had lost around 2,000 men killed by military action and nearly 9,000 by disease. The number of Indians who died, sepoy and civilian, will never be known, but was certainly more than 100,000.

What enabled the British to overcome the rebellion? In military terms, once they survived the first phase of the storm and rallied Punjabis and Gurkhas, they remained a formidable force. Armed with Enfield rifles and cannon, they outgunned sepoy units. While sepoys fought bravely and proved adept in defence, British troops constantly showed a ferocious aggression that carried the day against heavy odds. The sacrificial honour code of their officer corps, demanding displays of extreme physical courage (a social phenomenon as yet unexplored), may have been a critical factor: half the British officers in the Delhi assault were to die in the struggle.[66] The rebel forces suffered by contrast from the lack of organized leadership. In political terms, the eventual return of a large British army restored the balance of terror to British advantage, correcting the 'imbalance' between coercion and collaboration that had imperilled their Raj.

The Indian rebellion thus cannot be seen as a war of Indian independence: it lacked the organization, the ideology, and the mass solidarity. It found no foreign friends. It was confined to North India. Its outbreak required the special characteristics of the Bengal native army, as a declining and resentful martial peasant elite. Even in North India, the revolt was very uneven. Many Indians rejected rebellion as dangerous and futile; many more might have done so had it been safe to remain loyal. In a pattern repeated elsewhere, in trying to pre-empt an uprising, the British often took action that merely served to ignite it. The war of reprisals they fought helped to stiffen resistance and then to prolong it. For these kinds of reasons, disentangling the motives of rebels and loyalists is an uncertain business. Some rebels were hanged protesting their innocence, victims of circumstance, malice or British obtuseness. The British themselves were crucially aided by Indian support and often survived by Indian courage and kindness. Their wiser officials were at pains to dispel some of the uglier rumours about sepoy atrocities. It was definitely not true, wrote the intelligence chief at Agra, that white women had been raped.[67] Indeed, they soon became anxious that reprisals would make their task harder once the violence died down.

As might be expected, such a massive upheaval left a huge mark. The Queen's Proclamation in November 1858, on the Crown's formal assumption of constitutional authority from the discredited Company, spoke of reconciliation and promised equal treatment between religions and races. But in many respects, the British had carried through a second conquest of India. It left its physical signs. Delhi's Muslim population was expelled from the city. Parts of Lucknow were razed and rebuilt as broad boulevards – and better firepaths.[68] The fatal well at Cawnpore became a site of remembrance and martyrdom – a deliberate reminder to the British in India that race solidarity was a paramount virtue. Politically, the rebellion persuaded the British to reconcile with the princes, reassure rural elites and stress the 'oriental' and 'traditional' ethos of their rule. Hence the self-conscious symbolism by which the British Queen became 'empress', while her subjects paid homage at Disneyesque *durbars*. The lesson that was drawn by almost all Indians was that attacking the British by force could only lead to catastrophe. When the Indian National Congress was formed in 1885, its leaders constantly stressed their allegiance and loyalty, and their abhorrence of violence.

The military consequence was also dramatic. The British disbanded what was left of their old Bengal army, including its European regiments (some of which were absorbed into the British army at home). When they reformed it, it was smaller in size and recruited almost entirely from loyal Punjabis and hardy hill peoples – so-called 'martial races'. The rebellious high-caste peasants of the North Indian plains were carefully excluded. And an iron rule was imposed that, whatever the size of Britain's Indian army, it should never exceed the all-British garrison by more than two to one – a massive insurance policy, the costs of which fell on all Indian taxpayers. Finally, there was a huge psychological legacy. One British official remembered a case from his youth when Indian merchants at Cawnpore had signed a commercial petition. When it was presented to the British Commissioner, he remarked to the principal signatory: 'I came across your father during the Mutiny: he was one of those who should have been hanged.' The implication was obvious. The signatories withdrew in confusion and the petition collapsed.[69] It became almost a cliché that the British ultimately ruled by the sword – or the threat of its use – and that their guard could never be dropped. Perhaps the last terrible gasp of this 'mutiny' spirit was seen at Amritsar in April 1919, when (Indian) soldiers under General Dyer shot dead nearly 400 unarmed demonstrators after five Europeans had been killed in the city. Dyer was disgraced. But to many British in India, he was the hero who had stopped a new mutiny in the nick of time.[70]

REBELS AND SETTLERS

Rebelling against British rule had cost Indians dear. But it had not led to their wholesale subjugation and dispossession because the British were too few and needed the cooperation of Indians to govern. Other peoples were less lucky. Resistance and rebellion by indigenous or first peoples against *settler* states and communities were in that sense more dangerous. Settlers had much stronger motives to impose total defeat and demand total subjection. They had less need to rely upon local power-brokers and make the concessions they sought – or so they believed. And once their settler bridgehead had reached a critical size, the settler mentality crossed a psychological threshold. The land they had occupied now became home (if not Home). It now was, or should be, a white man's country, whose indigenous people were at best a resource to exploit, at worst a menace to crush. The result was a shift in moral awareness of enormous importance. What might once have been thought of as the rights of original inhabitants were re-imagined instead as the barbaric hangovers of a redundant society. It is easy at this distance to deplore this transition; easier still to suppose that we would not have succumbed to the same moral temptation.

The signs of this struggle could be seen all along the settlement frontier of the nineteenth-century British empire: in Canada, Australia, New Zealand and South Africa. In Canada, the potential for conflict was lessened by the low population of native first peoples (partly the effects of imported disease)[71] and the orderly purchase of land; but far from completely avoided – as the Riel rebellions suggest.

In Australia (with the exception of Tasmania where a deliberate campaign by settler militia and troops forced the original Tasmanians into deadly exile offshore after 1830), much of the settler onslaught on Aborigines was local, unofficial and (where it involved any organized killing) kept deliberately quiet.[72] Since Aborigines lacked land rights, were reduced by disease and could not offer large-scale resistance, actual rebellion – disrupting settler power or renouncing its claims – was rarely an option. In New Zealand and South Africa, this was far from the case.

British authority was extended over the whole of New Zealand by the Treaty of Waitangi in 1840, whose ambiguous terms were agreed by Maori chiefs in the North and South Islands. In British eyes, therefore, Maori were British subjects, owing allegiance to the Crown and obedience to its laws. In fact, the hard edge of theory was softened by compromise. Maori were left to settle their internal disputes provided these did not harm British settlers or conflict too egregiously with British-made law. It was accepted *de facto* that there were really two New Zealands, one Maori one *pakeha*, held together in practice by the governor's authority over the chiefs on the one hand and the settler politicians on the other. The British response to displays of Maori defiance was resolutely pragmatic: where force was deficient a blind eye was turned. But by 1860 this 'limited liability' approach was under great strain from two different quarters. First, there was a growing demand within settler society for the sale of more land by its tribal proprietors, whose rights were enshrined in the treaty. Under the rules it had first to be sold to the colonial authorities and then resold to settlers. But, second, there was a growing anxiety among some Maori leaders that, sooner rather than later, land loss would trigger a social and cultural collapse.

What followed was a stand-off and then an explosion. In parts of the North Island, Maori began to put pressure on those who were willing to sell to the white man. The so-called 'King Movement' signalled the feeling that Maori needed a louder political voice to make themselves heard in Government House against the roar of the settlers' assembly and their vociferous press. The imperial government in London took a calm view of this new Maori politics. The settlers (by now enjoying a wide degree of self-government) did not. From their point of view, to allow a political movement that discouraged Maori land sales (by intimidation, they alleged) would frustrate any prospect of a viable settler society and hurl the colony back into a quasi-tribal economy. To foment a conspiracy that prevented the free sale of land was, they insisted, a rebellious act.

For much of the decade after 1860 large areas of the North Island, including Taranaki, the Waikato, the Bay of Plenty and the East Coast, were consumed by the 'fire in the fern' – the war between 'rebel' Maoris on one side and the British (settler militia as well as regular troops) and their Maori allies (the *kupapa*) on the other. Wherever they gained the upper hand in the struggle, the settlers applied a simple, self-serving logic. Plotting to resist the free sale of land was an act of rebellion. The penalty for rebellion was, among other things, the confiscation of land. Those who could prove that they had not been rebellious might claim compensation later – if they were lucky. The land could be sold by the government to help meet the costs of repression, and meet the settlers' land hunger. The Suppression of Rebellion Act of 1863 provided the legal machinery.[73] Large-scale confiscations marked the end of the conflict and persisted thereafter. Sixty years later, a judicial commission concluded: 'The Natives were treated as rebels and war declared against them before they had engaged in rebellion of any kind, and in the circumstances they had no alternative but fight in their own self-defence.'[74]

The ruthless deployment of a grossly one-sided procedure, backed up by military force, was a clear demonstration of settler intent. Yet the Maori were spared the worst fate that unlimited settler power could inflict. They retained a good deal of land and a constitutional voice in the settlers' assembly. They largely escaped the racial contempt with which settler politicians treated indigenous peoples in other colonized regions. Settler 'moderation' reflected New Zealand circumstances. There was little demand to conscript Maori labour. The Maori land that remained in the remote central uplands ('King Country') and in the East Cape had little appeal for the moment. The confiscation procedure ground to a halt when its administrative burden threatened to bankrupt the state.[75] It risked the creation of a desperate Maori resistance and yet more fire in the fern. And the Maori themselves roused ambiguous feelings. Their rights under the treaty and their claims on the Crown could not be denied. That they also seemed doomed to demographic collapse and eventual extinction made this easier to bear. Some whites were affected by the sentimental appeal of these now harmless relics of history. They became interesting.

Unlike colonial New Zealand, South Africa was a vast and turbulent subcontinent where the extension of sovereignty was piecemeal and contested. The trekkers (or Boers) who had left British-ruled Cape Colony in the late 1830s carved out their conquest states in the landlocked interior where African polities had been badly disrupted by internecine wars, the *Mfecane* or 'grinding'. They rejected British sovereignty and denied their allegiance. They seized African land, demanded African labour and tried to restrict African access to guns. They regarded British missionaries with the deepest suspicion and denounced David Livingstone, the plaster-saint of Victorian Protestantism, as a mischievous gun-runner (Livingstone did not deny the charge).[76] But from the 1840s to the 1880s, Boer expansion was tempered by caution. Their principal state, the ramshackle 'South African Republic', lacked the cash and the firepower to impose effective control over its African neighbours: the Pedi, Swazi and Zulu to the east, the Ndebele to the north, the Tswana to the west. Confrontation, not rebellion, would be a better description for the endemic violence this bred.

It was on the Cape's eastern frontier and in British Natal that the cause and effects of rebellion could be seen much more clearly. In the last major uprising in what became the Transkei, some 3,500 Xhosa were killed by the British, their cattle were seized and large numbers of adult survivors dispatched to the Cape as indentured labour. The violence had begun between communities crowded together as older landholdings were conquered or confiscated. Controlling access to guns was a prime source of tension. In 1873, a Natal chief, Langalibelele, defied the injunction to register the firearms in his tribesmen's possession and insulted the messenger sent to remind him. Martial law was declared and the settler militia called up. Fearing the worst, the tribe fled its territory but not before it had clashed with white troops and left several dead. The result was a mayhem of killing, burning and cattle-lifting as the settler militia exacted revenge. Langalibelele himself was hauled into court to be judged under native law for the crime of rebellion. There followed a pantomime in which the colony's governor in his guise as Supreme Chief conducted the trial in a tent on his lawn, sometimes wearing his helmet and sometimes a head-ring with a feather stuck in it.[77] Judge, prosecution and jury were enrolled in one panel, a cost-cutting convenience. But somewhat oddly, perhaps, the chief was sentenced to perpetual imprisonment on Robben Island – a punishment soon vetoed in London as beyond the governor's powers.

Natal's history belies the popular myth that the British treatment of Africans was more kindly and liberal than that of the Boers. Natal was granted (settler) self-government in 1893. Its white population (some 46,000 in 1891, 97,000 by 1904) was overwhelmingly British in origin.[78] But its outlook was ruled by a deep-seated fear of an African uprising, and by the shadow long cast by the Zulu state to the north. The Zulu kingdom was dismantled after the Anglo-Zulu War of 1879, and London eventually permitted settler Natal to annex its remnants in 1897. Two years later the colony was engulfed in the South African War of 1899–1902. It was after the war, and in the depression that followed, that the trouble began.

The trigger was taxation. The settler government had decided to recoup its battered finances by levying a poll tax on adult African males. White opinion regarded the native as lazy by nature and employers complained bitterly about the shortage of labour. The poll tax would force the unemployed into work. The chiefs were required to present all those liable at a magistrate's office. It was hardly surprising that this was badly received, that chiefs sought to prevaricate and that when the men did assemble their demeanour was not reassuring to the settler officials. What happened next turned discontent to rebellion.

During 1906, in three different parts of Natal, the reluctance to pay brought on confrontation and extraordinary violence. In the early months of the year, two policemen were killed in a fracas not very far from the colony's capital. The colony's ministers mobilized a 'field force' of settler militia. Its tactics were simple. It marched through the region where rebellion was suspected demanding submission (a contemporary photograph shows the militia drawn up on a hill behind its machine gun facing a chief and his followers while a huge Union Jack flutters above them).[79] Cattle were confiscated and villages burned where their inhabitants, not unwisely, had absented themselves. Having met no resistance the column disbanded. Meanwhile, further north on the fringes of Zululand, a chief was deposed on suspicion of resisting the poll tax. This was Bambatha. But Bambatha evaded the force that was sent to arrest him, fled to the forest and began a guerrilla campaign against his successor. The field force gathered again and deployed the same tactics. Its firepower and mobility conferred a massive advantage. On 10 June, it trapped Bambatha and his followers in the Mome Gorge. Perhaps 1,000 were killed by shrapnel, bullet and bayonet. Few, if any, escaped. But a third phase was to follow in the Maphumulo district, much closer to white farms and plantations spreading in from the coast. Here the violence was triggered not so much by dislike of the poll tax, as by the means used to enforce it. The white troopers who came were an ominous presence. The confiscation of cattle, casual brutality (including casual murder), beating and burning formed their main repertoire. It invoked an obvious response. Africans fled at their arrival and gathered together for mutual protection. Some sought reprisal. But when three whites were killed, this police operation turned into a war. Perhaps fearing the worst, perhaps hoping for help from Zulus further afield, the local chiefs and their followers moved into the bush and got ready for battle. When the field force arrived in early July, it made short work of the rebels: in two successive engagements more than 900 were killed. Resistance collapsed but more punishment followed: cattle-looting, hut-burning, killing and beating. The whole district 'wiped out and burnt ... a black pall of smoke hanging over the valley for miles', noted one official report.[80] A party of American missionaries who arrived shortly after '"rode along highways strewn with the unburied putrefying carcasses of the slain ... multitudes were dead"'.[81] The death toll for Natal cannot be known, but must have run into thousands.

How can we explain the extreme and indiscriminate violence of the settler reaction? The white outlook was ruled by an overmastering fear. Any act of resistance was seen as the possible prelude to a general uprising – and alarms of this kind raced through the province during the events of that year. Although the Zulu state had been broken, a

Zulu *revanche* was constantly feared and the Zulu paramount king always closely surveilled. Whites were also deeply suspicious of African religion and ritual, and quick to assume its malign influence and intent. They imagined a skein of 'war doctors' pulling the strings of revolt. When a white man was killed during the violence in Maphumulo and his body parts taken to 'strengthen' the rebels, it confirmed their belief that they faced a barbarous foe on whom pity was wasted and who understood nothing but force. Nor were African Christians exempt from this view. Indeed, independent African churches – the so-called 'Ethiopians' – were strongly suspected of rebellious sympathies, perhaps because African Christians were more vocal in grievance and enjoyed some outside support. John Buchan's *Prester John*, published soon after, was a vivid fictional version of a widespread white feeling. Perhaps, above all, a white settler government in which the farming interest was dominant was acutely aware of the demand by whites in the countryside for 'untouchable' status. The only security that many whites felt was the ever-present awareness in their African neighbours that a hand raised against them would bring retribution of unimaginable horror.

There was one other factor. Despite the network of spies on which white officials depended, their effective control in the tribal reserves was curiously limited. If the chief was uncooperative, they had very few means of picking out those who were causing them trouble. It was this defect of power that encouraged the crudest forms of coercion. All were deemed guilty. Punishment was collective. Terror was preferred since the formal process of law was slow, accident-prone and more likely to act as the focus of grievance than serve as dire warning. It was precisely these features of settler coercion that so often widened revolt, and turned momentary turbulence into real rebellion.

9

Converts and Cultures

The history of empire is often presented in a single dimension: the assertion of dominance by imperial officials (or settlers) and the experience of oppression by indigenous peoples. But as we have seen this is not the whole story. If rule was to work it required a second dimension: in almost all cases, both sides came to rely on a form of political bargain, or what has sometimes been called 'collaborative politics'. Collaboration allowed local elites to protect their own social privileges and helped them to control the vertical links binding their districts to imperial rule. Many castes, communities, tribes and individuals were also well placed to offer their services – as soldiers, clerks, policemen and teachers – to the colonial regime and reap the reward. The third dimension of empire was economic and commercial. Empire existed to profit its 'owners' – in theory at least the British people at large. If the share-out at home was skewed in favour of those with social privilege and power, in colonial societies the economics of empire also created both winners and losers: those who could gain from new commercial connections, and those left on the sidelines or trapped in serf labour. To many 'colonials', this economic dimension (and its unpredictable changes) was what mattered most. But there was also a fourth dimension to empire whose effects were less tangible. If its influence is harder to measure than some of the others, it was no less profound.

The fourth dimension was a matter of minds. Of course, many aspects of the colonial relationship turned on how they were 'seen' by rulers and ruled. Willingness to collaborate politically, or to cooperate economically, reflected a judgement – calculated or intuitive – about likely alternatives and their probable cost. But the British Empire depended on more than such pragmatic calculations. It projected a moral and cultural authority, the implication of which was that British values, beliefs, institutions and habits were the norm against which all others should be measured – and usually found wanting. The deeper implication was that the colonial regime or British connection, far from inflicting oppression or the denial of freedom, was liberating, empowering (not a word the Victorians would have used) and progressive (a word they certainly did). Those who opposed it were not just a nuisance, they were backward, foolish and ignorant. Their civilizations were at a standstill, if not in actual regression. Worse still, 'history' was against them: their failure was certain.

Made into a system, this cultural assertiveness might almost be seen as a form of mind control. When George Orwell's Winston Smith glances up at the white concrete façade of Oceania's Ministry of Truth, he reads its familiar slogan: 'War is Peace. Freedom is Slavery. Ignorance is Strength'.[1] Smith's colonial opposite number, seeing the buildings the British erected, the names they conferred on the streets, the statues and monuments that marked their triumphs and conquests, and reading the language of official reports, might have thus decoded their message: 'Colonialism is good for you. It is here to stay. You had better get used to it.' Indeed, a powerful school of writers has forcefully argued that the deliberate reshaping of colonial minds, the deliberate remaking of what was thought of as 'knowledge', was an essential, perhaps *the* essential, part of the apparatus of colonial domination. Such 'epistemic violence' underwrote the more visible means of control.

The most brilliant exponent of this seductive idea was the American literary critic Edward Said. In his *Orientalism* (1978), he took up the idea that all public discussion is governed by rules laying down what can or can't be said. Those who wish to converse in public must accept the terms of the 'discourse' or be regarded as ignoramuses, criminals, cranks or madmen. Those who manage the discourse are thus able to exercise enormous power, all the more formidable because its sanctions are silent, invisible and intellectually lethal. An idea left unsaid, or disparaged as meaningless, is an idea without power. In Said's notorious description, a coterie of Western intellectuals was able to disparage the intellectual and cultural life of every part of the world beyond Europe as stagnant at best, retrogressive at worst; and the societies that sustained it as variously corrupt, despotic, cruel and effeminate – when not actually barbaric. European colonial regimes – the British foremost amongst them – he saw as zealous enforcers of this self-serving doctrine. By the relentless condemnation of indigenous cultures and the systematic promotion of forms of 'colonial knowledge' that favoured their power, they destroyed the cultural self-confidence of those they ruled over. The application of Western science and technology, the imposition of Western geopolitical forms (the territorial state), the dissemination of Western literary forms (especially the novel), even the writing of history itself, added up to the claim that there was only one escape from tradition (and backwardness) and only one form of modernity: the one purveyed by colonial rule.

As might be expected, this sweeping analysis proved hugely attractive, and has continued to be so despite a robust critical onslaught. It chimed with the widespread belief that the persistence of racism in the post-colonial world sprang from the 'deep' mental structures that had sustained colonialism in its prime and which remained as its legacy. It affirmed the conviction that Western modernity and European empires (of which the British was the biggest) had been brothers-in-arms. As a challenge to previous complacency or indifference, the 'orientalism' formula has been a powerful addition. But, as is often the case, by exposing its assumptions, we can edge a bit closer to the more complex reality that it is in danger of masking.

There are three obvious ways in which orientalism falls short as a convincing description of the cultural impact of British expansion. Firstly, it ignores the importance of time and change, as if a single attitude and a uniform approach prevailed over the whole period up to 1914 and beyond. In fact, British thinking about non-Western peoples and cultures passed through a series of changes in the eighteenth and nineteenth centuries, amounting at times to the dramatic reversal of previous orthodoxy. Secondly (a point that has often been made), Said's thesis is almost quaintly monolithic. It assumes that British opinion towards the non-Western world was all of a piece; that no major debates upset the smooth ideological mould; that cultural practice was invariably draconian; and that those who formed opinion and governed the discourse were the willing allies and agents of the imperial state – as intellectuals were to be later in the Nazi and Stalinist states. Thirdly (and worst), it treats the 'victims' of this 'cultural imperialism' as precisely that: hapless and helpless. The rich and fascinating record of non-Western responses to Western ideas – exploiting, adapting, embracing, rejecting, revising, recycling – disappears into a crude caricature in which only two reactions were possible – resistance or compliance – and only one permitted.

The actual picture was much more confused and complicated. This is not just an obvious and tedious truism, but goes to the heart of the cultural impact of empire. For its most striking feature was the strength of mutual ambivalence. Of course, in any colonial setting there were those who celebrated imperial power, the colonizing 'mission' and its supposed triumphs of 'progress'. But there were always those who were doubtful, dismissive, uneasy or critical – both on the spot and at home. Their influence was intermittently but sometimes critically powerful. Among the colonized there were many who resented – deeply, bitterly and uncompromisingly – the alien cultural intrusion for a number of reasons, not all altruistic. But there were also many who looked towards it for group opportunity, spiritual promise and personal liberation. They sought to propitiate, serve, manage and exploit it for purposes to which their foreign political masters were often quite blind. There were even those orphans of history whose security, identity and even ethnicity came to be bound up with it. We shall catch up with them later.

KNOWLEDGE AND EMPIRE

An overseas empire produces a vast sea of paper. From the earliest period of English colonization, a stream of reports and accounts, instructions and laws, invoices and payments, as well as a mass of personal correspondence, were exchanged between the administrators, soldiers, merchants and colonists in the colonies and their correspondents at home: officials, business partners, customers, creditors and families. By the late eighteenth century, this had turned into a flood. A huge torrent of information about the most distant parts of the world now flowed back to Britain. It formed a vast database of imperial knowledge on which the British could draw. It came in all sorts: governmental reports and statistics; charts, maps, surveys and plans; diplomatic correspondence; the semi-official record of embassies, like Lord Macartney's to Beijing in 1792–3; the propaganda of colonization companies, such as the New Zealand Company, enticing investors and emigrants; the accounts of explorers, like Mungo Park, whose description of West Africa was compiled from notes he had hidden in his hat, or Richard Burton, whose dangerous journey to Mecca in disguise was sponsored by the Royal Geographical Society; the journals of scientific travellers such as Sir Joseph Banks (who had sailed with Cook), Charles Darwin or Alfred Russel Wallace; the uplifting experience of pioneer missionaries (the most famous was David Livingstone's 1857 *Missionary Travels and Researches in South Africa*, an enormous bestseller); overseas newspaper coverage, particularly the columns of special correspondents for whom colonial wars were a virtual gold rush; the stream of trophies and artefacts, some bought, some looted, some animal, some human, put on public display; and, not least, the vast gallery of pictorial images, the result of official commissions (Cook and Macartney had taken artists with them; the East India Company had employed William Hodges) or of wandering freelance artists, looking for subjects and fame.

We can see that this huge treasure trove of information and images might serve two distinct functions. Organized into a system or archive, it allowed the British to map the human and physical landscape of the regions to which they were drawn by commercial, strategic or evangelical motives.[2] The histories of dynasties, the state of their armies, the flows of regional commerce, the migrations of peoples and tribes, religious practice and rituals, social hierarchies and conflicts, indigenous knowledge systems and their guardians, as well as the natural and physical world: all were surveyed and assessed by a cohort of observers, private and public. Collated in handbooks, codified in regulations, circulated and recycled in bowdlerized versions, crushed into stereotypes, they embodied the British understanding of the new worlds they had entered. Indeed, without the mental framing they promised, the rules of thumb they enjoined, or the geographical orientation they offered, it is hard to see how the British could have functioned in alien and exotic environments, except in the most hand-to-mouth fashion or in very small groups. The sheer scale of their presence in the non-European world, and the intense interaction between their different activities, demanded something like the mass production of knowledge and its swift circulation to a wide range of interests.

The second of these functions partly grew out of the first. The collection, collation and circulation of knowledge required a grand entrepot, a great emporium of data. Here it could be gathered and processed, discussed and distributed, bought and sold. The grand entrepot for the British Empire and, as the nineteenth century wore on, for the world as a whole, was London. A flotilla of institutions, some highly specialized, some informal and private, sprang up to package this knowledge for subscribers at home as well as users abroad: professional and scientific societies, commercial associations, museums, libraries and galleries. To many interests in Britain, the service they offered had a practical value. But they also supplied, in effect, much of what was known about empire by the wider domestic audience in Britain, and shaped the ways in which it was discussed and imagined.

However, it would be wrong to suppose that this torrent of knowledge created a common perception of empire in British opinion. There were two reasons for this. Firstly, the information assembled in Britain was drawn from a wide range of informants and sources. It resisted reduction to a formulaic world-view that justified conquest and empire or offered crude vindication of British superiority. The voluminous reports of the East India Company's activities sent back every year to appease its critics in Parliament (and probably to anaesthetize them) had the unintended effect of convincing most British opinion that the further expansion of Company rule would be a dangerous folly. The evidence presented by a large body of witnesses persuaded the parliamentary Select Committee on 'Aborigines' (i.e. indigenous peoples) in 1837 that colonial expansion risked doing them irreparable harm. Much that was written about empire by insiders took the form of complaints – about injustice, unfairness, waste and incompetence. Writers rarely wrote without purpose, if only to make money. But their purposes varied, as did their agenda and interests. Some widely read authors, such as Park and Wallace, were at pains to demolish disparaging notions about 'uncivilized' peoples. Others openly warned, among them John Malcolm, a senior British official in India, in his *Political History of India* of 1826, against the idea of transplanting British institutions to India and meddling too much with existing political customs. Among settler propagandists, it made little sense, if the aim was to encourage migration, to portray indigenous peoples as too barbaric and dangerous – unless a frontier war was in progress and help was needed from home. Missionaries had to persuade potential donors in Britain that 'heathen' populations were in urgent need of salvation, but not too far gone to make their redemption unlikely. Commercial promoters pictured the promise of untapped new markets (China was much favoured) but had to be careful not to paint them as wastelands from which no return could be hoped for.

Secondly, the audiences at whom these writers directed their words were also fragmented by interest and outlook. The empires they saw could be remarkably different. For naval and military men, it was a chain of overseas stations, a frontier of small wars, a source of fame and preferment. For gentlemen-scientists, it was a vast deposit of specimens. For manufacturers and merchants, the empire Britain ruled over was (after *c.* 1840) the lesser half of the empire of free trade they wanted to conquer. They regarded the East India Company (still India's ruler until 1858) as a corrupt and wasteful obstruction to India's commercial development. For the missionary interest, the spread of white settlement was unwelcome at best. For the colonization lobby, and the families of migrants, the empire that mattered was in Canada, Australia and New Zealand. For the network of Anglo-Indian officials and their allies at home, a vociferous, letter-writing fraternity, the settlement colonies were an annoying distraction from Britain's real empire. In the great public debates in which empire was caught up, imperial lobbies could be found on both sides: over slavery and free trade and in the Edwardian controversy over tariff reform and imperial federation.

Of course, British opinion about empire was not just a patchwork of lobbies and interest groups. It coalesced around certain broad propositions that were vague enough to command general agreement. However, these changed over time and their influence was variable and depended on circumstance. And they always left room for entrenched oppositions and dug-in cabals. In fact, public opinion can be seen more realistically not as a real and omnipotent force but as something imagined by contending opinion-formers who asserted that *their* views commanded the greatest public support. Victory could be claimed if the larger proportion of newspapers and journalists echoed these views and leading public men also deferred to them – in public at least. It was one of the hazards of political life that predicting the direction that opinion might take and how long it would last before a new mood set in was exceptionally difficult in a country where already by 1830 some 3 million people read newspapers, newscarrying publications ran into the thousands, and regional differences were cross-cut by those of religion, occupation and class as well as political loyalty.[3]

In the mid eighteenth century, the high ground was taken by those who regarded the pattern of Europe's colonial expansion as shameful and dangerous. It was possible, like William Robertson in his *History of America* (1777), to see the voyages of Columbus and Vasco da Gama as a great turning point that allowed Europe to become a truly commercial society.[4] Indeed, commerce was seen as the most advanced social stage – above hunting and agriculture – and the essential condition for a liberal and enlightened society. But European colonization – in the Americas above all – (this was Robertson's point) had betrayed a noble ideal. For the French thinker Diderot, a contributor to Raynal's collective *Histoire des Deux Indes* (1780), its motives were 'atrocious'. Far from promoting the true aims of commerce – the free and equal exchange of goods and ideas – it had led to the conquest and annihilation of peoples. The effect on Europeans had been almost equally bad: their feelings were corrupted and coarsened by the violence and misery they inflicted.[5] Indeed, trying to rule colonies that were geographically remote as well as ethnically different was politically risky and certain to fail. These views were influential among thinkers and writers in Britain, including Hume and Edward Gibbon, whose *Decline and Fall of the Roman Empire* (1776) had famously warned against the danger for an empire of reaching 'immoderate size'. In *The Wealth of Nations* (1776), Adam Smith had looked forward to the time when those the Europeans had been able to oppress 'with impunity'[6] would restore the balance of power. Edmund Burke's famous polemic against the corruption and cruelty of the British presence in India reflected the same disenchanted view of European behaviour overseas and its destructive effects on other cultures and peoples.

So it was not entirely surprising that when the convict colony was established at Botany Bay in 1788, Arthur Phillip, the first governor, was determined to promote friendly relations with the Aborigines and prevent his own men from using force against them. Australia was not to be a second America. Phillip even named Manly Cove (in today's Sydney Harbour) for what he saw as the Aborigines' 'manly' bearing. The ideal of free commerce as the path to enlightenment chimed with the rise of humanitarian feeling (itself supercharged with evangelical fervour) whose pre-eminent cause became the abolition of slavery. Planters and slave-owners in the British West Indies were tarred with the same brush of degraded brutality as their Spanish and Portuguese counterparts, long favourite targets for British abuse. But while these liberal opinions were widely proclaimed, they were not universal. The slave interest fought back: Edward Long, the son and grandson of planters, in his 1774 *History of Jamaica* defended slavery as giving order and discipline to 'sub-human' Africans. Another planter-historian, Bryan Edwards, urged amelioration but not abolition. Even in the 1820s the abolition of slavery could be agreed as a principle but not as a practical measure, given the political strength of its champions.[7] British ministers had already (in 1810) dismissed as absurd the notion that representative government could be extended to 'free people of colour'.[8] The reservations Burke had voiced about the perils of extending British rule over Indians were swept aside in the wars against Tipu Sultan and the Marathas – justified as pre-empting the imperial ambitions of France under Bonaparte. The imperative need to place British not Indians in every position of administrative power became a cardinal rule in the mid 1790s – and an article of faith among the clamorous throng of British job-seekers chasing these golden appointments. Meanwhile British views on the likely survival of Asia's great empires became increasingly negative.

China, said Lord Macartney after his abortive mission to Beijing in 1792–3, was barely afloat. Thirty years later, the Ottoman Empire was dismissed by Lord Aberdeen, then Foreign Secretary, as 'this clumsy fabric of barbarous power [that] will speedily crumble to pieces from its own inherent causes of decay'.[9]

Thus the great wave of humanitarian feeling that reached its climax with the abolition of slavery (1833) and the Select Committee *Report on Aborigines* (1837) coexisted with less generous views about the status and prospects of non-Western cultures and practical, if not theoretical, distinctions of colour and race. Indeed, the 1830s marked the gradual transition towards what became the dominant idea in Victorian Britain about its place in the world. The cosmopolitan outlook of the eighteenth-century 'philosophers' and the willingness of writers such as the great oriental scholar Sir William Jones to concede intellectual parity to other civilizations were undermined by the visible signs of the West's military and technical superiority. At the same time, the great intellectual movement of utilitarianism – so influential in Britain – was losing its claim to be the master-key of social progress. Its psychological doctrine – that men's actions were driven by the urge to maximize pleasure and minimize pain – left too many questions unanswered, not least why ideas of pleasure and pain varied so much across different societies. Its insistence that a universal model of institutional change would yield a just and progressive society whatever the setting buckled under the strain of actual experience, not least in India. Instead, there was an increasing recognition that what the utilitarians had denounced as the 'dead hand of history' might be of decisive importance in shaping social institutions, the law above all. In Britain, especially, the ferment of social and cultural ideas had two highly volatile elements. Industrialism and its discontents bred visions of anarchy and utopia; and religious certainties began to dissolve in a storm of theological and scientific controversy.

A straw in the wind was an outburst by Thomas Carlyle, the sage (and scourge) of early and mid Victorian Britain. In characteristically violent language, Carlyle denounced what he saw as the moral abdication implicit in conventional humanitarian attitudes, utilitarian thinking and the laissez-faire doctrines of the 'political economists'.

The target he chose, designed to create maximum offence, was the abolition of slavery. Its result, he declared, had been to ruin the British West Indies and to leave the freed slaves to fester in idleness. Carlyle's explicit assertion that blacks should be made to work under whites, and his resort to the crude epithets of a pro-slavery agitator, provoked general outrage.[10] Carlyle's polemic did not mark the sudden arrival of a new racist mood in British opinion (as some excitable commentators have suggested), and his friends, including John Stuart Mill, were appalled by his language. But it was symptomatic of wider discontent with the facile prescriptions he dealt with so savagely.

In the new social theory that took shape in the 1840s and 1850s, 'evolution' was the pivot. This was not the biological evolution of Charles Darwin and *The Origin of Species* (1859), which it long predated: 'When the cradle of evolutionary theory was being prepared,' remarks its witty historian, 'Darwin was in his hammock and three thousand miles away.'[11] Evolution's principal value lay in offering a framework for understanding why some societies had achieved more rapid and far-reaching change than others. It retained the eighteenth-century idea of successive social stages: the hunter-gatherer, the agricultural and the commercial. It was the shift up the scale that evolution was meant to explain as a process of continuous adjustment to aspiration and need. Part of its intellectual and moral attraction was to keep intact the belief in the unity of mankind, on which much European religious and philosophical thinking depended, while also explaining why mankind varied so much in its social and cultural behaviour. A second attraction was that social evolution could be equated with progress and moral achievement because successful adaptation required making the right choices – social, intellectual and ethical. Social evolution had one further great merit. As a theory by which to make sense of the world, it was extraordinarily flexible. Its devotees could combine it with a wide range of cults and claim its authority for all sorts of beliefs, banal or bizarre. Perhaps that is what explains its extraordinary influence and intellectual longevity.

Social evolution focused intellectual attention on the web of custom, law and religion that bound peoples together and on the divergence between the most powerful and prosperous states and the less fortunate rest. It was a short step to argue that increases in wealth and power were the visible signs of successful evolution; commercial stagnation or political breakdown the hallmarks of a stationary state or actual regression. But selecting the *active* ingredient that explained why some peoples advanced while others stood still was a matter of choice. Protestant churchmen laid great weight on the socially virtuous behaviour that Protestant Christianity encouraged, or on the unique insight that it gave into the intentions of Providence: Protestants worked with the grain of God's plan for the world. Lawyers pointed to property law: the individual's right to own property, to inherit or bequeath it, free from interference by a predatory ruler, explained the accumulation and wise use of wealth. Politicians eulogized the role of representative government; writers and journalists the right to free speech; moralists the absence of oriental indulgence. Intellectually, evolution was a club open to all, an idea whose simplicity (and circularity) made it an ideal mass product. It was perfectly timed for an industrial age. It entered the Victorians' bloodstream and lodged there for good.

Charles Darwin's biology did not inspire evolution, but it added several strings to the evolutionists' bow. It gave much wider currency (and scientific credibility) to the notion that all life was a 'struggle for existence': 'natural selection' carried with it the threat of extinction.[12] The influence of heredity could be conscripted by those for whom inherited characteristics could be equated with race. The link between adaptation and physical attributes encouraged the notion that measuring head shape or nose size would allow the expert observer to rank the cultural capacities of different peoples and races. The appeal of eugenics sprang from the fear that physical degeneration (for which Darwin's theory allowed) would impede social progress and even impose retrogression. But three points should be noted. Firstly, 'Social Darwinism' was not a manifesto for imperial aggrandizement. To many of its followers, in the struggle for existence consolidation and caution, not feckless expansion, appeared the best course. It was also widely believed that Europeans could not flourish in a tropical climate. They lived there like divers on the sea bed, wrote one Social Darwinist. Secondly, the use and abuse of Darwin's ideas was largely a by-product of the excitable atmosphere of the 1890s, when imperial, international and industrial competition seemed to rise sharply, and public debate became more frenetic. Fear of Russian, French and German colonial expansion as well as the industrial ascent of the United States, fuelled the alarm. Thirdly, in Britain at least, the usual explanations for progress, or its absence, were couched in cultural not biological terms. Law, language, institutions and beliefs, not physical attributes, were what held peoples back or encouraged them forward. The most influential Social Darwinist of the 1890s and after, Benjamin Kidd (1858–1916), rejected biological arguments for the 'social efficiency' that explained European primacy.[13] 'Scientific racism' was a convenient addition, not the nub of the argument.

As a result, social evolution left room for quite different responses to the British encounter with non-Western peoples. Disillusionment with the results of ending black slavery, the great Indian rebellion and the tepid if not hostile response to British missionary efforts persuaded many observers that order and progress in non-Western societies required the forceful assertion of British authority. But no simple logic connected this view with the annexation of non-Western states, the denial of rights to non-Western peoples, or the systematic belittling of non-Western cultures. The 'vulgar racism' that belittled all foreigners and especially those with dark skins was not all-pervading. Much British opinion rejected the atrocity stories about the Indians' treatment of whites in 1857, amid a deep sense of unease about the British treatment of Indians.[14] Indeed, one near-contemporary account, Montgomery Martin's *Mutiny of the Bengal Army* (1861) presented the sepoys as victims and British 'war heroes' as pathological mass murderers.[15] The savage repression of the 1865 Jamaica uprising was fiercely condemned by an enquiry commission as 'barbarous, wanton and cruel'.[16] London insisted on a 'colour-blind' franchise when it conceded self-government to its South African Cape Colony; the number of non-whites who qualified was small but in certain districts significant. Nor was there always agreement as to where a particular society stood on the scale of social advance. In the 1880s, the British occupation of Egypt evoked a furious reaction among Liberals against the throttling of Egyptian democracy. Much British opinion at home disliked the racial arrogance and authoritarianism of British officials in India. One Liberal minister likened them to 'tchinovniks', the repressive bureaucracy of tsarist Russia.[17] The dislike and mistrust were warmly reciprocated. The settler treatment of indigenous peoples attracted regular criticism. Behind these reactions lay the growing suspicion that far from assisting social evolution and progress, officials and settlers were crushing their promise and conspiring against their true local champions.

In fact, British ideas about their place in the world, and about the meaning of empire, agreed on generalities but differed in detail. Few Late Victorians would have denied that Britain enjoyed a central position in global affairs: its industrial, financial, naval and imperial power ensured such pre-eminence. Few would have doubted that it also derived in large part from British success in evolving more rapidly into a civilized, efficient and dynamic society than anywhere else on the globe. But there was much less agreement on how best to preserve this exceptional status, or whether indeed it could be sustained. There was quite wide disagreement on how Britain should deal with less advanced cultures. The orthodox view was that Islam should be treated with pragmatic respect as a creed that imposed a strict social discipline, while regarded intellectually as an historical relic of stagnant scholasticism. But this coexisted with a much more romantic response to Islamic societies, especially those of the desert (a tradition made famous by Wilfrid Blunt, Charles Doughty and, later, T. E. Lawrence). It was commonplace to distinguish between 'manly' or 'martial' peoples (to be co-opted if possible) and those classified as obedient peasantries ('sturdy peasants') or as 'criminal tribes', a designation used by the British in India. A major fault-line in Victorian opinion lay between those who showed sympathy for the modernizing ambitions of Asian and African proto-nationalist elites (like the leaders of the Indian National Congress, founded in 1885), and those who dismissed them as bogus and counterfeit, tiresome, unrepresentative microscopic minorities, whose motive was position and power for themselves. The other side of this coin was the search for authentic tradition among indigenous peoples, the (limited) willingness to clothe the colonial regime in some of its trappings, and the selection of princes and chiefs as true representatives. Both schools of opinion debated the merits of segregating 'backward' peoples from whites.

Preserving intact the cultural elan and racial cohesion of the progressive whites struck some late nineteenth-century observers as an urgent precaution in a fully colonized world. But segregation also appealed to those for whom the opposite danger seemed more real: that the corrosive effects of white commerce, culture and power would turn native peoples into demoralized, impoverished and landless proletarians, a vast reserve army of explosive resentment.

The multiple streams of knowledge, the wide range of contacts, the profusion of interests that connected Britain to its empire thus produced, not surprisingly, both a degree of consensus and much variation in perceptions and attitudes. Among the numerous constituencies with a stake in British expansion – colonial officials, soldiers, merchants, settlers, missionaries, explorers and travellers, as well as those social reformers who looked to empire abroad to relieve social tensions at home – priorities and sympathies were bound to be different. For a radical few, empire was the prop of a corrupt and oppressive social structure in Britain: social justice at home required its demolition (in part).[18] For all its ironclad exterior, official thinking about empire was periodically troubled by moral unease, or swayed by the roar of vociferous lobbies. More important in the long run, colonial peoples and their leaders were rarely without some friends and supporters in Britain to encourage their hopes of eventual release into a free 'British world'. And far from imposing a common culture on their colonies, the British could neither agree on what it should be, nor on whether to risk the political fall-out that might follow any attempt to enforce it.

MISSIONARY WORK

A missionary, Lord Salisbury (1830–1903) remarked in his youth, is 'a religious Englishman with a mission to offend the religious feelings of the natives'.[19] This is not a view he would have ventured in public when leader of the Conservative Party or in office as prime minister. The Victorians' enthusiasm for missionary work is perhaps the hardest of their public emotions for a secular age like our own to imagine. Their theological anxieties, even more than their spiritual strivings, are a closed book to us. Yet a sense of missionary duty informed much of the public understanding of empire from the 1790s until 1914 and even beyond. Many Victorians were inspired by their platoon of missionary saints with David Livingstone at its head. Indeed, once placed in his tomb in Westminster Abbey (his body was brought back from Africa in April 1874), Livingstone's influence was more compelling than ever. But the missionary was not just an agent of religious fervour at home sent by the pious to win the heathen for Christ. Nor did he act as the cultural auxiliary of colonial power (the condescending assumption of secular-minded historians) – a point forcefully made in the best modern study of the British Protestant missions.[20] And far from enjoying unchallenged moral and religious authority, the missionary found himself uneasily poised between those he was meant to convert, the official men on the spot, an often hostile settler opinion, and his sponsors at home, eager for news of his spiritual triumphs. The strain was sometimes unbearable.

Before 1790, missionary zeal in Britain was largely concerned with the religious well-being of the British abroad. The 1790s were a watershed. Half a dozen societies sprang up to recruit, train and fund a corps of spiritual messengers to the non-Christian world, among them the Baptist Missionary Society (1792), the non-denominational London Missionary Society (1795) and the Anglican Church Missionary Society (1799). The coincidence is striking and suggests a certain competitiveness. But the deeper cause was the growth of an intense evangelical culture that was a dominant force in Victorian Britain and whose influence was still felt as late as the interwar years. The evangelical movement of the 1730s and 1740s, with its revivalist meetings and demotic expression, had been viewed with suspicion by the social elite. But the 'sentimental revolution' in the second half of the century made evangelicalism respectable.[21] It reacted against a 'mechanical' view of human motivation and stressed the importance of 'sensibility' and empathy as guides to social behaviour. It required the individual to cultivate his or her own moral growth, to produce the right feelings that would conduce to right conduct. The evangelical message fitted perfectly with this mood. What the Christian believer should strive for was a personal connection with God through meditation and prayer. The aim was a state of heightened spirituality and (thus) a keener awareness of spiritual duty. It followed quite logically that the evangelical Christian should spread the good news (of his spiritual breakthrough) and help others to do so. By his own direct action, or through aid to third parties (such as the missionary societies), he would proclaim his evangelical faith.[22]

This impulse was strengthened by unease at the moral effects of headlong urbanization and by the claim that action was needed to restore social discipline among the unruly poor. The reformation of manners and morals was the evangelical cause. The arduous struggle with France (1793–1815) and the social strain it imposed made moral cohesion seem all the more urgent. Its victorious conclusion bred a double belief: that Britain's survival was part of God's plan and that this imposed on its people an evangelical duty. At much the same time, as new worlds came into view from the late eighteenth century in the Pacific, India, China and the interiors of West and South Africa, this sense of divine purpose was partly diverted abroad. From this moment on, British ideas about empire were injected with a serum of religious and humanitarian feeling that they never quite lost.

The societies' first task was to find the recruits for their self-imposed burden. Missionary work, it turned out, had little appeal for the comfortably off. Those who stepped forward came from the artisan class, literate and respectable but not highly educated. William Carey, the first Baptist missionary in India, was a Northamptonshire shoemaker. Robert Morrison, who pioneered the Protestant presence in China, had been trained to make boot-holders. His colleague Walter Medhurst was a printer. Hudson Taylor, who founded the China Inland Mission, was the son of a chemist. Samuel Marsden, the first missionary to New Zealand, was the son of a butcher. Of those who went to South Africa, James Read had been a carpenter and Robert Moffatt a gardener, while his famous son-in-law, David Livingstone, had worked in a cotton mill before saving enough to begin medical training. These modest origins were not a coincidence. The pioneer conditions of missionary work repelled those with better prospects at home. When Samuel Marsden came to Britain in 1811 (he was then in Australia) to recruit for his mission to New Zealand, he found the Maori reputation for cannibalism had travelled ahead of him. 'No clergymen ...

offered their services . . . The character of New Zealand was considered more barbarous than that of any other country,' he complained to his journal.[23] He found two 'mechanics' instead. What may have attracted such recruits was that they could be ordained as a missionary without the formal education required for a career as a cleric at home. Missionary work promised social ascent as well as religious fulfilment. Indeed, those who did the recruiting treated formal education as of lesser importance than spiritual conviction. Perhaps they were wise. The skills of a gardener or carpenter were of more practical use than 'gentlemanly' accomplishments. Utter commitment, not a sceptical intellect, was a better defence against the bleak disillusion that most missionaries faced.

But of course not all missionaries were cut from this cloth. The mission societies relied early on, and for many years after, on foreign recruits, mainly from Germany. The first CMS missionary in East Africa was Johan Ludwig Krapf (1810–81), the son of a Württemberg peasant, who arrived in Mombasa in 1844. Germans formed the bulk of the CMS strength there for the next thirty years.[24] In West Africa, much of the missionary effort was the work of 'Liberated Africans' from Sierra Leone. The great Anglican missionary statesman of British West Africa was Samuel Ajayi Crowther (1807–91), a Yoruba from today's western Nigeria. At the age of fifteen he was sold as a slave captive and placed on a Portuguese slave ship (perhaps bound for Brazil), but recaptured the next day by a Royal Navy patrol. He was sent as a Liberated African to Sierra Leone where freed slaves from the Americas and former slave captives formed a creole society with its own Christian college at Fourah Bay in the colony.[25] With its ready supply of Christian believers, Freetown's trade links along the West African coast, and the ties that were formed by the Yoruba diaspora, Sierra Leone became the vital 'sub-station' for the Christianization of West Africa. Crowther himself (who was received by the Queen) was appointed bishop of 'the countries of Western Africa beyond the limits of our dominions' in 1864.[26] In East Africa, so-called 'Bombay Africans' – freed slaves taken first to Bombay and then to a miniature Freetown ('Freretown' near Mombasa) – played (much more modestly) a similar role.[27]

Despite its conventional image, missionary work was not a purely male preserve. For, early in the nineteenth century, the value of 'missionary wives' to the evangelical effort was widely acknowledged. Indeed, they were sometimes explicitly referred to as 'female missionaries' as in Jemima Thompson's compilation *Memoirs of British Female Missionaries*, published in 1841.[28] Ironically, women were being increasingly excluded from preaching in Britain by the organized churches, but from the late 1850s single women were being actively recruited as salaried missionaries. The CMS sent sixteen women abroad between 1873 and 1883, and was employing over 400 world-wide some twenty years later.[29] Half of its eighty-strong missionary force in Uganda in 1907 were women. Indeed, one scholar has calculated that by 1900 nearly two-thirds of all British missionaries were actually women, although they rarely held positions of religious authority.[30] The recruiting of women missionaries reflected in part the importance attached to reaching women secluded in Hindu and Muslim societies, as well as recognition that if Christianity was to enter the home the allegiance of women as mothers was vital. 'Without the aid of pious females,' declared the great China missionary Charles Gutzlaff, 'no permanent impression can ever be made upon families . . . hence the necessity of female labourers of the same stamp as the . . . male agents.'[31]

Recruitment was one thing, deployment another. How was the missionary to reach his (later her) chosen field? This was not a trivial matter. There was no reason to think that his message or her presence would be welcomed, even by their own compatriots. The British East India Company, nervous of Indian reaction, barred missionaries from its territories until forced to give in by the clamour at home in 1813, when its charter was debated in Parliament. In the British West Indies, they were suspected (not without reason) of fomenting slave discontent. In China, they had to wait until British military power forced open the door in two Opium Wars. They might be deterred by the fearsome reputation of the locals, as Marsden complained, or by the flat refusal of rulers to allow them to stay. If, as Johan Krapf found in East Africa, they were suspected of plotting to disrupt the slave trade, or seen as a soft target for theft (Krapf had a rifle but could not bring himself to fire it *at* anyone), their lives were at risk.

In fact, except where they could enter a region as the camp-followers of empire, missionaries had to climb over two practical barriers. They had to find ways not only of transporting themselves and their families to the chosen location but of maintaining regular contact thereafter since missionaries had to be paid, supervised (to ensure their compliance with the society's rules and their theological conformity), and also supplied. As well as his and his family's clothes, a medical chest and 'civilized' necessities such as coffee, sugar and tea, he would need some 'equipment' to make his presence effective: a stock of Bibles and books; the tools he would need for minimal self-sufficiency (spades, axes and saws) as well as those he would encourage his converts to use. The missionary could rarely operate very far from an established trade route or too far in advance of the trader's frontier. Indeed it was sometimes convenient to become a trader himself. So determined was Samuel Marsden to rescue the Maori from the Prince of Darkness (his phrase) that he bought his own ship (he had become a rich man) and sailed the 1,200 miles from Sydney to the North Island of New Zealand to buy Maori flax in exchange for his trade goods. It was the way to win friends and Marsden quickly made contact with Maori communities around the North Island's coast. Forty years later, David Livingstone won over the Makololo people (in modern Zambia) with the promise to help them to sell ivory at the faraway coast.[32]

To be sure not just of a welcome, but of permission to stay, the missionary usually needed to offer more than spiritual benefits – perhaps the least desired of his gifts. He might be pressed to supply guns – and find it hard to refuse as James Read discovered in 1813, since these were the trade goods that his hosts valued most.[33] Indeed they could plausibly claim that their very survival required them in an increasingly violent age. The missionary could seem useful as the arbiter of local disputes (a role Livingstone played), as the diplomatic agent to deal with the colonial authorities, or as a vocal champion against settler encroachment. Where they were competent linguists, missionaries might be key intermediaries in the colonial encounter. It was a missionary who translated (not, it seems, very well) the Treaty of Waitangi that annexed New Zealand to Britain in January 1840. Their medical skills were another attraction. It was these that helped Gutzlaff break the ban on outsiders when he landed in China, and commended the missionaries to Mpande, the Zulu king, in 1850. For some African rulers, the real appeal of a mission was its contribution to state-building. Like the 'convert-kings' of Anglo-Saxon England, they grasped the importance of religious identity in snapping the bonds of kin, clan and lineage and building a wider allegiance – provided, of course, that there was no falling out between church and state. But it usually seemed wise not to put all their eggs in one theological basket. The kings of Buganda invited both Muslims and Christians to their court and kept each of them guessing – although this was a tactic that later backfired.[34] The Lesotho ruler Moshoeshoe encouraged conversion, but shrewdly refrained from committing himself to Christianity until on his death-bed.[35]

Missionaries might be welcome for a number of reasons but perhaps chiefly because they promised the benefits of external contacts – skills, information, trade and diplomacy – but without external control. But this was no guarantee that they would be allowed to start 'fishing for souls'. They were unlikely to stumble on a spiritual vacuum or face no competition. In almost every society there were spiritual specialists whose prestige (and prosperity) derived from their claim to supernatural powers, to be able to drive away evil in all its numerous forms and protect the community. They were bound to resent the arrival of such strident intruders and use every means to discredit them. The missionaries, for their part, had to hit on a strategy that would allow them to shatter the grip of established belief quickly and peacefully. This was to be a tall order.

The usual platform for the missionary presence was the mission station. There were thirty-four in Cape Colony when a census was taken in 1849, the largest of which held 2,000 people although the average was much lower.[36] Typically a station would have a church, a school, a workshop, a row of houses for the missionary and his flock, as well as gardens and ploughlands for food. The Christian calendar, the clock and church bell would regulate time.[37] Square-built houses (not circular huts) with two separate rooms for marital privacy were designed to enhance the household status of the (single) wife – a missionary preoccupation – and separate the nuclear family from the rest of their kin. In South and West Africa, the missions adopted the slogan 'the Bible and the Plough' attributed to the great evangelical abolitionist Sir Thomas Fowell Buxton. It went without saying that the convert must know and ideally read his Bible. Adopting the plough would make his spiritual revolution complete. It meant regular work, a permanent settlement (not shifting cultivation) and earning the means for the civilized garb (cotton trousers and dresses) that modesty and morality demanded. Using the plough meant rejecting the hoe, and the old division of labour by which women worked in the fields while men fought, foraged or hunted or (as the missionaries suspected) sat around and got drunk. The plough was man's work. It sent him to the fields and kept his wife in the home to practise its skills and look after her children. The Bible for the mind, the plough for the body, would bring a godly thorough reformation.

But who would come to the missions and accept their arduous demands? Their very existence as separate locations was a revealing admission. The naïve expectation that the missionary could preach direct to the people and convert by mass meeting was rarely borne out. Mission stations were enclaves in a hostile or indifferent terrain. In what became southern Nigeria, separate mission houses were built to showcase the new way of life and limit the tug of customary rites.[38] Here the congregations were largely composed of African migrants from along the coast and African traders. In South Africa, especially, those who came to the missions were chiefly the desperate and displaced, victims of the subcontinent's wars between blacks and blacks as well as whites and blacks. The LMS station at Bethelsdorp (near modern Port Elizabeth) was a refuge for Khoikhoi, sometimes called 'Hottentots' or later 'Cape Coloureds', avoiding serf labour on the colony's farms. Where missions were granted reserves of land (as occurred in Natal), or missionaries bought farms (as at Edendale in Natal), they attracted a following. Sceptics like the journalist-traveller Winwood Reade (whom we met on the Gold Coast) contemptuously dismissed mission converts as frauds. 'Every Christian negress I met with was a prostitute, and every Christian negro a thief,' he told the Anthropological Society of London in 1865.[39] Observers in China referred disparagingly to what they called 'rice Christians' – those looking for shelter and food not religious enlightenment. Similar accusations were made about the 'untouchable' converts drawn to the missions in India. Indeed, for those who enjoyed status in traditional society, conversion was costly.

For once in the mission, the convert risked burning his boats. He would come under pressure to sever his ties with the rest of his kindred and reject their mutual obligations as impious and immoral. From this arose a dilemma.

Missionaries were bound to be anxious that their converts were genuine. Part of the reason for imposing the drastic life-changes that conversion required was to discourage backsliding. But they were also reluctant to deter would-be believers by demanding too much. A key issue here was polygamy. There was hardly a tenet more precious to evangelical Christianity than the sanctity of the marriage bond, the foundation of family life. But forcing male converts to set aside all but one of their wives, many missionaries argued, was asking too much and threw on the missions the odium of much social disruption. John Colenso, the Bishop of Natal, and Samuel Crowther, later Bishop in West Africa, pressed their superiors at home to show flexibility.[40] Baptism should not be denied a polygamous wife, urged Crowther. The CMS committee would have none of it. 'Polygamy is an offence against the law of God,' they bluntly told Crowther. Another issue was slavery. Could Christians keep slaves? The obvious answer was no. Yet in West and East Africa household slavery (as opposed to Caribbean-style field labour) was too deeply entrenched in social relations to be quickly abandoned. Perhaps surprisingly, mission headquarters at home was more willing to compromise. Actual practice on the ground is hard to know at this distance. But it seems that Christian converts in South Africa were allowed to continue 'lobola' – the practice of buying a wife (usually with cattle) – so central to kinship connections and marriage alliance.

But what was the role of the missionary once he had recruited his followers and created a settled community? This too was fiercely debated. Some argued in favour of careful consolidation to maintain the continuity of pastoral care. But others, including David Livingstone, Johan Krapf and Samuel Crowther, urged a more radical policy. The missionary, they said, should be the advance-guard, founding a chain of new stations, not lagging behind among the converted. To Livingstone, who was bored by the round of pastoral life, this had a special appeal. It gave free rein to his ambition to explore the unmapped interior of south-central Africa and diverted attention from the curious fact that this great 'missionary-saint' seems only ever to have made one (short-lived) convert.[41] It also went to the heart of a critical question: how was the missionary effort around the world to be funded? And was it meant to provide pastoral care indefinitely? The societies depended on private donations, assiduously gathered by a vast range of support groups, the mission committees and activists attached to most churches and chapels. They paid the missionaries' salaries and funded their pensions. But the societies had to compete for public attention with other charitable objects. Missionaries were expected to send home reports that could be plundered for copy in the numerous missionary papers and journals, or for missionary stories in Sunday School teaching. Missionaries on leave lectured and preached as part of this effort. Dramatic adventure made better copy than the humdrum of pastoral life. Livingstone's sudden fame after his epic crossing of Africa was a boon to his employer, the London Missionary Society, then much in debt. Livingstone's posthumous fame (he died in 1873) was to prove a huge asset to the missionary cause. His heroic and pious reputation was carefully cultivated by a succession of biographers. In life, however, he was not so easily managed. As a mid Victorian celebrity, he took his image very seriously, declining to drink alcohol on public occasions and ostentatiously wearing his explorer's peaked cap. But he quietly renounced the LMS for a more generous commission from the Royal Geographical Society (and a salary from government) as leader of the ill-fated expedition to promote Christianity and commerce along the Zambezi.

'Commerce, Christianity and civilization' was Livingstone's formula. 'I go back to Africa to make an open path for commerce and Christianity', he told the audience who came to his lecture in Cambridge in 1858.[42] 'We ought to encourage the Africans to cultivate for our markets, as the most effectual means, next to the Gospel, of their elevation.'[43] Without the transformation that commerce would bring, he strongly implied, Christianity could never be properly rooted, and the missionary freed to go further and deeper. This chimed with the views of Henry Venn (1796–1873), the CMS secretary and Victorian grand strategist of the missionary effort. In a famous report, Venn had laid down the missionary's objective: to make himself redundant as quickly as possible. 'The breath of life in a native church', he insisted, depended on 'self-government, self-support, self-extension'[44] so that the 'mission and all missionary agency should be transferred to the "regions beyond"'.[45] But in many parts of the world, the self-supporting native church remained a pious white hope and mission communities fragile and small. The wave of civilization and commerce on which they were to float was often disappointingly puny: they were left to splash in its shallows. Missionaries proved reluctant to hand over control to native-born converts. In West Africa, indeed, the late nineteenth century saw not the replacement of white men by black but precisely the opposite. Africans were now deemed to lack the needed zeal and efficiency.[46] Self-interest, careerism and a strengthening racism may have been part of the story. But in China and India, the expatriate missionaries could make more of a case.

This was because here in particular the pace of conversion was desperately slow. These were (partly) literate societies where missionaries faced confident, articulate and determined opponents. In China, the efforts of 350 Protestant missionaries yielded only 6,000 converts by 1870.[47] In British-ruled India, the record was better, but hardly impressive. After three decades of mission work in the Punjab, there were barely 5,000 converts in the province.[48] Worse still, so some missionaries thought, by accepting untouchable converts, they were 'raking in rubbish', tainting Christianity in the eyes of Muslims and caste Hindus. The way out, it seemed, was to put the missionary effort into something that even high-caste Indians would admire. Elite education became the missionary cause. In the Punjab they established a number of secondary schools including St Stephen's College in Delhi, founded on the model of a Cambridge college (with a 'high table' in its hall). The missionaries who taught there were not the ex-artisans sent to rough it in the South African bush but Oxbridge men and classical scholars like Charles Freer Andrews (1871–1940), who joined the Cambridge Brothers in Delhi in 1904 – and later became a disciple of Gandhi. The mission schools made no attempt to convert: that would have driven their pupils away. Indeed most of their students and 70 per cent of their teachers were non-Christians.[49] Instead they inculcated the ideals of social service, the importance of extra-curricular activity, the necessity of character-building and (in some cases) the virtues of manliness. The aim was transparent: if they could not preach Christianity, they would teach the Christian ethos. Its gradual penetration of the Indian elite – this was the hope – would dissolve the moral foundations of Hinduism and Islam and thus open the path for Christian conversion at the top, as well as the bottom, of Indian society. But the drawback was obvious. Far from promoting an autonomous church, this educational strategy reinforced the dependence on Britain for expatriate teachers and the money to pay for them.

By the end of the century there were some 4,000 British Protestant missionaries abroad (that figure reached 7,500 by 1916).[50] They maintained a vast infrastructure of religious activity. In South Africa alone there were some 610 mission stations and a further 5,000 out-stations, as well as schools and from 1916 the South African Native College at Fort Hare.[51] Although not immune from patriotic feeling and the racial and cultural assumptions that evolution implied, missionaries tried for the most part to distance themselves from the agents of imperial rule because they needed the trust and acceptance of their converts. That applied even more strongly to their relations with white settlers. Commerce and civilization for Livingstone meant excluding white settlers, not encouraging them. But for all their efforts to reconcile their local commitment with their external con-nections, missionaries encountered a deep-rooted resistance to their evangelical message.

This was despite the fact that much of the idiom and apparatus of Christianity proved very attractive to these reluctant converts. Mis-sionary styles of teaching and preaching, the writing and singing of hymns, the biblical imagery of the Fall, the Flood and the Second Coming, were adopted by indigenous practitioners. It was not such a paradox. The missionaries' methods were a challenge to established religions as much as their message: so they encouraged innovation as a means of resistance. But as long as traditional beliefs could still draw support from traditional forms of authority, and their spiritual prac-tices still commanded prestige, Christianity could make only a gradual advance. Even among converts, there was by the late nineteenth cen-tury, a growing resentment against spiritual rule by outsiders. From the 1880s, independent African or 'Ethiopian' churches sprang up in

South Africa, and a growing number of Africans gained theological qualifications at black colleges in the United States. They asserted the claim 'Africa for the Africans', and attracted suspicion and hostility from white settler authorities as well as from missionaries. They were followed in the twentieth century by the 'Zionist' churches, where the missionary emphasis on teaching and preaching was replaced by the rituals required for the struggle against evil spirits and sorcery: baptismal immersion in a 'Jordan' or 'Bethesda'; speaking with tongues; wrestling with demons.[52]

Indeed, in Africa and elsewhere, the great expansion in the number of Christian believers was delayed until after 1900. The twentieth century, not the Victorian, was the great Christian century. This was not really surprising. The Victorians' belief that they could create Christian communities by charismatic example and preaching was heroic but not wise. They were most successful among those for whom traditional social forms and beliefs had failed or been broken. Across much of the world, that process – involving far-reaching social, economic and technological change – had to wait until the late nineteenth century and after, and until indigenous Christians were numerous and organized enough to carry their message in a more accessible idiom. The high-tide of empire and the spring-tide of conversion did not coincide.

WHO DO YOU THINK YOU ARE?
EMPIRE AND IDENTITY

Christian conversion was perhaps the most dramatic way in which an external influence could transform the sense of personal identity by imposing new obligations, as well as cutting off old ones, demanding new loyalties, and bringing new solidarities – in each case transcending old local or even regional ties in a new web of connections. But we might expect empire itself to reshape the sense of identity among those that it ruled over (including the British at home) – although not always in ways that its rulers might welcome.

How far the possession of an empire was *decisive* in shaping the outlook of people in Britain is hotly contested. To one school of

thought, the effects are so obvious as to make inquiry almost superflu-
ous. Racism and racial violence, the insistence on distinct gender
roles, a culture of aggressive masculinity, a virulently exploitative
view of the natural world and its creatures, militaristic values, an
excessive deference to authority, and a tenacious class system: all
could be traced back to the ways in which external domination had
validated hierarchies of class, gender and race and stifled the voice of
dissent. Under the relentless bombardment of imperial propaganda,
preached by the church, purveyed by the press, promoted in literature,
theatre and music hall, and crudely repackaged as 'patriotic' emotion,
the British at home reinvented themselves as an imperial people, with
imperial attitudes and imperial vices. To the opposite school, most of
these claims rest on a methodological fallacy. If the 'real' meaning of
empire is ruling directly over Asians and Africans, there was little sign
that it roused more than a minimal interest outside the small social
groups from whom imperial officials were selected. For everyone else
it was largely irrelevant, a vague, distant blur barely on their horizon.
And while approving references to empire, or even an interest in its
workings, could be found in some items of popular culture, they were
utterly dwarfed by the volume of non-empire references, suggesting at
most a marginal impact on public awareness.[53] Indeed, the very stri-
dency with which empire was preached by imperialists told its own
tale: the propagandists for empire had to shout to be heard.

Consensus on this question is not very likely. But three points are
crucial. First, 'empire' was understood in a variety of ways by people
in Britain, and not just (or even very much) as the vicarious enjoyment of racial overlordship. For the largest segment of British
opinion, empire meant emigration (mainly to countries whose indigenous populations had become all but invisible). For most British
people before 1914, the empire that mattered was the countries of
settlement (not India or tropical Africa), whose societies were more,
not less, democratic than Britain's. British workers (by 1900 some 60
per cent of adult males had the vote) favoured free trade as the key
to prosperity, not imposing closed markets on tropical peoples, and
free trade remained British policy from the 1840s until the economic
catastrophe of 1931. Indeed free trade was widely regarded as much
the most promising way to encourage modernity and representative

government in the non-Western world. And while British opinion was certainly not free from racial condescension, for a vocal division of the Victorian public empire was equated with the assault upon slavery and the protection of Christians abroad from non-Christian oppressors. Empire fed a commitment to humanitarian values, a tradition that persists. These different imaginings of empire – humanitarian, authoritarian, democratic, protectionist, free-trading, religious-minded and militaristic – existed because so many different interest groups in Britain saw it as an arena where their values and aims could be given expression. Empire, in that sense, was not so much a source of identity as a cockpit or battleground where different versions of Britishness competed for space.[54]

Secondly, because empire was imagined and experienced in such various ways, it was highly unlikely that a coherent set of values, or a common sense of identity, could be derived from its shadowy presence – or that British society was decisively influenced (the fashionable word is 'constituted') by its engagement with empire. Insofar as it was, the effects of emigration, free trade ideology and missionary endeavour were likely to have been a great deal more powerful than feelings of racial superiority, or any other emotion aroused by the vicarious enjoyment of colonial mastery. It was in the end the protean nature of empire as a political idea, the extraordinary range of interests and purposes to which it could be rhetorically harnessed (including preparing colonial peoples for self-rule) that allowed its demise amid a mood of public indifference. Thirdly, what might be described as this 'confusion' about empire reflected in part a general uncertainty about where empire started and finished, who or what was included, and where Britain's writ ran. 'The Ocean is . . . a British possession,' declared two Victorian defence experts echoing the popular anthem.[55] Many parts of the world beyond the limits of rule acknowledged a predominant British influence. The precise relation of Egypt (under 'temporary occupation' from 1882) to Britain was a riddle preserved by a sphinx-like diplomacy. A verbal convenience, coined in the 1880s, sanctioned this vagueness. The *Pax Britannica* extended wherever British power was exerted, but its obvious corollary was that maintaining 'British Peace' under very varied conditions required something more subtle than pure domination.

This very vagueness about what empire might mean was what

made it acceptable to such a broad range of opinion and to very different communities. Subscribing to empire did not exclude other ties and identities and might even reinforce them. It has been persuasively argued that for Scots and Welsh, and for many Irish as well, empire was not only a vast field of emigration and opportunity but also supplied a collective focus of loyalty less overweeningly English than the three unions with England out of which the United Kingdom had been made. The Scottish case is the strongest. Glasgow's rise to become a great commercial metropolis, the active share taken by Scots businessmen in Indian and African trade, the part played by Scots in the settlement colonies, the Scottish commitment to missionary endeavour (hugely boosted by Livingstone's fame), the imperial campaigns in which Scottish regiments served, had a double effect. They were a reminder – if reminder were needed – that Victorian Scotland without empire would have been a poor relation of England. And they were a huge reinforcement to Scots self-belief: the conviction that Scotland could survive as a distinct national community, with distinctive traditions and its own path to modernity.[56]

But how far could the British impose an imperial identity on the peoples they colonized? In their spheres of overseas rule in Asia and Africa, they could draw new lines on the map, impose new systems of law, invent new rules about representation, and proclaim new ideals of civilization and progress. They could classify, categorize and sometimes even count their colonial populations (their first census in India was in 1871; in much of tropical Africa, they barely got round to this before the end of their rule). They could reward those who displayed loyalty and punish those who did not. They could erect statues and monuments to signal their intention to stay on indefinitely. But reshaping local identities to an *imperial* design was rarely in their power. Across most of their empire they lacked the resources to reach down very far towards the colonial grass-roots. Mass education was far too expensive for their colonial regimes – and for the mission societies on whom the educational effort was largely devolved, especially in Africa. Nor could they hope to exert their cultural hegemony on the local elite: indeed, what such a thing would amount to in practical terms was bafflingly vague if not completely nonsensical.

In fact, the limits on their strength, and on their manpower above all, meant that the British had to rely on collaboration with the local gatekeepers of culture: indigenous teachers, clerics and law-givers (like the Muslim *ulama*) and the guardians of oral tradition. This was all the more necessary because the British as rulers were obsessed with the need to codify custom. They wanted fixed schedules of rights and claims so that their men on the spot should not be too much in the dark. They consulted the learned men of the district, and turned to chiefs, pundits and *maulvis* for help with their law codes. It was hardly surprising that these experts should claim that their views were embodied in immemorial tradition, and that their privileged status as law-givers enjoyed universal acceptance. In India, for example, the British adopted the Brahmins' version of history: that India had always been a caste-bound society, and that all other castes deferred to Brahmin authority.

Thus far from assaulting local cultural traditions, the British more often allied with the interested parties to fabricate a 'neo-traditional' order, in which the past was re-invented to their mutual convenience. Their motive was obvious and not entirely Machiavellian. They assumed that without the backbone of tradition, the peoples they ruled over would dissolve into fragments, a prey to fanatics and demagogues, rootless and ungovernable. But, crucially, this bargain left room for local cultural elites to respond to the challenge of Western thought and technology. They had time to exploit the new modes of communication and teaching to widen their own reach and reinforce their own message. In the nineteenth century, Muslims, Hindus and Theravada Buddhists among others felt the urge to 'self-strengthen' spiritually. This meant a big effort to 'purify' their belief-system by driving out heresies: the relics of local spirit-worship, reverence for unauthorized gods or saints, or practices borrowed willy-nilly from other religions (many Indian Muslims, for example, had adopted caste status). It meant reasserting the power of the original holy texts. It meant reaching down to the poorest, to reclaim their allegiance and re-impose moral authority. It meant adopting new methods to diffuse religious belief: the Western-style classroom and the medium of print. It meant exploiting the railway and steamship to increase the numbers of pilgrims, who would return as the vectors of a purified faith. It meant, for Muslims especially, mobilizing the faithful – the *umma*

– and awakening their consciousness of a collective identity. Since this religious activity mostly posed no open challenge to colonial authority, the British remained largely indifferent. But they reacted with anger and fear when religion was harnessed to political movements and directed against them. The 'martyrdom' of General Gordon at the hands of Mahdist 'fanatics' at Khartoum in 1885 etched itself deeply on their view of Islam.

Religious revival was not the only cultural activity inside colonial societies, nor the only agent of change in the sense of local identity. Colonialism created the space for a new social class to mediate between rulers and subjects – although that space was much smaller in settler societies where indigenous peoples had been pushed to the margins. This was a new service class fluent in the language and cultural peculiarities of the white master class. It included the bureaucrats, lawyers and doctors adept in the administrative, legal and medical technologies that arrived with colonialism. It also included the teachers whose role was to train this English-speaking elite as well as the writers and journalists who helped these 'new men' to communicate with each other, and with the larger world to which empire now linked them. Their British masters might have hoped that their cultural ambitions would merely equip them as loyal servants of empire. But there was no chance of that. Instead three powerful impulses shaped the outlook and sympathies of this new social elite.

The first was a paradox. To many of those who now served the new rulers, the British arrival had brought liberation. It had allowed escape from the clutches of traditional princes and chiefs, or from rulers more oppressive than the British themselves. To the Hindu *bhadralok* – the 'respectable people' – the overthrow of Bengal's Muslim ruling class after the battle of Plassey (1757) was an historic release. With the British regime came commercial and bureaucratic opportunity. Calcutta became the metropolis of *bhadralok* ambition. Bengal was remade as the *bhadralok*'s country. It was hard not to feel that this dramatic transformation was a providential event. Indeed the 'providential' nature of the British conquest of India was often invoked (with no sense of irony) by those who attended the meetings of the Indian National Congress before 1914.[57]

But this social and cultural remaking was not without strain and set off an anxious debate. In the more open society of colonial Bengal, what did it mean to be honourable, or respectable? How was personal ambition now reconciled with religious obligation or the demands of the family: especially the Hindu 'joint family' with its 'corporate' life? What role, or rights, should women enjoy? – a highly sensitive question when social convention had required the 'seclusion' of women. What forms of dress were tasteful and moral? What forms of leisure? What kind of reading? What should education be teaching and who should be teachers? Discussing these questions prompted new kinds of writing and the use of new media. Novels (such as those of Bankim Chandra Chattopadhyay, Bengal's first modern novelist) and newspapers (like the *National Paper* founded by the wealthy Tagore family), pamphlets, poems and plays became the literary arena where social questions were asked and new social types were paraded and parodied. A new literary language was fashioned to carry new kinds of message. It encouraged a new sense of place, a new feeling for landscape, a new sense of history, and a new sense of nation.

The third impulse was patriotic and political. It reflected the feeling that social and cultural transition would remain incomplete until the colonial community was welded into a nation. It sprang from resentment among the educated elite at the racial contempt displayed by the British, and at their exclusion from power. It echoed the belief, to which liberals in Britain subscribed, that self-rule was the key to moral and political virtue: without it a people would be stunted at best. Its most vehement spokesman in colonial Bengal was Surendranath Banerjea (1848–1925). Banerjea was an ardent reformer. He denounced caste-distinctions, the practice of child-marriage, the ban on widows' remarriage and the seclusion of women. The British mission in India was to help 'in the formation of a manly, energetic, self-reliant Indian character' and introduce 'the arts of self-government'.[58] Through his newspaper *The Bengalee* and his political movement, Banerjea pressed for constitutional change and for the removal of British officials in favour of Indians.

But, oddly enough, neither Banerjea nor the other politicians from west and north India who formed the Indian National Congress in 1885 demanded the end of the connection with Britain. On the contrary: they insisted that they wished to preserve it, and that Indian self-government would bring them closer to Britain. This is often dismissed as tabby cat politics, as if they were afraid to strike hard at the Raj or rouse a mass movement against it. These complaints are naïve. The Congress politicians understood perfectly well the constraints that they faced. They could have raised a mass movement, but only by playing upon religious emotions or social and caste grievances. Both would be sources of intense division and danger. They grasped instead that a nation in India must be built from the top down, by gradually drawing the masses towards its core institutions, above all a parliament. They learned this from Britain, and from the example of Gladstone. Indeed, they were converts to liberalism rather than disciples of nationalism. But they faced a dilemma that became increasingly cruel. They had to persuade the British officials to hand over power willingly, not to force them to fight, risking upheaval and conflict. Their tragedy was that the British valued India too much to let it go easily, while they themselves had no means to drive them from power. The frustrations this caused helped breed an extremist minority: terror by bomb began in pre-1914 Bengal.[59] In the interwar years it fired the mass nationalism that Gandhi inspired. But as the first Congress leaders foresaw, the mass emotions it fed on proved a fatal source of division.

The first generation of Indian political leaders had embarked on a conscious attempt to graft what they saw as British political virtues on to an indigenous stem: to make a nation from above. There were other social groups in Asia and Africa for whom the British connection became a key part of their local identity and social cohesion. The most obvious cases were among coastal communities who enjoyed a privileged status as commercial intermediaries between British merchants and interior peoples. The so-called 'Straits Chinese' – Chinese born in the Malayan peninsula – were very well placed when the British arrived in Southeast Asia at Penang in 1786 and Singapore in 1819. As trade with China grew rapidly, they became agents and compradors for British merchants and traded on their own. They controlled the opium traffic in the region, the source of much British revenue in Singapore as in India. Wealthy, propertied and English-speaking, they filled the official posts that the British created to manage the rising population of migrant Chinese who came to Singapore, the boom city of the region. They founded newspapers and schools, and managed the civic and ritual life of the Chinese majority. They attacked superstition and debased ritual practices in favour of 'rational Confucian reform'. They abandoned the queue ('pigtail') and adopted a distinct style of dress to reflect an Anglo-Chinese outlook: waistcoats and bow-ties, with Chinese-type jackets and mandarin collars. They expressed fervent loyalty to the British Empire: a huge demonstration celebrated the British capture of Pretoria in June 1900, fondly imagined at the time as the end of the South African War.

But the Straits Chinese were not British puppets nor mere mimicmen. They retained a keen sense of their Chinese culture and origins. They fostered their connections with China and expressed public devotion to their 'ancestral country'. They cast themselves in the role of bringing modernization to China at a time (c. 1900) when its collapse and partition seemed a probable fate. With the British behind them, they might expect a large influence. The British, for their own reasons, encouraged this ambition, and indulged their dual loyalty. It was only once China's revolutionary course had become more pronounced after 1918, and the British started to treat Chinese nationalism as a threat to their empire, that the Straits Chinese began to look inwards, and imagine a political future without British rule.[60]

Like the Straits Chinese, the Krio, or Creoles, of West Africa were a commercial diaspora that clung to the Coast and throve under British protection. Their 'home' was Freetown in Sierra Leone, ruled by the British but colonized by black freedmen and ex-slaves from British America and 'Liberated Africans' taken from slave-ships by Royal Navy patrols.[61] The Krio elite saw themselves as the agents of Christianity, commerce and civilization. They spread along the West African coast as merchants and missionaries, teachers and clerks. They linked the British firms in the ports with their inland suppliers and customers. They included 'mulattoes' – the offspring of whites and African women. They esteemed education and the forms of bourgeois respectability (temperance was an issue). They adopted British styles of dress and deportment. They were the 'Black English': some called England 'home'. Facing inland towards the 'barbarous' kingdoms of Dahomey and Ashanti, the warring Yoruba states and the Muslim emirates to the north, it was hardly surprising that they regarded British expansion as a highly desirable change in the region's geopolitics.

But like the Straits Chinese, the Krio Black English had their own local agenda. They saw themselves as the vanguard of British influence on the Coast but also inland. They dreamed of an 'Imperial British West Africa', perhaps one day to be a great self-governing dominion (like Canada) but under their command.[62] They resented the arrival of ever more British expatriates – as administrators, businessmen, missionaries and doctors – towards the end of the century. They resented even more their own gradual demotion as a troublesome minority when the British decided to rule their new inland empire through traditional chiefs and customary (not English) law. Though some were prosperous enough, they were too few and too scattered to stage an effective resistance, or to play the same political role as the Straits Chinese. Freetown was not Singapore: Imperial West Africa was four separate colonies. By the interwar years, when their resentment began to boil over, they could make little headway against colonial regimes that rested on indirect rule and the British alliance with traditional leaders.

But perhaps the most remarkable group made by the British connection was the Mfengu or Fingoes of colonial South Africa. It is hard to be sure how they first began to emerge as a distinctive community. The most convincing suggestion is that they began as the victims of the so-called *mfecane* or 'grinding' – the intra-African conflicts over people and land set off by the rise of the Zulu warrior state in the late eighteenth century.[63] As refugees among the pastoralist Xhosa, they became grain cultivators ('women's work') and then traders, low-prestige occupations that attracted growing mistrust as the Xhosa conflict with whites began to intensify. The key moment came in the 1835 war between Xhosa and British. The Mfengu broke with their Xhosa overlords and allied with the British.[64] Their reward was a land grant in what became the Ciskei, where they were settled as a buffer on the new eastern frontier. Their formation as a distinct ethnic group under British protection was symbolized in a great public act still remembered today. In May 1836, led by John Ayliff, a missionary, some 17,000 Mfengu swore a three-fold allegiance to God, the mission and the British Crown under a milkwood tree in the frontier hamlet of

Peddie.[65] They became British subjects. For the next fifty years the Mfengu were to serve as British auxiliaries in the Cape's frontier wars, and to take their reward in cattle and land.

The Mfengu were quick to take advantage of mission education and the skills it provided. By the late nineteenth century, they settled as far afield as Kimberley and Rhodesia (modern Zimbabwe). Within the Cape Colony, they formed an African elite. 'When I was a boy,' remembered Nelson Mandela (a Xhosa), 'the amaMfengu were the most advanced section of the community, and furnished our clergymen, policemen, teachers, clerks and interpreters. They were also among the first to become Christians . . . they confirmed the missionaries' axiom that to be civilised was to be Christian and to be Christian was to be civilised.'[66] The Mfengu were loyalists, but their loyalty was not blind. They were among the first Africans to use the vote (under the Cape's qualified but colour-blind franchise) and to mobilize against discriminatory laws. A Mfengu, John Tengo Jabavu, became the leading Cape African politician and newspaper editor. As with the Krio and Straits Chinese, their British connection conferred a sense of political purpose as well as a distinctive identity. In May 1908, they celebrated 'Fingo Emancipation Day', a blunt reassertion of their British allegiance just at the time when the negotiation to unify South Africa under white domination was reaching its climax. The message was obvious. The Mfengu were not alone in believing that their British connection was the only defence against settler oppression: among mixed race 'Cape Coloureds' it was felt even more deeply.[67] But like the Krio they found that their claims counted for little against the brutal realities of collaborative politics. It was whites in South Africa, like traditional rulers in West Africa, who held the high cards.

Empire – as foreign rule – was an agent of cultural change. But it was only one among several. It often arrived in harness with others: the expansion of trade; new kinds of consumption; swifter methods of transport; the codification of language in script; the widening of literacy; new communication techniques, including regular letter post and the telegraph; new kinds of schooling; new forms of literature, not least newspapers and pamphlets; new medical knowledge; new notions of leisure and taste; a different and demanding religion. Some or all might have arrived in a region before empire itself and sprung from local initiative: the best example is Egypt. Empire might act to strengthen the impact of such changes and exploit their potential for imperial advantage. But its men on the spot just as often displayed a timid desire to shore up the old order, both cultural and political. They usually found allies who were eager to help them. Yet there were also very many in every colonial society to whom the new cultural forms were deeply attractive. They offered a new individualism: the liberation from custom, worn-out religious ritual, the iron grip of lineage or a prescribed occupation. It was this promise of escape from the grinding rigidity of their own social systems – not least in the treatment of women – that they wanted the British to honour. Indian liberals such at Banerjea or Motilal Nehru (father of Jawaharlal) would have been astonished to learn that they were the victims of what recent writers have called 'epistemic violence' – the wrecking of old knowledge systems by colonial power.

Perhaps it should go without saying that culturally, as politically, empire was disruptive but also creative. But as a cultural force it had little coherence. Both at home and abroad, empire took different forms and assumed different meanings. It attracted different allies, often with little in common. Its mystique was invoked to support multiple causes, some contradictory. In the non-Western world, it sometimes appeared as a juggernaut crushing all in its path, sometimes as a creaky under-engined jalopy barely able to stay on the road or carry its passengers. Its political agents were rarely self-confident of its cultural power. They avoided confrontation with major religions and dreaded arousing suspicion by seeming too close to their own. They could hardly prevent adept local elites from borrowing the techniques and ideas that colonialism brought with it, but they had little control over the uses they made of them. The wider impact of empire as an alien force to resist by religious or cultural revival was beyond their administrative grasp and perhaps their comprehension. Since they could not know the future, they were mainly impressed by the brittle stationary state of the local cultures they met and the danger of chaos if they were challenged too directly. Their shrill calls for progress concealed their suspicion that it would be painfully slow in the deeper interiors of the non-Western world. The modern complaint that they were remaking the world as a crude imitation of the West or its cultural lackey would have struck them as strange. From the other side of the hill, the local guardians of culture took a more urgent view. But neither had any idea of the dramatic acceleration in the pace of social and cultural change that was to set in after the mid twentieth century. It is really the shadow of that which has so hugely transformed our current perspective on the impact of empire.

10
Defending Empire

THE GOUTY GIANT

'Once the British Empire became world-wide,' it was once shrewdly remarked, 'the sun never set on its crises.'[1] This moment had come during the Seven Years' War of 1756–63, when the British added an empire in Asia to their Atlantic possessions. From then on their thinking was forced to be global. It was not just the case that their restless expansion multiplied the list of their enemies, adding Marathas and Rohillas to Shawnees and Delawares, and to their old rivals in Europe, Spain, France and the Dutch. This global dimension contained a new threat. For it was now all too likely that a frontier war in South Asia or an American rebellion would suck in British troops and divert British sea power just at the moment when they were needed elsewhere to foil the designs of their European foes, or repel an invasion at home. The price of empire on a global scale was not just the means to contain an endless succession of crises in different parts of the world, but also the resources to cope when a chain reaction occurred, when danger in one zone exposed weakness in others. From that point of view, the imperial triumph of 1763 was merely the prelude to a fifty-year lesson in what could go wrong.

As we shall see, victory in 1815 after nearly twenty years of world war eased the worst of these fears for more than five decades. But by the late nineteenth century, the strategic dilemmas that had obsessed British statesmen before Waterloo and Trafalgar came back to haunt them. Their empire had become a territorial colossus. The extent of their holdings dwarfed those of their rivals, in population and wealth as much as in area. They had taken a lion's share in the partitions of Africa and Southeast Asia (in Burma, Malaya and Borneo). They had reacted with outrage (some of it genuine) when European 'interlopers' intruded upon regions like West and East Africa or the Persian Gulf that they had reserved for themselves as 'spheres of interference',[2] if not of protection or rule. Their calmer advisers warned against the collective resentment that this attitude bred. 'It has sometimes seemed to me,' wrote one, 'that to a foreigner reading our press, the British Empire must appear as a huge giant sprawling over the globe, with gouty finger and toes stretching in every direction which cannot be approached without eliciting a scream.'[3]

To make matters worse, the whole balance of world politics now seemed to have shifted against Britain. Two aggressive new claimants to overseas empire, Germany and Italy, demanded their place in the tropical sun. Britain's most dangerous rivals, Russia and France, formed an alliance in 1894, the so-called '*Franco-Russe*', with French capital fuelling the Tsar's Asian ambitions. Small fry, like Portugal or the king of the Belgians, were emboldened by this to twist the lion's tail or pull at his whiskers. Public opinion in the colonial powers, great and small, was whipped into hysteria by the fear of exclusion from the as yet uncolonized world with its eldorados of trade or mineral wealth. The communications revolution of the late-century world encouraged this mood. The steamship and railway turned every part of the globe into a potential province of Europe and sharpened the appetite of all empire-builders. A line of rail laid down in the African sand was as good as economic annexation. It created an interest that must be defended. The web of telegraph wires destroyed the illusion of distance. It brought every squabble or jostle between freelance imperialists, however remote, unseemly or trivial, into the public arena within a matter of hours to stir patriotic emotions. British diplomats raged vainly against France's 'reptile press', forgetting their own. Amid the hubbub of prospectuses, propaganda and projects (not to mention the blizzard of fraudulent schemes), it was easy to think that the competition of empires had entered the end-game. The frontiers were closing, and not just in America. The division of the world was now under way.

To be left out in the cold, without a fair share, was to risk future attrition by the premiership of 'world-states'.

Indeed, after 1900 it seemed increasingly likely that those parts of the world that had so far escaped the net of partition would soon begin to crack open. The weight of Europe's commercial, techno-logical and ideological onslaught would divide and demoralize, or simply demolish, the surviving *anciens régimes* in China, Korea, the Ottoman Empire, Iran, Morocco and Ethiopia. A vast belt of terri-tory from the Atlantic to East Asia would come up for grabs in an unpredictable sequence, made even more baffling by a mass of local actors and accidents. The world-states would be forced into a scram-ble with far more at stake, and far less scope for concession, than in the partition of Africa, that bargain basement of empire. The win-ners this time would have scooped the pool. An indefinite hegemony might be the reward.

We know now with hindsight that it did not turn out like this. But those charged with safeguarding Britain's interests and spheres could not assume that it wouldn't. Their task was far from straightforward. To defend Britain's empire was not simply a matter of building fleets and fortresses, or stationing gunboats and garrisons, however numer-ous or far-flung. It turned instead on an extraordinary range of theoretical and practical problems, both strategic and political, that persisted as long as the empire itself.

At the root of all these was the peculiar geography of British expansion. The shape of Britain's empire reversed every notion of military logic. A properly planned empire, it might be supposed, would expand steadily outward. Its metropolitan core would be carefully guarded by its most trustworthy provinces. Beyond them would lie in graduated succession the less valuable zones and, out on the edge, the buffer-states and client-kingdoms that could be dis-pensed with if necessary. The well-designed empire, when it came under strain, could expect to fall back on its wall: the Roman *limes*; the 'Great Wall' of China; the *chert* lines that guarded the Russian-occupied steppe; Hitler's 'West Wall'. Behind these defences, it could restore its morale, recoup its strength and rethink its war plans. But if this was the model of designer-imperialism, the British version of empire was a ridiculous parody. Its head and centre lay only twenty-two miles from what had usually been its most dangerous enemy. Its most valuable territories were not compact provinces arrayed close to the centre but lay on the other side of the world, six months away by sail, and at least three weeks by steam. After 1860, nearly half the British army was stationed in Indian cantonments, many miles and days from the nearest seaport. Much of the empire, with the exception of India and Canada, resembled a vast archipelago strewn round the world from Hong Kong to the Falkland Islands. 'The British Empire is, for the purpose of a war with any Power except Russia and the United States, equivalent to a number of islands scattered over the oceans,' remarked a Late Victorian expert.[4]

This bizarre configuration was not without benefits. But it raised many issues. One of the most crucial, a source of constant debate, was Britain's connection with Europe. It was a plausible view that involvement in Europe, the cockpit of dynastic intrigue and, by the late nineteenth century, of competitive militarisms, was a deadly distraction from Britain's true destiny. The open sea and the outer world were where her real interests lay: they yielded the biggest returns and imposed the least cost. Here Britain's advantage in sea power, already apparent by 1700, could be exploited to pillage her rivals' possessions, while protecting the Home Islands against any chance of invasion. This (in the eighteenth century) was the 'American' or 'Blue Water' strategy.[5] It remained deeply attractive into the late 1930s when fear of a second Great War made Europe's internecine conflicts an object of loathing. To waste Britain's strength defending an indefensible peace treaty seemed the 'midsummer of madness', not least to the leaders of the white dominions, Canada, Australia, New Zealand and South Africa. The veteran imperialist Leopold Amery, later a member of Churchill's War Cabinet, even hoped for a German *Mitteleuropa* that would leave the British Empire alone.[6] But this strategy contained, so its critics insisted, a fatal misjudgement.

A blue water strategy assumed that, if it came to a crisis, Britain could stand against any combination of foes. Although this had sometimes been possible, it came at a very high price. One difficulty was that it required a huge navy, not just one bigger than that of any likely opponent, but larger than those of any combination of foes. But a much greater danger loomed in the shadows. From the time of Elizabeth, British leaders had always been mindful that Europe's volatile politics might destroy the balance of power between its quarrelsome rulers. If one of Europe's great powers were to win the struggle for mastery and defeat the others, it would command the resources of the whole of the mainland: its armies and navies as well as its trade, treasure, industries, shipping and manpower. It would control the Baltic and also the Mediterranean. It could wreck British commerce (for which the European market was vital). Above all, it would soon have the means to threaten invasion and perhaps to carry it out. To avert such an appalling catastrophe, argued the critics of blue water imperialism, required constant attention to the shifts and alignments of the European powers, monitoring the minutest adjustments in the balance of power like a modern seismologist on the lookout for earthquakes. That was merely the start. The real purpose behind this ceaseless flow of intelligence was to exert British influence and (if need be) to choose Britain's allies so that no single power could become hegemonic in Europe. The grim logic of that was that if diplomacy failed, Britain must be willing to make entangling alliances, to spend freely on allies and, if it came to the worst, to send armies to fight in the continent's wars. Indeed, again and again, despite the siren appeal of blue water isolation, British leaders had accepted that Britain and its empire must be defended in Europe: in the Nine Years' War of the English Succession (1688–97); in the War of Spanish Succession (1702–13); in the War of the Austrian Succession (1740–48); the Seven Years' War (1756–63); in the Revolutionary and Napoleonic Wars (what the Victorians called the 'Great War' of 1793–1815); and in the First and Second World Wars of the twentieth century. 'Those who talk of confining a great war to naval operations only,' said Pitt, Britain's grand strategist in the Seven Years' War, 'speak without knowledge or experience.'[7]

Yet a continental commitment was bound to make them very uneasy – for at least four different reasons. They knew very well – and from bitter experience – that wars on the continent were extremely expensive. Each major war from 1690 onwards had created huge debts, increased the burdens of tax, and caused widespread domestic unrest as the strains made themselves felt. It was pressures like these that had pushed British ministers towards taxing America after 1763, with disastrous results. Secondly, when the size of armies exploded and mass conscription became general among the European powers (a nineteenth-century development), there were many voices to warn that fighting in Europe would make conscription inevitable in Britain itself and break British freedom on the militarist wheel. Thirdly, there was deep hesitation among governments dependent on parliamentary support (and hence on public opinion) to bind themselves into any long-term alliance with another European state, for fear that when their support was invoked, opinion at home would refuse them its backing. Yet to insist on a free hand in all their diplomatic relations was bound to deepen mistrust among their neighbours in Europe and perhaps to weaken their voice at a critical time (one view of the reason why the Germans discounted intervention by Britain in July 1914). Fourthly, it could also be argued that defending the borders of their imperial estate, especially in India, was already burden enough for a relatively small army (between 120,000 and 180,000 for most of the century before 1914). Nor was it easy to see how an army that was usually employed in far-flung locations and against 'uncivilized' foes, could be quickly deployed against 'first-class' opponents trained to fight under modern conditions and with heavy equipment. To Lord Salisbury (no great admirer of generals) to train for such an event was merely play-acting. 'Our army will not find itself in that condition in a blue moon,' he remarked in 1899. 'What they ought to practise is the rapid expedition of a relatively small force to any point in the Empire where it might be wanted. Your business is that of a military fire brigade . . .'[8]

It is easy to see why, whatever their views on a continental commitment, most British leaders remained studiously vague over where and how they would act militarily if Europe's balance of power came to be seriously threatened. Indeed, quite apart from the European complication, defending the empire was controversial enough. The most basic dispute turned on which threat was most real and whose need was most urgent. In the eighteenth century, planters in the British West Indies vied with the American colonists to demand

British protection against attack by the French. In the nineteenth century, governors in Cape Colony competed with settlers in New Zealand (fearful of Maori), consuls in China and viceroys in India for the line battalions of infantry, the spear of British imperialism. In the twentieth century, London faced fretful demands to make the defence of Australia, the safeguarding of Egypt (the Clapham Junction of empire), the protection of the Home Islands or of the Atlantic sea-lanes its greatest priority. Bound up with these quarrels was the question not just of whom to defend but of where and how. On almost every frontier of empire and along its main routes, a case could be made for a further advance: an anchorage here, a coastline there, a fortress, a river, a mountain, a hill, a state in decay, a vital oasis, a recalcitrant tribe. Annexation, occupation, or a military presence would shorten the line, lower its costs and strengthen the empire. Or so it was argued. Seasoned politicians had learned to be sceptical. 'If you believe the soldiers,' Salisbury told an excitable viceroy, 'nothing is safe.'[9] His nephew A. J. Balfour, one of the few British prime ministers to study strategy seriously, was also a sceptic. When Lord Curzon insisted in 1918 that the protection of India required the occupation of Persia and perhaps of the Caucasus, Balfour remarked that the gateways to India were 'getting further and further from India and I do not know how far west they are going to be brought by the General Staff'.[10] But as Balfour found out, it was not always possible to resist the demand, and not always wise. Much of the strange shape that the British Empire had taken was dictated in fact by the need to guard its sea-lanes, and to hold the bastions and buffers that permitted the imperial archipelago to be ruled on a loose rein.

In times of anxiety the most pressing question of all was where to station the navy, Britain's prime weapon. During the wars of the long eighteenth century (1690–1815), it seemed obvious that the 'wooden wall' of the navy was needed to keep Britain itself safe from invasion. But how best that could be done caused sometimes bitter dispute. Should the navy maintain a close blockade of the main French naval base (at Brest in Brittany) to stop the French fleet from venturing into the Channel? Perhaps, but the wear and tear of blockade was notoriously costly, and there was no guarantee that in a fog or a gale, it might not fail altogether.[11] It also required a large preponderance in numbers since worn-out ships and crews had to be rotated periodically. But there was also the question of whether the navy's firepower should be diverted elsewhere. France maintained a large fleet at Toulon on its Mediterranean coast. If it was allowed to break out, and support the fleet based at Brest, it might tip the balance of strength in the Channel. A British Mediterranean squadron was required to guard against this. But where should *it* be stationed in wartime? So far from its home base, it could not blockade Toulon closely.[12] It might fall back on Gibraltar and seal the gateway into the Atlantic. But that would allow the French fleet to control the central and eastern Mediterranean, destroy British trade, and (worse still) join forces with Spain. There was no easy answer. Another conundrum was posed by the demand for protection by mercantile shipping, the prey of enemy cruisers. When shipping entered the Western Approaches to the Irish Sea and the Channel, it was especially vulnerable. But guarding a convoy was a huge distraction from what the navy's leaders saw as its main task in war.

This task was personified in the heroic figure of Nelson, perhaps its greatest exemplar. It was expressed in the maxim that the object of maritime war was 'command of the sea'. That could be gained only by a decisive engagement with the enemy fleet to ensure its destruction or capture. Once that was secured, policing the sea-lanes would minimize the losses to commerce, and naval power could be used to damage the enemy further. The logic of this was not the stalemate of blockade but finding a way to bring the foe to a battle at almost all costs. The deeper logic, of course, was that naval power must be concentrated in the likeliest arena of combat. As we shall see, this logic was not always welcome, especially to those faraway colonies on the other side of the globe who feared a local invasion. 'If the British Fleet were defeated in the North Sea,' Winston Churchill (then First Lord of the Admiralty) declared in 1913, 'all the dangers which it now wards off from the Australian Dominions would be liberated ... The situation in the Pacific will

14. The Royal Navy and its stations, 1875 and 1898

In 1875 the total number of ships in commission was 241, of which 20 were ships of the line. Naval estimates amounted to about £9.5m and some 34,000 seamen, boys, and marines were employed.

In 1898 the total number of ships in commission was 287, of which 52 were battleships. Naval estimates amounted to about £23.8m and some 97,000 seamen, boys, and marines were employed.

Wellington

Fiji ▲

Cape York ▲
Sydney ●
Melbourne ●
Adelaide ●   Australia 11
                              16
Perth ▲

Weihaiwai ▲   China 22
                       27
                Hong Kong ●
                East Indies 13
                             10
Labuan ●
Singapore ●

Calcutta ●

Trincomalee ●
Colombo ●

Bombay ●
Aden ●
Seychelles ▲
Mauritius ●

Mombasa ▲
Zanzibar ▲

Heligoland ●
Mediterranean 18
               38
Ionian Islands ■
Malta ●   Cyprus ▲
Alexandria ●
Lagos ●   Cape and 11
               West Africa 20
               Cape Town ●

Home 52
      15

Gibraltar ●
Gambia ●
Sierra Leone ●
Ascension ●
St Helena ●

Halifax ●
Bermuda ●
North America 15
West Indies 15
Antigua ●
St Lucia ●
Trinidad ●
Jamaica ●

Falkland Islands ●

Pacific 8
         9

Esquimalt ●

● bases 1848 and 1898
■ bases in 1848 relinquished by 1898
▲ additional bases acquired by 1898

Number of ships   Home 52   1875
based on station   15   1898

be absolutely regulated by the decisions on the North Sea.'[13] But Australian and New Zealand politicians, nervous of Japanese sea power, found it hard to believe that a navy based in the Orkneys was the real guarantee of their regional safety. In fact, the pattern of sea war in 1914–18 justified Churchill's assertion. But after 1919, when it was no longer clear whether the main naval threat would come in Northern Europe, the Mediterranean or from Japan in East Asia, the problem of where to concentrate Britain's naval power, and how it would be able to achieve command of the sea, became a great deal more complex. When Britain was faced with the prospect of a combined onslaught by Germany, Italy and Japan – as seemed increasingly likely after 1936 – it appeared almost insoluble. Indeed, the final eclipse of British sea power (masked by victory in the Second World War) was now very near.

For an empire that depended so much on its maritime links, on the profits of trade, and, at its centre, upon imports of food (critically so by the late nineteenth century), the size, deployment and firepower of the navy were bound to seem critical. But as we have seen these were not the only considerations that those defending the empire were forced to weigh up. They had to determine where and how to preserve British influence in Europe, partly if not mainly for Britain's own safety. They had to balance their friendships in Europe against the urge to expand on the frontiers of empire, the source of much friction. They had to decide whether extending the empire, or its sphere of influence, at any particular place or time would improve its security or risk (in a modern phrase) 'overstretch' – often a fine calculation not easily made. Above all, perhaps, they had to be mindful of three fundamental conditions which (with the advantage of hindsight) we can see held the key to British world power. The first was the need to avoid isolation. 'There is no such thing as isolation, least of all for an island state seated on the world's highway and the centre of a maritime empire,' remarked a Late Victorian commentator.[14] An active diplomacy was always required to fend off such a nightmare. The second was the danger that an empire strung round the world might be overwhelmed by a great concentration of power on the 'super-continent' of Eurasia, perhaps by one superpower, perhaps by an alliance. This was the peril, most brilliantly spelt out by Halford Mackinder in 1904, which haunted the policymakers.[15] The British had to decide how far they could diminish this threat by a 'forward movement' in Asia – and made a dramatic and fateful decision in March 1918 (as we will see in a moment). Thirdly, in ways that were glimpsed only dimly before 1930, what made their world empire strategically viable at bearable cost was a world-historical accident. It was the unique combination of a real European balance of power after 1815 and the weakness of East Asia that created the space for Britain's global imperialism. When those conditions broke down, as they threatened to do by the mid 1930s, it was an open question whether the 'great liner' (Churchill's colourful phrase) could survive at all.

THE ROLLERCOASTER OF WAR
1755–1815

On 8 June 1755, without a declaration of war, a British squadron in the Western Atlantic intercepted a convoy of French troop-transports bound for Quebec. Most escaped in the fog, but two were captured. Over the ensuing six months, the British seized more than 300 French ships before 'peace' was formally ended. For much of the next sixty years, the British were at war to defend their safety at home, their position in Europe and their overseas empire. They lurched from victory to disaster, and from recovery to stalemate. In an astonishing climax, they passed from victorious peace in 1814 to the prospect of renewed struggle in Europe (had Napoleon won at Waterloo) and to the grand geopolitical triumph that Wellington's victory assured in June 1815. In the ninety-nine-year interval that followed, the British enjoyed almost uniquely favourable conditions to expand overseas. They took full advantage of them.

In the 1750s, however, the task was largely defensive. In their American colonies, they were alarmed by the signs that the French were tightening their grip on the transmontane interior, controlling the Ohio and Mississippi from the two ends of their empire in Quebec and New Orleans. An expedition under General Braddock, a veteran of the gaming tables, dispatched to seize the French forward position at Fort Duquesne (today's Pittsburgh) was a costly fiasco. For the next three years the British and their colonial militias struggled to make headway against the ring of French forts that fenced in British America: Duquesne, Ticonderoga, Louisbourg (on Cape Breton Island) and, above all, the fortress-citadel of Quebec. In Europe, their position looked, if anything, grimmer. In a dramatic reversal of existing alliances, France and Austria, the continent's principal military powers, formed a new partnership. Since Austria then ruled the southern Low Countries (modern Belgium) – the historic launch-pad for the invasion of Britain – and the Bourbons reigned in both France and Spain, Britain's bitterest rivals in the Atlantic and Americas, this new constellation looked exceptionally threatening. It was little more than a decade since France had supported the last great Jacobite Rising in Britain (that of Bonny Prince Charlie); and both an invasion of Britain and a settling of Atlantic accounts could not be ruled out. So to avoid isolation and restore the balance in Europe, the British threw in their lot with Frederick of Prussia, Austria's *bête noire*, whose land-grab of Silesia (an Austrian province) had provoked Habsburg wrath. It seemed a desperate expedient.

Against all the odds, however, Frederick turned out to be an inspired army commander. Kept afloat by British subsidies, he scored a series of remarkable victories over his much grander opponents.[16] Meanwhile, the tide turned in the American theatre and in the maritime war. In 1758, the British captured Duquesne and Louisbourg, opening the way into the western interior and the Gulf of St Lawrence, and 1759 was the 'year of victories'. In September, almost at its last gasp, the expedition under James Wolfe sent to capture Quebec scrambled up from the river to confront the French garrison on the Heights of Abraham. In a short bloody struggle, they forced its surrender, and with Quebec in their hands now held the key to French North America. Two months later, in a dramatic pursuit, Admiral Hawke's Channel squadron chased France's Brest fleet into the dangerous rocks and shoals of Quiberon Bay and destroyed it there.[17] The wreck of French naval power ended all risk of invasion and exposed France's Atlantic empire (including its

Caribbean sugar colonies) to ruin. In India, meanwhile, a powerful French squadron sent to disrupt British trade and strengthen French influence (in South India especially) was kept at bay, until in January 1761 the British captured Pondicherry, France's main base in India. And in a curious finale, when Spain eventually entered the war – perhaps to limit the scope of British success – its reward was disaster. In 1762, the British captured Havana, Spain's Caribbean Gibraltar guarding its sea-route to Mexican silver; and also Manila in the Western Pacific, with a scratch force of fewer than 1,000 men – British regulars and sepoys from the East India Company's army.[18] When Russia – which had joined France and Austria against the Prussian *parvenu* – withdrew from the war, it was effectively over.

The scale of British gains was astonishing. A 'defensive' war had yielded imperial bounty beyond the wildest dreams of 1755. At the Peace of Paris in 1763, the British received the whole of North America east of the Mississippi, including Spanish Florida, as well as Senegal in West Africa, a slave-trading sphere. France abandoned its claims in South India and renounced the right to maintain a military presence in Bengal, the scene of Clive's victory at Plassey in 1757. But there was a large European fly in this sweet colonial ointment. Handsome as their overseas victories had been, the British had not been able to defeat France *in Europe*. Nor did they want to prolong their war with Spain. Colonial concessions were necessary to persuade France and Spain to make peace; to secure France's withdrawal from the German lands it had occupied (a key protection for Prussia); and to deny Austria allies with which to continue the war. French Guadeloupe, Havana and Manila were all handed back – to a furious popular outcry in Britain. A British overseas empire free from all rivals, or the fear of attack, was not to be had after all. Indeed, there soon began to be signs that the British had overextended themselves. And then – worse still – that even the victory that they had won was not great enough to ease the longstanding constraints of their situation in Europe: the need to avoid isolation and maintain a 'friendly' balance of power to prevent a grand coalition being formed up against them.[19]

This might not have mattered so much except for the breach with their American subjects. That too was a cost of their victory in war. To limit their military burdens, British ministers decided to restrict white American settlement of the Indian interior behind the 'Proclamation Line' of 1763 – a line drawn through the woods to pin back the frontier farmers and avaricious land speculators (of which George Washington was a conspicuous example) for whom Indian land was an irresistible lure. To reduce their war debts and head off resentment at home, they also resolved to tax the Americans modestly for their imperial protection. Both schemes turned out to be catastrophic politically. By the mid 1770s, they faced a serious settler revolt. That was dangerous enough. But in 1778, it got very much worse. For it was now that the French, having patiently awaited their chance for revenge, intervened in the struggle on the American side. In 1779, they were again joined by Spain and in 1780 by the Dutch, both eager to trounce the overconfident British and check their Atlantic and Asian expansion. (As well as their Caribbean possessions, Curaçao, St Eustatius and Surinam, the Dutch ruled Ceylon, Java, Sumatra and the Spice Islands.) In 1780, an Armed Neutrality, orchestrated by Russia, aligned the rest of Europe against Britain behind the demand that neutral shipping should not be affected by the British blockade. In these appalling conditions, the American struggle became almost a side-show. The British faced invasion at home and the loss of their Caribbean 'crown jewels' – chief amongst them Jamaica. With some ninety sail-of-the-line (i.e. battleships), they were badly outnumbered by the total (116) that France and Spain could muster against them. By furious efforts, they parried the threat in home waters and, in Rodney's Caribbean victory of 'the Saints' (named after the group of islets between Guadeloupe and Dominica where the battle was fought) in 1782, regained control of the Atlantic. But for the American war, it was too little too late. In the critical phase when its Atlantic lifeline was cut, Cornwallis's army, their main American strike-force, was squeezed into surrender at Yorktown.[20] With no will to go on, the British went to the conference table desperate to break up the coalition against them. Conceding American independence was the only sure way to end the colonies' alliance with France – the worst of all worlds – and preserve their commercial connection with Britain.[21] The one bright spot in this darkness was their naval successes in India where French efforts to help Haidar Ali – the Company's great foe in South India – had been decisively thwarted.[22] Had the French squadron succeeded in blockading the British base in Madras, and cut its vital links with Bengal, Haidar Ali might have crushed the ill-supplied Company armies and the history of India might have been very different.[23]

Under William Pitt the Younger (prime minister 1783–1801, 1804–6), the British began a naval and diplomatic recovery. In 1790, they were strong enough to face down Spain's longstanding claim to exclusive control over the Pacific coast of North America, and extract a formal acceptance that the Pacific Ocean was no longer its monopoly zone (the so-called 'Nootka Sound crisis'). Three years later they were at war with France in the twenty-year struggle whose outcome decided the fate of their global expansion. This was a conflict whose scale and duration would have been hard to sustain even thirty years earlier: on one side a land power whose capacity to mobilize the human and physical resources of Europe (by collaboration and force) astonished and appalled contemporary opinion; on the other a sea power whose resistance depended in critical part on the extraordinary growth of Europe's colonization and trade in the non-European world since c. 1760 – in the Americas and South Asia above all. It was this 'double revolution' in both Europe and non-Europe that made this a 'war of the world', even, perhaps, a 'war for the world'. What began as Britain's effort to defend its island safety at home was to determine the shape of Europe's place in the world for a century or more.

Defence was certainly needed, and at the most vulnerable point of Britain's imperial system. 'Let us be master of the Strait for six hours,' said Napoleon, 'and we shall be masters of the world.'[24] Naval command of the Straits of Dover and the Narrow Seas and, by extension, keeping the Low Countries free from a rival great power, were the key to British security. It was to counter this northward expansion of revolutionary France that they first went to war. But as the struggle went on, and the revolutionary mobilization of France was supercharged by Napoleon's military genius and grandiose vision, the threat to their empire grew wider and wider: in the Mediterranean, the Caribbean, the Indian Ocean and India, and to their far-reaching commerce. It was not easy, as British strategic vacillations revealed, to decide how best to resist, let alone how the war might some day be won.

The obvious step was to drive France away from the estuary of the Scheldt, the launch-pad for invasion. But when Holland collapsed and its Patriot party went over to France, this was no longer an option. It was already apparent that the containing of France would require a coalition of powers, with Austria in the lead. To keep a coalition in the field, the British would have to be willing to advance the financial support that its armies required. It would also be vital to keep part of their navy in the Mediterranean, to encourage their allies and prevent the French domination of Mediterranean Europe. That was not all. Once driven from the mainland, the British had to be constantly vigilant against the threat of invasion, not just against Britain but into the rebellious island of Ireland. Close watch and ward of French naval ports, and of the intentions of Spain, briefly Britain's ally, but then that of France, was the supreme priority. But at the same time, it was very tempting indeed to adopt a blue water strategy: to use Britain's amphibious power to seize the colonial possessions of her enemies, after 1795 the Dutch and the Spanish as well as the French. Nor was this mere opportunism. Henry Dundas, Pitt's right-hand man and his unofficial director of strategy, insisted that from Britain's 'insular situation, our limited population not admitting of extensive continental operations, and from our importance depending ... upon the extent of our commerce and navigation', the conclusion was 'obvious'. Britain should aim above all to enlarge its own maritime power and destroy that of the enemy: 'we ought as early as we can at the commencement of a war to cut off the commercial resources of enemies [and] infallibly weaken their naval resources'.[25] What made this even more urgent was the closure of their usual markets to British manufacturers and the consequent damage to trade.

What Dundas understood was that there was an intimate link between overseas trade and empire and Britain's peculiar role in the European war: that of paymaster and banker to its military allies. If British trade were to falter, and with it the intricate system of credits and loans that was managed in the City, financial disaster would follow. This was partly a matter of confidence. Thus it was vital to safeguard Britain's Caribbean possessions, still the jewel in the crown. 'The loss of Jamaica,' said Dundas in August 1796, 'would be complete ruin to our credit.'[26] Losing its exports, remittances and the revenue from sugar duties would be a shattering blow. Dundas thought the same about India (where three of his brothers had sought their fortune). Indeed, it had long been acknowledged in London that the East India Company was 'too big to fail'. But even fighting a naval or maritime war against an opponent commanding the navies of the Dutch and the Spanish as well as his own was no easy matter. The British use of blockade alienated possible friends. Naval warfare required large supplies of naval stores, the timber and tar needed for repair and construction – a consideration that made the Baltic and even Corsica strategically vital. It required secure bases where ships could refit and crews could recover, in the eastern world especially. In the Bay of Bengal, the British had no safe harbour where their ships could ride out the hurricane season that arrived when the south-west monsoon became the north-east monsoon in the month of October. Above all, it required the willingness to take risks in an age when communication was slow and unreliable, when tracking the enemy's fleet was painfully difficult, and when wind and weather could thwart the best-laid plans. 'When the enemy's force by sea is superior to yours and you have many remote possessions to guard,' Admiral Kempenfeldt had remarked during a critical phase of the American war of 1775–83, 'it renders it difficult to determine the best means of disposing of your ships.'[27]

Whatever its benefits, the attack on French colonies could make no real contribution to the crucial arena where victory mattered most: the European war. And it cost the British dear: some 66,000 men died (mostly of disease) in the Caribbean expeditions of 1794–1801.[28] In 1797, the coalition against France fell apart when Napoleon smashed his way into Italy. Fearful of invasion (a small French expedition actually landed in Wales), with their finances in disarray and the navy threatened by mutiny, the British abandoned the Mediterranean. The decision to return the following year – the price of inveigling Austria back into the war – seemed to carry huge risks. It coincided unwittingly with Napoleon's grand scheme for the conquest of Egypt, the first stage (it seems likely) of a great eastern empire and an eventual assault upon India. 'We take the earliest opportunity of acquainting you,' the East India Company's directors in London warned their Indian governor-general in June 1798, 'that we have received information . . . that a very large armament of ships, troops, military stores &c has been lately fitted out at Toulon and sailed . . . [on 19 May] . . . it is not improbable . . . that its destination may be for India, either (having first taken possession of Egypt) by way of the Red Sea or by Bussora [Basra].'[29] There the governor-general had already decided to attack Tipu Sultan, ruler of Mysore, long suspected of a secret understanding with the French to eject the British from South India and perhaps from the whole subcontinent.[30] The French army did indeed invade Egypt. But before Napoleon could exploit his coup further, his plans were wrecked by Nelson's complete destruction of his fleet at the battle of the Nile on 1 August in an action of extraordinary daring and brilliant execution: Nelson's plan had required sailing part of his fleet between the anchored French fleet and the shore and risked grounding his ships in unsounded waters. The huge advantage he gained from this dangerous manoeuvre was 'doubling' the French – attacking their ships from two sides at once, a lethal onslaught.[31] The battle of the Nile and Wellesley's crushing victory over Tipu Sultan at Seringapatam the following year ended the French threat to India. But neither this, nor the foiling of the French invasion of Ireland to coincide with the uprising of 1798, could secure the balance of forces in Europe that British safety demanded.

The apparent impossibility of defeating Napoleon on land drove the British to seek a compromise peace in 1801. It quickly broke down when the French refused to withdraw from the Low Countries or the British from Malta (captured earlier by Nelson). In the second phase of the struggle between 1803 and 1814, the British secured the command of the sea that had eluded them earlier. Nelson's great victory at Trafalgar over the French and Spanish fleets on 21 October 1805 had one crucial result: the British were now free to pick off the overseas possessions of their enemies without danger at home.

They added Cape Colony, Mauritius and Java to their earlier conquests of Trinidad and Ceylon (Sri Lanka). When Napoleon imposed his Continental System in 1809 to exclude their commerce from Europe, it leaked like a sieve as well as enraging his vassals. When his army invaded Spain to suppress the anti-French rising, a naval supply line immune from French interference sustained Wellington's army in Portugal and permitted its gradual advance into Spain. But the conundrum remained. As long as Napoleon was master of Europe, the British could not be sure when he might next try to invade them, or build a new fleet, or rally new allies. Meanwhile, they remained at full stretch to maintain a large army as well as the navy. By the latter part of the war, government spending consumed nearly one quarter of national income to pay for defence and to service the huge public debt that fighting the war had created. It was economic expansion at home, including the great increase in steam power, that made the burden of tax and inflation politically tolerable.[32]

The stalemate was broken by Russia's revolt against Napoleon's hegemony, and by the catastrophic defeat of his invasion of Russia in 1812. In its wake, a grand continental coalition of Austria, Prussia and Russia assembled against the wounded emperor. Its crushing victory at Leipzig in 1813 was the prelude to the invasion of France and the exile of Napoleon to Elba. Wellington's army, advancing from Spain, had played its part in the victory. But its more critical role was to break Napoleon's frantic attempt to restore his military and political fortunes in the 'Hundred Days' of 1815. The battle of Waterloo in June 1815 was (for the British) the counterpart of Trafalgar – although it seems likely that even a French victory would not have saved Napoleon from the crushing advance of the Russian, Austrian and Prussian armies gathering nearby.[33] It confirmed France's outright defeat on land as on sea. This precondition was vital to British hopes of retaining their key wartime gains, and to their global expansion after 1815.

The reason was simple. In previous wars, as far back as the 1690s, the British and their allies had fought France to a standstill, but not to defeat. To achieve a peace settlement, the British had had to throw much of their winnings back on to the table: Guadeloupe,

Pondicherry, Cuba and Manila in 1763. After 1805, their global position had become immensely stronger both strategically and economically. Unlike the other European states, they could draw on the resources of the rest of the world, in both the Atlantic and Indian oceans, to sustain their war effort and subsidize others. The defeat of Napoleon *on land* (partly the consequence of Britain's extra-European power) allowed the British to capitalize fully on this crucial improvement in their geostrategic position. In 1815, the need to keep the unpopular Bourbons afloat in Paris (as the best guarantee against a Napoleonic revival) meant returning their sugar colonies. To help the new 'Kingdom of the Netherlands' to guard the Low Countries against France, Java – its treasure-chest – was restored to the Dutch. But the British kept their hands on Malta, the Ionians, the Cape, Mauritius and Ceylon. They soon forced the Dutch to concede their claim to Singapore. Neither France nor Spain, let alone the Dutch, were in a position to challenge these maritime gains: Britain's European allies had little interest in doing so. Hence the exceptional conjuncture of 1815 turned Britain's arduous campaign of empire defence into a geopolitical triumph. With the Cape, Mauritius and Ceylon (with its storm-proof harbour at Trincomali), they held all the main stations on the trunk route to India. From Malta's Grand Harbour they could watch the eastern Mediterranean, and the 'short' road (as yet overland) to the east. With these as well as their Irish, North American and Caribbean sea bases, they now held the keys to lock up the world in a sailing ship age.

THE 'BRITISH PEACE', 1815–1914

After 1815 the British seemed to enjoy almost perfect conditions in which to defend their existing possessions and add new tracts to their empire. The strength of their navy made a home invasion unlikely – despite periodic fears of a French lightning attack. Their iron grip on the sea lanes secured by their bases made a naval attack on their empire (common enough in the previous century) almost fantastically improbable. Swifter communications, by steamship, railway and telegraph, made it gradually easier to move their stock of ships and infantry battalions to meet any local emergency. Just as important was the critical change in Europe's power politics. The profound shock of war, revolution and Napoleon's military genius had jolted Europe's statesmen into a new kind of diplomacy. To preserve Europe's fragile stability, they agreed on a 'concert system'. Henceforth any change in territorial control that might alter the balance between Europe's five powers (Russia, Austria, Prussia, France and Britain) would require general agreement. Any power breaking this rule would find the others united against it.[34] For almost a century, the concert principle held – to the huge relief of the British. The supreme threat to their empire – a Europe united against them – receded into the shadows.

In practice, of course, matters were not quite so straightforward. The British were nervous of Russian expansion: slow but unstoppable, like a glacier, some said. Russia's vast army, its inscrutable politics, its invulnerability to sea power and the apparently unlimited scale of tsarist ambition encouraged a form of 'Russophobia' in Britain. Nicholas I showed the 'same hatred to England which was felt by Napoleon', said Palmerston.[35] Signs of military life along its inner Asian frontier were treated as proof that the tsars planned the conquest, or at least the disruption, of Britain's Indian Raj. 'The Cossak and the Sepoy, the man from the Baltic and he from the British islands, will meet in the centre of Asia,' was Palmerston's graphic prediction.[36] Suspicion of France also quickly revived, along with French power, founded as always on its large and well-equipped army. The British were deeply suspicious of French intentions in Belgium and insisted on a treaty guaranteeing its neutrality in 1839 (the famous 'scrap of paper' that the Kaiser ignored in 1914). They opposed the reassertion of French influence in Spain and also in Italy. When Napoleon's nephew, Louis Napoleon, became first president and then emperor (in 1851) their mistrust was redoubled. Castlereagh, Canning, Palmerston, Aberdeen, Disraeli and Salisbury, the great shapers of British foreign policy in the nineteenth century, all understood that Britain's world interests required an active diplomacy in Europe to check what they saw as the instinctive aggression of some of its rulers. It was alliance with

France, and a grudging Austrian emperor, that ensured Russian defeat in the Crimean War. As long as Europe was 'quiet', Victorian statesmen believed, they could deal with the threats to their imperial authority posed by local resistance. To suppress the great Indian revolt of 1857–9, they sent most of their (British) army deep into the Indian interior. Even so, they kept their eye on their Irish back door. 'The smallest outbreak in Ireland', said Palmerston at the height of the crisis in India, would 'go further to shake the impression of our power than all that can happen in India'.[37]

There were three 'hot spots' where Victorian anxieties about the external defence of the empire were concentrated. The first and least serious of these was the long border between Canada and the United States. The weakness of the US federal government, the prevalence of 'filibusters' – unofficial expansionists who gathered an armed gang to invade neighbouring territories – and periodic phases of tension between London and Washington meant that this danger was real, if spasmodic. During and after the American Civil War, it was briefly acute, and the British had to consider how to strengthen their meagre garrison in Canada, especially in winter when the St Lawrence River was frozen.[38] The second was on India's north-west frontier, where the advance of Russian influence from the Caspian Sea into Central Asia was monitored closely. The third and most serious was the vast region that the Victorians called the 'Near East' – extending from Greece to the eastern borders of Persia. For it was here that they expected to have to defend their short route to India (after 1869, the Suez Canal), and exclude any rival from Egypt or the land approaches to the Persian Gulf, with its access to India.[39] India, indeed, became the central obsession of imperial defence – because it was vulnerable and because it was valuable. The 1857 revolt left a curious double legacy. It bred something close to paranoia among the British about the dangers of a second Mutiny, and made them hypersensitive about any challenge to their *izzat* – their prestige as the ruler or *sarkar*. A military setback or the close approach of a rival to the frontiers of India might spark a new uprising. It was partly to insure against this that 60,000 to 70,000 British soldiers – around one third of the army – were kept in India after 1860. On the other hand, India's rapid commercial development after 1860, its role as a hub for the

15. Distribution of British troops, 1881

Hong Kong 1,167
Straits Settlements 1,028

India 69,647
Native troops 125,000

Ceylon 1,224

Cyprus 420

Mauritius 355

Malta 5,626

Sierra Leone 441
Gold Coast 191

Cape 4,848

St Helena 210

Britain 65,809

Ireland 25,353

Gibraltar 4,158

Bermuda 2,200

Canada 1,820

Honduras 247
Bahamas 101
Jamaica 778
Barbados 813
Trinidad 121
British Guiana 246

Cape 4,848 number of troops based at garrison

vast maritime region between East Africa and China, made it more and more valuable, as market, supplier and investment. Not only that, the large British garrison stationed there at Indian expense and the reformed Indian army became the strategic reserve for the empire in Asia, the spear-point for its sea power, and India itself the springboard for further expansion. A British Empire without India had become inconceivable.

Defending India and the empire thus also meant a strong diplomatic and naval British presence in the Near East where Russia or France, together or separately, might try to break up the Ottoman Empire and share out its provinces. Russia's claim to protect the Ottomans' Christian subjects, their forward base in the Caucasus, where they maintained a large army, and the tsars' longstanding ambition to rule Constantinople (Tsargrad) and master the Straits, were a source of constant unease. Neither did the British forget Napoleon's Egyptian invasion: all French interest in Egypt was viewed with suspicion. The main means of defence was a large naval squadron, the Mediterranean fleet with its main station at Malta, to deter French or Russian advance and stiffen the Ottomans. But in the 1830s, at the time of the Crimean War and after 1875 it was not enough. On each occasion agile diplomacy was needed to enlist European allies against Russian expansion. Then, in the early 1880s, the British were forced to take a further long step. A crisis in Egypt threw up an anti-foreign regime. British concern for their *izzat*, the fear that chaos in Egypt would trigger great power intervention beyond their control, and the ever-growing importance of the Suez Canal, pushed Gladstone's cabinet into a 'temporary occupation' in 1882. It was a risky commitment that exposed them to fierce condemnation by the other great powers. They appeased and divided their European critics by making concessions during the African 'scramble'. Little by little, their temporary occupation on the Nile became the 'veiled protectorate', and Lord Cromer, their 'agent', the 'whisper behind the throne' in Cairo.[40] The day of departure was put off indefinitely. And Egypt became the kernel of a future Middle Eastern empire – acquired to defend India.

By the mid 1890s, British leaders were inclined (incorrectly) to look back to the middle years of the century as a golden age of security.

They began to suspect that the huge scale of their empire was turning it into an albatross, and that they were losing the will and the means to advance British claims with Mid-Victorian *machismo*. This mood was induced by two disturbing developments. The first was what seemed the increasing aggressiveness of European ambitions beyond Europe – a throwback to the age of mercantilism before 1815. France and Russia, their most dangerous rivals in the Near East, Asia and Africa, formed a defensive alliance. Wilhelmine Germany adopted *Weltpolitik* as its motto, demanded a place in the imperial sun, and began building a navy. The chance of collision with a powerful opponent loomed ever larger. The second was the growth of new epicentres of crisis in the non-European world, where a large British interest existed. The partition of China seemed more and more likely as its Manchu rulers' grip slackened. Russia, France, Germany and Japan (a new regional power) all had large claims: the British might have to fight hard for their share.[41] At almost exactly the same time, the rise of the gold-rich Transvaal upset the local balance of power in South Africa. It raised the grim prospect of an independent Afrikaner republic courting French or German support and corroding Britain's grip on the Cape, one of the keys that locked up the world. When the Transvaal president, the old frontier-fighter Paul Kruger, pre-empted Britain's military build-up by invading the Cape and Natal in October 1899, the British found themselves in a war. When they suffered a string of early defeats, just as the Boxer rebellion and the arrival of foreign armies in Beijing warned that China's dissolution was at hand, the reaction in London verged on panic. Their dilemma was obvious to Kruger's closest adviser. The British Empire consisted, wrote Jan Christiaan Smuts in 1899, of 'great countries inhabited by antagonistic peoples (Cape Colony, India, Egypt &c.) without any adequate military organization in case of disturbance or attack. The dominion that the British Empire exercises . . . rests more upon prestige and moral intimidation than upon true military strength.'[42]

Smuts was too optimistic. But the fear of finding themselves in conflict with France and Russia in the Near East and East Asia, while war dragged on in South Africa, galvanized opinion in Britain. 'We must have a force which is reasonably calculated to beat France and Russia,' declared Lord Selborne, the First Lord of the Admiralty, in January 1903, 'and still have something in hand against Germany.'[43] By 1905, spending on the navy was 50 per cent higher than in 1899. The British embarked on the great naval race, at first to outbuild Russia and France, and after 1908, to see off the challenge of the German High Seas fleet. To some eager imperialists this was only a start. Joseph Chamberlain's great scheme for an imperial federation of the white settlement colonies, bonded together by tariff reform and the end of free trade, was meant to rally its offspring to the now 'weary titan'. But protection was an albatross, and the Conservatives scrapped it after two election defeats. Others favoured the building of a great conscript army. That too was a fantasy: no British government would then have dared impose it in peacetime. Still others urged an alliance with Germany against the *Franco-Russe*. But the diplomatic price was too high: Britain would have been committed to defending the ramshackle empire of the Habsburgs with its turbulent nationalities. In fact the British were lucky. Their often tense relations with the United States improved greatly with the new century. Both sides saw the advantage of a tacit maritime partnership. British naval supremacy, remarked Theodore Roosevelt, was 'the great guaranty of the peace of the world'.[44] An opportunist alliance with Japan yielded an astonishing dividend when the Japanese disabled Russia's sea power at Tsushima in May 1905. By that time the British had also persuaded the French to settle their (mainly) African differences in the entente of 1904. A weakened Russia followed suit with a second entente in 1907, easing the tensions in Central Asia and Persia.[45] That left the Germans.

The calculation here was a complicated one. The German strategy was to build a large enough fleet to deter the British from entering a European war or acting against them. A powerful battle fleet that broke out of the North Sea and attacked British shipping and colonies could inflict massive damage. It would cripple Britain's ability to intervene on the continent, perhaps for the critical period in which a decisive battle occurred. For the British in turn, there was a double imperative in containing that threat. As Winston Churchill insisted, the best defence of the empire was to prevent the enemy's navy from leaving the seas around Europe. But there was a deeper side to the argument. If Britain were unable to act as one of Europe's great powers, to prevent a dangerous shift in its geopolitical balance, then it had no means of averting the greatest danger of all: a Europe united against it by force or diplomacy. So the British embarked on a huge naval programme to achieve an unbeatable lead in the 'all big-gun' battleship or 'dreadnought'. To drive home their message, they assembled this armament at Scapa Flow in the Orkneys, to block the German navy's escape from the North Sea to the Atlantic. To make it invincible, they stripped the Mediterranean (and everywhere else) of almost all their modern warships. Of all the keys that locked up the world, Scapa Flow was the grandest.

It ought to have worked, and, as we will see, in many ways did. But it was not a sufficient deterrent against German hopes of a triumph in Europe, founded on faith in their knock-out blow against France – the Schlieffen Plan. So when an obscure Balkan quarrel plunged first Austria and Russia, and then the Germans and France into Europe's first general war for a century, the British could not stay out – though their ostensible motive was Berlin's violation of Belgian neutrality. By the time that peace came, the task of defending their empire looked almost startlingly different.

IMPERIAL WAR, IMPERIAL PEACE 1914–1935

Between 1914 and 1918, the British fought on three fronts – in Europe, at sea and in the Middle East – to defend their empire, as well as embarking on several lesser campaigns to seize Germany's colonies in the Pacific and Africa. Australian and South African troops captured German New Guinea and German South West Africa (Namibia) respectively. South African and Indian troops bore a large share of the fighting in German East Africa (Tanzania).[46] The Western Front war to expel Germany from French and Belgian soil, was really a war to prevent Europe's subjugation to one dominant power, the greatest threat to British world power. The war at sea was fought partly to keep the German High Seas fleet in its ports. There was no need for a second Trafalgar, although the admirals longed for one.

The battle of Jutland in May 1916 was a tactical stand-off, but a strategic success. The German fleet went home and stayed there. But to a much greater extent than in the previous Great War, the British now depended on imports of food and materials. The rapid advance of submarine warfare, and the huge scale of their shipping losses, forced them on the defensive at sea until the balance was changed in late 1917 by the addition of American sea power in the North Atlantic. The third major war was the most obviously imperial. When the Ottoman Empire threw its lot in with Germany and Austria-Hungary in October 1914, its armies posed an immediate threat to two key British interests: the Suez Canal, close to Ottoman Palestine; and the large Anglo-Persian Oil Company depot at Abadan near Basra. Behind the need to protect these great installations lurked a less tangible but no less urgent imperative. In their Indian Empire, the British ruled over millions of Muslims for whom the Ottoman Sultan was the *khalifa* – the 'Commander of the Faithful' – to whom allegiance was owed. A shock defeat, a failure to win quickly, might stir Muslim excitement, set off a *jihad*, or encourage the unconquered Pathans to test British nerves along the North West frontier.[47] It was an added complication that they had to rely on their Indian army – with its large contingent of North Indian Muslims – to fight their Middle East war.

The British had intended – as so often before – to wage a war of limited liability. A small expeditionary force (in European terms) to stiffen the French; a naval blockade; some colonial campaigns; and heavy use of their 'fourth arm' – finance and supply – to bolster the French and the Russians whose mass conscript armies would bear the brunt of the land war.[48] But – as so often before – that quickly went wrong. The weight of the German attack forced the deployment of a huge volunteer army sent over the top in the great Somme offensive in July 1916. The scale of the losses forced the resort to conscription. But in 1917, despite another costly offensive, the Western Front was at stalemate. In the Middle East war, the desperate attempt to take the Dardanelles and open the Straits to supply the Russian war effort was another costly disaster. And although Russian armies attacked the Turks from the Caucasus, the British forces in Palestine and Iraq made very slow progress (the British captured Jerusalem in December 1917 but their advance then stalled). Then after more than three years of war, they were plunged into the vortex.

It began with the collapse of Russia's war effort after the Bolshevik coup of October 1917. In the following March, the 'surrender' treaty of Brest-Litovsk left the Germans free to recall much of their Eastern Front army, to control the Ukraine and its vast grain reserves, and send military help round the Black Sea to their Ottoman allies. Two glittering prizes, Russia's huge oilfield at Baku, and command of northern Iran and its road to Central Asia, Afghanistan and eventually India, lay in their grasp. But it was in the west that the outlook was darkest. A massive German offensive threatened the vital breakthrough, splitting the French and the British, seizing the coast and forcing both a British withdrawal (a 1918 'Dunkirk') and a French surrender.[49] As late as July 1918, the British confronted the grim prospect that both France and Italy might abandon the war. If, in the meantime, the Germans linked up with the Ottomans, the whole Middle East might fall into their hands. The British now faced their imperial nemesis, said Lord Milner, the principal director of strategy in Lloyd George's War Cabinet.[50] 'We must be prepared for France and Italy being beaten to their knees,' he told Lloyd George in June 1918.

> In that case it is clear that the German-Austro-Turko-Bulgar bloc will be master of all Europe and Northern and Central Asia up to the point where Japan steps in to bar the way . . . It is clear that unless the remaining free peoples of the world, America, this country and the Dominions, are knit together in the closest conceivable alliance . . . the Central bloc under the hegemony of Germany will control not only Europe and most of Asia, but the whole world . . . If all these things happen . . . these islands become the exposed outpost of the Allied positions encircling the world – a very disadvantageous position for the brain centre of such a combination.

The fight, he concluded, 'will now be for Southern Asia and, above all, for Africa (the Palestine bridgehead is of immense importance)'.[51]

Milner's nightmare vision receded. By August 1918, the Germans had run out of steam. Their armies began to implode. The huge reinforcement of American manpower now made the outcome inevitable. The collapse of Austria and the Ottomans soon followed. But the desperate fear that the British Empire would be cut in half left a huge legacy. It became a British obsession that no other power should have a position of strength in the Middle East, and that the Canal and the Gulf must remain in their grip come what may. And although they were forced to give ground in the aftermath of the war, when constraints on their manpower and military budget combined with Turkish, Arab and Iranian resistance to reduce the full scope of their power in the region, in strategic and military terms, they were now masters of the Middle East, and determined to remain so.[52] They had made a huge forward movement of empire of exactly the kind that they had loudly forsworn before 1914. In fact, the narrow escape of 1918 fused with new strategic and technological developments to raise still further the imperial value of their Middle East mastery. After 1918, the two largest navies that might challenge British command of the sea were the American and the Japanese. To shuttle their fleet between West and East quickly, the Suez Canal was more vital than ever. And then there was air power. Cairo was already emerging as the hub of air movement, civilian and military, linking Britain to India and soon to Australia via the Middle East air corridor. 'The Gulf is becoming,' wrote a *Times* correspondent in 1935, 'the Suez Canal of the air, an essential channel of communication with India, Singapore and Australia.'[53]

But as British leaders well knew, what mattered most was what happened in Europe. Without a balance in Europe, they could never be safe: defending their empire would be an intolerable burden. From that point of view, the defeat of Germany and Austria-Hungary had been inconclusive. For all the sanctions imposed on Germany by the peace treaty of June 1919 (a miniature army, the loss of its navy, the subtractions of territory and financial reparations), it remained a great and discontented power. The means to create a new balance in Europe were sadly lacking. The hope that the United States would act as a guarantor of the peace settlement and join the new League of Nations was soon dispelled by its Senate. Nor would Russia fulfil its old role as the barrier to German expansion. To its Bolshevik rulers the other European states were not would-be allies but the ideological enemy: a feeling fiercely reciprocated by Western politicians. Eastern Europe was now a mass of small or weak states. Meanwhile, Franco-German antagonism, embittered by disputes over unpaid reparations, threatened renewal of a continental war into which Britain might be dragged, especially if (as seemed not unlikely) the two great losers – Russia and Germany – chose to join forces.[54]

What seemed the way out of this geopolitical labyrinth was eventually found. The Locarno Treaties of 1925, in which France and Germany settled their differences and their mutual frontier was 'guaranteed' by Britain and Italy, marked the German desire to enter a new concert of Europe. The British relaxed. Indeed, their global position now looked far more secure than it had done for decades, certainly since the early 1890s. The worrying symptoms of America's naval ambition had largely subsided, and the Americans had agreed to build a navy no larger than Britain's (and split by necessity between the Atlantic and Pacific). Despite the loud murmur of revolutionary plotting, Soviet Russia was a weak military power that posed a negligible threat to Britain's Middle Eastern hegemony. The Germans had been forced to accept the loss of their colonies to match that of their navy. Japan was now the third largest naval power – a thought that caused shudders in Canberra and Wellington. But the idea that Japan would risk a conflict with the 'Anglo-Saxon' powers was dismissed by Winston Churchill, then Chancellor of the Exchequer, as a transparent ruse by ship-hungry British admirals. 'Why should there be a war with Japan?' he asked in December 1924. 'I do not believe there is the slightest chance of it in my lifetime.'[55] In the post-Locarno world, there was no great power rival with the means and desire to attack a British world empire that was now, territorially, larger than ever before. There was a further reassuring corollary. With no other great power willing or able to threaten their imperial authority, the British could deal with any nationalist movement, in India, Egypt or China, as a localized problem to be managed, appeased or repressed as their interests dictated.

This pleasing scenario lasted for less than a decade. Japan's all-but annexation of Manchuria in 1931 (where Tokyo created the puppet state of Manchukuo) and its flagrant violation of the rules of the League could be dismissed with regret as a local anomaly with only limited significance (as it seemed at first) for Britain's interests in Asia. But a much louder alarm was sounded in January 1933. The arrival in power at Berlin of a strident nationalist leader – the way Hitler was viewed – who rejected the Versailles Treaty and the reconciliation of Locarno threw a large and dangerous spanner into the fine-tuned machinery of 'imperial defence'. Indeed, almost immediately, the British began to rethink their strategic assumptions and plan for rearmament. Another European war was no longer unthinkable. But when they tried to balance the dangers now posed by an aggressive Japan on the one hand (not least to the two Pacific dominions), against those of the 'ultimate enemy', Germany, on the other, against the background of depression and the need for economy, the planners fell out.[56] It was the familiar dilemma of a globe-spread empire: which threat would come soonest? Where would attack be most dangerous? Which deterrents would work? And where to deploy them? These were hard questions. What made them much harder was a geopolitical landscape swept by revolutionary change. By the mid 1930s, of the world's larger powers, only Britain and France retained any commitment to the existing world order and its distribution of wealth. British leaders grasped little of the ethnic and ideological conflicts that had galvanized Europe. They were poorly prepared for the brutal contempt that Hitler displayed towards diplomatic convention and towards those he regarded as his racial inferiors. In this vertiginous world, to which the past was no guide, they groped their way blindly into the last and worst crisis of the British world-system.

THE ROAD PAST SINGAPORE
1936–1945

The rearming of Germany and the potential threat from Japan created an acute strategic dilemma.[57] What turned it into a crisis was Italy's attack on Ethiopia in 1935. London denounced Mussolini's brazen campaign of conquest, but shrank from the naval confrontation and probable losses to which intervention might lead. The British got the worst of both worlds. They failed to prevent Mussolini's war of expansion, but drove him instead into a tripartite alignment with their principal enemies. From 1937 on they faced an unprecedented accumulation of dangers: a possible war on three fronts separated by thousands of miles. Lacking decisive strength in each sector, they had to decide which to make their priority – and run the risks this entailed for the others.[58] Of course, this was not the first time they had met a triple combination of foes. In 1779, they had come under attack from France, Spain and the Dutch while struggling to crush the American rebels. The example was hardly encouraging. What made matters worse 160 years later was the vast distance involved: a rapid concentration of forces to overwhelm their opponents was simply out of the question. And there was also no parallel with the situation they had faced before 1914. Then too they were challenged by a triple alliance. But they had two *de facto* allies in Russia and France and could blunt the main danger by a huge naval concentration at home. Their situation by 1937 was incomparably weaker. There was deep mutual mistrust between Britain and France, not least because London resisted involvement with France's weak East European allies, and even deeper mistrust between London and Washington. With such a grim outlook, it was hardly surprising that Neville Chamberlain's policy appeared the most credible. Chamberlain's plan, partly driven by fear of financial collapse if defence costs ballooned, was to focus British resources on a huge bomber force to deter a German attack. If the threat of a knock-out blow was averted, so the reasoning went, the Germans would not dare to embark on another long and unwinnable war. That would leave time for peace-building diplomacy and the gradual improvement in Britain's naval position – and deter Japan. This was the logic that led to the search for agreement at Munich in September–October 1938.

The second stage of the crisis now began to unfold. Within six months of Munich, Hitler had broken its terms and signalled his aim to impose German hegemony. The British scrambled to keep up by scattering 'guarantees' to Poland, Greece and Turkey.[59] They still pinned their faith on Hitler's unwillingness to fight a long war. If he could not break through in the West, or knock Britain out with a surprise air attack (two basic assumptions), a stalemate would follow. This faith began to unravel. When Hitler settled with Stalin in August 1939 on the share-out of Poland, he also gained access to Russian supplies, including its oil. A blockade would not hurt him. When war began in September, its early course seemed to confirm the prognosis of stalemate. But 'phoney war' was revealed as a strategic illusion. In May–June 1940, Hitler's Wehrmacht demolished the Anglo-French armies. With France's outright defeat and the expulsion of Britain from the mainland, Hitler was master of Europe. From this crushing strategic defeat, the crisis soon spread to the rest of the empire.

For it was now that the threat posed by Italy and Japan became dangerously real. Even Winston Churchill had reckoned in March 1939, that unless Britain suffered defeat in the West, the Japanese would hold back.[60] Encouraged by France's defeat, and already engaged in the ever-deeper invasion of China, the Japanese moved into French Indo-China, soon the jumping off point for the invasion of British Malaya and the Dutch East Indies. Mussolini was emboldened to try to seize Egypt and the Suez Canal, and before very long dragged Germany after him. The British at home faced the almost hourly threat of invasion, stalled for the moment by victory in the Battle of Britain. But with control of the French coast, Hitler could now turn on them their own noose of blockade: his submarine warfare threatened supply and survival. Meanwhile, every saleable asset (that mainly meant dollars) was pledged to the purchase of desperately needed equipment from neutral America where goods could be bought only for cash on the nail. With no ally in Europe – or anywhere else – the British were thrown back on their own white dominions and their Indian Raj for help in the struggle. They could only watch nervously for signs of a Japanese onslaught, since the naval strength to oppose it (let alone the air power) could not be spared from the Atlantic and Mediterranean theatres.[61] Even the German invasion of Russia in June 1941 promised little relief. Hitler's early successes and the chaos and confusion of the Soviet defence seemed likely to yield another staggering victory. The battle-hardened Wehrmacht would swing through the Ukraine and round the Black Sea. The British in Egypt would be taken from the front and the rear. Here was a vision of catastrophe to exceed Milner's nightmare of 1918. The British Empire might be broken before America entered the fight.

The chain of disaster was not yet complete. In October 1940, the Japanese formally entered an alliance with Germany and Italy. For the time being, however, they made no move against Britain: their titanic struggle in China consumed much of their military strength. When Hitler attacked Russia, they remained carefully neutral. But the growing tension with the United States, and the American embargo on oil, forced them on to the offensive. In early December 1941, they struck east and west, landing in British Malaya a few hours before their attack on Pearl Harbor. Almost within days, they overwhelmed the British defences by lightning advance and complete command of the air. *Prince of Wales* and *Repulse*, two of the Royal Navy's most powerful ships, sent by Churchill to deter a Japanese invasion, were destroyed from the air. By the middle of January 1942, the Japanese had taken the Malayan capital; by 4 February, they were outside Singapore. On 15 February, Singapore surrendered: 130,000 British, Australian and Indian troops were taken prisoner by a Japanese force of around half that number. By 9 March, the Japanese were in Rangoon, the capital of British Burma, nearly capturing General Alexander 'who escaped by sheer luck'.[62] British rule in Burma collapsed in an agony of chaos, shame and betrayal.[63] By the middle of May, after a 900-mile retreat, the last British forces had fallen back into India. Defeat in Asia had followed defeat in Europe. In July 1942, it looked as if these would be followed by defeat in the Middle East as well. As the Axis armies advanced towards Cairo, hasty plans were being made to abandon the city. If that were to happen, the South African prime minister, Jan Christiaan Smuts, insisted, the Eighth Army's South African contingent should retreat up the Nile.[64] As the Middle East front seemed about to cave in, its commander posed a grim choice. To save India from Japan the British might have to abandon their great Middle East base. 'India is vital to our existence,' General Auchinleck told Churchill, 'we could still hold India without the Middle East, but we cannot hold the Middle East without India.'[65]

The British were saved from an invasion of India by an early monsoon that turned all roads into mud. It was, perhaps, also the case that, by mid 1942, Japan's lightning expansion was reaching its limit. At the naval battle of Midway in June, the Americans restored their command of the central Pacific. There was now no question of sending a large Japanese fleet into the Indian Ocean. With a huge effort in India, the British began to assemble a volunteer army of more than 2 million men with which they held the line in Assam and eventually forced their way back into Burma and Malaya in 1944–5.[66] Meanwhile, Montgomery's triumph at Alamein in November 1942 – the first real British victory – relieved the pressure on Egypt. The German retreat from North Africa began. Fifteen hundred miles to the north, the German advance through South Russia ground to a halt in the killing ground of Stalingrad. But if the flood tide of German and Japanese power had now reached its crest, the ebb tide turned out to be desperately slow.

By the time that peace came in Asia in August 1945, the British had reclaimed their lost colonies and had even asserted their military power more robustly than ever across the Middle East. They were one of the three victor powers. But their great strategic defeats of 1940–42 – far greater than any since 1781 – had inflicted four indelible injuries on their system of empire from which it would never recover. The first was the end of their intense special relationship with the four white dominions. After Dunkirk and Singapore they would never again regard Britain as their ultimate shield and protector, on whose survival their own freedom depended. Canada, Australia and New Zealand all turned instead towards the United States – though not without misgivings. Indeed both Australia and New Zealand were keen to preserve close relations with Britain. The second was the precipitate end of British power in India. In the desperate circumstances of 1942, the British had promised independence at the end of the war. They jailed thousands of activists to crush the 'Quit India' uprising in August 1942. But they lost control of India's politics and lacked both the strength and the will to reassert their authority at the coming of peace.[67] They had meant to insist on a united Indian 'dominion' that would play its old part in imperial defence as the adjunct of British power in the Middle East and Southeast Asia. These hopes proved fantastic as their Raj dissolved in the chaos of 1946–7. The great auxiliary motor of British world power since the 1780s had seized up for good.

The third result of defeat was economic disaster. Neville Chamberlain's plan had been to stall German aggression and then throttle Hitler's ambitions with an economic blockade. Even *Fortune* magazine, the voice of corporate America, thought that Britain and France had the upper hand economically.[68] Drawing on their overseas income and their vast web of suppliers, the British would ride out the storm with their commercial strength unimpaired. Hitler's *Blitzkrieg* made nonsense of that. Total war mobilization, a fire-sale of assets to buy American goods, and – under the terms of Lend-Lease – a strict limitation on production for export, turned Britain into a great debtor nation, grossly dependent on American aid by the end of the war.[69] The economic profits of war had crossed the Atlantic. To remain a great power at all meant continued privation at home and new exploitation abroad. Both were imposed. Neither was sustainable.

The fourth result was perhaps the most decisive. When the British and French lost the battle for Europe in June 1940, there was no going back. Hitler's triumph was so great that it took Soviet and American power to reverse it completely. The great victor in Europe in May 1945 was not the British but Stalin. There was no postwar settlement to make Europe 'safe'. Instead, the risk of a new war for Europe stretched British resources to their limit and increased their dependence on the United States, the new guardian of 'free' Europe after 1948. In Asia, the British had turned defeat into victory – of a sort. But there too they had little control over the postwar balance of power. With the collapse of Japan's parvenu empire, it was the United States, Soviet Russia and Nationalist – then Maoist – China that filled the vacuum. The British without India were no longer an Asian great power. Only in the Middle East and sub-Saharan Africa did their imperial writ really run.

The full extent of this great geopolitical change took some time to unfold. The British were buoyed up by their heroic defence against Hitler and their hard-won recovery. But the terms on which they had built and guarded a world-wide empire had been utterly changed by two years of catastrophe. A new world order, with new institutions, new ideologies and a new balance of power, began to take shape in the hour of the British defeat. As the British were soon to discover, the defence of their empire had reached the last ditch.

There was nothing straightforward about the end of the British Empire. Despite the huge sacrifice of the Second World War, and the costs of postwar recovery, British leaders saw no reason to abandon the empire. The consequences of their geostrategic disaster of 1940–42 that were sketched in the last chapter were not as yet obvious. They were forced out of India and Burma by their turbulent politics. They gave Ceylon (Sri Lanka) independence to conciliate its nationalist leaders and preserve a 'special relationship'.[1] But they clung on in Malaya and in the enclave of Hong Kong. And while their mandate in Palestine ended in ignominy in 1948, they were more determined than ever to impose their *imperium* on the Arab Middle East and control the Suez Canal. Self-rule in Africa they thought at least a generation away. And they did not think that building a welfare state at home would conflict with rebuilding their empire abroad. Indeed, quite the contrary. Even more ruthlessly than in previous eras, they imagined the empire as a vital support for Britain's economic wellbeing and its strategic security.

Before *c.* 1960, there was little sign that British opinion entertained many doubts about the value of being a great power, although it was fiercely divided over the reckless venture of Suez. Disquiet at the methods of colonial counter-insurgency in Malaya, Kenya and Cyprus was confined to a small fringe.[2] That Britain's future prosperity lay in its trade with the empire and Commonwealth, rather than with Europe, remained the orthodox view into the late 1950s. The West European nations were regarded as weak and unstable, a drag on British recovery not contributors to it.[3] Nor did British leaders accept that their ideas about empire were now out of date. In fact, they acknowledged the need to widen representative government, to prescribe a timetable for self-rule, and – in a small number of cases – to offer swift independence. 'Empire' was gradually excised from their working vocabulary. They reinvented the 'Commonwealth' (understood before 1939 as the club of white dominions) as a multiracial association of Britain's ex-colonies, ready and willing – or so it was hoped – to follow Britain's lead in world affairs. They insisted that the end of colonial *rule* symbolized the success of the British method of empire, and was merely the prelude to a new and more equitable partnership. They saw only very late that Britain was grossly under-equipped to act the role of the metropole in such an informal empire. Despite their obvious differences, Harold Macmillan and Harold Wilson, the dominant figures in British politics from 1957 to 1970, agreed upon one thing: that Britain must be a world power and play a world role. That grand illusion crashed to earth in January 1968. But its shadowy afterlife has been strangely persistent.

LEAVING INDIA

For more than 150 years India was the second centre of British power in the world, the stronghold from which they dominated Southern Asia. India had been the commercial base from which British merchants had advanced into China. Troops from India were the crowbar that forced open its ports. The Indian navy (the 'Bombay Marine') had imposed British sea power on the Persian Gulf and its statelets. Indian labourers and traders helped build the export economies of Burma and Malaya, Britain's Southeast Asian empire. Indian merchants and peddlers were the commercial pioneers of what became British East Africa, while coolies from India constructed the Uganda Railway to link the inland protectorate to the sea at Mombasa – it was in the hope of making it pay that London encouraged white farming in Kenya. From Aden (governed from India until 1937) to Burma, and north to Afghanistan, Tibet and Nepal, British interests in Asia were essentially Anglo-Indian, watched over from Simla, Calcutta and later New Delhi. Indeed, across a large part of the world East of Suez, it would have been more accurate to talk not of a British but an Anglo-Indian empire.

This was as true after 1900 as it had been before. The First World War, which dragged the British into a huge Middle Eastern conflict, hammered this home. It was on Indian manpower that they were forced to rely more and more as the war reached its climax. But after 1918, it became harder and harder for the British to rule India to serve their imperial convenience. Political change within India, in part a response to the growing demands of the colonial state, in part an outgrowth of both religious revival and new cultural movements, forced them into concessions: to associate more 'representative' Indians with the Raj and its workings. After 1920, they faced a new political foe: the Indian National Congress, founded originally in 1885 as a genteel pressure group of impeccable loyalty, was transformed by the genius of Gandhi into a subcontinental mass movement. Its boycotts, *hartals* (shutdowns), demonstrations and tax protests (such as Gandhi's 'salt march' to the sea to make untaxed salt) and the whole panoply of *satyagraha* (literally 'truth force') – a doctrine of moral liberation – were aimed at destroying the *habit* of deference to British authority on which the Raj depended so much. Congress lacked the strength to force the British from India. By 1930, it had largely lost the support of the big Muslim minority. It was divided between those willing to share power with the British and those who (rightly) suspected that the British were trying to break up the Congress by 'federalizing' India into self-governing provinces – an ingenious new version of 'divide and rule'. And while the Indian army and police remained loyal, and the British kept a large all-British garrison of some 70,000 men in India, a revolutionary coup was the wildest of dreams. Yet, with its disciplined cadres, its enormous mass following and the charisma of Gandhi, Congress still had the power to extract important concessions. When provincial self-government was granted in 1935, it set out to build on its provincial power bases to capture supreme power at the centre. How soon it could do so remained deeply uncertain.

This was how matters stood at the outbreak of war. Congress politicians ruled some of the most populous provinces (but not Punjab or Bengal). But the more elaborate scheme devised by the British to make India a 'federal dominion', theoretically equal in status to the white dominions which enjoyed complete sovereignty, but actually bound by extensive safeguards to protect British interests, had made little progress. The Princely States (around 600 in number), on whose willing adhesion implementing the federal constitution had to wait, showed an understandable preference for the devil they knew: their treaty relations with Britain. To keep India quiet, the British intended to reduce its role in the war to the minimum: the stalemate in Europe in 1939–40 suited their Indian plans admirably. But when the war exploded sensationally in June 1940 to embroil the Middle East, and eighteen months later the Pacific and Southeast Asia, this anaesthetic approach was no longer an option. Now it was urgent to raise a huge Indian army, to create a vast war economy, and to justify the world-struggle in ideological terms as a 'battle for freedom'. As a method of galvanizing Indian political life into frenetic activity, this would have been hard to improve on.

The reaction was not long in coming. Indeed, in the very first months of the war, the Congress politicians had demanded further constitutional concessions in return for their help. When the British refused they resigned in a body to harass the hard-pressed British officials who now took their place. Throughout 1940–41, the British resisted the Congress demand for more power at the centre. But when Japan invaded Malaya and Burma in 1942, they faced a colossal new crisis. A Japanese invasion of India was now widely expected; Japanese warships had appeared on the coast. To rally the Congress (and thus Indian opinion) to the cause seemed more vital than ever. London dispatched a mission to Delhi under Sir Stafford Cripps, a senior member of the government, and (some thought) Churchill's likely successor if the war continued to go badly. But negotiations broke down over the Congress leaders' insistence on a larger share of control over India's war effort – one issue on which Churchill's views were immovable.[4] The mission went home. But it left an indelible legacy. To win Indian sympathy and put pressure on Congress, the British had now committed themselves to giving India self-government at the end of the war. Command of the timetable of constitutional change, always carefully reserved to London's discretion, had been surrendered for good.

Even if India had remained calm and orderly, this postdated promise would have raised expectations and created uncertainties in perhaps equal measure. In a subcontinent acutely divided by caste, religion and class, a coming new order was bound to be seen as a political call to arms. But India did not remain calm. In August 1942, perhaps in anticipation of a Japanese attack, perhaps in frustration at the Cripps mission's failure, Gandhi and the Congress called for mass civil disobedience to force the British to leave. The 'Quit India' movement was a massive emergency – the gravest threat to the Raj since the 1857 rebellion. It was suppressed by the British (India was full of their troops) and tens of thousands of Congressmen were thrown into gaol. The Congress itself was placed under a ban. But there were two ineluctable consequences. The Congress now became more determined than ever to demolish the apparatus of rule as soon as it could and a bitter mood of mistrust clouded its view of British intentions. Secondly, as the Congress was driven from the political field, the Muslim League was left free to become what it had not been before, a Congress-like movement. In the second half of the war, the causes of mass grievance and fear also grew quickly. Inflation, food shortage (the Bengal famine of 1943 may have killed more than 2 million people), the recruitment of soldiers for India's huge volunteer army more than 2 million strong, and the movement of labour to the centres of industry, piled up resentments between Indian and Indian as much as they did between Indians and British. Emergency rule blocked their expression as long as war lasted. But with the coming of peace in August 1945, the restoration of normal political life, far from paving the way to a transfer of power, ignited a powder-keg. Parties, factions, communities, families and individuals battled for advantage or looked for protection. Armed bands and self-defence groups began to be formed. Social and religious divides became toxic with hatred. Muslims in the United Provinces (today's Uttar Pradesh), Hindus in Bengal, Hindus and Sikhs in Punjab, landowners, untouchables, land-deprived peasants, the mass of urban unskilled on the very margins of poverty: all had something to fear – and hope for – from the collapse of the Raj. In this intense and volatile atmosphere the end of empire began.[5]

London was largely oblivious to these cumulative strains that were soon to demolish its rule. It had other things on its plate. The new Labour government, in which Stafford Cripps was a key figure, was determined to honour the promise of Indian independence, but to do so in ways that met Britain's wider requirements. Thus India would become a dominion like Canada or Australia and remain in the Commonwealth. The king would still be its head of state, and command Indians' allegiance. More to the point, India would remain undivided as a great federation. The great virtue of this, so London thought, was to preserve the old Indian army, so vital in wartime, and make it available for the postwar organization of Commonwealth defence – in Southeast Asia especially. For Whitehall found it hard to believe that the new men ruling India would want to shake off its ties to the West and not feel the need to continue their British connection. But the first year of peace brought an end to illusion.

As the first stage of transition, elections had been held and an interim government of Indian ministers formed. But it quickly became obvious that the two major parties, Congress and the Muslim League, would not cooperate. The League led by Jinnah stuck to its claim for a separate Muslim nation – Pakistan – to be carved out of India, although its territorial boundaries and constitutional relationship with India remained studiously vague.[6] A British 'Cabinet Mission', sent out in 1946, tried and failed to secure an agreement on a three-level India, in which two groups of provinces, one mainly Muslim, one mainly Hindu, would be joined at the apex to form a single, decentralized federation. While the politicians wrangled in Delhi, British power on the ground was swiftly seeping away. It was becoming ever more difficult to keep local order as social and communal tensions rose. Many British officials in India, exhausted by war service, longed to go home. British soldiers in India were just as eager to leave and get back to civvy street. Worse still, there were worrying signs that the Raj's military backbone might suddenly snap. In early 1946, Indian sailors of the Royal Indian Navy mutinied in Bombay. The police mutinied in Bihar. The trial of those soldiers who had deserted in wartime to join the Indian national army and fight with Japan revealed the deep popular anger at any effort to punish them. Fear that the contagion of mutiny might spread to the army began to infect British thinking. To the Viceroy, Lord Wavell, it was increasingly obvious by mid 1946, that the physical power to rule India – already stretched to its limits – could not last more than a year. If the

Congress chose to make trouble, there was little the British could do: 'I doubt whether a Congress rebellion could be suppressed,' wrote the Viceroy's adviser on internal security.[7] The rod of coercion – on which the Raj's survival had rested for more than a century – had finally shattered.

A new factor now began to make itself felt. The British had struggled to broker agreement between the League and the Congress to keep India united. By the end of 1946, their priority had changed. Their main concern now was to get out of India before their Raj and the subcontinent became engulfed in civil war, the signs of whose coming seemed to multiply daily. Some 5,000 people were killed in Calcutta alone in the first days of August. Prime Minister Attlee's own notes revealed the sense of impotent fear that now reigned in London. Could British control be restored, Attlee asked himself. The answer, he wrote, 'must clearly be no', because, he went on

(a) In view of our commitments all over the world we have not the military force to hold India against a widespread guerilla movement or to reconquer India
(b) If we had, public opinion especially in our party would not stand for it
(c) It is very doubtful if we could keep the Indian troops loyal. It is doubtful if our own troops would act.
(d) We should have world opinion against us . . .
(e) We have not the administrative machine to carry out such a policy British or Indian.[8]

But Attlee was equally clear that the British could not simply withdraw province by province as Wavell suggested without rousing a storm of outrage at home. It was in desperation, then, that he turned to Mountbatten, who knew India well as chief of the wartime South East Asian Command, to find a solution. The last Viceroy would have a free hand and the will to use it to the full. Before leaving London, he extracted a crucial concession: a public declaration that the Raj would come to an end by mid 1948.

Mountbatten arrived in India in March 1947 still committed officially to preserving one India. But he decided with astonishing speed that the only way out was to accept the partition that Jinnah demanded and force the Congress and Nehru to see that any further delay would plunge India in chaos. 'Unless I act quickly,' he wrote home in April, 'I may find the beginnings of a real civil war on my hands.'[9] 'I am very much afraid,' he wrote a fortnight later, 'that partition may prove to be the only possible alternative.'[10] Mountbatten's main challenge lay in persuading Nehru and the Congress high command to accept what they had sworn to prevent. It was less his powers of persuasion, perhaps, than their own realization that the Congress itself might collapse as a political force if the communal conflict between Hindus and Muslims turned into a war that obtained their grudging acceptance. At the end of June, Mountbatten telegraphed triumphantly home: '[W]e can look upon the creation of Pakistan on 15 August as legally decided upon.'[11] He had already agreed, as part of the bargain, that independence would come not in June 1948 but in August 1947. At breakneck speed, the lines of partition were drawn on the map through Punjab and Bengal, but deliberately kept secret to avoid further upheaval and violence.

Thus India (and Pakistan) reached what Nehru famously called its 'tryst with destiny'. The aftermath was horrific. Far from cauterizing the communal hatreds, partition brought with it the prospect of plunder, the chance for revenge, the fear of mass killing, and the desperate urge to escape. It created a mood of mass madness in which at least 1 million people died and more than 12 million were displaced from their homes, often to far distant places. The two new states then fought a short war for Kashmir, destined like India to suffer partition. But in a revealing demonstration of collective amnesia, all the main parties to this catastrophic termination of Britain's two-century Raj presented the transfer of power as a political triumph. In India and Pakistan this was perhaps understandable. Deep wounds had to be healed and painful failures forgotten in the struggle to build nations. The British case was more complex.

The way in which India became independent was a disaster for Britain as well as for Indians. A self-governing India, free but united, still closely aligned with its old ruling power, was one thing. A divided 'two-nation' India, embittered by conflict and deeply resentful of the way the Raj ended, was another matter entirely. There was no question now of India's contributing to a Commonwealth defence system

349

in Asia. For a time it seemed doubtful whether it would even remain in the Commonwealth. The frailty of Pakistan as a state quickly became obvious. Yet the British preferred to remember that they had honoured the promise to give India self-rule. That India did stay in the Commonwealth preserved the outward appearance of a graceful transfer of power. In fact the end of the Raj did not, as some feared, signal the immediate break-up of the empire. But it marked a critical break in its internal cohesion, and an irreparable loss of the vital resources – military above all – without which Britain's empire elsewhere in Asia became soon enough an intolerable burden. Perhaps even more poignantly, the fate of India revealed that if the transfer of power could be seen as a political triumph, the carefully stage-managed demission of redundant authority, it was also a terrible warning of how political failure at the moment of change could inflict intense human suffering. In the tryst with destiny freedom could be won and lost at the same midnight hour.

THE PARADOX OF DECLINE

Indian independence left a huge hole in Britain's system of empire. But its impact on British thinking was much less dramatic. In reality, it was hardly surprising that there was no sudden rejection of empire at the end of the war. An imperial mentality was still deeply entrenched at all levels of British society: among those who hoped to migrate to Australia or South Africa, as well as among those who saw themselves dispensing justice in the bush. Well into the 1950s, popular fiction, for young readers especially, portrayed the British as an imperial people: in the pages of an 'improving' comic like the *Eagle*, first published in 1950, or in the novels – some reissued in the 1950s – of the Victorian writer G. A. Henty.[12] The sufferings of war had not undermined British self-confidence. Quite the reverse. It was widely believed that ultimate victory was a vindication of British institutions and Britain's social cohesion. It could also be seen, with some justification, as a remarkable tribute to Britain's scientific prowess and resourcefulness, as well as the huge range of skills that its industrial workforce possessed.[13] The war had also inspired a sense of social renewal most strikingly visible in the proposals for social insurance advanced by Lord Beveridge, in his great manifesto *Full Employment in a Free Society* (1944), and in the 1944 Education Act which envisaged (among other things) a nationwide system of free grammar schools as a well-spring of talent. The British entered the postwar world with renewed confidence in the value of their political system as a model for others. As the progenitors of both parliamentary government and modern industrialism, they were profoundly convinced of their continued centrality in world affairs. It was a short step to believing that in some form or another Britain must act as the pole of a great system of influence. Empire was its lot and also its duty.

Hence Churchill's truculent warning, 'I have not become the King's First Minister to preside over the liquidation of the British Empire,'[14] uttered in 1942, cast a long shadow over postwar politicians. Far from boldly embracing the idea of India's independence (an historical myth that has been eagerly peddled), Attlee's Labour government had been terrified by the prospect that declaring its intent to withdraw would be seen as 'the first step in the liquidation of the British Empire'. Any such statement should be redrafted to present British withdrawal not as 'the first step in the dissolution of the Empire' but as 'a voluntary transfer of power to a democratic government'.[15] The appearance of a 'scuttle' would be fatal. 'I am convinced,' Ernest Bevin (then Foreign Secretary and the second most powerful man in the government) told Attlee, 'that if you do that our Party in this country will lose irrevocably . . .'[16] Indeed Bevin had urged Attlee to stand firm in India and reassert British authority. It was too late for that, replied Attlee. Of course, British socialist sympathy for Indian aspirations went back a long way – although it was far from uncritical.[17] But for other parts of the world, there seemed no contradiction between socialism as a gospel of social and moral improvement and an enlightened colonial trusteeship. What was wrong with the British Empire, many socialists argued, was that it had neglected the duty of social reform and fallen into the hands of exploitative settlers abroad and business interests at home.

The imperial habit of mind did not survive in a vacuum. It was powerfully reinforced by urgent self-interest. The British ended the war with their debts piled around them. But one economic problem surpassed all the others. To rebuild their industrial economy they must buy 'dollar' goods, since for practical purposes the only source was America. But with the end of Lend-Lease in August 1945 the flow of dollars dried up. Worse still, the terms of the loan that Washington afterwards granted required the British to make their storm-beaten pound freely convertible (that meant into dollars) as quickly as possible. The result was fiasco. When convertibility came in mid 1947, the pound's value sank like a stone: no one wanted to hold it. With Washington's grudging agreement, exchange control was restored. In the new economics of siege, the commercial value of empire rose like a rocket. London now looked to its tropical colonies for the means of survival. They would supply the basket of goods craved by the home population – on still shorter rations than during the war (now bread and potatoes were rationed): cocoa for chocolate, tea, coffee and margarine from ground nuts (butter was a luxury). Better still, they could be paid in 'soft' pounds, at prices below the world market level, and in deferred funds. In other words, their right to buy British goods with the pounds that they earned could be put off till later by a form of compulsory saving. This allowed British exports to be sent to those markets where they could earn precious dollars.

Colonial commodities promised a further reward. Cocoa exports also earned dollars. Even more valuable were strategic materials such as rubber and tin from Malaya and copper from Northern Rhodesia (today's Zambia) for which America's industrial expansion and its postwar rearmament created an insatiable demand. The dollar income these brought did not go back to the colony: it flowed instead into London's 'dollar pool', to be spent as London decided. Malaya's dollar earnings were crucial to sterling's recovery from the devaluation crisis of 1949. Indeed all those countries whose currency was tied to sterling – including Australia, New Zealand and South Africa – were forced to accept central control of their dollar spending, and buy sterling goods whenever they could. The result by 1950 was that Britain sent a larger proportion of its exports to empire countries than at any time in its history. The logic was obvious. Colonial administrators were no longer expected just to keep order and balance their budgets. Now they were charged with raising colonial production and modernizing their laggard economies at breakneck speed. The colonial state had to spring into life, to reach deeper than ever into rural localities, and chastise the commercially sluggish. It was armed with new regulatory powers and encouraged to find new political allies to replace its old-fashioned friends (usually chiefs) in the countryside. This was no time to relax Britain's grip on colonial resources: the point was made forcibly when the cabinet considered the threat posed by Communist insurgents in Malaya. In much the same way, it seemed vital to stand guard over the Middle East's oil (supplying some 60 per cent of British consumption) and the vast British-owned refinery at Abadan in Iran.[18] For those who stood in its path, it was easy to think that British imperialism, far from fading away, had acquired an aggressive new edge.

Such economic colonialism was not just a British response: all the West European countries with overseas empires regarded their colonies as a tool of domestic recovery. But the British had a second powerful incentive to maintain their imperial prerogatives. The main threat to their safety posed at the end of the war had been the westward expansion of Russia. The failure to settle their differences over the treatment of Germany at the postwar conference at Potsdam, the scale of Soviet military power and the uncertainty over how far the United States was committed to Europe's defence, raised the grim question: how could Britain and a convalescent France deter Stalin from imposing a Russian solution on Western Europe as well? The British had air power – a huge bomber force. But it lacked the range to attack Russian cities, especially if French airfields came under attack. There was an answer of sorts. The British could attack the Soviet industrial heartland in south Russia from their Middle East airbases. That meant maintaining Britain's special position as the regional hegemon, and keeping the huge Suez Canal base with its workshops, stores, camps and training grounds – a great military enclave whose western boundary was a stone's throw from Cairo.[19] So when Attlee proposed a grand withdrawal from the Middle East in 1946, leaving, as he put it, 'a wide glacis of desert and Arabs' between the Soviet Union and Britain's empire in Africa, he was shouted down by Bevin and the chiefs of staff. To withdraw, said Bevin, 'would be Munich all over again, only on a world scale, with Greece, Turkey and Persia as the victims . . .' It would shatter American faith in British resilience, encourage India to move towards Russia and have an 'incalculable effect' on the dominions. If it coincided with Britain's withdrawal from India (Bevin was writing in January 1947), it 'would appear to the world as the abdication of our position as a world power'.[20] Here was the inkling of a much larger claim: that if the British were to remain a world power (on which there was no disagreement) they had to retain the *substance* of empire as far as they could. Once they left India, control of the Middle East would be their greatest geopolitical asset. To give it away, far from easing the pressure on Britain's straitened resources, might destroy what was left of its great place in the world.

The British stayed on, despite the surge of anti-British nationalism in Egypt and Iraq. They stayed on in Malaya to crush the Communist insurgents and preserve Singapore as their prime regional base, part of the chain of connections that ran between Britain and Australia, via Suez or the Cape. For this was still a seaborne age across much of the world. They were willing to be flexible in handling their colonies: violent protest in the Gold Coast (modern Ghana) in 1948 was appeased with the promise of more self-government. Despite their rapid exit from India in August 1947, the British still cherished the hope of a special Anglo-Indian relationship in trade and defence. They still looked on India as a huge reserve tank of military manpower. So when the Indian prime minister, Jawaharlal Nehru, told Attlee that India was to become a republic (a step then thought to mean leaving the Commonwealth), Attlee was aghast. A republic, he told Nehru, was against India's traditions.[21] 'Does a republic really appeal to the masses in India? . . . [R]epublicanism is an alien import from Europe.'[22] When Nehru persisted, London anxiously searched for a formula to reconcile republican status with Commonwealth membership. India's exclusion from the Commonwealth, argued a cabinet committee, 'would encourage her to concentrate her attention on the creation of an Asiatic bloc, isolated from and possibly hostile to the Western Powers'.[23] The eventual solution in 1949 was to replace allegiance to the Crown as the hallmark of Commonwealth membership, with recognition of its role as 'head of the Commonwealth' – a compromise that endures to this day.

Indeed, far from treating the Commonwealth as the dignified relic of an obsolete empire, the Labour government of 1945–51 was determined to make it a dynamic new vehicle for British world influence. Free from the authoritarian, acquisitive and exploitative traditions of the old version of empire, it would make the British connection voluntary, democratic and mutually beneficial. Oppressed as they were by their burdens of debt and defence, British leaders (and British opinion more generally) retained what in hindsight seems a grandiose vision of their future and destiny. 'More stress should be laid,' Ernest Bevin told his colleagues, 'on the need to build up a Commonwealth defence system which together with Western Union, would result in a bloc equivalent in strength to the United States or the Soviet Union.'[24] 'If it is our aim,' wrote the Cabinet Secretary in March 1948, 'to achieve the leadership of a Western Union sufficiently powerful to be independent of both the Soviet and American blocs, we must be at the heart of a Commonwealth of nations that is as large and powerful as we can make it.'[25] Britain must be both the guardian of Europe and a global great power; the two were inseparable. Underlying this aim were two no less powerful assumptions, the product perhaps of attitudes formed before 1914.[26] The first was belief that sooner or later Britain would recover its pre-1939 role as the world's greatest trader, investor and ship-owning power, reinforced by recent scientific achievements in atomic energy and aerospace. The premium value now placed on the food, raw materials and strategic minerals produced in its colonies would be an added advantage in a world afflicted by shortages. The second, made explicit in Bevin's formulation, was that the British would not be content to follow in America's shadow. Once they had rebuilt their strength, and weathered the storms of the aftermath, they would reclaim their place as one of the three great powers of the world, equal in status and power to the new 'superpowers', and with a vast and valuable sphere to set against theirs.

But, as it turned out, the course of economic and geopolitical change turned these hopes into ashes in little more than a decade.

THE LAST CHANCE FOR EMPIRE

For the moment, however, they seemed not unrealistic. There were numerous signs that Britain's position was easing after the *annus horribilis* of 1947 when the threat of disaster in India coincided with economic crisis at home. One critical change was the ever-closer alliance with the United States. Despite Bevin's brave talk, it was an enormous relief to secure American backing from 1948 onwards to defend Western Europe against Soviet aggression. Moreover, fear of Communism's global expansion, soon to be sharpened by the loss of China to Mao, had made the break-up of empires a much less urgent priority in American eyes than it had been in wartime.[27] Now it seemed sensible to keep the Europeans' empires afloat lest a vacuum appear that Communism could exploit. So, far from loudly demanding when the British planned to retire from their career as imperialists, it now suited Washington to urge them (and the French) not to throw in the towel but stand to their duty. In the Middle East, sub-Saharan Africa and parts of Southeast Asia, it was the French and the British who would defend the West's interests. Tacit backing was given to the British assertion of their regional primacy in the Arab Middle East. 'It would be a grave error,' remarked a State Department official, 'to press at this time for the withdrawal of the British from the Suez Canal Zone.'[28] There was even less reason to press for political change in colonial Africa. Washington blithely accepted the imperialists' claim that their rule would combine economic and social improvement with a timely advance towards local self-rule.

Harnessing empire to the task of Cold War containment gave it a new lease of life. By presenting their influence as a vital barrier to Communism, the British could extract diplomatic support and material assistance from the United States, and strengthen their claim to be America's partner and not its dependant. The pattern of superpower rivalry also worked in their favour. The triumph of Mao and the threat of a Communist takeover of the whole of Korea – dangerously close to an unsettled Japan – brought a huge new extension of America's global commitments, sharply raising the value of its friendship with Britain. The British were lucky. Much of their empire was sheltered from a direct Soviet attack. In Malaya, they were fortunate that the Communist insurrection (mainly confined to ethnic Chinese) had no ready access to outside support (unlike the Communist armies in northern Vietnam). Most surprising of all, despite some early warnings, Stalin made no open challenge to Britain's Middle Eastern position, where the British were at their most vulnerable. Indeed, the main British hope was to stabilize the spheres of great power predominance – the object of the 'summit conferences' which Churchill was eager to hold[29] – in ways that conserved this favourable pattern and gave them a breathing space for an economic recovery.

Nor for a time did such a recovery look too optimistic. By dint of grinding austerity at home, and a ferocious concentration on exports, the British raised the value of goods sent abroad from some £400 million in 1945 to £2.5 billion in 1951. Even in volume terms (to allow for inflation) this was 75 per cent higher than the level prewar. This huge effort was needed not just to pay down Britain's debts but to help compensate for the loss of invisible income from capital invested abroad but sold off in the war. It was also assisted by a large devaluation of the pound, enforced by a crisis in the balance of payments in 1949: from over $4 to the pound to a new figure of $2.80. Aided by this, and by the surging demand for dollar-earning colonial produce, the British economy staged a rapid and reassuring recovery – although, as we will see, it was depressingly short-lived.

A further reason to hope that time was on Britain's side could be found in the pattern of politics across much of the empire. Of course, the huge upheaval in India, and the rapid exit from Burma, had brought down the curtain on most of Britain's Asian empire – though not in Malaya or Borneo. There had been postwar disturbances in British West Africa – in both the Gold Coast and Nigeria. But the British made a tacit distinction between what were still called 'Asiatics' and other colonial peoples. They thought Asiatics, with their ancient, deep-rooted high cultures, intense and tightly organized religious identities, their vast peasant masses and numerous great cities, and their large and sophisticated intellectual elites, were much more susceptible to nationalism and xenophobia than peoples elsewhere. The crisis of empire in 1945–8 had been an Asian crisis of empire. As their willingness to accommodate India in 1949 had revealed, the British accepted that Asians had to be treated with considerable tact if they were to be kept on friendly terms with the West. But there was little reason, they thought, to expect Africa to follow in the footsteps of Asia, or not, at least, for many decades to come. There were no great nationalist or Communist movements in Africa to rival the Indian National Congress, the Chinese Guomindang, the Viet Minh or Mao's Chinese Communist Party. In much of sub-Saharan Africa, the most powerful non-local religion was mission-centred Christianity. Africa's modern elites were small and as yet modest in their political claims. Across much of the continent, traditional leaders were still enormously powerful, and displayed little interest in promoting nationalist mass movements that they would not control. If British rule had encountered a frustrating resistance among its subjects in Asia, by contrast it seemed that African societies were considerably more pliable and easier to manage. Lacking the huge burden of Asian tradition, they would respond more positively and develop more quickly under colonial 'guidance'.

These ideas now seem quaint, perhaps even comic. What gave them some credence was the deceptive hiatus in African political life. Before 1939, much of British-ruled Africa had followed the policy of extreme localization. Power was largely devolved downwards to the tribal locality, where 'native authorities' (i.e. chiefs) asserted customary authority under the watch of a British district official. Very little space was permitted where non-traditional politicians might gather a following. All this had made sense in a period when colonial economies were mired in depression, and balancing an exiguous budget was the main task of government. But after 1945 (as we have seen) British priorities changed. To transform its stagnating backwaters into dynamic new assets, London was willing to advance credits and loans, to dispatch technicians and experts, to impose strict new controls on wasteful agricultural practices, and demand ambitious new schemes for agricultural improvement. African farmers now had to be taught (and if need be compelled) to protect their livestock and plants from disease, and their soil from erosion. That meant imposing the laborious practice of 'dipping', the burning of diseased cocoa trees and backbreaking labour to construct the soil contours that would stop run-offs after rain. It is easy to see how what historians have labelled a 'second colonial occupation' would have struck rural populations who found it hard to believe that these burdensome novelties were for their benefit, and not that of their colonial masters. They gained little or nothing from the huge demand for their produce because London was setting its prices and hoarding the dollars it earned.[30] They were even less likely to welcome the new tide of settlers that London encouraged in Kenya and the Rhodesias, who demanded more land and labour. But, except on the Gold Coast, there was for the moment only a muted reaction. It was not long in coming.

Indeed by the early 1950s there were worrying signs that even a rebranded British Empire had only limited prospects. The Korean War (1950–53) was a milestone. On the one hand, it was bound to make Britain a more valuable ally to a hard-pressed United States. But, on the other, as American policymakers began to see their task of 'containment' as global in scale, they became more willing to see nationalists in colonial or (like Egypt) semi-colonial settings as potential allies against Communism. They were less and less happy to be seen as the friends of old-fashioned imperialism lest that encouraged nationalist leaders to look east towards Moscow. For the British, the widening global confrontation that Korea betokened had other unwelcome effects. It increased the pressure in Europe and forced them into making a permanent commitment *on land* to the defence of West Germany (this was the British Army of the Rhine, a force as large as the old British garrison in India). It demolished their hope, perhaps never well founded, of a Commonwealth–West Europe combination that London would lead. For Korea helped to persuade newly independent Afro-Asian states to refuse their support to either side as the rift between East and West grew wider. This was the Non-Aligned Movement, proclaimed at the Bandung Conference in 1955. It was an unambiguous rejection of the West-leaning post-colonial association that the British had intended their multiracial Commonwealth to become. It attracted colonial nationalist politicians (such as the Gold Coast's Kwame Nkrumah) as well as leaders like Nasser. The leading part taken by India, and by Jawaharlal Nehru personally, crushed any lingering hope that Delhi would be drawn into a new

Indo-British defence agreement in the Indian Ocean and Southeast Asia.

Korea also provided a painful reminder of the continuing fragility of the British economy. The soaring price of imports in wartime was one source of difficulty. The Attlee government also committed itself, under pressure from Washington, to an enormous new programme of rearmament, diverting precious manpower and money from the civilian economy and its export drive. The results were soon felt in another huge crisis over the value of sterling. Although the incoming Conservative government under Churchill (1951–5) quickly reversed much of this programme, staring into the economic abyss had been salutary. The priority now was to cut Britain's defence bill as quickly as possible. Large overseas garrisons were an economic hostage to fortune. A key part of their aim was the increasingly desperate effort to make sterling stronger by building up a favourable balance of trade and reclaim its old role as the currency in which other nations preferred to do business and which they would use as a store of hard currency. Before 1939 (and even more before 1914) this had been one of the secrets of the City of London's wealth – and of Britain's power. But the Korean crisis had shown that sterling's convalescence would be very protracted (at best), and that the margin of safety was very narrow indeed.

This was the setting in which the Suez crisis exploded in 1956, with the force of a mine under the bows of a battleship.[31] The crisis began when the Egyptian leader Colonel Nasser, charting a treacherous course from military coup to populist dictatorship, nationalized the Suez Canal and its revenues. Nasser's perilous gamble (as it seemed at that moment) was prompted by outrage at the withdrawal of American-led funding for constructing the Aswan High Dam, his regime's signature policy. For the British prime minister, Anthony Eden, forcing Nasser into a U-turn, and restoring the Canal to its 'rightful' owners, the Anglo-French Canal Company, became the critical test of his own and Britain's prestige. When he failed to win Washington's backing to threaten an obdurate Nasser with force, he resorted instead to the infamous tactic of a collusive secret agreement with Israel. Britain and France would invade the Canal Zone under the pretext of protecting the waterway from the effects of an Israeli attack upon Egypt which they had secretly urged Israel to launch. Nasser's crushing defeat would ensure his political downfall – or worse – an outcome to which London, Paris and Tel Aviv (for different reasons) all looked forward with pleasure. Notoriously, this intricate scheme went badly wrong. The Anglo-French operation was aborted within days when Washington, carefully left in the dark, declared its furious opposition. A humiliating withdrawal was to follow. Eden's health and his premiership collapsed. Nasser became, in the eyes of much of the world, the hero of the hour: a nationalist David who had slain the Goliath of empire.

Eden's motives for embarking on such a risk-laden venture have been debated ever since. Even at the time, it was denounced by critics inside and outside his government as reckless, ill-conceived and unlawful: inflicting irreparable damage on Britain's reputation. It brought down on his head the public castigation from Washington. It provoked a ferocious response from the Afro-Asian leaders – and from Nehru especially – whom the British had been hoping to cultivate. Most Commonwealth countries expressed disapproval.[32] Eden's secretive methods, his angry dismissal of unwelcome expert advice, his volatile mood and highly charged language, unnerved those around him. 'Anthony, are you mad?' Eisenhower is said to have asked him in what must have been an uncomfortable phone call. But there was more method in Eden's madness than is sometimes supposed.

Eden was neither a warmonger nor an old-fashioned imperialist ready to die in a ditch. Before the Second World War, he had been an ardent internationalist, a champion of 'collective security' and the League of Nations. At the Geneva Conference in 1954, he had refused to back the American threat of war against China and favoured instead Vietnam's peaceful partition. In the same year, he faced down Churchill's opposition to force through the Suez Agreement that (ironically) had brought the withdrawal of all British troops from the Canal Zone in mid 1956. His aim was to end a commitment of limited military value and ease relations with Cairo. But Eden had no intention at all of giving up Britain's role as the Middle East's regional hegemon, and for a very good reason. He saw it, as had Bevin before him, as the greatest geostrategic asset still in Britain's hands. Quite apart from its value as a barrier to Soviet expansion, or its oil, Britain's Middle Eastern *imperium* was what allowed London to claim co-leadership of the Western Alliance, to resist what it saw as Washington's ill-thought-out policies (as in Vietnam), and to keep open the chance that, when the world settled down, Britain could resume its old role as an independent world power.

Nasser's bold stroke exposed the fragile supports on which this vision now rested. Eden's judgement of Nasser had been badly flawed. Nasser was bolder and far more ambitious than the British had thought. He was also more desperate. He suspected the British of backing his enemies in Iraq and Jordan. He found, perhaps to his surprise, that the British attempt to invoke international sanctions against him and regain the Canal made little headway. Once that was clear, it was Eden who was desperate. He knew that Britain's prestige in the region as the maker and breaker of governments was now on a knife edge. Nasser's successful 'rebellion' would inflame Arab nationalism. If Britain's regional allies (especially the Hashemite monarchs in Iraq and Jordan) were to fall, the British *imperium* would quickly be over. Britain's place in the world would be badly affected. The fund of authority on which Eden had drawn, and on which he relied to reassert (among other things) Britain's influence in Europe, would soon drain away. Yet he could hardly forget that Britain's claim to leadership in world affairs also depended on being seen to act in the spirit of the United Nations Charter, and to uphold the letter of international law. It was this ghastly dilemma that he hoped to evade by recourse to collusion with Israel. Perhaps he expected that a swift *fait accompli* would mollify Eisenhower, who himself had no love for Nasser. It was a disastrous mistake.

Humiliation at Suez did not trigger a British decision to abandon their empire. They had already decided to grant independence to some of their colonies: the Gold Coast and Malaya were set to receive it in 1957. The lessons of Suez (some not immediately visible) were more subtle. What they revealed was that Britain had lost the capacity for acting alone without a nod of approval from Washington. That was at least partly because the long-awaited economic recovery had failed to materialize. It was the weakness of sterling that broke London's nerve in November 1956. When the pound's value fell at news of the British invasion, the White House made it clear that no help would come unless the British withdrew. The threat was enough. What Suez had shown was that Britain lacked the resources – of financial muscle, military power and geopolitical leverage – to sustain an empire of influence, and certainly not in a region as rough and dangerous as the postwar Middle East. There were two other insights (both perhaps more obvious in hindsight) that the crisis could offer. Firstly, it signalled that the age of tripartite 'great power-dom' – if it had ever existed – was now definitely over. The simultaneous crisis in Hungary, where Soviet Russia conducted what was in effect a successful 'Suez' operation, revealed the tacit acceptance in Washington that Hungary was part of the Soviet sphere. What mattered now was to check Soviet influence in the world of new nations – in the Middle East and (soon) in Africa. In this fresh phase of rivalry, there was no place in the West for colonial adventures like Suez that upset Washington's plans for making friends among new national leaders. Secondly, as had been brutally clear, the British had lost touch with the ideological climate. Their much-vaunted claim to be the champions of freedom and progress had been exposed as a fraud. Far from deserving the sympathy of progressives and democrats, they stood revealed as imperialists, who sought to subvert the emerging world order of free sovereign nations that the United Nations Charter embodied. Although proof of British collusion only came later, for the fast-growing majority of Asian and African states who were filling the seats of the UN General Assembly, the British were 'public enemy number one', henceforth to be treated with the acutest mistrust.[33] It had been a steep fall from grace.

COUNTING THE COST

For the moment, however, British leaders still coveted the status of the world's third great power, morally if not materially equal to the two superpowers. Eden's successor as premier was Harold Macmillan, a Churchillian protégé unlike his main rival, R. A. Butler. Macmillan had been an ardent supporter of Suez. 'It is absolutely vital to humiliate Nasser . . . We must do it quickly or our M[iddle] East friends . . . will fall. We must do it quickly or we shall ourselves be ruined,' he had noted in an echo of Eden as the crisis approached.[34] He was also the first to sound the retreat as sterling gave way, uttering (as Chancellor of the Exchequer) dire warnings of approaching disaster. 'First in, first out', sneered his critics. Under Macmillan there was no inquiry into Suez. Instead, he set out to rebuild close relations with America – Eisenhower was an old wartime friend – and the Commonwealth countries, and smooth over ill-feeling with a large dose of charm.

Like Eden, Churchill and Bevin before him, Macmillan believed that Britain *must* be a great power, one of the Big Three. This conviction depended on three usually tacit assumptions. The first was that Britain's prosperity was chiefly derived from her global connections: with markets, suppliers and those who made use of British finance and shipping. British-owned enterprises could be found in every part of the world outside the Communist bloc – an empire of property that great power prestige could protect. To preserve and enhance this field of economic endeavour required the constant exertion of influence – not least in an age when capitalist free trade was opposed by both Marxism and nationalism. Secondly, in common with most British opinion, Macmillan regarded American leaders as too inexperienced and impetuous to manage the West's interests alone. In a phase of such global tension, world peace could not be left in their hands and those of Stalin's successors in Moscow. This condescending approach towards American leadership was strangely at odds with Washington's striking successes in Japan and West Germany. Its real source might be found in the instinctive resentment of a power in decline. Thirdly, Macmillan assumed (as did his Labour Party opponents) that the gradual transformation of what was still in 1957 a huge colonial empire into a self-governing Commonwealth would require active management for an indefinite period if it was to yield Britain its expected dividend of goodwill and influence. On all these three grounds, it was vital to assert British claims, and display – in public at least – a breezy self-confidence in British capacity.

Indeed, far from accepting that Britain's failure at Suez marked the end of an era, Macmillan believed that the new phase in world politics offered the chance to consolidate Britain's place as the West's second world power. Under Nikita Khrushchev, Soviet influence was exerted with growing self-confidence in the emerging 'Third World' of ex-colonial states. Soviet technological prowess, symbolized in the launch of the Sputnik in 1957, the aura of economic success that surrounded Khrushchev's agrarian schemes (the environmental costs were only revealed later) and the intellectual prestige of 'state socialism' as a fast track to industrialization, lent the Soviet leader a considerable if rather boorish charisma. The race for the Third World might tip the balance of world power. To Macmillan it was obvious that Britain must take the lead in many parts of the world in repelling Soviet influence and encouraging West-leaning regimes – a fact that Washington would be forced to acknowledge. Macmillan meant to capitalize on this by pressing for 'summit conferences' between East and West as a way of reducing the tensions of the Cold War (a device that Churchill had also favoured), insisting of course that Britain (and he) should attend.

At first, things went well. Macmillan hoped that modest affluence at home ('You've never had it so good')[35] and diplomatic success abroad would win his Conservative government wide electoral backing. The transition from empire to Commonwealth could be presented (for public consumption) as an act of far-sighted statesmanship, a triumph of vision, not a failure of nerve. The emergence of new nation-states, with British-type constitutions, still loyal to the Crown as head of the Commonwealth, could be skilfully painted as the successful fulfilment of Britain's imperial mission. The voices of sceptics and die-hards could be drowned by invoking patriotic emotion: the monarchy was carefully entwined around the idea of the Commonwealth. It seemed to work. In October 1959, Macmillan won a great victory in the British general election: he had become 'Supermac'. But on the morrow of victory, the tide began to go out. Macmillan's schemes started to unravel, perhaps because they were founded ultimately upon an illusion of strength and not the reality.

Macmillan had made the practice of summit diplomacy the crux of his plans. A summit conference to which he would go as the formal co-equal of Khrushchev and Eisenhower would confirm Britain's privileged place in a superpower world. Macmillan could deal directly with Khrushchev. He could add to his leverage with his American allies. He could signal to Commonwealth leaders, colonial politicians and his critics at home that Britain was still an independent great power, and one still worth courting. But the long-awaited summit in May 1960 was a diplomatic disaster. It was wrecked by the row that erupted when the American U-2 spy-plane was shot down over Russia. Despite Macmillan's desperate efforts to patch over the quarrel, the summit collapsed. His response was despair. It was the moment, said his private secretary, when he 'suddenly realized that Britain counted for nothing'.[36]

This high-level catastrophe coincided with signs that the economic recovery that had helped him to victory in 1959 was dangerously fragile. Building up Britain's surplus on its balance of payments to strengthen the pound (and also the City) while suppressing unemployment and containing inflation was a trick that had eluded all postwar governments. It eluded Macmillan as well. Without a strong British economy, sending services, manufactures and investment abroad, Britain's influence would wither. The prospect of winning an economic advantage was one of the reasons why Macmillan decided that Britain must enter the European Economic Community – the so-called 'Six' of France, West Germany, Italy, the Netherlands, Belgium and Luxembourg – in 1961. He was also concerned to reassert Britain's claim to lead Western Europe and retrieve the prestige that summit failure had lost him. But after arduous negotiation, and amid bitter divisions in his own party at home, the application was brusquely rejected in January 1963 by General De Gaulle's famous and unequivocal 'non'. Macmillan's humiliation was total. His premiership was in ruins. With one brutal syllable, De Gaulle had revealed the real limits on Britain's 'world power'. De Gaulle's alliance with West Germany (without which his veto would have been a dead letter) swept aside Britain's claim to a European role. The roof was falling in.

While this was happening in Europe, a vast crisis was brewing in Africa. The British had hoped to transform their African empire gradually to become part of a wide zone of influence that also embraced the Persian Gulf and South Arabia, and the maritime corridor of the Indian Ocean, linking Southeast Asia, Australia and New Zealand. By 1960, they had already conceded that their two main West African colonies should become independent: Ghana in 1957; Nigeria in 1960. Both were expected to retain close ties with London: neither had settlers to complicate matters. Elsewhere in Africa, British plans were more cautious. In Kenya, where there *were* British settlers, they had suppressed the great Kikuyu insurgency called Mau Mau with considerable brutality and a large loss of (Kikuyu) life.[37] Since Kikuyu were the largest and most politically active of Kenya's numerous tribes, increasing the African share in the colony's politics was bound to be difficult. The real British plan was to stage a 'go slow' while they constructed a federation of East Africa that included Uganda and Tanganyika (in today's Tanzania). A federal system, they reasoned, would dilute the bitter land politics that had helped to trigger Mau Mau, create a more viable state and promote economic development. In Central Africa a federation had already been formed between the self-governing settler-ruled colony of Southern Rhodesia (modern Zimbabwe) and the two northern protectorates of Northern Rhodesia (Zambia) and Nyasaland (Malawi). It was a constitutional cat's cradle. Some powers had been granted to the federal government, elected almost entirely by local whites; but others, including internal security in the two northern protectorates, had been retained by the British. Progress towards independence, implicitly promised by London when the federation was set up in 1953, required the British government's approval, as did any constitutional change. London hoped that its mildly liberal example (racial segregation was not quite as entrenched as it was further south) would also encourage a less fiercely white suprema-cist outlook among South Africa's Afrikaner nationalists. For it still regarded the Union as an extremely valuable partner, both economic and strategic.

It was never going to be easy to square so many circles – or such bitter antagonists. By the late 1950s the African colonies were no longer a backwater sunk in political slumber. The aggressive expan-sion of the colonial state – regulating, restricting, conscripting – and the arrival of more and more whites as farmers, miners, officials and experts aroused ever-increasing resentment among African peoples, not least among the traditional chiefs on whom the colonial apparatus relied. The Mau Mau uprising had been an early expression of this.

The fear of losing more land to a settler invasion was widespread and intense.[38] When the British conceded more political rights, aiming to win over the African 'moderates' (a favourite if fictional category), they found that the protests grew louder and the moderates more troublesome. It became harder and harder to insulate African politics from the ideological contagion of upheaval elsewhere in the world – with its promise of freedom from alien rule. Nor was it easy to bundle the new nationalist spokesmen into detention or exile, without risking outrage abroad and unease at home. Yet on the eve of the hurricane that blew them from Africa, they remained surprisingly confident that the pace of political change was still in their power. It was not an unreasonable view, but it was almost totally wrong.

Behind this misjudgement lay two (mis)calculations. The first was the belief that African leaders who demanded swift independence (usually labelled 'extremists') would find it hard to rally a following in the countryside where most Africans lived. The rural population was thought immune to ideology (unlike more excitable townsmen), while the rural elite would accept in good faith the concessions doled out by the colonial regime. There was therefore plenty of time before the decentralized politics of the colonial era would become recognizably national. The key error here was to ignore the depth and scale of rural bitterness – or to think that its sting had been drawn by schemes for agrarian improvement. The most ambitious of these was the 'Swynnerton Plan' to create a new class of African 'yeomen' in Kenya: contented land-owning proprietors, hostile to upheaval and moderate in politics.[39] Far from being indifferent to a populist nationalism, the countryside was a huge reservoir of potential support for it. The second calculation was closely linked to the first. The British assumed that their gimcrack colonial states would be able to deal with any likely disorder. Nationalist leaders who got too big for their boots, or who threatened unrest, could be thrown into gaol and their supporters dispersed by the colonial police and the scattered battalions of colonial troops. In the era of Mau Mau, this might seem a curious delusion. But the British had broken the Mau Mau rebellion, largely relying on loyal Kikuyu. No other tribe had joined in the struggle. Elsewhere in Africa, there seemed little reason to think that Mau Mau conditions existed: the intense pressure on land; an active political leadership, symbolized in Jomo Kenyatta who was gaoled for complicity; and a forested hinterland that favoured a guerrilla campaign. So long as the colonial regime retained the monopoly of force in a disarmed population, those it condemned as extremists had only two options: to accept its concessions or languish in gaol.

From early 1959 onwards these political 'certainties' were dethroned with astonishing speed. The effect on officials and ministers – however disguised by their elegant prose – was to cause something like panic. The alarm bell was sounded in March. The setting was Nyasaland, the impoverished protectorate that London had shoehorned into the federal scheme for Northern and Southern Rhodesia (where there were many more whites). The timing was not accidental. It had been widely announced that 1960 would be the year of decision in Central Africa, when London would choose whether to grant the Federation its full independence. It was also widely assumed from London's nods and winks that its answer would be yes – and on terms that maintained the effective control of the minority whites. Among many Africans, this caused intense trepidation, especially in overcrowded Nyasaland. Independence under white rule was expected to bring a reallocation of land in favour of white settlers (as had happened in Southern Rhodesia) and the substitution of whites for blacks in public employment. So when Dr Hastings Banda, the most charismatic figure in the Nyasaland African Congress, returned from his exile (first in Scotland then in Ghana) in 1958, to lead the campaign for more African rights, the political temperature rose exceptionally quickly. Attracting crowds of up to 20,000 people, Banda attacked the government's agrarian rules and urged his listeners to fight for freedom and against federation. The Nyasaland governor, Sir Robert Armitage, was convinced that Banda's intention was to make the protectorate ungovernable. Armitage had a deeper dilemma. It was still London's policy (and hence his duty) to support federation. It was also well understood that to make the Federation's independence more palatable (not least internationally) the Nyasaland Africans must be granted more political voice and some greater degree of self-rule. Yet it was obvious from the impact that Banda was making that a louder African voice would mean only one thing: a huge roar of protest against all that Federation represented.[40]

The sequel was dramatic. Amid growing signs of disorder, and under pressure from the Federation's prime minister, the rumbustious Roy Welensky, the Nyasaland government decided to stop Banda in his tracks. On 3 March 1959, Armitage declared an emergency. Banda was arrested and flown to gaol in Southern Rhodesia. The Nyasaland African Congress was declared unlawful and more than a hundred of its activists detained. Police and military units spread out across country to arrest those listed as 'militants'. The reaction was sharp. Crowds gathered, perhaps in self-defence.[41] There were riots and demonstrations. More than fifty Africans died, twenty in a single incident at Nkata Bay. But although the scale of the violence made an inquiry inevitable, the Nyasaland government and its masters in London thought they had little to fear. Armitage claimed to have evidence that Banda and his colleagues had planned the murder of whites, Asians and moderate Africans. The emergency could be justified as the timely prevention of a violent Mau Mau-like uprising. Better still, an inquiry would reveal that Banda and his friends were dangerous extremists who could not be allowed to obstruct the Federation's advance. But it did not turn out like that.

Instead, the inquiry under Sir Patrick Devlin, a high court judge, framed a crushing indictment of the Nyasaland government. It dismissed the 'murder plot' as an implausible fiction, denounced the government's tactics as those of a 'police state' (with a horrible echo of Europe's all too recent travails) and roundly declared that federation was deeply opposed by most Nyasaland Africans.[42] For Macmillan and his ministers, as much as for Armitage and the settler politicians, it was a major disaster. 'I have since discovered,' Macmillan raged to his diary, 'that [Devlin] is (a) Irish – no doubt with the Fenian blood that makes Irishmen anti-Government on principle, (b) a lapsed Roman Catholic.'[43] A major effort was made to discredit Devlin's report when it appeared in July 1959 and the government survived a parliamentary debate. But for Macmillan especially, the Nyasaland crisis contained an implacable message. Henceforth no British government should find itself dragged into confronting African popular movements. The potential humiliation outweighed any imaginable gain. At all costs London must find representative Africans with whom it could deal and to whom more power could be granted. In the famous speech that marked the climax of his African tour in early 1960, Macmillan lectured the South African parliament with the passion of a convert. 'The wind of change is blowing through this continent,' he told his all-white audience, 'and whether we like it or not, this growth of national consciousness is a political fact . . . The great issue,' he went on, rehearsing a favourite theme, 'in the second half of the twentieth century is whether the uncommitted peoples of Asia and Africa will swing to the East or to the West.'[44] In South Africa at least, all this fell on deaf ears. The bloody events at Sharpeville followed six weeks later.

A tenacious legend proclaims that, from October 1959 onwards, Macmillan and Iain Macleod, whom he appointed as Colonial Secretary, had decided to end British rule in Africa at maximum speed and hand over power to African nationalists; and that their tough-minded liberalism averted disaster for Britain. The legend derives in large part from Macleod's own vigorous myth-making. In fact, both men held their cards very close to their chest (Macleod had been a professional bridge-player) and for a good reason. Neither had any clear view about how to proceed and each harboured doubts about the rapid transfer of power. In the Federation, where Macmillan engaged in much double-talk,[45] their main idea was to try to preserve it by persuading white settler opinion and the African nationalists to accept a more decentralized version. Neither would do so. Despite the Devlin report, Macleod was unwilling to let Nyasaland leave – because the African leaders in Northern Rhodesia would then demand the same right of secession, and the Federation's death warrant would follow. Far from admiring Hastings Banda, Macleod, when he met him, dismissed him as 'a very vain and ignorant man'.[46] He hoped nonetheless to detach him from his 'extremist' friends and persuade him by judicious concession to support federation.[47] It was an absurd (but revealing) misjudgement. The British were torn between their desire to conciliate African leaders and their fear that the whites, who controlled all the military force in the region, would simply seize independence – 'doing a Samson' in Whitehall slang. Macmillan did not want to be blamed for the Federation's collapse, and provoke a backbench revolt by his party's right wing. The result was a series of abortive political fixes, but no settled plan. By early 1962 it was clear that the British had lost control on the ground and had no will to regain it. Without using force, they could neither prevent African nationalist parties from coming to power in Zambia and Malawi nor remove the settler minority who ruled Southern Rhodesia. All that was left was to dissolve the Federation in 1963 and divide up its assets, leaving behind (as a glaring symbol of British impotence) the white settler regime in Southern Rhodesia whose unilateral independence declaration was only a matter of time.

Between Macmillan's 'wind of change' speech and the Federation's demise, the African scene had radically changed. One sign of this (and an embarrassment to the British) was De Gaulle's sudden offer of independence to France's African colonies in 1960 (although not yet to Algeria). Much more significant was the 'Congo Disaster'. The Belgians had rushed their vast African colony into independence in January 1960, perhaps in the hope that they could then safely install a client regime.[48] The result was catastrophe. The copper-rich province of Katanga quickly split off, with the open encouragement of Belgian mining interests. Rule from the centre broke down elsewhere. The prime minister, Patrice Lumumba, was kidnapped and murdered with Belgian and perhaps American connivance.[49] Meanwhile the local Congolese army or *force publique* broke out in a mutiny, killing dozens of whites, including women and children. A torrent of white refugees poured down through the white-ruled Federation towards the South African ports and the safety of home. As the Congo split up into rival regional satrapies, the Soviet Union began (just as Macmillan had warned) to appeal to African nationalists, denouncing Western intrigue and blaming capitalist greed for the Congo's fate.

There can be little doubt that the long-drawn-out horror of the Congo concentrated British minds. It strengthened still further the aversion they felt for being trapped in an African conflict. 'The Prime Minister and Colonial Secretary then said that they did not want an Algeria,' noted Macmillan's private secretary in November 1960.[50] The Congo was worse – because it was much nearer to Britain's remaining possessions in Central and East Africa. It also heightened the fear that the siren call from Moscow would become more seductive with every month that passed until independence was granted. Tanganyika and Uganda, both Congo neighbours, were rushed into sovereignty in 1961 and 1962. The same effects can be seen in the other difficult case: the settler colony of Kenya.

In the aftermath of Mau Mau, the British were anxious to devise a regime that would rally loyal Africans and defuse their main grievances against the white settlers. They had already begun to move cautiously towards equalizing the political representation of whites, Asians (Kenya's other immigrant minority) and Africans. At the same time, the demonization of Mau Mau and the much publicized dangers to which whites were exposed made them nervous of courting a settler howl of betrayal. Macleod's solution was ingenious. He seized on the emergence of a moderate settler faction, the 'New Kenya Group', in which his own brother was active, to summon a conference in London in January 1960 at Lancaster House in St James's. No timetable for independence was drawn up, but African majority rule was laid down as the colony's destiny. Macleod's real aim was to induce an alliance between the New Kenya Group and moderate Africans – in reality the non-Kikuyu groupings that came together as the Kenya African Democratic Union or KADU. The bait was a gradual transfer of powers to an African-led ministry which would have the means (and the patronage) to build up support and contain the extremists. 'I am delighted to read your excellent news showing firming up of support for a KADU-based government,' Macleod wrote to the governor in April 1961, when the first elections were held. 'If this comes off, it will be wholly consistent with our constitutional hopes at Lancaster House.' Macleod left no doubt about his political aim. 'I want to emphasize,' he told the governor, 'how much I welcome a government based primarily on KADU and the New Kenya Party, and [the] very good chance there seems to be of leaving Kenyatta behind.'[51] The 'leader of darkness and death' – Governor Renison's famous description of Kenyatta – would watch from the sidelines (he was still in detention) while Kenya marched into the future.

This was delusion. It soon became clear that the KADU moderates lacked the skill and cohesion to compete with the Kikuyu-Luo combination of KANU (Kenya African National Union). To win more support, it was they who begged London to release Kenyatta from gaol. Once free, Kenyatta soon asserted his political authority as leader of KANU. London twisted and turned, hoping against hope to revive the idea of East African federation (by now quite forlorn), to federate Kenya itself, or to promote a split within KANU – anything but declare another emergency. Dread of a new confrontation was the real master-key of its policy. There were 80,000 ex-Mau Mau detainees in Kenya, reported *The Times*. By early 1962, the game was nearly up. As a new constitutional conference approached, Macleod's successor as Colonial Secretary, Reginald Maudling, punctured any remaining illusions of power. 'The best we can hope to achieve,' he warned his cabinet colleagues, 'is an orderly transfer of power to an African dominated government which is genuinely anxious to see Kenya develop as a modern state to avoid chaos, civil war or a relapse into tribalism.' It was too much to hope (by now) that it would be pro-Western; merely that it would resist Communist penetration.[52] To convince any doubters, Maudling raised the spectre they all feared most. 'Over everything broods the threat of Mau Mau, the influence of the ex-detainees [on KANU] and the persistence of personal violence.'[53] It was the turning point. Months of manoeuvre elapsed before Kenyatta worked out an agreement with the minority tribes, but effective political power had passed into his hands. In December 1963, in circumstances barely imaginable only three years before, Kenya became independent with Kenyatta as president.

What had happened in Africa was not in the plan. The British had retained the appearance of power up to the point of departure, but not its reality. The influence they expected to wield while conceding instalments of political power quickly dribbled away. They discovered that no halfway house could be found between rule and abdication. The African leaders they favoured as moderates could not survive on half a loaf of political power: to keep their supporters and fight off their rivals they needed it all. And once the British decided that they could not risk using force, they had few cards to play against a determined opponent. They displayed, nonetheless, considerable skill in masking their weakness and in devising the institutional machinery that allowed a peaceful withdrawal. But this was not just their own work. Those who aimed to succeed them were all too aware that their own mandate was fragile and their control incomplete. Engineering a mechanical breakdown of the British-run state was not in their interests: they needed to step into the driver's seat while the engine was still running. Constitutional legitimacy and the symbolic inheritance of colonial authority were valuable prizes. So once the die of decolonization was cast and the timetable decided, they had every incentive to display an obsequious gratitude for the British 'gift' of their freedom. The transfers of power were thus amicable, stately affairs, decorated by royalty. It was a pleasing pantomime in which all could delight.

Britain's relations with the Old Commonwealth countries were also affected by the great changes in its global position after 1945. Before 1939, all the four white dominions – Canada, Australia, New Zealand and South Africa – had looked towards Britain (with varying degrees of enthusiasm) as the ultimate guarantor of their interests and safety. This was emphatically true of Australia and New Zealand, whose sense of isolation as white British countries in the lee of Asia promoted an almost neurotic attachment to their British connection. In South Africa, by contrast, the Afrikaner majority among whites found a degree of detachment from Britain and Europe much more appealing. In Canada, where there was a British majority, domestic stability required the careful appeasement of French-Canadian hostility to imperial commitments. Nevertheless, at the outbreak of war, all the dominions had joined Britain's side, South Africa by a narrow parliamentary vote.[54]

Britain's strategic disasters in 1940–42 marked a great change. Canada, Australia and New Zealand (though not South Africa) discovered their strategic dependence on American power. Their status as sovereign countries, acknowledged in theory since 1926, became increasingly real: Canada, in particular, became a major military and industrial power and its navy was crucial to winning the war of the sea lanes in the North Atlantic. But although Britain's relative decline as a great power – by both strategic and economic criteria – brought an irreversible shift in the dominion relationship, this took some time to become obvious. After the war, Australia, New Zealand and South

Africa, as 'sterling' countries, were closely bound to London's dollar-saving arrangements. All three were key markets for British manufactures. Canada, however, was a 'dollar' country, whose trade links with America became tighter and tighter. Australia, New Zealand and Canada were all key destinations for postwar British migration, and all three retained the British Crown as their head of state. So too did South Africa (where few British emigrants went) – despite the triumph of the National Party in 1948. Cold War anxieties and the importance of British investment (not least in its gold fields) trumped, for the moment, the appeal of republican isolation, symbolized by the *Vierkleur* – the old Transvaal flag.

Until 1960, it was still possible to think that despite the war and its aftermath, and a growing unease about South Africa's racial politics, a special relationship with the Old Commonwealth lay at the heart of Britain's claim to world power. Australia and New Zealand had been vociferously loyal over Suez in 1956. Indeed, from one point of view, Australia's relations with Britain became closer than ever because Canberra was London's invaluable partner in developing and testing the British nuclear deterrent, at Woomera in South Australia. By 1970, however, the Old Commonwealth link had been greatly diluted where it had not vanished completely. The most dramatic break was South Africa's withdrawal from the Commonwealth in 1961, in effect an expulsion on which the Afro-Asian members insisted to Macmillan's great chagrin.[55] In Canada, the 1960s saw a subtle but profound redefinition of the country's identity. The old emphatic assertion of Canada's Britishness disappeared in the wake of the great 'flag debate', when the Maple Leaf flag replaced the Red Ensign but without the Union Jack quartering. The Canadian prime minister, Lester Pearson, even toyed briefly with Canada's becoming a republic.[56] In Australia and New Zealand, the shock of Britain's application to join the European Economic Community in 1961 ended the longstanding presumption that, economically and culturally, they would go on looking to Britain.[57] Between the collapse in 1960 of the 'Blue Streak' programme to develop Britain's own nuclear missile and the announcement of British withdrawal from Southeast Asia in 1968, the Anglo-Australian 'alliance' gradually faded away. In both Australia and New Zealand what followed was growing acceptance of a multiracial (not British) identity, and increasing acknowledgement that Asia not Britain held the key to their futures.

ALMOST THE LAST ACT

Between 1945 and 1964, the hopes and ambitions of British leaders had been tossed on the waves of Cold War competition and their own economic misfortunes. Glimmers of triumph (such as Macmillan's 'grand design') were succeeded by crises and failures – and the humiliations dealt out by Nasser and De Gaulle. By 1964, the mood was more sombre. Shortly before the 1964 general election (and the end of Conservative rule) the Foreign Secretary, R. A. Butler, drily summed up Britain's 'special relationship' with the United States. 'As much the weaker partner ... we find American support for our overseas policies virtually indispensable. They find our support for theirs useful and sometimes valuable.'[58] It was a brutal epitaph on the dream of Anglo-American interdependence to which Macmillan had clung. Meanwhile, it was recognized that the frantic pace at which colonial rule was giving way to sovereign independence would have to continue until all but the smallest and poorest of territories had become a new nation. Indeed, between 1961 and 1966, independence was granted to Sierra Leone, Tanzania, Western Samoa, Jamaica, Trinidad and Tobago, Uganda, Zanzibar, Kenya, Malawi, Zambia, Malta, Singapore, Gambia, the Maldives, Guyana, Botswana, Lesotho and Barbados. In those that remained, it was not British reluctance that imposed a delay but mainly the challenge of reaching agreement *between* local communities or of rushing into existence the basic institutions of statehood. The empire, it seemed, was being wound up as quickly as was practicably possible.

Yet this was not the whole story. In October 1964, a new Labour government came into power. The incoming prime minister, a veteran of Attlee's cabinet, was Harold Wilson. Wilson had led the attack on the old-fashioned Conservative attitudes which, he insisted, obstructed Britain's modernization. This was in tune with the wave of critical commentary in the press and elsewhere (the 'satire boom' was one manifestation) in which the fusty, hierarchical attitudes associated with empire and its delusions of grandeur were blamed for economic stagnation and the failure to build a technocratic meritocracy. A new Britain must be forged, declared Wilson, 'in the white heat of scientific revolution'.[59] Once in office, however, these radical attitudes were subtly transformed. Wilson was soon found discoursing enthusiastically on Britain's world role. There was, after all, a strong Bevinite tradition among Labour's trade union supporters (and also perhaps among many working-class voters) that was deeply attached to the idea of Britain's 'greatness' – and Winston Churchill, its heroic symbol, was still alive (he died in January 1965). Wilson also inherited, if in much more threadbare condition, Macmillan's glittering mantle: the belief that Britain was – at the very least – America's first lieutenant in the Western alliance. To maintain that status, at whatever cost, became an overriding priority.

Britain's world role was code for this claim. Its concrete expression was what became known as the 'East of Suez' commitment. Here, in a vast maritime zone that stretched from East Africa to Australia, and included the Persian Gulf and former British Malaya and Borneo (now the Federation of Malaysia), the British would act as the guardian of Western interests, and the protector of friendly regimes. In more grandiose moments, the old claim to watch over India made a late reappearance. 'Britain's frontiers are on the Himalayas,' said Harold Wilson in June 1965: a gesture of support for India in its conflict with China.[60] Its real military burdens were guarding the fragile South Arabian Federation into which the great military base at Aden had been thrust; and defending the newly created Malaysia (especially its Borneo territories) against Indonesia's claim to embrace the whole Malay world.[61] East of Suez was also a means of reinforcing Britain's link with Australia, still an important trade partner and still the prime target of British migration. But the bill was mounting. To remain a credible military presence across this oceanic expanse, the British needed sea power and air power: new aircraft carriers and planes as well as the bases from which to deploy them. Yet within weeks of coming to power, the Labour government was confronted with a fresh sterling crisis requiring drastic reductions in overseas spending. In June 1965, just as Wilson stood (figuratively) foursquare on the Himalayas, the cabinet decided that Britain should leave its Singapore base as soon as the confrontation with Indonesia was over, and retain only a small Middle East military presence. Under fierce American pressure (the struggle in Vietnam was reaching its peak), this plan was shelved for the moment. But Wilson and his colleagues were caught in a vice. They were desperate to stave off unemployment at home – which meant more public spending and a widening gap in the balance of payments. They were even more desperate not to devalue the pound (whose value was threatened by the huge payments deficit), as the symbol of British determination to keep their economic place in the world.[62] And a key group of ministers, including Wilson himself, dreaded falling through the 'status barrier' – the ironic description of one of their cabinet critics[63] – the fate they assumed that withdrawal from East of Suez would mean. 'He would never deny Britain the role of a world power,' said Wilson in June 1966 to a group of Labour backbenchers.[64] But something had to give.

For the next two years, London's policy twisted and turned between the rival imperatives of solvency and prestige.[65] In the spring of 1966, it was announced that British forces would stay in Malaysia and Singapore for the foreseeable future. Almost exactly a year later, the decision was taken to withdraw in two stages, in 1970–71 and 1975–6. In late 1967, the British left Aden after a long futile struggle against rival factions of urban guerrillas: the South Arabian federation was left to its fate.[66] Meanwhile, a British minister was sent to assure the Persian Gulf rulers that, whatever happened in Aden, the British intended to stay in the Gulf.[67] This compromise formula did not last very long. In early November, the value of sterling came under more intense pressure than ever. On 18 November, perhaps to avoid the indignity of supervision by the International Monetary Fund,[68] Wilson and his colleagues swallowed the medicine they had resisted for so long. The pound was devalued by 15 per cent, and a new Chancellor of the Exchequer was appointed to manage the economic recovery. This was Roy Jenkins, an ardent Europeanist and a no less ardent opponent of 'redundant' post-imperial commitments. A bitter struggle now followed, this time in Whitehall. For Jenkins, appeasing backbench hostility to the deep cuts at home that recovery demanded was an urgent necessity. A great symbolic sacrifice was required. Against fierce opposition, he forced through the decision to end Britain's military presence in both the Gulf and South East Asia by 1971. On 16 January 1968, Wilson announced the end of Britain's East of Suez commitment. His speech marked the terminus of Britain's three-century career as a great Asian power. It also signalled the final collapse of the postwar campaign to remain a world power. Three years later, a new Conservative government successfully negotiated Britain's entry into the European Community. Its triumphant manifesto of Britain's European destiny bluntly rejected the fading vision of Commonwealth, that nebulous shadow-empire. 'The member countries of the Commonwealth,' it coldly remarked, 'are widely scattered in different regions of the world and differ widely in their political ideas and economic development . . . their political relations with the United Kingdom have greatly changed and are still changing.'[69] 'Goodbye' was the message.

But it was not quite over. Some colonial possessions remained, clinging like barnacles to the old hull of empire. A handful were too small and too poor to be forced into sovereignty. Others (such as Gibraltar) resisted London's unsubtle attempts to drop them over the side. Three in particular caused British governments no end of trouble. The first was Rhodesia, for which London remained – to its chagrin – constitutionally responsible. After November 1965, when the white settler regime had seized independence, three efforts were made to reach an agreement that conferred lawful independence in exchange for representation of the African majority. All three came to nothing.[70] Meanwhile London writhed under the scorn of African governments, whose own political record received caustic attention in Britain. The turning point came when the collapse of Portuguese rule in Mozambique and Angola in 1974 undermined the Rhodesians' ability to contain guerrilla incursion and unnerved their South African backers. In a situation largely contrived by American and South African pressure on the rebel regime, the British acted as brokers. Their hereditary right to confer constitutional legitimacy made London the stage for the independence agreement, while troops and observers from Britain and Commonwealth countries superintended a ceasefire in which the guerrilla armies were gathered at supervised camps. With its usual sure grasp of African politics, Whitehall expected the elections that followed to sideline the less moderate faction (ZANU-PF) under Robert Mugabe.[71] But to its relief, a victorious Mugabe stuck to his promise not to seize the land of white farmers. Disillusionment came later.

A far more dangerous crisis arose in 1982 over another relic of empire, the Falkland Islands in the remote South Atlantic.[72] Here too London had longed to be rid of a tiresome attachment. But the Falkland islanders (who were ethnically British) resisted White-hall's mandarin schemes to make them Argentine subjects on the instalment plan – by ceding the islands to Argentina and leasing them back. They had an understandable suspicion of bureaucratic *bona fides*. Their case was made stronger by the fascistic behaviour of the Buenos Aires regime, and the support of Conservative back-bench opinion in London. But when negotiation broke down in 1982, and the Argentinians invaded the colony, the British faced a dilemma. Their chances of bringing sufficient international pressure to bear to force an Argentinian withdrawal were extremely remote. The logistical difficulties of a counter-invasion at such a huge distance were daunting: the risk of disaster was real. Yet to accept the *fait accompli* would inflict considerable injury on British prestige. There was much on the record since the mid 1960s to suggest that a British government would draw back from a conflict that turned on its claim to a faraway colony. In fact, the outcome was startling. The Prime Minister, Margaret Thatcher, with the enthusiastic support of her chief naval adviser, immediately ordered the dispatch of a task force.[73] She was warmly supported by her Labour opponents (in striking contrast with Suez). The issue was skilfully packaged as a question of self-determination for the Falklanders, not as a claim to territory. And after weeks of fruitless diplomacy, the British (not without losses in ships and men) fought their way back on to the islands, and swiftly defeated the poorly led conscripts with which they were garrisoned. The result was a triumph and a surge of self-confidence after the decades of imperial retreat. But the British had been lucky. They were able to see the intelligence that Washington gleaned (perhaps the reward for Mrs Thatcher's close understanding with President Reagan). And they were saved from potential disaster by geographical accident: the Falklands lay at the extreme edge of Argentinian air power. With only a few minutes' flight-time over the islands, Argentina's formidable air force could not destroy the main British fleet, which sat just out of range. But the margin was narrow.

The third case was Hong Kong. This too was an oddity. Most of Hong Kong (though not its central district in Victoria) was held on a lease that expired in 1997. But its overwhelmingly Chinese population showed little desire to see its return to Chinese control. There was no question, of course, of resisting rendition if China insisted. The British at first hoped to persuade the Beijing regime (newly emerged from Maoist seclusion) to renew their tenancy and preserve Hong Kong as a British Crown colony. This was delusion. But as negotiation ground on, they exploited Beijing's reluctance to risk the critical role that Hong Kong already played as the great port of South China and (more to the point) as the entrepot of finance for East Asian trade and for Beijing's 'special economic zone' on the mainland. In the final agreement reached in 1984, China's right to recover Hong Kong, including the territories originally ceded to Britain, was acknowledged and the timetable for handover in 1997 laid down. In exchange, Beijing agreed that Hong Kong would enjoy administrative and financial autonomy and keep its own British-based legal system for at least fifty years. 'The current social and economic systems in Hong Kong will remain unchanged, and so will the life-style. Rights and freedoms, including those of the person, of speech, of the press, of assembly, of association, of travel, of movement, of strike, of choice of occupation, of academic research, and of religious belief will be ensured by law . . .'[74] There followed a fraught period in which democratic activism in Hong Kong, the sudden British desire to entrench a democratic tradition before the moment of handover (a policy mainly associated with Hong Kong's last governor, Christopher Patten), and Beijing's suspicion that a trap was being laid for its long-awaited return, created a three-cornered quarrel and recurrent bursts of alarm. In fact, both sides had too much at stake to risk a political breakdown. The transfer of power in 1997 went ahead smoothly. The last British colony of major importance was now (if somewhat ambiguously) foreign soil.[75]

RETROSPECT

Historians have usually been kind to the British decision to wind down their empire without protracted resistance and often contrasted it with the 'dirty' wars waged by the French in Indochina and Algeria. A pervasive historical myth (enthusiastically endorsed in political memoirs) suggests that the British excelled in the practice of 'managed decline': the pragmatic adjustment of imperial ambition to shrinking resources. As we have seen, it was certainly true that they were extremely reluctant to resist mass political movements, whether in India after 1945 or in Africa after 1959. But they were much less unwilling to use military force where the odds were more promising and the incentives were greater: as in Malaya, Cyprus and Kenya. Nor was it true – as this chapter has shown – that British leaders quickly adjusted their vision of Britain's place in the world to its reduced physical power and economic potential. The reverse was the case for much of the time. The supposed apostle of pragmatism, Harold Macmillan, was anything but. His grandiose scheme for preserving British world power betrayed a flawed understanding of European politics and (much more understandably) almost no comprehension of the complex realities of African politics. This is not to deride an acute politician, for the unpredictable shifts in Britain's postwar position, and the inevitable lag in conventional attitudes, made a rational diagnosis of British decline by contemporary policymakers all but impossible.

In fact, the long series of 'misjudgements' that we have traced in this chapter – the false hopes of India, the false expectations in Africa, the vision of Britain as the third world power, the economic grand strategy built round the revival of sterling, the struggle to keep a Middle Eastern *imperium* (the real cause of Suez), the dream of an enduring but somehow inexpensive world role ('Britain's frontiers are on the Himalayas') – reveal something more interesting than the wisdom of hindsight. They suggest that *predicting* historical change is a hazardous business: there are too many factors at play and far too much noise to decode the correct signals. They remind us especially that empires rarely decline at a predictable speed and even more rarely along a predictable path. The Ottoman Empire, to take an example at random, suffered a long series of setbacks from the mid seventeenth century. It was widely despised as the 'sick man of Europe'. Yet it only broke up after 1918 at the end of an arduous military struggle against two of the world's greatest powers. The second example is even more salutary. Less than a decade before its sudden collapse, the Soviet Empire was regarded as an impregnable power and immune from the strains that dented American confidence in the aftermath of Vietnam. Its fall astonished the world. So it was hardly surprising that British leaders did not predict Britain's future correctly. Neither did anyone else.

The final thought that might strike us is that *explaining* why empires collapse is often no easier than predicting their fall. Perhaps the most straightforward cases arise from defeat on the battlefield – although explaining *defeat* may be a part of the problem. The causes most often invoked fall into four groups: external defeat or geopolitical weakness; ideological contagion and the loss of legitimacy; domestic enfeeblement at the centre of empire – the loss of political will and economic capacity; and colonial revolt. Although it is sometimes attractive to see one cause as decisive (thus nationalists usually favour the effects of revolt), this rarely convinces – and certainly not in a large complex empire like that of the British. It may be better to see the break-up of empires as a kind of unravelling, in which failure in one sector sets up intolerable strains in other parts of the system. Adjusting to these creates further unpredictable stresses, until the whole system breaks up or is absorbed piecemeal into a stronger successor. The argument in this book is that in the case of the British the long fuse was lit by their great geostrategic defeats of 1939–42. Thereafter, the whole balance of their system was badly upset, its legitimacy corroded, and the terms of collaboration with its clients and subjects decisively (if not immediately) altered. After 1945, British leaders struggled in vain to correct the imbalance, not least the fatal imbalance that shifted the burdens of empire so much more on to Britain itself. They planned to relieve the main stresses by conceding self-government and sometimes independence while preserving a prime influence in the old zones of rule. They were heartened by signs that their efforts were working and misled by the caution of their opponents and rivals. Until 1960, it was still possible to think that much of the fabric of empire (in its more decentralized form) would still hold together. The threads had been loosened, not finally severed. But with one final tug (of economic and geopolitical change) all the connections were broken and the whole fell to pieces. It only remained to re-imagine the future – and invent a new past.

12

The Last and Largest Empire?

'To the last and the largest empire, to the map that is half unrolled', sing the white settlers in Kipling's poem 'The Native Born' (1894). The British Empire was certainly not the last of empires but – if we discount the empire of influence that America built after 1945 – it was at its zenith perhaps the largest in world history. Although its era of global pre-eminence was comparatively brief (from the 1830s to the 1940s), an empire ruled from London endured for more than 500 years if we include (as we should) its medieval foundations. We should resist the idea that the British Empire was unique, since empire has been one of the commonest forms of political unit for most of world history. Portugal, Spain, France and the Netherlands rivalled Britain in creating overseas empires; so later on did Germany and Italy. Russia became master of much of North Asia, and remains so today. Nor were British motives and methods so utterly different from those of the great Asian empires to which they were forced to pay court until the mid eighteenth century. The Chinese ideal of a scholar-mandarin bureaucracy, serving a far-away emperor in provinces where they had no local ties, was ironically echoed in the British-staffed Indian Civil Service, the so-called 'steel frame' of British rule in South Asia. The British borrowed much of their system of governance in India from their Mughal predecessors. And like the Ottomans, they often preferred to divide up their subjects by their religious allegiance, or by some other marker of ethnic identity (imagined or real), rather than rule them *en masse* as a common body of subjects.

Like all empires, perhaps, the British made theirs by exploiting connections. It is now a commonplace that the movement of people, goods and ideas over short distances or long has been the great shaping force of human history, perhaps the greatest driver of historical change. Much of this has occurred outside the control of rulers or states, or against their opposition. Its effect was to create new forms of connectedness within regions, between them, or even globe-wide. New trading connections, new religious ideas, new migrant communities (sometimes all three) constantly unsettled established societies. They created new opportunities, challenged old interests, threatened old hierarchies. They could create the conditions for a stealth invasion by outsiders bearing gifts: a prestigious material culture; a seductive religion; the promise of commercial advantage. This dynamic environment favoured those states best placed to exploit these forms of connection on which they fastened like parasites, and to insert their own agents into regions previously closed to their influence. Great empires and small have followed this path to aggrandizement, sometimes close by, sometimes across continents and, in a few cases, from one side of the world to the other.

The British were able to build a world empire because they exploited the opportunities of global connectedness more fully than their rivals. But they had to wait until the means of connection lay ready to hand, and until their own cocktail of assets could be used to advantage. It was the Spanish who pioneered Europe's lasting Atlantic connection (the Scandinavian link with North America failed), and the Portuguese who found the maritime route to the East. The Dutch first devised the commercial apparatus to control the supply of Asian commodities to Europe by sea. The British came late to the party. But by the end of the seventeenth century, they had begun to command the crucial resources required for success in these new global ventures. Firstly, although not completely ideal in terms of wind systems, their offshore position placed them at the crossroads of Europe's main sea-going trades: between northern Europe and the Mediterranean and between Atlantic Europe and the Americas. They were exceptionally well placed to serve as the entrepot for the trades that grew fastest. Secondly, despite the turmoil of civil war and revolution between 1640 and 1660, the means to construct a strong central state had survived. A well-funded 'fiscal-military' state, capable of dispatching a large army to Europe (as in the War of Spanish Succession 1702–13) and, more to the point, of maintaining a large deep-sea navy, played a critical role in protecting (and sometimes extending) the commercial connections that their rivals were eager to strangle. Thirdly, the British had begun to enjoy the advantages of the well-integrated domestic economy so brilliantly portrayed in Daniel Defoe's *Tour Through the Whole Island of Great Britain*. Indeed, London was already beginning to play its part as the central place where market information was exchanged and financial arrangements were made for trade within Britain, across the Atlantic and with mainland Europe. Its crucial combination of roles as the centre of government (and of public finance), as the greatest consumer of domestic production and its principal market, and as a great mercantile seaport for overseas commerce, conferred a major advantage over its European competitors.

But perhaps the strongest card that the British were able to use in exploiting and expanding Europe's global connections was to be so adaptable. The hallmark of British imperialism was its extraordinary versatility in method, outlook and object. As we saw in an earlier chapter, the British imagined different kinds of empire, sought different kinds of relations with client peoples and subjects, and pursued a wide range of interests that were sometimes in conflict with one another. They were able to appeal to the self-interest or sympathy of a multitude of partners, allies, compradors, collaborators and converts in different parts of the world. The British connection was, more often than not, a set of British connections. Those who disliked one face of British imperialism could usually find an alternative, more liberal, humane or respectful. This was no accident. It reflected the fact that by the eighteenth century at latest, Britain had become a remarkably pluralistic society, tolerating different religions, sustaining different subcultures (regional, religious, intellectual and class-based), and with a political system open to new wealth and new ideological influences (evangelicalism and anti-slavery were the two prime examples). This pluralistic society threw up not one kind of motive for overseas empire, nor one kind of technique with which to construct it, but an enormous variety. Gentry hoping to fuel their social ambitions with an overseas fortune, courtiers exploiting Crown rights of monopoly, patrons and placemen thirsting for colonial appointments, Catholics and Puritans wanting places of refuge, slaveowners (of whom there were many thousand in Britain) looking to keep their human property safe, abolitionists intent on suppressing the slave trade, merchants and manufacturers scouting for markets, migrants craving free empty lands overseas, churchmen and missionaries pursuing the 'Empire of Christ': all these and more enlisted British resources in their imperial ambitions, as well as scanning the globe for new opportunities.

They could do this all the more freely because this was in the main a private enterprise empire. The role of the state was largely confined to the granting of charters that conferred commercial monopoly or jurisdictional power on companies or proprietors. Colonizing America, like trade with the East, depended on private capital and was at private risk. Slowly the state began to interfere more directly in this overseas enterprise and assume its protection. But action was spasmodic and regulation generally light. Since the prime motive was profit, and not the glory of Church or king, this was an empire of commercial experiments not an empire of rule by design. Economic survival required the ready adoption of new kinds of crops, new ways of farming and new sources of labour. English immigrants had been replaced by African slaves on the Barbados plantations within thirty years of the colony's founding. Colonies were also forced to compete with each other since they often exported the same kind of produce (sugar, tobacco, lumber, wool), and looked to Britain for credit and capital and sometimes for manpower. They had a powerful incentive to be attractive to all three – with obvious implications for their property laws, taxation and distribution of land. Settlers, planters and merchants tried to maintain a strong lobby in London to laud their colony's promise, ward off 'interference' (like the abolition of slavery), or demand naval and military help. They were eager for news from the centre of empire and even more eager to plant their own news in Fleet Street and Grub Street. When necessary, they promoted associations and societies to recruit wider support – like Cecil Rhodes's Imperial South Africa Association. And although planters and settlers were particularly good at this game, Indians and Africans quickly saw its potential for circumventing the 'official mind' and finding influential allies and friends in Britain. It was a lobby like this that helped to keep India's claim to self-government on the British political agenda after 1900.[1]

Empire-building was thus a higgledy-piggledy process in which government policy, or decisions taken in Whitehall, were only a part (sometimes a small part) of the story. By the late eighteenth century, however, we can see that Britain's overseas empire had begun to be sorted into four different divisions, almost different sub-empires. After *c.* 1830, the British were unique in possessing a large number of self-governing colonies (in North America, the Caribbean and Australasia) ruled by settlers or planters in elected assemblies. Although the original number was whittled down by amalgamation or (in the Caribbean case) the loss of planter self-government, the existence of so many dependencies over whose internal affairs London had almost no control, mystified both foreign observers and much opinion in Britain, for whom a colony, as they were still called, was a colony and 'responsible government' a constitutional riddle. Stranger still, perhaps, was the tendency of the settler societies in Canada, Australia and New Zealand (and the British fraction of South African whites) to stress more and more not their difference from Britain but their claim to shared Britishness, even better Britishness – an improved version of the original. In the twentieth century, that sense of shared Britishness, as much as self-interest, inspired extraordinary levels of sacrifice in two world wars.

Self-governing colonies may have seemed an imperial oddity. But it was Britain's possession of India that made it a great Asian power, and for much of the nineteenth century, *the* Asian power. No other European state acquired an overseas territory on remotely this scale, or one which conferred such astonishing benefits. With India in their hands, the British had the means to exert their power across a huge swathe of the world from the Persian Gulf to the South China Sea, and even for a time into the Sea of Japan. This was partly because India supplied so many mercantile assets (Indian merchants as well as cotton and opium). But India's unique value lay mainly in the fact that it gave the British an army. After the Mutiny, when the Indian army was shrunk, and the all-British garrison enlarged, two thirds of Britain's regular forces (Indian and British) were paid for by the Indian taxpayer. The India-based forces could be, and were, used for imperial purposes – a category easily blurred. If India's contribution (fiercely resented by Indian nationalists) is fitted into the larger scheme of the empire's military power, it is easy to see its significance. London was able to spend much more modestly on its army in peacetime than would otherwise have been possible, and much more generously on its navy. Defence spending was thus far less of a political issue in Britain than it might have been otherwise. But there was a sting in the tail that became increasingly painful. Because India's defence budget was so crucial to public spending in Britain, India could not be given self-government on white colony terms, in case its elected assembly declined to pay the Home Charges – the rent for the British garrison – or for the huge cost of the army. Right up to 1939, this issue – which lay at the heart of India's constitutional progress – remained unresolved.

The third kind of empire was really a ragbag: a mass of small or (usually) less valuable territories. They were bases and fortresses such as Gibraltar, Malta, Hong Kong and St Helena (originally acquired as a way station for East India Company ships sailing to and from India); a clutch of tropical colonies, some like Ceylon and Malaya highly profitable plantation colonies; maritime bridgeheads with a straggling interior (as in East and West Africa); decaying 'old' colonies with a great future behind them (much of the British West Indies); booming trade entrepots like Singapore and Hong Kong; and a sprinkling of minnows acquired for no discernible reason but hard to abandon. They were ruled by authoritarian methods, like so many 'little Indias' although with much local variation. They were really the offspring of two sorts of power: naval power based in Britain and military (and some naval) power based in India. Their seemingly random distribution reflected in fact the overlapping fields of these two magnetic poles of imperialism. They helped to make the British Empire less a recognizable bloc with boundaries and limits than a vast archipelago, strewn across the world. Politically, like India, they were garrison states in which a band of British officials resisted the claims of creole politicians – however anglicized, christianized or loyal – to a share of administrative power, proclaiming instead the need to acknowledge tradition and seek traditional allies. This was often the high road to a form of 'caretaker imperialism': hold on, hang on, do nothing.

There was a fourth kind of empire that was nearly invisible. Informal empire existed without benefit of governors or flags, annexation or sovereignty. It relied upon the influence of merchants and bankers, consuls and diplomats, sometimes with gunboats and garrisons not far away. Its classic expressions were Britain's business empires in Argentina and Uruguay, the temporary occupation of Egypt (1882–1956) and treaty port China. It helps to remind us that staring at maps can sometimes delude. For the invisible empire was functionally inseparable from its visible counterpart. Informal colonies were often much more valuable commercially (like Argentina) or strategically (Egypt above all) than the formal variety. Some formal colonies – the bases and depots – derived much of their value from the informal empire that had sprung up nearby; this was true of Hong Kong and perhaps of the Falklands. But informal empire was also an unstable category. British power was exerted informally because the cost and effort of rule seemed unnecessary, or because rule would have been too hard to impose. It was a compromise that depended on the cooperation of locals and the absence of rivals. When these preconditions broke down, hard choices had to be made: between asserting much more control (with its commitments and risks) and accepting much less authority. On the China coast after 1920, with Chinese nationalism in front and Japanese imperialism behind, the British felt this dilemma with particular sharpness.

In one sense, of course, the imperial archipelago, whether formal or informal, was the outgrowth of more than naval and military power. Much of the human capital that sustained British expansion derived from the propensity of the British to migrate. It was the huge emigrant stream that made the British the greatest exponents of demographic imperialism, not merely ruling but physically occupying so much of the globe. Twice as many people emigrated from the British Isles between 1815 and 1930 as from any other part of Europe (the total was 19 million; Italy came second with 9 million). Although migration can be driven by many different impulses, in the British case it was closely related to the demands of a dynamic economy. Rapid economic development encouraged population growth. Diverging prospects made some British regions into importers of people and some into exporters. In parts of Scotland and Ireland (where ecological hazard added a grim extra twist) the outflow was huge. By the later nineteenth century, a similar exodus affected rural England as well. But, as if in compensation, it was Britain's commercial and industrial economy that supplied a solution – harsh and inhumane as it might have appeared. It was the commercial development of what became settlement regions (in North America above all) that equipped them to absorb the great influx of people and employ them productively. It was Britain's industrial economy that made it the world's largest consumer of imported produce, raw materials and food stuffs, from *c.* 1800 to 1940 and thus a huge market for the settlement regions. The flows of migration from the British Isles can be seen as part of a huge rearrangement of the domestic economy in which much of the work of growing food and other materials was transferred overseas, along with the labour that was needed.

Of course, the expansion of Britain into a world-spanning power depended from the beginning on commercial success. Its precocious development as an integrated commercial economy was then supercharged (the two are not unrelated) by industrialization – carried further and faster in Britain than anywhere else in the nineteenth century. The commercial origins of Britain's overseas empire shaped its whole character. In an agrarian empire, the ruler must tax his subjects directly if he is to profit from power. He must exert close control (with its costs and risks) to prevent his agents from defrauding him and diverting his revenues into their own pockets. The effort and burden of doing this tended to set limits to imperial ambition, since the remoter the province the harder it was to supervise from the centre. A commercial empire was largely free from this constraint. It had no interest in raising a direct local revenue, and therefore no need for an oppressive close rule. It relied instead on the profits of trade, taxed at the point where collection was easiest – in the home ports. When the British departed from this golden rule (as they did in the 1770s in America), disaster soon followed. Nevertheless, a check did exist on the scope of commercial empire. As long as the profits of commerce were thought to derive from the careful exclusion of rival empires of trade, an expensive apparatus of sea power was needed to enforce the monopoly. Nor was it any coincidence that the great expansion of trade between Europe, the Americas and Asia in the long eighteenth century up to 1815 was marked by prolonged periods of naval and colonial war between the European states.

Famously, the loss of the American colonies in 1783 was the prelude not to Britain's decline and fall as an imperial power (as many jeremiads of the day proclaimed) but to an extraordinary transition. After 1815, the British Empire became the one genuinely global empire – a status it maintained until 1940. That the British were able to make such an empire required the conjunction of two epoch-making changes in their global position. The first was the achievement of naval primacy, secured at Trafalgar in 1805, and jealously guarded thereafter. By destroying the maritime power of their principal rivals, they broke down the barriers that had restricted their trade and erased the threats that made it so expensive to guard. Henceforth, the whole world was their market – in theory at least. The costs of a globe-wide empire came tumbling down. But the promise this offered would have been much less had it not coincided with Britain's conversion from a commercial into an industrial and commercial economy. Indeed, it is easy to see that without industrialization, the effort to maintain a commercial empire on a global scale might have become unsustainable. It was coal, cotton and capital, not derring-do or district officers, on which Britain's world empire was built.

This was partly because a steam-driven empire, soon bound together by telegraph wires, was much more efficient than one dependent on winds and currents for its motive power. The swifter movement of information and people accelerated economic development, increased the volume of trade and allowed resources to be switched quickly between places and purposes. One obvious convenience lay in the deployment of troops. The telegraph and the steamship allowed the relatively small British army of around 150,000 men, and its Indian counterpart, to be shuffled quickly round the globe to imperial emergencies – like a fire brigade always on call. Steam-powered vessels extended Britain's reach up rivers (such as the Yangtze) and along previously inaccessible coastlines, like that of the Red Sea. With the building of railways – a core British technology – vast new areas of the world came within reach, both commercial and military. Railways turned the British, hitherto mainly a sea power, into a land *and* sea power, a huge increase of capacity. Armed with cheap textiles (steam-driven spinning and weaving allowed a massive reduction in the costs of manufacture), the British now had the means to penetrate markets world-wide. Advancing cheap credit, building cheap transport, they drew a growing mass of producers in the Americas, Asia and Africa into their web.

Thus the great advantage of an industrial empire lay in its ability to *integrate* a wide range of regions, however remote, into a single system of wealth and power. This worked in three ways. Firstly, by producing for export either to Britain or through Britain, colonial or semi-colonial economies became dependent on the commercial apparatus for long-distance trade that the British provided – at a cost. Once they were hooked up to this link, and reliant upon it for local prosperity, withdrawal was difficult and likely to be painful. Indeed, the tendency was to conform more and more to the demands that it made, to become more and more specialized in the economic functions it rewarded. Secondly, economic integration had social and cultural consequences. Vested interests grew up for whom the British connection was the indispensable mainstay of their status and wealth. They were keen to promote it, not whittle it down. The wealth created by trade encouraged the social and cultural emulation of the imperial metropolis. It stimulated a fast-growing volume of information exchange: the circulation of news, legal opinion, commercial and scientific inquiry, imaginative literature and private correspondence between the different parts of the empire, and even the emergence to varying degrees of a common imperial culture. Thirdly, the growth of an industrial society and economy in Britain brought an increasing diversity in its needs, outlook and tastes. By the mid nineteenth century, Britain was also a predominantly urban society – restless and mobile. The demands of the urban consumer, for food and cheap luxuries (like tobacco or chocolate), as well as entertainment and knowledge, swelled the volume of imports (the value of tobacco imports rose by 30 times between 1826 and 1913). There was almost no part of the world whose produce could not find a market in Britain or whose commercial prospects did not appeal to British investors, merchants and adventurers. And at the heart of this urban-imperial nexus was London whose extraordinary growth (London's population rose from 1 million to 7 million between 1801 and 1911) into a global metropolis played a critical role in the integration of empire, as much culturally as commercially. London stood at the centre of (and had helped to create) a network of imperial port cities – Montreal, Cape Town, Colombo, Bombay, Calcutta, Singapore, Hong Kong, Melbourne, Sydney and Auckland – between which much of the business of empire was transacted. It was not just in Britain that the British Empire was an urban phenomenon. It was from these urban bridgeheads that British influence was expected to reach into the backward interiors of the colonial world.

Free trade was the ideology of this great outward movement. The British quickly forgot that their own rise to world power before 1815 had relied upon a heavy dose of protection. Free trade, they insisted, was good for everyone and not just for them. By opening their empire to the trade of all nations, the British assumed that they had made it acceptable to the rest of the world. Up to a point that was true: it may have helped to discourage the formation of grand coalitions against them. But this ignored the extent to which free trade was dependent on the application of British power. 'Did Lancashire realize that it was by force that the free import of cottons was imposed on India?' asked Halford Mackinder, a vehement protectionist, in 1919. 'Both Free Trade of the *laissez faire* type and Protection of the predatory type are policies of Empire and both make for War.'[2] The British had used sea power to make a free-trading world empire. Germany had built its own high seas fleet to create a protectionist one. A collision was inevitable, said Mackinder – with some advantage from hindsight.

But the growth of empire was not simply the sum of economic and strategic decisions, nor a rational calculus of the costs and benefits that might accrue to Britain. Empire-building was driven by visions and fantasies, and sustained by myth and delusion. Those who tried to direct it had to remember that British opinion (whose support and approval they needed) was flighty at best. Enraged by reckless adventures in Afghanistan and South Africa, the electorate hurled Disraeli from office in 1880. Twenty years later, as Lord Salisbury complained, he was forced into war in South Africa by a 'jingo hurricane' at home. In large parts of the empire, British rule had been established by force and was maintained by coercion. But violence against natives was habitual, not just instrumental. 'I noticed in all the hotels in India the significant notice, "Gentlemen are earnestly requested not to strike the servants",' reported Charles Dilke in 1869.[3] African mine labour, as we saw in an earlier chapter, was treated with a routine brutality that verged on the psychopathic. Of course, such indiscriminate violence was partly the product of a violent culture at home: the British flogged their own soldiers but not their Indian sepoys. But it also derived from their tenacious belief in a scale of racial capacities in which they stood at the top.

This 'vulgar racism' may have owed its origins to the practice of slavery and to the 'logic' behind its public defence in the anti-slavery debate of the late eighteenth century. But it is easy to see why it became so widely diffused in the British version of empire. Its fortunes were linked to the rise of social evolution as the grand explanation for the differential performance of states, nations and peoples in the acquisition of wealth and the building of states. 'Scientific' or 'biological' racism was really top-dressing for older, deeper and primarily cultural prejudices. Intellectually, social evolution strengthened its grip long into the twentieth century – indeed up to and after the Second World War. Vulgar racism itself was not intellectual, but a set of linked assumptions and attitudes. It postulated not only a civilizational hierarchy but also the need for those at the top to guard against 'dilution' or overthrow by the world's 'lesser breeds'. It prescribed racial separation and race solidarity as the best form of protection against the two great dangers that threatened: the loss of civilizational impetus by racial mixing and the loss of control were the 'lower races' to revolt. In both the empire of settlement and the empire of rule, these racial prescriptions had an obvious appeal.

In the settlement colonies, even those like Canada, Australia and New Zealand where the indigenous population had shrunk to an embattled minority, the racial exclusion of non-European migrants had become a pressing concern by the later nineteenth century. This was partly because it was then that their economic expansion seemed likely to draw on Asian labour supplies – Chinese coolies helped build the Canadian Pacific Railway. But it was also because this was the era when the need to construct modern nations out of rough frontier communities acquired a new urgency. Temperance, education, stable family life, regular forms of employment, these were the attributes of a well-policed and well-regulated society. But their enactment required strong political will, an ideology and a model. The modernizers looked

– not surprisingly – mainly to Britain. They were anxious to claim that their societies were new Britains: fit destinations for the immigrant masses they longed to attract. To replicate Britain, and ideally to improve on it, to create a closely organized state that was based on consent, required, they believed, a high degree of cultural uniformity: that was the British model. Only a common British high culture in which the whole population could share would permit their advance to become true British nations in North America and the South Pacific. The racial exclusion of 'others' was the vital corollary of the nation-building project.

Of course, this high-minded objective was reinforced by less respectable motives: the fear of white labour that Chinese, Indians and Africans would drive down their wages. In those settlement colonies where whites were the minority, civilizational aspiration was the obverse of physical fear – that the subjugated majority would rise against them. In the empire of rule (as in the old slave colonies), the same threat of revolt – however remote – was the ultimate horror. Even if civilian in style, these were really garrison states in which a small alien group commanded the citadel. Power and authority depended upon – perhaps even derived from – the solidarity of the garrison. As British rule expanded in India, the need to insist on the separation of rulers and ruled became stronger and stronger. This was partly because of the danger that British officials might be drawn into partnership with local Indian networks of influence. (The 'disappearing' into local society of its administrative agents was the insidious form of subversion faced by all 'empires of domination'.[4]) But it was hugely reinforced by the fear and fact of rebellion, above all that of 1857. Henceforth, no white person in India could escape the constant reminder – by history, myth and commemoration – that racial solidarity was the price of survival. By the time that the British also became rulers in tropical Africa, this 'Indian' mentality had become commonplace. It derived enormous additional force from what might be called the 'trade union' outlook of white British officials. Again and again they insisted (in subtle mandarin prose) that skin colour was the only sure marker of political trust. To dilute white authority by making it subject to non-white assemblies or by recruiting non-white officials was the road to perdition.

Thus a vision of race solidarity common to the empire of settlement and the empire of rule was, alongside economic and military power and the empire-wide apparatus of institutions and laws, a crucial component of imperial cohesion. It found a strong echo at home, but only an echo. Opinion in Britain adopted many distinctly imperial beliefs – not least the assumption that British migration to 'empty' lands overseas was a British birthright. But contrary to what is some-times suggested, Britain was not in any obvious way a product of empire. It was not 'constituted' by empire – a modish but vacuous expression. The main reason for this was that its English core was already an exceptionally strong and culturally unified state (taking language and law as the most obvious criteria) long before it acquired an empire beyond Europe. Imperial attitudes entered Britain, but only (like the tea-drinking habit) after they had been suitably anglicized. When they confronted powerful home prejudices, such as the opposi-tion to slavery, support for free trade or the urge to evangelize the overseas heathen, they had little hope of prevailing. The cry of race solidarity proved no defence when British governments resolved to abandon the settler minorities in tropical Africa after 1960. Once the preservation of a territorial empire had become a seemingly unsus-tainable burden, domestic imperialism died with a whimper.

That all empires decline is an historical truism: so far, indeed, all empires have. It is only a short step to assume that decline was pre-dictable, and that the historian can point to the moment when its onset was inevitable. It is certainly true that in most of the empires we know of there were prophets of doom, forecasting disaster ahead without military, material or moral reform. In a society as pluralistic as Britain's there were always plenty of voices to speak against empire, but very little agreement as to what that empire was. Thus those who disliked the authoritarianism of British rule in the Raj would have been aghast at the idea that the connection with Canada or Australia should be broken. More usually they argued that extending repre-sentative government to Indians (and later to Africans) would win their lasting allegiance to Britain's liberal world empire. Even as extreme an anti-imperialist as the Marxist John Strachey could look forward (in 1932) to a Bolshevik Britain that would 'cooperate' with its colonies in much the same way that Moscow cooperated with the old tsarist empire.[5] In most mainstream opinion in Britain, certainly up to the Second World War, there was an extraordinary confidence that, while many adjustments might be needed, the empire would survive as a system of states centred on Britain, dependent on Britain for capital, technology and strategic defence, and British in values, institutions and ideas. Whence came this confidence?

It derived above all from belief that the British Empire was unique and incomparable. Three key characteristics would save it from the fate of all previous imperialisms. Firstly, the head and heart of the empire, in Britain itself, was an open society and politically liberal. The sclerosis that had overcome empires in the past, when entrenched oligarchies resisted economic and social change, would have no purchase there. The free exchange of ideas, the free expression of opinion and free representative institutions formed an iron guarantee that the spirit of government would be constant adaptation to new pressures and needs. Indeed, the British prided themselves on the unrivalled efficiency with which information and news from every part of the world was transmitted to London and circulated within Britain. They contrasted this openness with the closed political worlds of failed empires in the past and of those that collapsed after 1918. Their histories taught them that British society was uniquely progressive. Secondly, there was an equal conviction that the British economy was dynamic and adaptable, the reward of free trade. The American economy might be bigger, and German industry more efficient, but Britain remained up to 1939 the world's greatest trader and the world's largest investor. The deadweight of depression, when the British reluctantly abandoned free trade, was felt less severely in Britain and the sterling bloc than in either the United States or Germany. Thirdly, most – perhaps all – British leaders assumed that their empire would continue to enjoy exceptional geostrategic security as long as the right precautions were taken. This view became deeply entrenched after 1815. The empire's maritime character, its very limited exposure to any frontal attack, the remoteness of most British possessions from the cockpit of Europe, ruled out most of the dangers against which other great powers had to guard so expensively. The British could blockade enemy states in wartime, seize their overseas assets and drive their shipping from the seas – the prerogative of sea power. They were a formidable opponent, but one whose apparent detachment from Europe's inter-necine quarrels removed the obvious sources of friction with other large states, and made a coalition against them an unlikely event. And although the experience of the First World War might have demol-ished some of this confidence, its actual outcome did not. Until the late 1930s, it was the weakness and division of all the rival great powers that was the prime fact in world politics. That Britain would be unable to manoeuvre between them, to exploit their divisions and contain any threat, seemed almost absurdly improbable.

Indeed, geostrategic security was the sheet anchor of empire. So long as no external enemy broke into their empire, or so ran the rea-soning, the British could always suppress any internal disruption. So long as their prestige and authority were not diminished by defeat, they could overawe the separatist demands of nationalist movements. Indeed, so long as Britain remained a great independent world power in Europe *and* Asia, separatism (i.e. a complete break with Britain) would appeal only to the fringe of extremists: moderate, sensible nationalists would reject it as futile. With the advantage of hindsight, we might treat such views as naïve, or at best too optimistic. But we cannot be sure.

Explaining the end of empires is an uncertain business. The British case has attracted a host of historical experts. They invoke a legion of causes indicting economic, political, military, diplomatic, techno-logical, social and cultural failure. All may be true. But what made those failures so costly, and cumulatively fatal, was something much deeper. In the long view of world history, Britain's age of world empire was only a phase, an exceptional moment. Its chance was cre-ated by one of history's unpredicted conjunctures – when conditions in both Europe and East Asia were simultaneously favourable. A weak and passive East Asia, a Europe precariously in balance between its rival great states, combined with an introverted America and an Islamic world in disarray, provided the perfect conditions for British expansion. Naval supremacy, and the rise of steam power on the back of unlimited coal, helped the British to exploit this unforeseen opportunity at a cost they could bear. They weathered the storms of imperial competition in the 1880s and 1890s surprisingly comforta-bly. They survived the Great War, and enlarged their possessions. But when revolution and war convulsed both Europe and East Asia in the late 1930s, and when strategic disaster in Europe was followed by a cataclysm in Asia, the essential preconditions for British world power vanished for ever. A new world emerged. A new geopolitical order was born. There was no going back.

Notes

ABBREVIATIONS

CAB	Cabinet Office Records in the National Archives
CO	Colonial Office Records in the National Archives
PP	British Parliamentary Papers
PREM	Prime Ministers' Records in the National Archives
TNA	The U.K. National Archives, Kew, London
WO	War Office Records, in the National Archives

1. IMAGINING EMPIRE

1. See A. Zimmern, *The Third British Empire* (Oxford, 1926). Zimmern was a pioneer scholar of international relations.

2. This went down badly in Oxford: Williams's thesis was published in the United States in 1944 as *Capitalism and Slavery*, but only twenty years later in Britain.

3. See P. Maylam, *The Cult of Rhodes* (Claremont, 2005), pp. 10–11.

4. Ibid., pp. 36, 42.

5. 'Liberal' historians tended to resist inevitability; Marxist historians to assert it.

6. See V. Chaturvedi (ed.), *Mapping Subaltern Studies and the Post Colonial* (London, 2000) for an excellent survey.

7. For the European 'dark ages', see P. J. Geary, *The Myth of Nations: The Medieval Origins of Europe* (Princeton, 2002).

8. For a recent discussion, J. Goldstone and J. F. Haldon, 'Ancient States, Empires and Exploitation', in I. Morris and W. Scheidel (eds.), *The Dynamics of Ancient Empires* (Oxford, 2009).

9. J. Gallagher and R. Robinson, 'The Imperialism of Free Trade', *Economic History Review*, 2nd Series, VI, 1 (1953).

10. For a recent analysis, N. Draper, *The Price of Emancipation: Slave-Ownership, Compensation and British Society at the End of Slavery* (Cambridge, 2010).

11. These institutional foundations can be followed in the magisterial volumes of F. Madden (ed.), *Select Documents on the Constitutional History of the British Empire and Commonwealth* (8 vols., Westport, CN, 1985–2000), esp. vol. 1: '*The Empire of the Bretaignes*' (1985).

12. R. R. Davies, '*The First English Empire* (Oxford, 2000), p. 9.

13. See R. R. Davies, 'Colonial Wales', *Past and Present* 65, 1 (1974), 3–23.

14. Davies, *First English Empire*, pp. 121ff.

15. N. Rodger, *The Safeguard of the Sea: A Naval History of Britain*, vol. 1: *660–1649* (London, 1997), p. 100.

16. See L. Colley, *Britons* (London, 1992).

17. Rodger, *Safeguard*, pp. 229–30.

18. N. Canny, *Making Ireland British 1580–1650* (Oxford, 2001), p. 66.

19. See D. H. Sacks, *The Widening Gate: Bristol and the Atlantic Economy 1450–1700* (Berkeley, 1991); A. Peacock, 'The Men of Bristol and the Atlantic Discovery Voyages of the Fifteenth and Early Sixteenth Centuries', MA thesis, Bristol University, consulted online at http://www.bris.ac.uk/Depts/History/Maritime/Sources/2007mapeacock.htm; E. Jones, 'The *Matthew* of Bristol and the Financiers of John Cabot's Voyage to North America', *English Historical Review*, cxxi, 492 (2006), 778–95.

20. For Drake's activities, K. R. Andrews, *Drake's Voyages* (London, 1967).

21. This was Richard Hakluyt in 1595–8. See D. Armitage, *The Ideological Origins of the British Empire* (Cambridge, 2000), p. 108.

22. See M. Nicholls and P. Williams, 'Sir Walter Ralegh' in *Oxford Dictionary of National Biography* online.

23. See C. Hill, 'Ralegh – Science, History and Politics', in his *The Intellectual Origins of the English Revolution* (Oxford, 1965), p. 154.

24. Cited in E. Williams (ed.), *Documents of West Indian History 1492–1655* (Port of Spain, 1963), p. 269.

25. D. B. Quinn, *Raleigh and the British Empire* (pbk edn, London, 1962), p. 134.

26. G. Holmes, *British Politics in the Age of Anne* (London, 1967).

27. Quoted in Sacks, *Widening Gate*, p. 340.

28. For a recent survey, K. Morgan, 'Mercantilism and the British Empire 1688–1815', in D. Winch and P. K. O'Brien (eds.), *The Political Economy of British Historical Experience, 1688–1914* (London, 2002), pp. 165–92.

29. E. Williams, *Capitalism and Slavery* (new edn, London, 1994), p. 56.

30. Williams, *Documents of West Indian History*, p. 290.

31. Quoted in Jack P. Greene, 'Liberty and Slavery' in Jack P. Greene (ed.), *Exclusionary Empire: English Liberty Overseas 1600–1900* (Cambridge, 2010), p. 61.

32. P. Earle, *The World of Defoe* (London, 1976), p. 130.

33. Williams, *Capitalism and Slavery*, pp. 40–41.

34. Quoted in T. B. Macaulay, *History of England* (Everyman edn, London, 1906), vol. III, p. 278.

35. Speech on 'Conciliation with America', 22 March 1775, in *Burke's Speeches and Letters on American Affairs* (Everyman edn, London, 1908), p. 105.

36. The classic study of this is P. J. Marshall, *The Impeachment of Warren Hastings* (Oxford, 1965).

37. Macaulay in the House of Commons, 10 July 1833. A. B. Keith (ed.), *Speeches and Documents on Indian Policy 1750–1921* (Oxford, 1922), vol. 2, p. 244.

38. J. S. Mill, *Representative Government* (1861), ch. 18.

39. See E. T. Stokes, *The English Utilitarians and India* (Oxford, 1959).

40. For the Indian case, T.R. Metcalf, *Ideologies of the Raj* (Cambridge, 1995).

41. C. Dilke, *Greater Britain* (1869), p. vii.

42. J. A. Froude, *Oceana* (1886).

43. R. Cobden, *England, Ireland and America* (1835), p. 11.

44. R. Cobden, 'How Wars Are Got Up in India', *The Political Writings of Richard Cobden*, vol. 2 (1868), pp. 105ff.

45. C. W. Newbury (ed.), *British Policy Towards West Africa: Select Documents 1786–1874* (Oxford, 1965), p. 120: Palmerston's Minute, 22 April 1860.

46. H. J. Mackinder, 'The Geographical Pivot of History', *Geographical Journal* 23, 4 (1904), 231–47.

47. J.Swift, 'A Voyage to the Houyhnhnms' in *Gulliver's Travels* (1726).

48. For a graphic account of what they did, T. Burnard, *Mastery, Tyranny and Desire: Thomas Thistlewood and his Slaves in the Anglo-Jamaican World* (Chapel Hill, NC, 2004).

49. See Cobden, 'How Wars Are Got Up in India', pp. 105ff.

50. In his *The Empire* (1863).

51. Quoted in K. Knorr, *British Colonial Theories 1570–1850* (Toronto, 1944), p. 373.

2. MAKING CONTACT

1. See D. K. Richter, *Facing East from Indian Country* (Cambridge, MA, 2001), pp. 8–10.

2. See R. Law, *Ouidah: the Social History of a West African Slaving Port* (Oxford, 2004), ch. 1, for the practice of separate quarters in West Africa.

3. I have adopted this useful term from I. K. Steele, *The English Atlantic 1675–1740: An Exploration of Communication and Community* (Oxford, 1986).

4. See D. B. Quinn, *England and the Discovery of America* (London, 1974), p. 288.

5. See P. D. Morgan, 'Virginia's Other Prototype: the Caribbean' in P. C. Mancall (ed.), *The Atlantic World and Virginia 1550–1624* (Chapel Hill, NC, 2007).

6. P. P. Boucher, 'First Impressions: Europeans and Island Caribs in the Pre-Colonial Era, 1492–1623' in V. Shepherd and H. McD. Beckles (eds.), *Caribbean Slavery in the Atlantic World* (Oxford, 2000), p. 109.

7. See H. McD. Beckles, 'Kalinago (Carib) Resistance to European Colonization of the Caribbean', in Shepherd and Beckles, *Caribbean Slavery*, pp. 117–26.

8. See D. Buisseret, 'The Taylor Manuscript and Seventeenth Century Jamaica', in R. A. McDonald (ed.), *West Indian Accounts* (Kingston, Jamaica, 1996).

9. T. Burnard, 'European Migration to Jamaica, 1655–1780', *William and Mary Quarterly*, 3rd Series, 52, 4 (1996), 769–96.

10. For some of these ideas, see G. Lewis, 'Pro-slavery Ideology' and E. Goveia, 'West Indian Slave Laws of the Eighteenth Century', both in Shepherd and Beckles, *Caribbean Slavery*.

11. H. McD. Beckles, 'Property Rights in Pleasure: The Marketing of Enslaved Women's Sexuality', in Shepherd and Beckles, *Caribbean Slavery*, p. 701.

12. The case was Thomas Thistlewood (1721–86). See D. Hall, *In Miserable Slavery: Thomas Thistlewood in Jamaica 1750–86* (Basingstoke, 1989). For the motive/intention, T. Burnard, *Mastery, Tyranny and Desire: Thomas Thistlewood and his Slaves in the Anglo-Jamaican World* (Chapel Hill, NC, 2004).

13. R. S. Dunn, *Sugar and Slaves: The Rise of the Planter Class in the English West Indies 1624–1713* (Chapel Hill, NC, 1972), p. 231.

14. Quoted in A. G. Hopkins, *An Economic History of West Africa* (London, 1973), p. 87.

15. D. Eltis, 'The Relative Importance of Slaves and Commodities in the Atlantic Trade of Seventeenth-Century Africa', *Journal of African History* 35 (1994), 244–5.

16. For an introduction, see R. S. Smith, *Warfare and Diplomacy in Pre-colonial West Africa* (London, 1976); R. Law, *The Slave Coast of West Africa 1550–1750* (Oxford, 1991).

17. I have drawn on Law, *Ouidah*, for this description.

18. Smith's instructions can be found on the highly informative website *Virtual Jamestown, www.virtualjamestown.org*.

19. See D. Blanton, 'Jamestown's Environment' in *Virtual Jamestown*.

20. See S. Mallios, *The Deadly Politics of Giving: Exchange and Violence at Ajacan, Roanoke and Jamestown* (Tuscaloosa, AL, 2006).

21. See D. K. Richter, 'Tsenacommacah and the Atlantic World' in Mancall, *Atlantic World and Virginia*, p. 33.

22. Mallios, *Deadly Politics of Giving*, p. 85.

23. Richter, 'Tsenacommacah and the Atlantic World', p. 57.

24. See Kathleen M. Brown, 'Women in Early Jamestown' in *Virtual Jamestown*.

25. Richter, *Facing East*, p. 74.

26. V. W. Crane, *The Southern Frontier 1670–1732* (Durham, NC, 1928), p. 22.

27. Ibid. pp. 39ff.

28. Ibid., p. 256.

29. Richter, *Facing East*, p. 164.

30. N. Shoemaker, *Strange Likeness: Becoming Red and White in Eighteenth-Century North America* (Oxford, 2004), p. 131.

31. See J. M. Merrell, *Into the American Woods: Negotiators on the Pennsylvania Frontier* (New York, 1999), p. 130.

32. Ibid., p. 176.

33. See G. C. Rogers, *The History of Georgetown County, South Carolina* (Columbia, SC, 1970), p. 10.

34. This is the main theme of Merrell, *American Woods*.

35. See J. O. Spady, 'Colonialism and the Discursive Precedents of "Penn's Treaty with the Indians"', in W. A. Pencak and D. K. Richter (eds.), *Friends and Enemies in Penn's Woods* (University Park, PA, 2004), p. 21.

36. The classic study is F. Jennings, *The Invasion of America: Indians, Colonialism and the Cant of Conquest* (Chapel Hill, NC, 1975).

37. I owe this point to Richter, *Facing East*, p. 41.

38. Ibid., p. 51.

39. P. C. Mancall, *Deadly Medicine: Indians and Alcohol in Early America* (London, 1995), p. 14.

40. V. Lieberman, *Strange Parallels: Southeast Asia in Global Context c. 800–1830* (Cambridge, 2003), vol. 1, pp. 277–82.

41. For a fascinating survey, D. Lombard and J. Aubin (eds.), *Asian Merchants and Businessmen in the Indian Ocean and South China Sea* (Delhi, 2000).

42. This is a tiny selection from that extraordinary lexicon of Anglo-Indian speech, H. Yule and A. C. Burnell (eds.), *Hobson-Jobson: A Glossary of Colloquial Anglo-Indian Words and Phrases*, first published in 1886.

43. For these ventures, W. Foster, *England's Quest of Eastern Trade* (London, 1933).

44. See N. Hiromu, 'The Factories and Facilities of the East India Companies in Surat: Locations, Building Characteristics and Ownership', in Haneda Masashi (ed.), *Asian Port Cities 1600–1800: Local and Foreign Cultural Interactions* (Tokyo, 2009), p. 221 (quoting Sir Thomas Roe).

45. Ibid., p. 203, quoting the English traveller John Fryer.

46. J. Fryer, *A New Account of East India and Persia Being Nine Years' Travels 1672–1681*, ed. W. Crooke (Hakluyt Society, 2nd Series, 1912), p. 165.

47. For a detailed account of this period of Gulf history, W. Floor, *The Persian Gulf: A Political and Economic History of Five Port Cities 1500–1730* (Washington, DC, 2006), chs. 4, 5.

48. See G. W. Forrest, *The Life of Lord Clive* (London, 1918), vol. I, pp. 10–12.

49. H. Dodwell, *The Nabobs of Madras* (London, 1926), p. 9.

50. For two contemporary descriptions of *c.* 1700 by Thomas Salmon and Charles Lockyer, H. D. Love, *Vestiges of Old Madras* (4 vols., London, 1913), vol. 1, pp. 71–5, 80–84.

51. J. Talboys Wheeler, *Madras in the Olden Time: A History of the Presidency 1639–1702 from Official Records* (Madras, 1861), p. 252.

52. P. Spear, *The Nabobs: A Study of the Social Life of the English in Eighteenth Century India* (London, 1932), p. 11. The full list with names is in Love, *Vestiges*, vol. 1, p. 65.

53. See S. Mentz, *The English Gentleman Merchant at Work: Madras and the City of London 1660–1740* (Copenhagen, 2005); Dodwell, *Nabobs*, p. 21.

54. Wheeler, *Madras in Olden Time*, p. 224.

55. Dodwell, *Nabobs of Madras*, pp. 177–8.

56. Spear, *Nabobs*, p. 98.

57. Wheeler, *Madras in Olden Time*, p. 269.

58. Ibid., p. 199.

59. See I. B. Watson, 'Elihu Yale' in *Oxford Dictionary of National Biography* online.

60. Love, *Vestiges*, vol. 1, p. 60.

61. See P. Gauci, 'Thomas Pitt' in *Oxford Dictionary of National Biography* online.

62. The classic account of this undeclared war remains H. Dodwell, *Dupleix and Clive: The Beginning of Empire* (London, 1920), chs. 1–5. Dodwell was the archivist of the records in Madras. But see now P. J. Marshall, *The Making and Unmaking of Empires: Britain, India and America c. 1750–1783* (Oxford, 2005), ch. 4.

63. The best account of Clive's nerve-racking secret diplomacy, and the

doubts and fears that preceded the encounter at Plassey, is A. Mervyn Davies, *Clive of Plassey* (London, 1939), chs. 13–15.

64. For a recent survey, F. Furstenberg, 'The Significance of the Trans-Appalachian Frontier in Atlantic History', *American Historical Review* (2008), 647–77.

65. This expression was coined by the American historian Richard White. See his *The Middle Ground: Indians, Empire, and Republics in the Great Lakes Region 1650–1815* (Cambridge, 1991).

66. F. E. Maning, *Old New Zealand: A Tale of the Good Old Times by a Pakeha Maori* [1863], (Auckland, 1930), p. 1.

67. Ibid., p. 19.

68. For Raymond, W. Dalrymple, *White Mughals: Love and Betrayal in Eighteenth Century India* (London, 2003); for Martin, R. Llewellyn-Jones, *A Very Ingenious Man: Claude Martin in Early Colonial India* (Delhi, 1992).

69. For a superb study of this in the Dutch eastern empire, U. Bosma and R. Raben, *Being 'Dutch' in the Indies: A History of Creolisation and Empire, 1500–1820* (Singapore, 2008).

3. TAKING POSSESSION

1. PP 1862 [2982][3003], *Papers Relating to the Occupation of Lagos*: Acting Consul McCoskry to Lord J. Russell, 7 August 1861.

2. Ibid., Docemo to Queen Victoria, 8 August 1861.

3. C. M. H. Clark (ed.), *Select Documents in Australian History 1788–1850* (Sydney, 1950), pp. 25–6.

4. Quoted in N. Thomas, *Discoveries: The Voyages of Captain Cook* (London, 2003), p. 127.

5. S. H. Peplow, *Hong Kong, Around and About* (Hong Kong, 1931), p. 9.

6. F. Madden (ed.), *Imperial Reconstruction, 1763–1840: The Evolution of Alternative Systems of Colonial Government. Select Documents on the Constitutional History of the British Empire and Commonwealth*, vol. III (Westport, CN, 1987), p. 807.

7. The classic analysis is F. Knight, *Risk, Uncertainty and Profit* (Boston, MA, 1921).

8. See above, ch. 2.

9. F. Madden (ed.), *'The Empire of the Bretaignes': The Foundations of a Colonial System of Government: Select Documents*, vol. I (Westport, CN, 1985), p. 216.

10. Ibid., pp. 238–41.

11. Ibid., p. 258: this was the charter granted by Charles I in 1629.

12. Ibid., p. 239.

13. See for example, the 1600 charter of the East India Company. Ibid., p. 236.

14. Ibid., p. 240.

15. See for example, Elizabeth's charter to Sir Humfrey Gilbert in June 1578. Ibid., p. 214.

16. See below, ch. 6.

17. For this episode and Henry II's motives, W. L. Warren, *Henry II* (Berkeley, 1973), pp. 199–200.

18. Madden, '*Empire of the Bretaignes*', p. 48.

19. C. W. De Kiewiet, *A History of South Africa: Social and Economic* (London, 1941), p. 61.

20. Madden, '*Empire of the Bretaignes*', p. 339.

21. F. Madden (ed.), *The Classical Period of the First British Empire 1689–1783 . . . Select Documents* (Westport, CN, 1985), pp. 54–8.

22. Ibid., pp. 192–3: Privy Council Memorandum, 9 August 1722.

23. Ibid.

24. V. Harlow and F. Madden (eds.), *British Colonial Developments 1774–1834* (Oxford, 1953), pp. 78–9.

25. F. Madden, *Imperial Reconstruction*, p. 673.

26. Ibid., p. 704: Memo by P. Anstruther, 23 November 1840.

27. See E. Curtis, *A History of Ireland* (London, 1936), pp. 112–13.

28. For an authoritative account, N. Canny, *Making Ireland British 1580–1650* (Oxford, 2001).

29. J. C. Beckett, *The Making of Modern Ireland 1603–1923* (London, 1966), pp. 157–61, provides a summary.

30. Madden, '*Empire of the Bretaignes*', p. 78.

31. This was Lord Hardwicke. See the entry under his name in *The Oxford Dictionary of National Biography* online.

32. Madden, *Imperial Reconstruction*, p. 241. For Munro's 'great minute', B. Stein, *Thomas Munro: The Origins of the Colonial State and His Vision of Empire* (Delhi, 1989), pp. 287–98. Munro was governor of Madras.

33. Stein, *Munro*: Munro to Canning, 30 June 1821.

34. Madden, *Imperial Reconstruction*, pp. 232–3: Sir Charles Grey and Sir Edward Ryan to the Governor-General in Council, 16 October 1830.

35. The classic account of the Indian case is E. T. Stokes, *The Peasant and the Raj* (Cambridge, 1978).

36. Madden, '*Empire of the Bretaignes*', pp. 338–9: Cromwell's Manifesto, 26 October 1655.

37. See P. McHugh, *Aboriginal Societies and the Common Law* (Oxford, 2004), p. 66.

38. See C. Maxwell (ed.), *Irish History from Contemporary Sources (1509–1610)* (London, 1923), pp. 242–3: Scheme for the Plantation of Munster, 21 June 1586.

39. Ibid., p. 248: memorandum on the affairs of Munster, 1598.

40. S. Banner, *How the Indians Lost Their Land* (Cambridge, MA, 2005), p. 26.

41. Madden, *Classical Period*, pp. 521–3: Royal Proclamation, 7 October 1763.

42. Quoted in McHugh, *Aboriginal Societies*, p. 38.

43. James Stephen to Vernon Smith, 28 July 1839. Quoted in D. Ward, 'A Means and a Measure of Civilisation: Colonial Authorities and Indigenous Law in Australasia', *History Compass* I (2003), 7.

44. Madden, *Imperial Reconstruction*, p. 854: minute by James Stephen, 25 May 1830.

45. Ibid., p. 874: Treaty of Waitangi, 6 February 1840, Article Two.

46. The best recent study is R. Boast, *Buying the Land, Selling the Land: Government and Maori Land on the North Island 1865–1921* (Wellington, 2008).

47. See N. Penn, *The Forgotten Frontier: Colonist and Khoisan on the Cape's Northern Frontier in the Eighteenth Century* (Cape Town, 2005).

48. See the Natal Proclamation, 12 May 1843 in K. N. Bell and W. P. Morrell (eds.), *Select Documents on British Colonial Policy* (Oxford, 1928), pp. 496–7.

49. S. Trapido, 'Reflections on Land, Office and Wealth in the South African Republic, 1850–1900' in S. Marks and A. Atmore (eds.), *Economy and Society in Pre-Industrial South Africa* (London, 1980), pp. 350–59.

50. C. Palley, *The Constitutional History and Law of Southern Rhodesia 1888–1965* (Oxford, 1966), ch. 6.

51. Hutt to Lord John Russell, 10 July 1841, in Ward, 'A Means and a Measure', 13.

52. For some discussion of this, Bain Attwood, '*The Law of the Land* or the Law of the Land: History, Law and Narrative in a Settler Society', *History Compass* 2, 1 (2004).

53. For an excellent survey, D. C. M. Platt (ed.), *Business Imperialism 1840–1930: An Inquiry Based on the British Experience in Latin America* (Oxford, 1977).

4. SETTLING IN

1. G. N. Curzon, *The Place of India in the Empire* (London, 1909).

2. J. R. Seeley, *The Expansion of England* (1883), p. 12.

3. Ibid., p. 13.

4. N. Canny, *Making Ireland British 1580–1650* (Oxford, 2001), p. 146.

5. J. H. Ohlmeyer, ' "Civilizinge of those Rude Partes": Colonization within Britain and Ireland', in N. Canny (ed.), *Oxford History of the British Empire*, vol. 1: *The Origins of Empire* (Oxford, 1998), pp. 139–40.

6. T. C. Barnard, 'New Opportunities for British Settlement: Ireland, 1650–1700', in Canny, *Origins*, p. 324.

7. H. McD. Beckles, 'The "Hub of Empire": The Caribbean and Britain in the Seventeenth Century', in Canny, *Origins*, p. 222; Canny, 'The Origins of Empire', in ibid., p. 31.

8. J. Horn, 'British Diaspora: Emigration from Britain 1680–1715', in P. J. Marshall (ed.), *Oxford History of the British Empire*, vol. 2: *The Eighteenth Century* (Oxford, 1998), p. 30.

9. See R. S. Dunn, *Sugar and Slaves: The Rise of the Planter Class in the English West Indies 1624–1713* (Chapel Hill, NC, 1972).

10. K. Fedorowich, 'The British Empire on the Move, 1776–1914', in S. Stockwell, *The British Empire: Themes and Perspectives* (Oxford, 2008), p. 67.

11. PP 1877 (5), *Report and Statistical Tables Relating to Emigration and Immigration, 1876*, table X.

12. Ibid., table XIII.

13. Fedorowich, 'British Empire on the Move', p. 89.

14. E. Richards, *The Highland Clearances: People, Landlords and Rural Turmoil* (Edinburgh, 2000), p. 5.

15. J. M. Collison Black, *Economic Thought and the Irish Question 1817–1870* (Cambridge, 1960), ch. VII.

16. Mill's ideas can be followed in his *Principles of Political Economy* [1848] (People's edn, 1885), Book II, ch. 10.

17. See J. MacAskill, 'The Chartist Land Plan' in A. Briggs (ed.), *Chartist Studies* (London, 1959).

18. M. Fairburn, *The Ideal Society and its Enemies: The Foundations of Modern New Zealand Society 1850–1900* (Auckland, 1986).

19. Fedorowich, 'British Empire on the Move', p. 76.

20. See J. S. Donnelly, *The Land and the People of Nineteenth-Century Cork: The Rural Economy and the Land Question* (London, 1975), pp. 55–6.

21. Richards, *Highland Clearances*, p. 2.

22. Donnelly, *Land and People*, p. 128.

23. J. Lennox, 'An Empire on Paper: The Founding of Halifax and Conceptions of Imperial Space, 1744–55', *Canadian Historical Review* 88, 3 (2007), 403.

24. J. Reid, *The Upper Ottawa Valley* (Ottawa, 1990), p. xxii.

25. H. J. M. Johnston, *British Immigration Policy 1815–1830: 'Shovelling Out Paupers'* (Oxford, 1972), pp. 38–9.

26. Fedorowich, 'British Empire on the Move', p. 79.

27. B. Greenhill and A. Giffard, *Westcountrymen in Prince Edward's Isle* (Toronto, 1967), p. 103.

28. W. S. Shepperson, *British Emigration to North America: Projects and Opinions in the Early Victorian Period* (Oxford, 1957), p. 210.

29. See B. Bailyn and Barbara De Wolfe, *Voyagers to the West: A Passage in the Peopling of America on the Eve of the Revolution* (New York, 1986), pp. 604–37.

30. See A. Kulikoff, *From British Peasants to Colonial American Farmers* (Chapel Hill, NC and London, 2000), p. 51.

31. R. J. Grace, 'Irish Immigration and Settlement in a Catholic City: Quebec, 1842–1861', *Canadian Historical Review* 84, 2 (2003), 241.

32. Kulikoff, *British Peasants*, pp. 40–42.

33. Lennox, 'Empire on Paper', p. 405.

34. For a graphic description, G. Blainey, *The Tyranny of Distance* (Melbourne, 1966), pp. 179–86.

35. Puke Ariki Archives, New Plymouth, New Zealand, ARC 2001/373: Journal of Surgeon on the *Blenheim*, 1842.

36. P. Statham (ed.), *The Origins of Australia's Capital Cities* (Cambridge, 1989), pp. 27–8.

37. National Library of Australia, Online Collections: Sir Joseph Banks Papers: Bligh to Banks 12 August 1806.

38. See J. D. Wood, *Making Ontario: Agricultural Colonization and Landscape Re-creation before the Railway* (Montreal and Kingston, 2000), pp. 94–6.

39. J. Weaver, *The Great Land Rush and the Making of the Modern World 1650–1900* (Montreal and London, 2003), p. 207.

40. A. Schrauwers, 'Revolutions without a Revolutionary Moment: Joint Stock Democracy and the Transition to Capitalism in Upper Canada', *Canadian Historical Review* 89, 2 (2008), 236.

41. See L. F. Gates, *Land Policies of Upper Canada* (Toronto, 1968).

42. Wood, *Making Ontario*, p. 97.

43. *Historical Records of Victoria*, vol. 6: *The Crown, the Land and the Squatter 1835–1840*, ed. M. Cannon and I. Macfarlane (Melbourne, 1991), p. xvii: Bourke to Glenelg, 18 December 1835. Glenelg was Secretary of State for the Colonies.

44. Ibid, p. 36: J. Stephen to Colonization Commissioners, 27 October 1836.

45. J. Hall-Jones, *John Turnbull Thomson: First Surveyor-General of New Zealand* (Dunedin, 1992), p. 30.

46. E. Liebenberg, 'The Mapping of South Africa 1813–1912', in T. R. H. Davenport (ed.), *History of Surveying and Land Tenure: Collected Papers*, vol. 2 (Cape Town, 2004), p. 75.

47. For an excellent study based on New Zealand, G. Byrnes, *Boundary Markers: Land Surveying and the Colonisation of New Zealand* (Wellington, 2001).

48. Quoted in ibid., p. 24.

49. For a description of the technique, A. E. J. Andrews, *Major Mitchell's Map, 1834: The Saga of the Survey of the Nineteen Counties* (Hobart, 1992), p. 9.

50. Wood, *Making Ontario*, pp. 93–6.

51. Schrauwers, 'Revolutions', 239.

52. Reid, *Upper Ottawa Valley*, p. xxxiii.

53. See G. Martin, 'Wakefield's Past and Futures', in *Edward Gibbon Wakefield and the Colonial Dream: A Reconsideration* (Alexander Turnbull Library, Wellington, New Zealand, 1997).

54. E. G. Wakefield, *A Letter from Sydney* (1829). It was written not in Sydney but in Newgate Prison.

55. B. Wells, *The History of Taranaki* (New Plymouth, 1878), p. 59.

56. ARC 2001–12: Carrington's Journal, 11 January 1841.

57. Ibid.: Carrington's Journal, 10 March 1841.

58. Ibid.: Carrington's Journal, 13 April 1841.

59. Ibid.: Carrington to W. Hendry and G. W. Carrington, 11 April 1843.

60. ARC 2001–373, New Plymouth Company Confidential Correspondence: Liardet to Col. Wakefield, 28 November 1841.

61. ARC 2001–12: Carrington to Thomas Woolcombe, 4 May 1841; to New Zealand Company, 22 September 1841.

62. ARC 2001–373, Plymouth Company Confidential Correspondence: Liardet to Col. Wakefield, 28 November 1841.

63. *Letters from New Plymouth 1843: Letters from Settlers and Labouring Emigrants in the New Zealand Company's Settlements of Wellington, Nelson and New Plymouth* (1843).

64. ARC 2001–373: Wicksteed to Col. Wakefield, 22 August 1843.

65. See N. Prickett, *Landscapes of Conflict: A Field Guide to the New Zealand Wars* (Auckland, 2002), pp. 58–60.

66. For Taranaki's economic misfortunes, J. Rutherford and W. H. Skinner, *The Establishment of the New Plymouth in New Zealand 1841–1843* (New Plymouth, 1940), p. 230; B. G. Quin, 'Bush Frontier: North Taranaki 1841–1860' (MA Thesis, Victoria University Wellington, 1966), pp. 170ff.

67. Wood, *Making Ontario*, p. 85.
68. T. Dunlap, *Nature and the English Diaspora* (Cambridge, 1999), p. 42.
69. T. Flannery, 'The Fate of Empire in High and Low-energy Ecosystems', in T. Griffiths and L. Robin (eds.), *Ecology and Empire* (Edinburgh, 1999), pp. 49–51.
70. W. Cronon, *Changes in the Land: Indians, Colonists and the Ecology of New England* (New York, 1983), p. 48.
71. M. Mackinnon (ed.), *New Zealand Historical Atlas* (Auckland, 1997), plate 12; P. Holland, K. O'Connor and A. Wearing, 'Remaking the Grasslands of the Open Country', in T. Brooking and E. Pawson (eds.), *Environmental Histories of New Zealand* (Oxford, 2002), p. 72.
72. T. L. Mitchell, *Journal of an Expedition into the Interior of Tropical Australia* (1848), quoted in P. Carter, *The Road to Botany Bay* (London, 1987), p. 342.
73. V. De John Anderson, *Creatures of Empire: How Domestic Animals Transformed Early America* (Oxford, 2004), p. 245.
74. Cronon, *Changes in the Land*, pp. 147–50.
75. There are reported to be some 1 million feral camels in Australia today.
76. The classic study of this phenomenon is A. L. Crosby, *Ecological Imperialism: The Biological Expansion of Europe 900–1900* (Cambridge, 1986).
77. The writer saw such a sign near Tutira in the North Island.
78. H. Guthrie-Smith, *Tutira: The Story of a New Zealand Sheep Station* (Edinburgh and London, 1921).
79. J. M. Powell, 'Thomas Griffith Taylor (1880–1963)', *Australian Dictionary of Biography*, vol. 12 (Melbourne, 1990), pp. 185–8. Available online.
80. Quoted in S. Zeller, *Inventing Canada: Early Victorian Science and the Idea of a Transcontinental Nation* (Toronto, 1987), p. 263.
81. Carter, *Botany Bay*, p. 248.
82. R. Hughes, *The Art of Australia* (Harmondsworth, 1966), ch. 2; for the Canadian 'Group of Seven' who came together in Toronto before 1914, C. C. Hill, *The Group of Seven: Art for a Nation* (Ottawa, 1995).
83. See R. McGregor, *Imagined Destinies: Aboriginal Australians and the Doomed Race Theory 1880–1939* (Carlton, Victoria, 1997).
84. For a brilliant near-contemporary description of this, W. M. Macmillan, *Complex South Africa: An Economic Footnote to History* (London, 1930). The anodyne title – he was then employed in South Africa – masked its vehement message.
85. For New Zealand, J. Stenhouse and B. Moloughney, '"Drug-besotted sin-begotten sons of filth": New Zealanders and the Oriental Other', *New Zealand Journal of History* 33, 1 (1999), 43–64.

86. See R. A. Huttenback, *Racism and Empire: White Settlers and Coloured Immigrants* (Ithaca and London, 1976).

5. RESORTING TO WAR

1. TNA, WO 33/256, 'Cost of Principal British Wars', 23 December 1902.

2. An excellent survey is I. K. Steele, *Warpaths: Invasions of North America* (New York and Oxford, 1994).

3. See J. Connor, *Australian Frontier Wars 1788–1838* (Sydney, 2002); H. Reynolds, *The Other Side of the Frontier* (Harmondsworth, 1982); J. Belich, *The New Zealand Wars* (Auckland, 1986); N. Prickett, *Landscapes of Conflict: A Field Guide to the New Zealand Wars* (Auckland, 2002).

4. J. B. Peires, *The Dead Will Arise: Nongqawuse and the Great Xhosa Cattle-killing Movement of 1856–57* (Johannesburg, 1989); J. Guy, *The Destruction of the Zulu State: The Civil War in Zululand* (London, 1979); J. Laband, *The Rope of Sand: The Rise and Fall of the Zulu Kingdom* (Johannesburg, 1995); A. Keppel-Jones, *Rhodes and Rhodesia: The White Conquest of Zimbabwe 1884–1902* (Kingston, Ontario, 1983).

5. For this view, J. Darwin, *The Empire Project: The Rise and Fall of the British World-System 1830–1970* (Cambridge, 2009), ch. 6.

6. J. D. Hargreaves, *West Africa Partitioned* (2 vols., London and Basingstoke, 1974–85).

7. See J. Lonsdale, 'The Conquest State of Kenya 1895–1905' and 'The Politics of Conquest in Western Kenya 1894–1908', both in B. Berman and J. Lonsdale, *Unhappy Valley: Conflict in Kenya and Africa*; Book 1: *State and Class* (London and Athens, OH, 1992); D. A. Low, *Fabrication of Empire: The British and the Uganda Kingdoms, 1890–1902* (Cambridge, 2009).

8. See P. J. Marshall, *The Making and Unmaking of Empires: Britain, India and America c. 1750–1783* (Oxford, 2005), chs. 4, 7, 8; M. Yapp, *Strategies of British India 1780–1850* (Oxford, 1980); D. Omissi, *The Sepoy and the Raj* (Basingstoke, 1994).

9. R. Callaghan, *The East India Company and Army Reform 1783–1798* (Cambridge, MA, 1972).

10. For a superb account of this, Bill Nasson, *Abraham Esau's War: A Black South African War in the Cape 1899–1902* (Cambridge, 1991).

11. S. Alavi, *The Sepoys and the Company: Tradition and Transition in Northern India 1770–1830* (Delhi, 1995).

12. For the role of the *kupapa*, Belich, *New Zealand Wars*, pp. 211–13.

13. See below ch. 8.

14. The classic account is G. Mattingly, *Renaissance Diplomacy* (Harmondsworth, 1955); see also M. S. Anderson, *The Rise of Modern Diplomacy 1450–1919* (London, 1993).

15. For European ideas of international order, M. Wight, *Systems of States* (Leicester, 1977), chs. 4, 5, 6; H. Bull, *The Anarchical Society* (London, 1977); see also E. Keene, *Beyond the Anarchical Society: Grotius, Colonialism and Order in World Politics* (Cambridge, 2002).

16. Minute 22 April 1860, in C. W. Newbury (ed.), *British Policy Towards West Africa: Select Documents 1786–1874* (Oxford, 1965), p. 120.

17. J. L. Cranmer-Byng (ed.), *Journal of the Embassy to China* (Folio Society edn, London, 2004), p. 27.

18. Ibid., p. 108.

19. See J. K. Fairbank, *Trade and Diplomacy on the China Coast* (Cambridge, MA, 1953).

20. See M. Greenberg, *British Trade and the Opening of China 1800–1842* (Cambridge, 1951).

21. Cranmer-Byng, *Journal*, p. 165.

22. A brilliantly perceptive account of the debate within Chinese officialdom is in J. Polachek, *The Inner Opium War* (Cambridge, MA, 1992).

23. D. Southgate, *The Most English Minister* (London, 1966), p. 146: Palmerston to Sir J. Davis, 9 January 1847.

24. The standard account is H. B. Morse, *The Trade and Administration of the Chinese Empire* (London, 1908).

25. See J. Y. Wong, *Deadly Dreams: Opium, Imperialism and the Arrow War (1856–1860)* (Cambridge, 1998).

26. See his *Le conflit entre la Russie et la Chine* (Brussels, 1880).

27. G. R. G. Hambly, 'The Emperor's Clothes', in S. Gordon (ed.), *Robes of Honour* (Delhi, 2003), pp. 31–49.

28. See P. Stern, *The Company State: Corporate Sovereignty and the Early Modern Foundations of the British Empire in India* (Oxford, 2011), ch. 6.

29. A. B. Keith (ed.), *Speeches and Documents on Indian Policy 1750–1921* (Oxford, 1922), vol. 1, p. 111.

30. S. J. Owen (ed.), *A Selection from the Despatches, Treaties and Other Papers of the Marquess Wellesley* (Oxford, 1877), p. 4: memo by J. Webbe, 6 July 1798.

31. Ibid., p. 632: Wellesley to the Court of Directors, 13 July 1804.

32. E. Thompson, *The Making of the Indian Princes* (Oxford, 1943), pp. 283–4.

33. See W. Dalrymple, *The Last Mughal: The Fall of a Dynasty, Delhi, 1857* (London, 2006).

34. For the notorious firm of Palmer and Co, see Z. Yasdani, *Hyderabad during the Residency of Henry Russell 1811–1820* (Oxford, 1976).

35. Steele, *Warpaths*, p. 86.

36. See V. W. Crane, *The Southern Frontier 1670–1732* (Durham, NC, 1928).

37. See N. Penn, *The Forgotten Frontier: Colonist and Khoisan on the Cape's Northern Frontier in the Eighteenth Century* (Athens, OH, 2005).

38. See J. S. Marais, *Maynier and the First Boer Republic* (Cape Town, 1944).

39. Connor, *Australian Frontier Wars*, p. 33.

40. See P. D. Gardner, *Gippsland Massacres: The Destruction of the Kurnai Tribes 1800–1860* (3rd edn, Ensay, Victoria, 2001).

41. For their disastrous Pedi war of 1876, P. Delius, *The Land Belongs to Us* (Johannesburg, 1983), pp. 205–12.

42. See H. Dodwell, *Dupleix and Clive: The Beginning of Empire* (London, 1920), pp. 26–9.

43. This was Charles Dilke.

44. See *Hansard* 3rd Series, vol. 159, col. 370–71 (12 June 1860): statement by Sir Charles Wood.

45. C. E. Callwell, *Small Wars: Their Principles and Practice* [1896], (3rd edn, London, 1906), p. 25.

46. Ibid., p. 42.

47. Ibid., p. 44.

48. J. Keegan, *The Mask of Command* (London, 1987), p. 148. For British military tactics in India, G. J. Bryant, 'Asymmetric Warfare: The British Experience in Eighteenth-Century India', *Journal of Military History* 68, 2 (2004), 431–69.

49. Callwell, *Small Wars*, p. 82.

50. PP 1896, C.7924, *Report on Military Operations against Kabarega, King of Unyoro*: Cunningham to Jackson, 7 June 1895.

51. From Henry Newbolt's poem 'Vitai Lampada' (1897), of which the second verse reads in part:

> The sand of the desert is sodden red,
> Red with the blood of the square that broke;
> The Gatling's jammed and the colonel dead
> And the regiment blind with dust and smoke.

52. These and other failings are analysed in G. Chet, *Conquering the American Wilderness: The Triumph of European Warfare in the Colonial Northeast* (Boston, 2003), pp. 118–21.

53. See the argument in R. G. S. Cooper, *The Anglo-Maratha Campaigns and*

the Contest for India: The Struggle for Control of the South Asian Military Economy (Cambridge, 2003).

54. For a contemporary British view, C. Ross (ed.), Correspondence of ... Marquis Cornwallis, vol. 1 (1859), chs. 3, 4.

55. D. H. Cole, Imperial Military Geography [1924] (8th edn, London, 1935), p. 356; for a general survey V. Schofield, Afghan Frontier: Feuding and Fighting in Central Asia ([1984] pbk edn, London, 2003).

56. H. Brackenbury, The Ashanti War: A Narrative Prepared from Official Documents (1874), vol. 1, p. 219.

57. See the excellent short biography by I. F. W. Beckett in the Oxford Dictionary of National Biography online.

58. For the umbrellas, E. Wood, From Midshipman to Field Marshal (London, 1906), p. 183. Wood served under Wolseley.

59. W. Reade, The Story of the Ashantee Campaign (1874), p. 163.

60. Brackenbury, Ashanti War, vol. 1, p. 139.

61. Ibid., p. 117.

62. Ibid., p. 361.

63. Ibid., p. 170.

64. Reade, Ashantee Campaign, p. 239.

65. Brackenbury, Ashanti War, vol. 1, p. 367.

66. Wolseley to Lady Wolseley, 28 January 1874, in I. F. W. Beckett (ed.), Wolseley and Ashanti: The Asante War Journal and Correspondence of Major General Sir Garnet Wolseley 1873–74 (Stroud, 2009), p. 383.

67. Reade, Ashantee Campaign, p. 412.

68. Brackenbury, Ashanti War, vol. 2, p. 213.

69. Ibid., p. 239.

70. For the setting, D. M. Schreuder, The Scramble for Southern Africa 1877–1895 (Cambridge, 1980).

71. For an expert account, I. Knight, A Companion to the Anglo-Zulu War (London, 2008), pp. 132–6, 210–14.

72. See H. Bailes, 'Technology and Imperialism: A Case Study of the Victorian Army in Africa', Victorian Studies 24 (1980), 83–104.

73. The British often used impi to refer to a Zulu regiment or ibutho, but it could be used of a force of any size.

74. Knight, Anglo-Zulu War, p. 119.

75. For Wood's account, Midshipman to Field Marshal, ch. 31.

76. The best account of the campaign remains J. Maurice, The Military History of the Campaign of 1882 in Egypt (1887). Maurice had been on Wolseley's staff.

77. Ibid., p. 130.

78. See R. Marjomaa, *War on the Savannah: The Military Collapse of the Sokoto Caliphate under the Invasion of the British Empire, 1897–1903* (Helsinki, 1998), p. 108.
79. See Knight, *Anglo-Zulu War*, 'small arms'.
80. Quoted in Bailes, 'Technology and Imperialism'. The date was 1878.
81. For a recent account, P. Marsden, *The Barefoot Emperor: An Ethiopian Tragedy* (London, 2007).
82. Superbly reconstructed in Sean Doyle, *Crisis and Decline in Bunyoro: Population and Environment in Western Uganda 1860–1955* (Oxford and Athens, OH, 2006).
83. Ibid., pp. 85–91.

6. TRAFFIC AND TRADE

1. *England's Interest and Improvement*, in J. R. McCulloch (ed.) *Early English Tracts on Commerce* [1856], (Cambridge, 1954), p. 244.
2. *The Wealth of Nations* [1776], (Everyman edn, London, 1910), vol. 2, pp. 94ff.
3. R. Cobden, 'How Wars Are Got Up in India' (1853), in *The Political Writings of Richard Cobden*, vol. 2 (1868), pp. 105ff.
4. J. A. Hobson, *Imperialism: A Study* (London, 1902).
5. See M. Greenberg, *British Trade and the Opening of China 1800–1842* (Cambridge, 1951).
6. K. Dike, *Trade and Politics in the Niger Delta 1830–1885* (Oxford, 1956), pp. 42, 63.
7. See his 'Congo Diary' in J. Conrad, *Last Essays* (Harmondsworth, 1928).
8. J. Prestholdt, *Domesticating the World: African Consumerism and the Genealogies of Globalization* (London and Berkeley, 2008), p. 64.
9. D. C. M. Platt, *Britain and Latin American Trade* (London, 1973), p. 34.
10. See J. Stuart and D. McK. Malcolm (eds.), *The Diary of Henry Francis Fynn* (Pietermaritzburg, 1952), pp. 56ff.
11. See, for example, the business records of Newton and Chambers, the Sheffield ironworks, in Sheffield City Archives.
12. See J. R. McCulloch, *A Dictionary . . . of Commerce and Commercial Navigation* (rev. edn, 1869), p. 232.
13. Ibid., p. 1168.
14. See L. Colley, *Ordeal of Elizabeth Marsh* (London, 2007).
15. S. G. Checkland, *The Gladstones* (Cambridge, 1971), p. 18.
16. Ibid., p. 24.

17. For a fascinating attempt to codify commercial law in an independent Niger Delta state, see 'Equity Court Regulations, Old Calabar, 5 May 1862', in C. W. Newbury (ed.), *British Policy Towards West Africa: Select Documents 1786–1874* (Oxford, 1965), pp. 396–9.

18. Quoted in G. Jones, *From Merchants to Multinationals: British Trading Companies in the Nineteenth and Twentieth Centuries* (Oxford, 2000), p. 209.

19. Jamaica: Two Reports from Committees . . . in V. Harlow and F. Madden (eds.), *British Colonial Developments 1774–1834* (Oxford, 1953), p. 340.

20. For Customs revenue and government income, B. R. Mitchell, *Abstract of British Historical Statistics* (Cambridge, 1971), p. 388.

21. Ibid., pp. 310ff.

22. J. J. McCusker and R. R. Menard, *The Economy of British America 1607–1789* (Chapel Hill, NC, 1985), p. 57, cit. in J. Inikori, *Africans and the Industrial Revolution in England* (Cambridge, 2002), p. 214.

23. For a brilliant account of the British addiction to sugar S. Mintz, *Sweetness and Power: The Place of Sugar in Modern History* (Harmondsworth, 1985), ch. 3.

24. See the fascinating account in Inikori, *Africans*, ch. 6.

25. Ibid., p. 302.

26. See F. Armytage, *The Free Port System in the British West Indies: A Study in Commercial Policy 1766–1822* (London, 1953), p. 4.

27. Thomas Irving to the Committee for Trade, 28 November 1786, Harlow and Madden, *British Colonial Developments*, p. 322.

28. See A. Christelow, 'Contraband Trade between Jamaica and the Spanish Main and the Freeport Act of 1766', *Hispanic American Historical Review* 22 (1942), 309–43, cit. in S. J. and B. H. Stein, *Silver, Trade and War: Spain and America in the Making of Early Modern Europe* (Baltimore and London, 2000).

29. See B. W. Higman, 'Physical and Economic Environments', in V. Shepherd and H. McD. Beckles (eds.), *Caribbean Slavery in the Atlantic World* (Princeton and Oxford, 2000), Table 28.7, p. 387.

30. Compared with 7 per cent in Barbados. S. Carrington et al., *A-Z of Barbados Heritage* [1990], (new edn, Oxford, 2003), p. 2.

31. Assembly Resolution, 11 December 1823, Harlow and Madden, *British Colonial Developments*, p. 566.

32. Ibid., p.384.

33. R. S. Dunn, *Sugar and Slaves: The Rise of the Planter Class in the English West Indies 1624–1713* (Chapel Hill, NC, 1972).

34. I have drawn on the brilliant reconstruction in I. K. Steele, *The English Atlantic 1675–1740: An Exploration of Communication and Community* (Oxford, 1986).

35. See D. Hancock, '"A World of Business to Do": William Freeman and the Foundations of England's Commercial Empire, 1645–1707', *William and Mary Quarterly* 57 (2000), 3–34.

36. See B. Wood (ed.), 'The Letters of Simon Taylor of Jamaica to Chalenor Arcedekne 1765–1775', in B. Wood and M. Lynn (eds.), *Travel, Trade and Power in the Atlantic 1765–1884* (Cambridge, 2002).

37. R. Blackburn, *The Overthrow of Colonial Slavery 1776–1848* (London, 1988), ch. 6.

38. A. T. Mahan, *The Influence of Sea Power on History 1660–1783* (1890), p. 314.

39. See R. Davis, 'English Foreign Trade, 1700–1774', *Economic History Review*, New Series, 15, 2 (1962), 285–303.

40. For a superb description of the contemporary outlook, see P. Earle, *The World of Defoe* (London, 1976), esp. ch. 5.

41. See N. F. R. Crafts, *British Economic Growth during the Industrial Revolution* (Oxford, 1985).

42. A. Smith, *The Wealth of Nations* (Everyman edn, London, 1910), vol. 1, pp. 84–5.

43. See B. Bailyn, *The New England Merchants in the Seventeenth Century* (Cambridge, MA, 1955), pp. 182ff.

44. See H. E. S. Fisher, *The Portugal Trade* (London, 1971).

45. Newfoundland Fishery: Report of the Committee of Trade, 17 March 1786, in Harlow and Madden, *British Colonial Developments*, p. 370.

46. Liverpool to Lord Hobart, 15 May 1802, in ibid., p. 336.

47. See W. R. Brock, *Lord Liverpool and Liberal Toryism* (Cambridge, 1939), ch. 6.

48. D. P. O'Brien, *The Classical Economists* (Oxford, 1975), p. 41.

49. B. Hilton, 'Peel: A Reappraisal', *Historical Journal* 22 (1979).

50. A. Ellis, *Heirs of Adventure: The Story of Brown, Shipley and Co., Merchant Bankers 1810–1960* (London, n.d.), p. 27.

51. See D. Meinig, *The Shaping of America*, vol. 2: *Continental America 1800–1867* (New Haven and London, 1993), p. 155.

52. P. Gootenberg, *Between Silver and Guano: Commercial Policy and the State in Postindependence Peru* (Princeton, 1989), pp. 82–3.

53. R. Graham, *Britain and the Modernisation of Brazil* (Cambridge, 1968), pp. 80–81.

54. H. S. Ferns, *Britain and Argentina in the Nineteenth Century* (Oxford, 1960); P. Winn, 'Britain's Informal Empire in Uruguay in the Nineteenth Century', *Past and Present* 73 (1976).

55. The main exception was Napoleon III's disastrous attempt to regain Mexico for the Habsburgs in 1863.

56. In fact this scheme in 1862 fell through. See Sandford Fleming, *The Intercolonial: A Historical Sketch* . . . (Montreal, 1876), pp. 59–60ff.

57. The classic account is D. Creighton, *The Commercial Empire of the St Lawrence 1760–1850* (New Haven and Toronto, 1937); D. Creighton, *John A. Macdonald* (2 vols., Toronto, 1952–5).

58. See J. S. Galbraith, *The Hudson's Bay Company as an Imperial Factor* (Berkeley, 1957).

59. See Merrill Dension, *Canada's First Bank: A History of the Bank of Montreal* (Toronto, 1967).

60. See M. Westley, *Remembrance of Grandeur: The Anglo-Protestant Elite of Montreal 1900–1950* (Montreal, 1990).

61. A. R. Wallace, *The Malay Archipelago* [1869] (Oxford, 1986), p. 32.

62. See D. A. Farnie, *East and West of Suez: The Suez Canal in History* (Oxford, 1969).

63. The main shipping routes to Australia and New Zealand largely bypassing the Asian ports can be seen in G. Philip and T. S. Sheldrake (eds.), *The Chambers of Commerce Atlas* (London, 1928 edn), Plate 21.

64. For dhows see E. Gilbert, *Dhows and the Colonial Economy of Zanzibar 1860–1970* (Oxford, 2004).

65. See Greenberg, *British Trade*, ch. 6; generally, S. D. Chapman, *Merchant Enterprise in Britain from the Industrial Revolution to the First World War* (Cambridge, 1992); M. Misra, *Business, Race and Politics in India c. 1850–1960* (Oxford, 1999).

66. J. F. Munro, *Maritime Enterprise and Empire: Sir William Mackinnon and his Business Network, 1823–1893* (Woodbridge, 2003), p. 15.

67. See L. A. Mills, *British Malaya 1824–1867* [1925] (Kuala Lumpur, 1966), pp. 197–8.

68. See N. Green, *Bombay Islam: The Religious Economy of the West Indian Ocean 1840–1915* (Cambridge, 2011), ch. 4.

69. Greenberg, *British Trade*, pp. 162–3.

70. For a brilliant study of this social phenomenon, R. Bickers, 'Shanghailanders: The Formation and Identity of the British Settler Community in Shanghai, 1843–1947', *Past and Present* 159 (1998).

71. See N. Horesh, *Shanghai Bund and Beyond: British Banks, Bank Notes and Monetary Policy in China* (New Haven, 2009), p. 31.

72. I base much of what follows on the superb study by J. F. Munro, *Maritime Enterprise and Empire*.

73. S. Jones, *Trade and Shipping: Lord Inchcape 1852–1932* (Manchester, 1989), p. 13.

74. See J. Furnivall, *Colonial Policy and Practice: A Comparative Study of Burma and Netherlands India* (Cambridge, 1948), pp. 86–98.

75. The geographer Halford Mackinder in a speech of 1913: Mackinder Papers, Bodleian Library c/400.

76. W. Schlote, *British Overseas Trade from 1700 to the 1930s* (Oxford, 1952), pp. 140–41.

77. For a superb description of the City, D. Kynaston, *The City of London: Golden Years 1890–1914* (London, 1995).

78. The classic account of London's role in lubricating multilateral trade is S. B. Saul, *Studies in British Overseas Trade* (Liverpool, 1960).

79. See P. M. Acena and J. Reis (eds.), *Monetary Standards in the Periphery: Paper, Silver and Gold 1854–1933* (Basingstoke, 2000), p. 1.

80. R. C. Michie, *The City of London* (London, 1992), p. 109. By some calculations, it was as much as half.

81. Bodleian Library, Oxford: Alfred Milner Mss Box 2, Dawkins to Milner, 16 October 1893.

82. For a penetrating new study, A. Dilley, *Finance, Politics and Imperialism: Australia, Canada and the City of London c. 1896–1914* (forthcoming, 2012).

83. For a contemporary view, see H. B. Morse, *The Trade and Administration of the Chinese Empire* (London, 1908).

84. See N. Pelcovits, *The Old China Hands and the Foreign Office* (New York, 1948).

85. T. G. Otte, *The China Question: Great Power Rivalry and British Isolation 1894–1905* (Oxford, 2007) for a recent study.

86. See the gruelling account in G. H. Portal, *The British Mission to Uganda in 1893* (1894). The journey cost Portal his life.

87. See the description in I. Phimister, *Wangi Kolia* (Johannesburg, 1994).

88. See C. van Onselen, *Chibaro: African Mine Labour in Southern Rhodesia 1900–1933* (London, 1976), p. 50; Mitchell, *Abstract*, p. 37.

89. Van Onselen, *Chibaro*, p. 146.

90. See S. Sweeney, *Financing India's Imperial Railways 1875–1914* (London, 2011).

91. See Saul, *Studies in British Overseas Trade*.

92. This term was coined by the economist W. S. Jevons in *The Coal Question* (1865).

93. See H. J. Mackinder, 'Historical Geography of Britain', unpublished lecture, 1906, in Bodleian Library, Oxford: H. J. Mackinder Mss.
94. See L. Chiozza Money, *The Nation's Wealth* (London, 1914).

7. RULING METHODS

1. F. Naumann, *Central Europe* (Engl. trans., London, 1917), p. 184.
2. Ibid.
3. I. K. Steele, *The English Atlantic 1675–1740: An Exploration of Communication and Community* (Oxford, 1986), Table 4.4.
4. E. Burke, *Letters and Speeches on American Affairs* (Everyman edn, London, 1908), pp. 95–6.
5. M. Perham, *Lugard: The Years of Authority 1898–1945* (London, 1960), p. 477.
6. F. Madden (ed.), *Settler Self-Government 1840–1900: The Development of Representative and Responsible Government* (Westport, CN, 1990), p. 7: James Stephen to Earl Grey, 15 January 1850.
7. For Stephen's career, A. G. L. Shaw, 'James Stephen 1789–1859', *Oxford Dictionary of National Biography* online.
8. See B. Bailyn, *The Origins of American Politics* (New York, 1968); Jack P. Greene, *Peripheries and Center: Constitutional Development in the Extended Polities of the British Empire and the United States* (Athens, GA, 1987).
9. See below ch. 8.
10. Ibid.
11. For Durham's recommendations, C. P. Lucas (ed.), *Lord Durham's Report on the Affairs of British North America* (3 vols., London, 1912).
12. Madden, *Settler Self-Government*, p. 128: Lord Elgin to Earl Grey, 30 April 1849.
13. Ibid., p. 539: Sir P. Wodehouse to the Duke of Newcastle, 9 October 1861.
14. See J. Rutherford, *Sir George Grey: A Study in Colonial Government* (London, 1961), chs. 32–4; J. Belich, *The New Zealand Wars* (Auckland, 1986), part 3.
15. For the proconsular outlook, J. Benyon, *Proconsul and Paramountcy in South Africa 1806–1910* (Pietermaritzburg, 1980).
16. Madden, *Settler Self-Government*, p. 550: Earl Granville to Sir P. Wodehouse, 9 December 1869.
17. For this episode, D. M. Schreuder, *Gladstone and Kruger* (London, 1969).
18. See J. Darwin, *The Empire Project: The Rise and Fall of the British World-System 1830–1970* (Cambridge, 2009), ch. 6.

19. W. K. Hancock and J. van der Poel (eds.), *Selections from the Smuts Papers* (Cambridge, 1966), vol. II, p. 115: Smuts to T. L. Graham, 26 July 1902.

20. Edmund Burke on the Impeachment of Warren Hastings, 15–19 February 1788, in A. B. Keith (ed.), *Speeches and Documents on Indian Policy 1750–1921* (Oxford, 1922), vol. 1, p. 128. Burke was describing the unreformed era of plunder and profit, but the outlook he described lived on.

21. Ibid., p. 125.

22. See Goldwin Smith, *The Empire* (1863). Smith was professor of history at Oxford.

23. Macaulay in the House of Commons, 10 July 1833 in Keith, *Speeches on Indian Policy*, vol. 1, p. 236.

24. See E. T. Stokes, *The English Utilitarians and India* (Oxford, 1959), Part IV.

25. Proclamation by the Queen to the Princes, Chiefs and People of India, 1 November 1858, in Keith, *Speeches on Indian Policy*, vol. 1, pp. 383–4.

26. PP 1887 (332), *East India (Army) Return*.

27. Originally limited to six, the number of British officers in an Indian battalion was later increased to fourteen. In 1882 it was eight. See D. Omissi, *The Sepoy and the Raj* (Basingstoke, 1994), pp. 158–60.

28. Quoted in A. Yang, *The Limited Raj* (London, 1989), p. 93.

29. The authoritative study is I. Copland, *The British Raj and the Indian Princes: Paramountcy in Western India 1857–1930* (Bombay, 1982).

30. R. Kipling, 'Arithmetic on the Frontier', published in his first collection of verse, *Departmental Ditties and Other Verses* (Calcutta, 1886).

31. Bodleian Library, Oxford, Mss Eng. Hist. c353, Macdonnell to Elgin (the Viceroy), 16 July 1897.

32. See M. Yapp, *Strategies of British India 1780–1850* (Oxford, 1980).

33. For this analysis see e.g. Report by Thackeray, 4 August 1807, in W. K. Firminger (ed.), *Fifth Report on East India Company Affairs, 1812* (3 vols., Calcutta, 1917), vol. 3, pp. 592–3.

34. For this process, see e.g. Firminger, *Fifth Report*, vol. 3, pp. 126–8: Proceedings of the Board of Revenue at Fort St George (Madras), 25 March 1793; B. Stein, *Thomas Munro: The Origins of the Colonial State and His Vision of Empire* (Delhi, 1989), pp. 84ff.; D. Ludden, *Peasant History in South India* (Princeton, 1985), ch. 4.

35. Firminger, *Fifth Report*, vol. 2, p. 726: Dowdeswell's Report on Police in Bengal, 29 September 1809.

36. Yang, *Limited Raj*, pp. 71–2.

37. Firminger, *Fifth Report*. vol. 1, p. 178: Madras Government to East India Company Court of Directors, 7 May 1793.

38. J. Beames, *Memoirs of an Indian Civilian* (London, 1961), p. 103.

39. Ibid., p. 126.

40. See R. Frykenberg, *Guntur District 1788–1848* (Oxford, 1965).

41. Yang, *Limited Raj*, pp. 102, 110; Ludden, *Peasant History*, p. 128.

42. See A. Seal, 'Imperialism and Nationalism in India', in J. Gallagher, G. Johnson and A. Seal (eds.), *Locality, Province and Nation* (Cambridge, 1973).

43. See H. V. Lovett, 'District Administration in Bengal 1858–1918', in H. H. Dodwell (ed.), *Cambridge History of the British Empire*, vol. V: *The Indian Empire 1858–1918* (Cambridge, 1932), p. 247.

44. A handful of nominated Indians had sat on the Viceroy's legislative council since 1861.

45. This was done by the transparent device of insisting that the entry examination was to be held only in Britain. See *Report of the Public Service Commission, 1886–87* (Calcutta, 1888), p. 50.

46. H. Yule and A. C. Burnell (eds.), *Hobson-Jobson: A Glossary of Colloquial Anglo-Indian Words and Phrases* (1886).

47. See M. Wight, *The Development of the Legislative Council 1606–1945* (London, 1946), ch. 2 for the classic account.

48. F. Madden (ed.), *The Dependent Empire and Ireland: Advance and Retreat in Representative Self-Government, Select Documents* (Westport, CN, 1991), pp. 159–61: Cardwell to Governor Eyre, 1 December 1865; pp. 266–8: C. P. Lucas, 'Constitutions of the West Indies', 14 February 1898.

49. The name 'Nigeria' was first used officially on 1 January 1900.

50. See M. Perham, *Lugard: The Years of Adventure 1858–1898* (London, 1956).

51. See J. Flint, *Sir George Goldie and the Making of Nigeria* (London, 1960).

52. Perham, *Lugard: The Years of Authority*, p. 146.

53. The best recent study is R. Marjomaa, *War on the Savannah: The Military Collapse of the Sokoto Caliphate 1897–1903* (Helsinki, 1998).

54. Perham, *Lugard: The Years of Authority*, p. 149.

55. See Lord Hailey, *Native Administration in the British African Territories*, Part III: *West Africa* (London, 1951), pp. 104–8.

56. F. Madden and J. Darwin (eds.), *The Dependent Empire 1900–1948, Select Documents . . .* (Westport, CN, 1994), p. 691: Lugard's Amalgamation Report, 9 April 1919.

57. C. Temple, *Native Races and their Rulers* (Cape Town, 1918); F. D. Lugard, *The Dual Mandate in Tropical Africa* (London, 1922).

58. Madden and Darwin, *Dependent Empire 1900–1948*, pp. 695–6: Sir Hugh Clifford's 'Kaduna Minute', 18 March 1922.

59. See Madden, *Dependent Empire and Ireland*, pp. 629–32: 'Uganda Agreement', 10 March 1900.

60. For a contemporary account of this journey stressing its hardships and dangers, G. H. Portal, *The British Mission to Uganda in 1893* (1894).

61. J. Lonsdale, 'The Conquest State of Kenya 1895–1905', in B. Berman and J. Lonsdale, *Unhappy Valley: Conflict in Kenya and Africa*, Book I: *State and Class* (London and Athens, OH, 1992), p. 26.

62. R. Waller, 'The Maasai and the British 1895–1905: The Origins of an Alliance', *Journal of African History* 17, 4 (1976), 529–53.

63. G. H. Mungeam (ed.), *Kenya: Select Historical Documents 1884–1923* (Nairobi, 1978), p. 87: Sir Charles Eliot to Lord Lansdowne, 18 June 1901.

64. Ibid., pp. 100–103: Memoranda by Sir P. Girouard, 18 May 1910.

65. Temple, *Native Races*, p. 26.

66. This was Lord Salisbury (1830–1903).

8. ACTS OF REBELLION

1. D. Morton (ed.), *The Queen v. Louis Riel* (Toronto, 1974), p. 372.

2. Ibid., p. 4.

3. See A. Atkinson, *The Europeans in Australia: A History*, vol. 1: *The Beginning* (Oxford, 1997), pp. 280–91, 300–307.

4. See R. S. Dunn, 'The Glorious Revolution and America', in N. Canny (ed.), *Oxford History of the British Empire*, vol. 1: *The Origins of Empire* (Oxford, 1998), pp. 463–5.

5. See K. Sinclair, *The Origins of the Maori Wars* (Wellington, 1957); J. Belich, *Making Peoples: A History of the New Zealanders* (Auckland, 1996), ch. 10.

6. G. F. G. Stanley, *The Birth of Western Canada: A History of the Riel Rebellions* (London, 1936), pp. 141–3; 159–61; 168.

7. See J. Lambert, *Betrayed Trust: Africans and the State in Colonial Natal* (Pietermaritzburg, 1995), chs. 10, 11.

8. K. N. Panikkar, *Against Lord and State* (Delhi, 1989), p. 67.

9. Ibid., pp. 71ff.

10. Sinclair, *Maori Wars*, pp. 235–6.

11. For some discussion of this, J. A. Scott, *Weapons of the Weak* (New Haven, 1985), pp. 317ff.

12. See M. Reckord, 'The Jamaican Slave Rebellion of 1831', *Past and Present* 40 (1968), 108–25.

13. See TNA, CO 879/119, H. R. Palmer, 'Report on a Journey from Maidugari, Nigeria to Jeddah in Arabia' (May 1919), pp. 22–3.

14. Reckord, 'Jamaican Slave Rebellion'.

15. Panikkar, *Against Lord and State*, pp. 70, 72, 81, 85.

16. See B. Bailyn, *The Ordeal of Thomas Hutchinson* (Cambridge, MA, 1974), pp. 35–8.

17. Ibid., p. 74.

18. The classic account can be found in B. Bailyn, *The Ideological Origins of the American Revolution* (Cambridge, MA, 1967).

19. Bailyn, *Ordeal*, p. 71.

20. See K. Lockridge, 'Land, Population and the Evolution of New England Society 1630–1790', *Past and Present* 39 (1968), 62–80.

21. R. H. Bloch, *Visionary Republic: Millennial Themes in American Thought 1756–1800* (Cambridge, 1985), p. 15.

22. For a brilliant dissection of Gage's outlook and tactics, D. H. Fischer, *Paul Revere's Ride* (Oxford, 1995).

23. In his *Declaration of the Causes and Necessity of Taking Up Arms* (1775). See G. W. Sheldon, *The Political Thought of Thomas Jefferson* (Baltimore, 1991), p. 31.

24. E. Foner, *Tom Paine and Revolutionary America* (New York, 1976), p. 79.

25. For Mackenzie's career, see *Dictionary of Canadian Biography* online: 'William Lyon Mackenzie'.

26. For the increasingly loyalist attitude of the Order, see H. Senior, 'The Genesis of Canadian Orangeism', in J. K. Johnson, *Historical Essays on Upper Canada* (Toronto, 1975), p. 258.

27. See C. Read, *The Rising in Western Canada, 1837–38: The Duncombe Rising and After* (Toronto, 1982).

28. W. R. Manning (ed.), *Diplomatic Correspondence of the United States: Canadian Relations 1784–1860* (Washington, DC, 1943), vol. III: *1836–1848*, pp. 472–3: Fox to Aaron Vail, acting Secretary of State, 3 November 1838.

29. PP 1839 (2), *Correspondence Relative to Affairs in British North America*, pp. 18off.: Durham to Glenelg, 23 September 1838.

30. Ibid.: evidence of Abraham Bechard.

31. Quoted in *Dictionary of Canadian Biography* online: 'Louis-Joseph Papineau'.

32. See A. Greer, 'From Folklore to Revolution: Charivaris and the Lower Canadian Rebellion of 1837', *Social History* 15, 1 (1990), 25–43.

33. PP 1839 (2), *Correspondence*, p. 222: Durham to Glenelg, 20 October 1838.

34. See ibid.: Colborne to Glenelg, 1 November 1838.

35. Ibid.: Colborne to Glenelg, 19 December 1838.

36. Ibid.: Durham to Glenelg, 3 August 1838.

37. Republished as C. P. Lucas (ed.), *Lord Durham's Report on the Affairs of British North America* (3 vols., London, 1912).

38. For Papineau's doubts about rebellion and his opposition to a second invasion attempt after fleeing to the United Sates, Ruth L. White, *Louis-Joseph Papineau et Lamennais: le chef des Patriots canadiens à Paris 1839–1845* (Montreal, 1983), chs. 1, 2.

39. For La Fontaine's role, see J. Monet, *The Last Cannon Shot: A Study of French-Canadian Nationalism 1837–1850* (Toronto, 1969).

40. The British chose selectively to ignore the claims of adoptive sons.

41. V. T. Oldenburg, *The Making of Colonial Lucknow 1856–1877* (Princeton, 1984), p. 3; for Delhi's Muslim culture and court, see the brilliant portrait in W. Dalrymple, *The Last Mughal: The Fall of a Dynasty, Delhi, 1857* (London, 2006), chs. 1–3.

42. For Nana Saheb, A. S. Misra, *Nana Saheb Peshwa and the Fight for Freedom* (Lucknow, 1961).

43. The great scholar of agrarian unrest was E. T. Stokes from whose *The Peasant and the Raj* (Cambridge, 1978) and *The Peasant Armed: The Indian Rebellion of 1857* (ed. C. A. Bayly, Oxford, 1986) these examples are drawn.

44. See S. Alavi, *The Sepoys and the Company: Tradition and Transition in Northern India 1770–1830* (Delhi, 1995), pp. 294–5; S. David, *The Indian Mutiny* (London, 2002), ch. 3.

45. S. P. Cohen, *The Indian Army* (Berkeley and London, 1971), p. 35; fifty-four out of seventy-four infantry regiments were affected. David, *Mutiny*, p. 19.

46. See K. A. Wagner, *The Great Fear of 1857: Rumours, Conspiracies and the Making of the Indian Uprising* (Oxford, 2010).

47. See *The Times*, 10 June 1857.

48. Quoted in *The Times*, 14 July 1857.

49. R. Guha, *Elementary Aspects of Peasant Insurgency in Colonial India* (Delhi, 1983), p. 310.

50. S. A. A. Rizvi and M. Bharghava (eds.), *The Freedom Struggle in Uttar Pradesh: Source-Material*, vol. III (Lucknow, 1959), p. 225.

51. By some accounts, Nana Saheb had been almost their prisoner. See the Deposition of Tantia Topi on his capture, 10 April 1859 in ibid., vol. III, pp. 582ff.

52. Ibid., vol. II (Lucknow, 1958), p. 116.

53. On 12 November 1857. Ibid., vol. I (Lucknow, 1957), p. 480. (The *Friend* was a missionary newspaper produced in Calcutta.)

54. David, *Mutiny*, p. 146.

55. See Stokes, *Peasant Armed*, p. 96.

56. Dalrymple, *Last Mughal*, p. 431.

57. David, *Mutiny*, pp. 236–7; K. Roy, 'The Beginning of "People's War" in India', in his *1857: Essays from the Economic and Political Weekly* (Hyderabad, 2008), p. 139.

58. Oldenburg, *Colonial Lucknow*, p. 23.

59. PP 1857–8 (2449), *Further Papers No. 9 Relative to the Insurrection in the East Indies*, pp. 896–7: Governor-General to Court of Directors, 9 January 1858.

60. *Papers relating to the Mutinies in the East Indies, 1857*, vol. III, pp. 144–5: Joint Magistrate, Gopelgunge to Commissioner, Allahabad, 24 September 1857.

61. For a classic case of this dilemma, E. Brodkin, 'The Struggle for Succession', in B. Pati (ed.), *The 1857 Rebellion* (Delhi, 2007), pp. 132–47.

62. *Freedom Struggle*, vol. I, p. 479, quoting 'Narrative of Events by Government of Bengal for 5–12 September 1857'.

63. R. Dunlop, *Service and Adventure with the Khakee Ressalah or Meerut Volunteer Horse During the Mutinies of 1857–58* (1858) in P. K. Nayar, *The Penguin 1857 Reader* (Delhi, 2007), p. 140.

64. See *Freedom Struggle*, vol. II, pp. 478ff.

65. Ibid., vol. III, p. 636.

66. See Stokes, *Peasant Armed*, p. 61.

67. See W. Muir, *Records of the Intelligence Department of the Government of the North West Provinces . . .* (2 vols., Edinburgh, 1905), pp. 367–72.

68. Oldenburg, *Colonial Lucknow*, pp. 34–5.

69. B. Fuller, *Some Personal Experiences* (London, 1930), p. 7.

70. It may not be irrelevant that Dyer himself was born in India. For an excellent biography, N. Collett, *The Butcher of Amritsar* (London, 2007).

71. For the Pacific coast peoples, see Cole Harris, 'Voices of Smallpox around the Strait of Georgia', in his *The Resettlement of British Columbia* (Vancouver, 1997).

72. See P. D. Gardner, *Gippsland Massacres* (3rd edn, Ensay, Victoria, 2001).

73. See B. Gilling, 'Raupatu: The Punitive Confiscation of Maori Land in the 1860s', in R. Boast and R. S. Hill (eds.), *Raupatu: The Confiscation of Maori Land* (Wellington, 2009), pp. 16–17.

74. Ibid., p. 23.

75. See V. O'Malley, '"A Mild Sort of Confiscation": War and Raupatu on the East Coast', in ibid., p. 210.

76. See J. A. I. Agar-Hamilton, *The Native Policy of the Voortrekkers* (Cape Town, 1928), pp. 143–51.

77. See W. K. Storey, *Guns, Race and Power in Colonial South Africa* (Cambridge, 2008), p. 163.

78. Some 76 per cent in 1904. See S. Marks, *Reluctant Rebellion: The 1906–07 Disturbances in Natal* (Oxford, 1970), p. 6.

79. This appears in Jeff Guy's superb history, *Remembering the Rebellion: The Zulu Uprising of 1906* (Durban, 2006).

80. J. Guy, *The Maphumulo Uprising: War, Law and Ritual in the Zulu Rebellion* (Scotsville, 2005), pp. 104–5.

81. Ibid., pp. 105–6.

9. CONVERTS AND CULTURES

1. G. Orwell, *Nineteen Eighty-Four* (London, 1949), p. 3.

2. This argument can be followed in: T. Richards, *The Imperial Archive* (London, 1993); C. A. Bayly, *Empire and Information: Intelligence Gathering and Social Communication in India 1780–1870* (Cambridge, 1996); J. Hevia, *English Lessons: The Pedagogy of Imperialism in Nineteenth-Century China* (Durham, NC, 2003), ch. 5.

3. See P. J. Jupp, *British Politics on the Eve of Reform* (Basingstoke, 1998), p. 338; sales of the leading London newspapers rose from 16 million a year in 1837 to 31.4 million in 1850. J. White, *London in the Nineteenth Century* (London, 2007), p. 230.

4. A. Pagden, *European Encounters with the New World* (New Haven and London, 1993), p. 99.

5. Ibid., p. 161.

6. A. Smith, *The Wealth of Nations* (Everyman edn., London, 1910), vol 2, p. 122.

7. See N. Draper, *The Price of Emancipation: Slave-Ownership, Compensation and British Society at the End of Slavery* (Cambridge, 2010) for a brilliant analysis of the scale of slave-owning in Britain, and of the rhetorical devices by which it was justified.

8. J. Darwin, 'Britain's Empires' in S. Stockwell (ed.), *The British Empire: Themes and Perspectives* (Oxford, 2008), p. 13.

9. Aberdeen to Gordon, 21 November 1829, in M. Chamberlain, *Lord Aberdeen* (London, 1983).

10. Carlyle's article 'Occasional Discourse on the Nigger Question' appeared

in *Fraser's Magazine*, December 1849. For his aims, and the reaction, J. A. Froude, *Thomas Carlyle: A History of his Life in London* (2 vols., 1884), vol. II, pp. 26ff.

11. J. Burrow, *Evolution and Society: A Study in Victorian Social Theory* (Cambridge, 1966), p. 100: a reference to Darwin's voyage in the *Beagle*.

12. See G. Beer, *Darwin's Plots: Evolutionary Narrative in Darwin, George Eliot and Nineteenth-Century Fiction* (London, 1983), pp. 111, 129, 141, 158.

13. See D. Crook, *Benjamin Kidd: Portrait of a Social Darwinist* (Cambridge, 1984).

14. See C. Herbert, *War of No Pity: The Indian Mutiny and Victorian Trauma* (Princeton, 2008).

15. Ibid., p. 15.

16. PP 1866 (3683), XXX, *Royal Commission into the Origins, Nature and Circumstances of the Disturbances in . . . Jamaica: Report*, p. 41.

17. This was the Secretary of State for India, John Morley. See Morley to Lord Minto (the Viceroy), 17 June 1908, in B. R. Nanda, *Gokhale* (Delhi, 1977), p. 297.

18. The classic expression of this view was J. A. Hobson, *Imperialism: A Study* (London, 1902).

19. A. Roberts, *Salisbury: Victorian Titan* (London, 1999), p. 42.

20. A. N. Porter, *Religion versus Empire? British Protestant Missionaries and Overseas Expansion 1700–1914* (Manchester, 2004).

21. For the 'sentimental revolution', P. Langford, *A Polite and Commercial People: England 1727–1783* (Oxford, 1989), pp. 463ff.

22. For a classic account, F. K. Brown, *Fathers of the Victorians: The Age of Wilberforce* (Cambridge, 1961).

23. J. R. Elder (ed.), *The Letters and Journals of Samuel Marsden 1765–1838* (Dunedin, 1932), p. 61.

24. R. W. Strayer, *The Making of Mission Communities in East Africa* (London, 1978), p. 32.

25. See J. F. A. Ajayi, *Christian Missions in Nigeria 1841–1891: The Making of a New Elite* (London, 1965), pp. 20ff.

26. Ibid., p. 206.

27. Strayer, *Mission Communities*, pp. 14ff.

28. See C. Midgley, '"Can Women Be Missionaries?": Envisioning Female Agency in the Early Nineteenth-century British Empire', *Journal of British Studies* 45, 2 (2006), 347.

29. E. Prevost, 'Married to the Mission Field: Gender, Christianity and Professionalisation in Britain and Colonial Africa, 1865–1914', *Journal of British Studies* 47, 4 (2008), 800–801.

30. J. Cox, *Imperial Fault Lines: Christianity and Colonial Power in India, 1818–1940* (Stanford, 2002), p. 152.

31. A. J. Broomhall, *Hudson Taylor and China's Open Century*, vol. 1: *Barbarians at the Gates* (London, 1981), p. 332.

32. I. Schapera (ed.), *Livingstone's African Journal 1853–1856*, vol. 2 (London, 1963), p. 330.

33. See A. J. Dachs, 'Missionary Imperialism: The Case of Bechuanaland', *Journal of African History* 13, 4 (1972), 648.

34. D. A. Low, *Fabrication of Empire: The British and the Uganda Kingdoms, 1890–1902* (Cambridge, 2009), pp. 60–65.

35. R. Beck, 'Monarchs and Missionaries among the Tswana and Sotho', in R. Elphick and R. Davenport (eds.), *Christianity in South Africa: A Political, Cultural and Social History* (Berkeley, 1997), p. 111.

36. R. Ross and R. Viljoen, 'The 1849 Census of Cape Missions', *South African Historical Journal* 61, 2 (2009), 389–406. Fifty-eight per cent of the inmates were children.

37. See J. Hodgson, 'Christian Beginnings among the Xhosa', in Elphick and Davenport, *Christianity in South Africa*, pp. 76ff.

38. Ajayi, *Christian Missions in Nigeria*, p. 217.

39. J. Guy, *The Heretic: A Study of the Life of John William Colenso 1814–1883* (Johannesburg, 1983), p. 75.

40. Ibid., p. 74; Ajayi, *Christian Missions in Nigeria*, p. 106.

41. For Livingstone's life, the best source remains T. Jeal, *Livingstone* (London, 1973).

42. C. P. Groves, *The Planting of Christianity in Africa* (4 vols., London, 1948–58), vol. 2, p. 176.

43. D. Livingstone, *Missionary Travels* (1857), p. 577.

44. Quoted in Ajayi, *Christian Missions*, p. 174.

45. Quoted in Broomhall, *Hudson Taylor*, p. 329.

46. See Ajayi, *Christian Missions*, ch. 8.

47. J. K. Fairbank, E. O. Reischauer and A. M. Craig, *East Asia: The Modern Transformation* (Boston, MA, 1965), pp. 331–2.

48. Cox, *Imperial Fault Lines*, p. 117.

49. Ibid., p. 196.

50. J. Cox, 'From the Empire of Christ to the Third World: Religion and the Experience of Empire in the Twentieth Century', in A. S. Thompson, *Britain and Empire in the Twentieth Century* (Oxford, 2011).

51. R. Elphick, 'The Benevolent Empire and the Social Gospel: Missionaries and South African Churches in the Age of Segregation', in Elphick and Davenport (eds.), *Christianity in South Africa*, p. 348.

52. For a graphic description, see the classic work by B. Sundkler, *Bantu Prophets in South Africa* (London, 1948).

53. This case is made trenchantly in B. Porter, *The Absent-Minded Imperialists: Empire, Society and Culture in Britain* (Oxford, 2004).

54. For a careful statement of this, A. Thompson, *Imperial Britain: The Empire in Britain Politics c. 1880–1932* (Harlow, 2000) and his wider study, *The Empire Strikes Back: The Impact of Imperialism on Britain from the Late Nineteenth Century* (Harlow, 2005).

55. C. W. Dilke and S. Wilkinson, *Imperial Defence* (1892), p. 34.

56. For Scotland, T. M. Devine, *The Scottish Nation 1700–2000* (London, 1999), p. 289; for Wales, A. Jones and B. Jones, 'The Welsh World and the British Empire, c.1851–1939', *Journal of Imperial and Commonwealth History* 31, 2 (2003), 57–81.

57. For these *bhadralok* attitudes see T. Raychaudhuri, *Europe Reconsidered: Perceptions of the West in Nineteenth-Century Bengal* (Delhi, 1988).

58. R. C. Palit, *Speeches by Babu Surendra Nath Banerjea 1876–1880* (Calcutta, 1891), vol. 1, p. 8.

59. See P. Heehs, *The Bomb in Bengal* (Delhi, 1993).

60. M. R. Frost, 'Transcultural Diaspora: The Straits Chinese at Singapore 1819–1918', Asia Research Institute, Singapore, Working Paper No. 10 (available online).

61. See C. H. Fyfe, *The History of Sierra Leone* (London, 1962).

62. For an expression of this, J. E. Casely-Hayford, *Gold Coast Native Institutions* (London, 1903).

63. See C. Hamilton, *The Mfecane Aftermath* (Johannesburg, 1995); J. Peires, 'Paradigm Deleted: The Materialist Interpretation of the Mfecane', *Journal of Southern African Studies* 19, 2 (1993), 295–313.

64. P. Fry, 'Siyamfenguza: The Creation of Fingoness in South Africa's Eastern Cape, 1800–1835', *Journal of Southern African Studies* 36, 1 (2010), 25–40.

65. L. Switzer, *Power and Resistance in an African Society: The Ciskei Xhosa and the Making of South Africa* (Madison, WI, 1993), pp. 56–60.

66. N. Mandela, *Long Walk to Freedom* (London, 1994), p. 14.

67. See Bill Nasson, *Abraham Esau's War: A Black South African War in the Cape 1899–1902* (Cambridge, 1991).

10. DEFENDING EMPIRE

1. J. Gallagher, 'The Crisis of Empire, 1918–1922', *Modern Asian Studies* 15, 3 (1981), 355.

2. For this phrase, W. C. Sellar and R. J. Yeatman, *1066 and All That* (London, 1930).

3. Memo, by Lord Sanderson, January 1907. G. P. Gooch and H. Temperley (eds.), *British Documents on the Origins of the War 1898–1914*, vol. III: *The Testing of the Entente* (London, 1928), p. 430.

4. S. Wilkinson, *The Command of the Sea* (1900), p. 49. Wilkinson later became Chichele Professor of War at Oxford University.

5. See R. Pares, 'American *versus* Continental Warfare, 1739–1763', *English Historical Review* 51, 203 (1936), 429–65.

6. See L. S. Amery to J. L. Garvin, 8 March 1937, J. L. Garvin Papers, Harry Ransome Research Center, University of Texas at Austin.

7. Pitt, then Lord Chatham, in 1770. See H. W. Hodges and E. A. Hughes (eds.), *Select Naval Documents* (Cambridge, 1927), p. 146.

8. Salisbury to Lord Lansdowne, 30 August 1899, Lord Newton, *Lord Lansdowne: A Biography* (London, 1929), p. 157.

9. Salisbury to Lord Lytton, 15 June 1877. Quoted in A. Roberts, *Salisbury: Victorian Titan* (London, 1999), p. 218.

10. Minutes of War Cabinet Eastern Committee, 9 December 1918. Quoted in J. Darwin, *Britain, Egypt and the Middle East: Imperial Policy in the Aftermath of War 1918–1922* (London and Basingstoke, 1981), p. 160.

11. The complications are brilliantly captured in A. T. Mahan, *The Influence of Sea Power upon the French Revolution and Empire 1793–1812* (1892), ch. 9.

12. See the arguments in J. Corbett, *Some Principles of Maritime Strategy* (London, 1911), pp. 190ff.

13. Churchill's memo. 'Imperial Naval Policy', read at the Committee of Imperial Defence, 123rd meeting, April 1913. N. Tracy (ed.), *The Collective Naval Defence of the Empire 1900–1940* (Navy Records Society, 1997), p. 198.

14. Wilkinson, *Command of the Sea*, p. 98.

15. In his 'Geographical Pivot of History', *Geographical Journal* 23, 4 (1904), 421–37.

16. The British funded as many soldiers in Europe as they did in America. See B. Simms, *Three Victories and a Defeat: The Rise and Fall of the First British Empire 1714–1783* (London, 2007), p. 451. For Frederick's career, T. Schieder, *Frederick the Great* (Frankfurt am Main, 1983; Eng. trans., London, 2000).

17. Graphically described in A. T. Mahan, *The Influence of Sea Power on History 1660–1783* (1890), pp. 299–304: the 'Trafalgar' of this war, said Mahan.

18. See N. Cushner (ed.), *Documents Illustrating the British Capture of Manila, 1762–63* (London, 1971).

19. Simms, *Three Victories*, chs. 18–22.

20. The best account of the war remains P. Mackesy, *The War for America 1775–1783* (Cambridge, 1964).

21. The classic account of British peace aims can be found in V. T. Harlow, *The Founding of the Second British Empire 1763–1793* (2 vols., London, 1952–64).

22. N. Rodger, *The Command of the Ocean: A Naval History of Britain 1649–1815* (London, 2006), pp. 356ff.

23. See the excellent recent account in P. P. Barua, 'Maritime Trade, Seapower and the Anglo-Mysore Wars 1767–1799', *The Historian* 73, 1 (2011), 22–40.

24. Quoted in J. Holland Rose, 'The Struggle with Napoleon, 1803–1815', in J. Holland Rose, A. P. Newton and E. A. Benians (eds.), *Cambridge History of the British Empire*, vol. II: *The Growth of the New Empire 1783–1870* (Cambridge, 1940), p. 96.

25. Dundas's speech in the House of Commons, March 1801. Quoted in H. Richmond, *Statesmen and Sea Power* (Oxford, 1946), pp. 338–40.

26. J. Holland Rose, 'The Conflict with Revolutionary France 1793–1802' in Holland Rose, Newton and Benians, *British Empire*, II, p. 66.

27. Admiral Kempenfelt, 6 January 1782. Hodges and Hughes, *Naval Documents*, p. 168.

28. Rodger, *Command of the Ocean*, p. 436.

29. East India Company Secret Committee to governor-general, Bengal, 18 June 1798. S. J. Owen (ed.), *A Selection from the Despatches, Treaties and Other Papers of the Marquess Wellesley* (Oxford, 1877), p. 1.

30. Minute of governor-general, 12 August 1798. Ibid., pp. 11–57.

31. For descriptions, Mahan, *French Revolution and Empire*, pp. 263–77; Rodger, *Command of the Ocean*, pp. 459–60.

32. See G. Stedman Jones, 'National Bankruptcy and European Revolution: European Observers on Britain, 1813–1844', in D. Winch and P. K. O'Brien (eds.), *The Political Economy of British Historical Experience, 1688–1914* (Oxford, 2002), p. 72.

33. See D. Lieven, *Russia against Napoleon* (London, 2009), p. 522.

34. For this revolution in statecraft, see P. W. Schroeder, *The Transformation of European Politics 1763–1848* (Oxford, 1994).

35. C. K. Webster, *The Foreign Policy of Palmerston 1830–1841* (London, 1951), vol. 2, p. 842: Palmerston to Melbourne, 8 June 1835.

36. Quoted in J. Darwin, *The Empire Project: The Rise and Fall of the British World-System 1830–1970* (Cambridge, 2009), p. 30.

37. E. D. Steele, *Palmerston and Liberalism, 1855–1865* (Cambridge, 1991), p. 317: Palmerston to Clarendon, 7 October 1857.

38. For these anxieties, Southampton University Library, Palmerston Papers PP/LE/230: Palmerston to Sir G. C. Lewis, 26 August 1861 (consulted online). (Ten thousand soldiers were sent.)

39. The classic account of this strategic preoccupation is J. Gallagher and R. Robinson, *Africa and the Victorians* (London, 1961).

40. The best modern study is R. Owen, *Lord Cromer* (Oxford, 2004).

41. See T. G. Otte, *The China Question: Great Power Rivalry and British Isolation 1894–1905* (Oxford, 2007).

42. W. K. Hancock, *Smuts: The Sanguine Years, 1870–1919* (Cambridge, 1962), p. 108.

43. D. G. Boyce, *The Crisis of British Power: The Imperial and Naval Papers of the Second Earl of Selborne, 1895–1910* (London, 1995), p. 154: Selborne to Lord Curzon, 6 January 1903.

44. See W. Tilchin, *Theodore Roosevelt and the British Empire* (New York, 1997), p. 236.

45. The best modern account of British diplomacy is G. Monger, *The End of Isolation* (London, 1963).

46. See H. Strachan, *The First World War*, vol. 1: *To Arms* (Oxford, 2001), chs. 6, 7.

47. For some of the symptoms of Muslim unrest, M. Hasan (ed.), *Mohamed Ali in Indian Politics: Selected Writings* (Delhi, 1987), vol. II.

48. The best account is D. French, *British Economic and Strategic Planning 1905–1915* (London, 1982).

49. For a recent account, D. Stevenson, *With Our Backs to the Wall* (London, 2011).

50. For Milner's role in the war, A. E. Gollin, *Proconsul in Politics* (London, 1964).

51. Bodleian Library, Mss Milner (Additional) c696: Milner to Lloyd George, 9 June 1918.

52. See Darwin, *Britain, Egypt and the Middle East*, Parts 2, 3.

53. *The Times*, 12 June 1935.

54. See memo. by Foreign Secretary Austen Chamberlain, 4 January 1925. *Documents on British Foreign Policy*, 1st Series, vol. XXVII (London, 1986), p. 256.

55. Quoted in Darwin, *Empire Project*, p. 368.

56. For the work of the Defence Requirements Committee and its arguments, see K. Neilson, 'The Defence Requirements Sub-Committee, British Strategic Foreign Policy, Neville Chamberlain and the Path to Appeasement', *English Historical Review* 118, 477 (2003), 651–84.

57. The best overall study is M. Howard, *The Continental Commitment* (London, 1972).

58. See L. R. Pratt, *East of Malta, West of Suez: Britain's Mediterranean Crisis 1936–39* (Cambridge, 1975).

59. For the guarantee to Poland, S. Newman, *March 1939: The British Guarantee to Poland* (Oxford, 1976).

60. See his memo on seapower, 27 March 1939 in M. Gilbert (ed.), *Churchill Companion*, vol. V, Part 3: *The Coming of War 1936–39* (London, 1982), pp. 1414ff.

61. For a brilliant description of Britain's eastern empire on the eve of war, Christopher Bayly and Tim Harper, *Forgotten Armies: Britain's Asian Empire and the War with Japan* (London, 2004), pp. 30–96.

62. Sir William Slim, *Defeat into Victory* (London, 1956), p. 27.

63. Mercilessly portrayed in Bayly and Harper, *Forgotten Armies*, chs. 3, 4.

64. J. van der Poel (ed.), *Selections from the Smuts Papers* (Cambridge, 1973), vol. VI, pp. 373–7: J. C. Smuts to F. H. Theron, 21 July 1942.

65. Quoted in Bayly and Harper, *Forgotten Armies*, p. 207.

66. N. Prasad, *Official History of the Indian Armed Forces in the Second World War: The Expansion of the Armed Forces and the Defence Organization 1939–1945* (Calcutta, 1956).

67. These events may be followed in G. Rizvi, *Linlithgow and India* (London, 1978); P. Moon (ed.), *Wavell: The Viceroy's Journal* (London, 1973); R. J. Moore, *Escape from Empire: The Attlee Government and the Indian Problem* (Oxford, 1983); A. Jalal, *The Sole Spokesman: Jinnah, the Muslim League and the Demand for Pakistan* (Cambridge, 1985); and, indispensably, in N. Mansergh (ed.), *Constitutional Relations between Britain and India: The Transfer of Power 1942–47* (12 vols., London, 1970–83).

68. *Fortune*, July 1940, p. 136.

69. See W. K. Hancock and M. Gowing, *British War Economy* (London, 1949); R. Skidelsky, *The Life of J. M. Keynes: Fighting for Britain* (London, 2000).

11. ENDING EMPIRE

1. For this calculation, TNA, CAB 129/26; Memo by Patrick Gordon Walker, CP (48) 91, March 1948.

2. See S. Howe, *Anti-Colonialism in British Politics 1918–1964: The Left and the End of Empire* (Oxford, 1993).

3. For this view in government, see minutes of discussion, 5 January 1949, in R. Clarke, *Anglo-American Economic Collaboration in War and Peace, 1942–49*, ed. A. Cairncross (Oxford, 1982), p. 209.

4. See R. J. Moore, *Churchill, Cripps and India* (Oxford, 1979).

5. This atmosphere has been brilliantly recreated in Y. Khan, *The Great Partition: The Making of India and Pakistan* (London, 2007).

6. Jinnah's uncertainties have been documented in A. Jalal, *The Sole Spokesman: Jinnah, the Muslim League and the Demand for Pakistan* (Cambridge, 1985).

7. N. Mansergh (ed.), *Constitutional Relations between Britain and India: The Transfer of Power 1942–1947* (12 vols., London, 1970–83), vol. VII, pp. 150–51: Thorne to Abell (the Viceroy's private secretary), 5 April 1946.

8. Ibid., vol. IX, p. 68: Attlee's notes n.d. but *c.* 14 November 1946.

9. TNA, CAB 127/111; Viceroy's Personal Reports, 2 April 1947.

10. Ibid., 17 April 1947.

11. Ibid., 27 June 1947.

12. In fact, only some of Henty's books were explicitly imperial in subject matter.

13. Recently emphasized in D. Edgerton, *Britain's War Machine: Weapons, Resources and Experts in the Second World War* (London, 2011).

14. In his speech on 10 November 1942. Quoted in W. R. Louis, *Imperialism at Bay: The United States and the Decolonization of the British Empire 1941–1945* (Oxford, 1977), p. 200.

15. Mansergh, *Transfer*, Vol. IX, pp. 427–31: Conclusions of Cabinet 108 (46), 31 December 1946, Confidential Annex.

16. TNA, PREM 8/564: Bevin to Attlee, 1 January 1947.

17. See N. Owen, *The British Left and India: Metropolitan Anti-Imperialism 1885–1947* (Oxford, 2007).

18. TNA, CAB 129/16: Joint Cabinet memo by Foreign Secretary and Minister of Fuel, 3 January 1947.

19. Just how close can be seen on the map annexed to the 1936 Anglo-Egyptian Treaty.

20. Bevin to Attlee, 7 January 1947, in R. Hyam (ed.), *British Documents on the End of Empire: The Labour Government and the End of Empire 1945–1951*, Part III, *Strategy, Politics and Constitutional Change* (London, 1992), p. 228.

21. S. Gopal, *Jawaharlal Nehru*, vol. 2 (London, 1979), p. 47.

22. TNA, PREM 8/950: Attlee to Nehru, Top Secret and Personal, 20 March 1949.

23. Ibid., Cabinet Committee on Commonwealth Relations, 8 February 1949.

24. TNA, CAB 131/5: Cabinet Defence Committee, DO 19 (48), 18 September 1948.

25. TNA, PREM 8/950: Sir Norman Brook, Draft Report on . . . Official Committee on Commonwealth Relations, 24 March 1948. 'Western Union' referred to Britain's 'junior partners' in Europe.

26. Attlee was born in 1883, Bevin in 1881.

27. The classic study of this change is Louis, *Imperialism at Bay*.

28. US National Record and Archive Administration, State Department Central Files, LM 89, Roll 37, Note by Stabler, 21 December 1950.

29. See K. Larres, *Churchill's Cold War* (London, 2002).

30. For the 'second colonial occupation', see D. A. Low and J. Lonsdale, 'Towards the New Order', in D. A. Low and A. Smith (eds.), *History of East Africa*, vol. 3 (Oxford, 1976), pp. 1–63.

31. The best overall studies are K. Kyle, *The Suez Conflict* (London, 1989), W. R. Louis and R. Owen (eds.), *Suez 1956: The Crisis and its Consequences* (Oxford, 1989). D. R. Thorpe, *Eden: The Life and Times of Anthony Eden* (London, 2003) offers a more sympathetic view of Eden.

32. See J. Eayrs (ed.), *The Commonwealth and Suez: A Documentary Survey* (London, 1964): the exceptions were Australia and New Zealand.

33. See W. R. Louis, 'Public Enemy Number One: Britain and the United States in the Aftermath of Suez', in his *Ends of British Imperialism: The Scramble for Empire, Suez and Decolonisation* (London, 2006).

34. Macmillan's diary, 15 September 1956, P. Catterall (ed.), *The Macmillan Diaries: The Cabinet Years 1950–1957* (London, 2003), p. 599.

35. What Macmillan actually said on 20 July 1957 in a speech at Bedford was 'most of our people have never had it so good'. See http//news.bbc. co.uk/onthisday. However, an eminent historian, Quentin Skinner, who was present as a schoolboy, remembers the more familiar version being used in response to a heckler. See *London Review of Books* 33, 18, 22 September 2011.

36. See P. Mangold, *The Almost Impossible Ally: Harold Macmillan and Charles De Gaulle* (London, 2006), p. 136.

37. Recent studies include D. Anderson, *Histories of the Hanged: Britain's Dirty War in Kenya and the End of Empire* (London, 2005) and D. Branch, *Defeating Mau Mau, Creating Kenya: Counterinsurgency, Civil War and Decolonization* (Cambridge, 2009).

38. The number of settler farmers in Kenya more than doubled between 1938–9 and 1960 – from 1,700 to 3,600. See R. M. A. Van Zwanenberg, *An Economic History of Kenya and Uganda* (London, 1975), p. 44.

39. For a contemporary (and optimistic) description, E. Huxley, *A New Earth: An Experiment in Colonialism* (London, 1960).

40. The best account of events in Nyasaland is C. Baker, *State of Emergency: Crisis in Central Africa, Nyasaland, 1959–1960* (London, 1997). See also J. Darwin, 'The Central African Emergency, 1959', *Journal of Imperial and Commonwealth History* 21 (1993), 217–34.

41. For this tendency, see ch. 8.

42. The Devlin Report was printed as Cmnd. 814 (1959), *Report of the Nyasaland Commission of Enquiry*.

43. A. Horne, *Macmillan 1957–1986* (London, 1988), p. 181.

44. The text of Macmillan's speech of 3 February 1960 can be found in *The Times*, 4 February 1960.

45. For an account from the white Rhodesian side based on the papers of Sir Roy Welensky, the federal premier, see J. R. T. Wood, *The Welensky Papers* (Durban, 1983).

46. *British Documents on the End of Empire*, P. Murphy (ed.), *Central Africa*, Part Two: *Crisis and Dissolution 1959–1965* (London, 2005), p. 131: Macleod to Macmillan, 3 April 1960.

47. Ibid., p. 182: Macleod's Minute for Macmillan, 29 November 1960.

48. See Crawford Young, *Politics in the Congo: Decolonization and Independence* (Princeton, 1965).

49. See Ludo de Witte, *The Assassination of Lumumba* (Eng. trans., London, 2001).

50. See R. Shepherd, *Iain Macleod* (London, 1994), p. 212.

51. TNA, CO 822/2235: Colonial Secretary to Governor of Kenya, 14 April 1961.

52. Memo. by Colonial Secretary for Cabinet Colonial Policy Committee, 30 January 1962. A draft is in TNA, CO 822/2238.

53. R. Hyam and W. R. Louis (eds.), *British Documents on the End of Empire: The Conservative Government and the End of Empire 1957–1964*, Part I: *High Policy, Political and Constitutional Change* (London, 2000), p. 531: Cabinet Memo by Colonial Secretary, 6 February 1962.

54. By a majority of thirteen, J. C. Smuts defeated the incumbent prime minister, J. B. M. Hertzog, and formed a new government.

55. Technically, on becoming a republic, South Africa had to seek re-entry as a Commonwealth member.

56. See P. Buckner, 'The Long Goodbye: English Canadians and the British World', in P. Buckner and D. Francis (eds.), *Rediscovering the British World* (Calgary, 2005), p. 202.

57. See S. Ward, *Australia and the British Embrace* (Melbourne, 2001); J. Belich, *Paradise Reforged: A History of the New Zealanders from the 1880s to the Year 2000* (Auckland, 2001), ch. 15.

58. Quoted in J. Darwin, *The Empire Project: The Rise and Fall of the British World-System 1830–1970* (Cambridge, 2009), p. 638.

59. The phrase appeared in Harold Wilson's Labour Party Conference speech on 1 October 1963. See *The Times*, 2 October 1963.

60. *Guardian*, 11 June 1965: 'Premier pledges support for India'.

61. See J. Subritzky, *Confronting Sukarno: British, American, Australian and New Zealand Diplomacy in the Malaysian-Indonesian Confrontation 1961–1965* (Basingstoke, 2000).

62. For these economic travails, A. Cairncross, *Managing the British Economy in the 1960s: A Treasury Perspective* (Basingstoke, 1996).

63. This was Richard Crossman, a self-styled opponent of the 'Great Britain school'. See his *Diaries of a Cabinet Minister*, vol. 2 (London, 1976), p. 639.

64. Ibid., vol. 1 (London, 1974), p. 539.

65. The authoritative account of policy towards Malaysia and Singapore in this period is now P. L. Pham, *Ending 'East of Suez': The British Decision to Withdraw from Malaysia and Singapore, 1964–1968* (Oxford, 2010).

66. Aden became the dominant element in the new state of South Yemen, later re-united with Yemen proper.

67. For British policy in the Gulf, see now S. C. Smith, *Britain's Revival and Fall in the Gulf: Kuwait, Qatar and the Trucial States 1950–1971* (London, 2004).

68. For this suggestion, *The Times*, 20 November 1967, Times Digital Archive.

69. Quoted in J. Darwin, *Britain and Decolonisation: The Retreat from Empire in the Post-war World* (Basingstoke, 1988), p. 324.

70. For the negotiations, E. Windrich, *Britain and the Politics of Rhodesian Independence* (London, 1978); for an account based on the papers of Ian Smith, J. R. T. Wood, *A Matter of Weeks Rather Than Months: The Impasse between Harold Wilson and Ian Smith: Sanctions, Aborted Settlements and War 1965–1969* (Trafford, 2008).

71. For a white Rhodesian insider account of the transition in Zimbabwe, Ken Flower, *Serving Secretly: An Intelligence Chief on Record: Rhodesia into Zimbabwe 1964 to 1981* (London, 1987).

72. For the Falklands war, M. Hastings and S. Jenkins, *The Battle for the Falklands* (London, 1983); L. Freedman and V. Gamba-Stonehouse, *Signals of War: The Falklands Conflict of 1982* (London, 1990).

73. I base this on a conversation with the late Sir Henry Leach (then First Sea Lord) in 1986.

74. Joint Declaration of the Government of the UK and of the People's Republic of China, 19 December 1984, 3 (5), in F. Madden (ed.), *Select Documents on the Constitutional History of the British Empire and Commonwealth,*

vol. 8: *The End of Empire, Dependencies since 1948* (Westport, CN, 2000), pp. 352–3.

75. For a survey, J. Brown and R. Foot (eds.), *Hong Kong's Transitions 1842–1997* (Basingstoke, 1997).

12. THE LAST AND LARGEST EMPIRE?

1. See N. Owen, *The British Left and India: Metropolitan Anti-Imperialism 1885–1947* (Oxford, 2008).

2. H. J. Mackinder, *Democratic Ideals and Reality* (London, 1919), p. 110.

3. C. Dilke, *Greater Britain* (1869), p. 446.

4. See M. Mann, *The Sources of Social Power*, vol. 1: *A History of Power from the Beginning to A.D. 1760* (Cambridge, 1986), p. 537.

5. See J. Strachey, *The Coming Struggle for Power* (London, 1932), p. 391.

Further Reading

This is not a full bibliography of the sources used in this book. The details of these are given in the notes and references that accompany each chapter. What I have included here are the books and articles that I have found most stimulating or helpful and which may allow the interested reader to pursue the topics discussed.

I. GENERAL

Readers in search of specialized topics should consult A. Porter, *Bibliography of Imperial, Colonial and Commonwealth History since 1600* (Oxford, 2002) which has some 24,000 entries, many running to dozens of volumes. S. Stockwell (ed.), *The British Empire: Themes and Perspectives* (Oxford, 2008) has an excellent – if somewhat shorter – bibliography. A. Jackson and D. Tomkins, *Illustrating Empire: A Visual History of British Imperialism* (Oxford, 2011) offers an interesting selection of imperial imagery. B. Porter, *The Lion's Share*, first published in 1975 but with several later editions, provides an excellent overview of the British Empire since 1850. W. R. Louis (general ed.), *Oxford History of the British Empire* (5 vols., Oxford, 1998–9) is now the most comprehensive account, beginning with N. Canny (ed.), *Origins of Empire* (Oxford, 1998). It has yielded a series of companion volumes on themes including gender, black experiences, migration, the history of settler and expatriate communities, and missionaries, as well as studies of the place of Ireland, Canada, Australia and twentieth-century Britain in the empire. D. Meinig, *The Shaping of America*, vol. 1: *Atlantic America, 1492–1800* (New Haven and London, 1986) brilliantly reconstructs the geographical and geopolitical setting for Britain's American empire. V. T. Harlow, *The Founding of the Second British Empire*, vol. 1: *Discovery and Revolution* (1952); vol. 2 *New Continents and Changing Values* (London, 1964) pioneered the idea of an imperial 'swing to the east' in the later eighteenth century. It should be compared with

C. A. Bayly, *Imperial Meridian: The British Empire and the World 1780–1830* (London, 1989). Conceptually, the study of British imperial expansion begins with the classic and irreplaceable essay by J. Gallagher and R. Robinson, 'The Imperialism of Free Trade', *Economic History Review*, 2nd Series, VI, 1 (1953). P. J. Cain and A. G. Hopkins, *British Imperialism 1688–2000* (2nd edn, Harlow, 2002) emphasizes the connection between British governments and the City of London and has stimulated much further research. R. C. Allen, *The British Industrial Revolution in Global Perspective* (Cambridge, 2009) is a powerful analysis of Britain's distinctive economic trajectory. A. Thompson, *The Empire Strikes Back: The Impact of Imperialism on Britain from the Late Nineteenth Century* (Harlow, 2005) is the best overall study of the domestic effects of empire. J. Darwin, *The Empire Project: The Rise and Fall of the British World-System 1830–1970* (Cambridge, 2009) emphasizes politics, economics and geopolitics. D. Lieven, *Empire: The Russian Empire and its Rivals* (London, 2003) presents a valuable comparison.

Among historical atlases, A. N. Porter, *Atlas of British Expansion* (London, 1991) is invaluable, but there are two gems: *The Historical Atlas of Canada*, published by Toronto University Press in three volumes from 1987; and M. Mackinnon (ed.), *New Zealand Historical Atlas* (Auckland, 1997).

2. IDEAS

A. P. Thornton, *The Imperial Idea and its Enemies* (London, 1959) is a grand overview. K. Knorr, *British Colonial Theories 1570–1850* (Toronto, 1944) is a marvellous compendium. D. Armitage, *The Ideological Origins of the British Empire* (Cambridge, 2000) traces imperial ideas from the time of Hakluyt. E. F. Heckscher, *Mercantilism* (2 vols, Eng. trans., London, 1935) is the classic account of the economic ideas that Adam Smith attacked in *The Wealth of Nations* (1776). P. Earle, *The World of Defoe* (London, 1976) discusses the economic assumptions of the late seventeenth and early eighteenth centuries. S. Pincus, *1688: The First Modern Revolution* (New Haven and London, 2009) challenges some of the received wisdom about British economic thinking in the 'mercantilist' era. A. C. Howe, *Free Trade and Liberal England* (Oxford, 1997) explains why free trade was an article of faith in Victorian Britain. C. Dilke, *Greater Britain* (1869), J. R. Seeley, *The Expansion of England* (1883) and J. A. Hobson, *Imperialism: A Study* (London, 1902) were the three faces of Victorian ideas about empire. Hobson's critique of empire is brilliantly analysed in P. J. Cain, *Hobson and Imperialism: Radicalism, New Liberalism and Finance 1887–1938* (Oxford, 2002). B. Porter, *Critics of Empire: British Radical Attitudes to Colonialism in*

Africa (London, 1968) and S. Howe, *Anti-Colonialism and British Politics: The Left and the End of Empire 1918–1964* (Oxford, 1993) set British 'anti-imperialism' in its contexts.

3. CONTACT AND CONQUEST

The creation of a dense and remarkably efficient system of communications is superbly described by I. K. Steele, *The English Atlantic 1675–1740: An Exploration of Communication and Community* (Oxford, 1986). The intriguing history of a half-colony, half-fishing camp can be found in the fascinating study by P. E. Pope, *Fish into Wine: The Newfoundland Plantation in the Seventeenth Century* (Chapel Hill, NC, 2004). W. Cronon, *Changes in the Land: Indians, Colonists and the Ecology of New England* (New York, 1983) explains the interplay of the human and environmental factors. F. Jennings, *The Invasion of America: Indians, Colonialism and the Cant of Conquest* (Chapel Hill, NC, 1975) was an onslaught on the complacency of much of the existing literature on 'settlement'. V. Shepherd and H. McD. Beckles (eds.), *Caribbean Slavery in the Atlantic World* (Oxford, 2000) contains a wide selection of essays on the early history of the region. R. Dunn, *Sugar and Slaves: The Rise of the Planter Class in the English West Indies 1624–1713* (Chapel Hill, NC, 1972) is the classic study of the switch to slave labour in colonial Barbados. Andrew Jackson O'Shaughnessy, *An Empire Divided: The American Revolution and the British Caribbean* (Philadelphia, 2000) contains a superb portrait of the mature plantation economy of the British Caribbean. W. Floor, *The Persian Gulf: A Political and Economic History of Five Port Cities 1500–1730* (Washington, DC, 2006) describes a region where the British were relative latecomers but which they were to turn eventually into a 'British lake'. P. J. Stern, *The Company-State: Corporate Sovereignty and the Early Modern Foundations of the British Empire in India* (Oxford, 2011) is the best recent account of the Company's political and administrative life in its first century. S. Mentz, *The English Gentleman Merchant at Work: Madras and the City of London 1660–1740* (Copenhagen, 2005) reveals the business practice and social ambitions of the Company's main centre in India until the 1760s. H. Dodwell, *The Nabobs of Madras* (London, 1926) is a pioneering social portrait of the raffish English colony there. The same writer's *Dupleix and Clive: The Beginning of Empire* (London, 1920) remains a classic account of the transition to empire. S. C. Hill, *Indian Record Series: Bengal in 1756–1757*, vol. 3 (London, 1905) vividly conveys the circumstances of the fall of Calcutta. M. Davies, *Clive of Plassey* (London, 1939) is much the best account of the nerve-racking prelude to the crucial encounter at Plassey in 1757. W. Dalrymple, *White Mughals: Love and*

Betrayal in Eighteenth Century India (London, 2003) brilliantly captures the era in which the British and other Europeans inserted themselves into Indian society rather than standing aloof from it. Bernard Smith, *European Vision and the South Pacific 1768–1850: A Study in the History of Art and Ideas* (Oxford, 1960) remains the classic account of the Europeans' cultural response. Inga Glendinnen, *Dancing with Strangers: The True History of the Meeting of the British First Fleet and the Aboriginal Australians, 1788* (Edinburgh, 2005) and Anne Salmond, *Between Worlds: Early Exchanges between Maori and Europeans, 1773–1815* (Auckland, 1997) reconstruct two encounters with quite different outcomes. M. Harrison, *Medicine in an Age of Commerce and Empire: Britain and Its Tropical Colonies 1660–1830* (Oxford, 2010) is a superb account of the aspect of contact that often weighed most heavily on its exponents.

4. SETTLEMENT

S. Constantine and M. Harper, *Migration and Empire* (Oxford, 2010) is now the authoritative study alongside E. Richards, *Britannia's Children: Emigration from England, Scotland, Wales and Ireland since 1600* (London and New York, 2004). K. Fedorowich, 'The British Empire on the Move, 1776–1914' in Stockwell, *British Empire* is much the best short study. B. Bailyn and Barbara De Wolfe, *Voyagers to the West: A Passage in the Peopling of America on the Eve of the Revolution* (New York, 1986) offers a fascinating account of the motives and methods of migration in the 1770s. Our understanding of the larger context in which British and other European settlement took place, as well as its social, cultural and political implications, has now been brilliantly illuminated by J. Belich's widely acclaimed *Replenishing the Earth: The Settler Revolution and the Rise of the Anglo-World, 1783–1939* (Oxford, 2009). A. L. Crosby, *Ecological Imperialism: The Biological Expansion of Europe 900–1900* (Cambridge, 1986) showed how settler expansion was able to exploit the often unintended effects of a parallel incursion by the biota they brought with them. The essays in E. Pawson and T. Brooking (eds.), *Environmental Histories of New Zealand* (Oxford, 2002) take up this theme in perhaps the most remarkable case of ecological colonization. J. D. Wood, *Making Ontario: Agricultural Colonization and Landscape Re-creation before the Railway* (Montreal and Kingston, 2000) explains how settlement did indeed require the making of a landscape. A. Atkinson, *The Europeans in Australia: A History*, vol. 1: *The Beginning* (Oxford, 1997), N. Penn, *The Forgotten Frontier: Colonist and Khoisan on the Cape's Northern Frontier in the Eighteenth Century* (Cape Town, 2005) and the essays in R. Elphick and H. Giliomee, *The Shaping of South African Society 1652–1840* (2nd edn, Cape Town, 1989) analyse the origins and early development of settlement in these regions. W. Anderson, *Cultivating Whiteness: Science, Health and Racial Destiny in Australia* (Melbourne, 2002) examines the preoccupation with racial purity.

5. WARFARE

H. Bull, *The Anarchical Society* (London, 1977), G. W. Gong, *The 'Standard of Civilisation' in International Society* (Oxford, 1984) and E. Keene, *Beyond the Anarchical Society: Grotius, Colonialism and Order in World Politics* (Cambridge, 2002) offer a framework for understanding the implications of imperial expansion for international order. L. H. Keeley, *War before Civilisation* (Oxford, 1996) attacks the mythology surrounding the relative harmlessness of 'primitive' warfare. C. E. Callwell, *Small Wars: Their Principles and Practice* [1896] (3rd edn, London, 1906) became the British manual on the conduct of colonial warfare. Its precept of exerting a 'moral effect' (i.e. terror) was invoked by General Dyer at the inquiry into the events at Amritsar in April 1919. B. Vandervort, *Wars of Imperial Conquest in Africa 1830–1914* (London, 1998) describes the actual record of warfare. I. W. F. Beckett (ed.), *Wolseley and Ashanti: The Asante War Journal and Correspondence of Major General Sir Garnet Wolseley 1873–74* (Stroud, 2009) gives an insight into the maestro of colonial warfare. D. Omissi, *The Sepoy and the Raj* (Basingstoke, 1994) and R. G. S. Cooper, *The Anglo-Maratha Campaigns and the Contest for India: The Struggle for Control of the South Asian Military Economy* (Cambridge, 2003) explain the evolution of British military power in India. I. Knight, *The National Army Museum Book of the Zulu War* (London, 2004) is comprehensive and fascinating. J. Connor, *Australian Frontier Wars 1788–1838* (Sydney, 2002) and J. Belich, *The New Zealand Wars* (Auckland, 1986) deal with the less familiar Australasian scene. N. Prickett, *Landscapes of Conflict: A Field Guide to the New Zealand Wars* (Auckland, 2002) reconstructs the battlegrounds in meticulous detail. R. Marjomaa, *War on the Savannah: The Military Collapse of the Sokoto Caliphate under the Invasion of the British Empire, 1897–1903* (Helsinki, 1998) explains the strengths and limitations of the advanced weaponry the British were able to deploy. C. Enloe, *Ethnic Soldiers: State Security in a Divided Society* (Harmondsworth, 1980) was a pioneering study of the use of indigenous 'martial races' to prop up colonial and post-colonial regimes.

6. TRADE

The motives behind the English turn to the Atlantic are explored in D. H. Sacks, *The Widening Gate: Bristol and the Atlantic Economy, 1450–1700* (Berkeley, 1991). The significance of the 'triangle trade' between Britain, West Africa and the Caribbean can be followed in S. Mintz, *Sweetness and Power: The Place of Sugar in Modern History* (Harmondsworth, 1985) and J. Inikori, *Africans and the Industrial Revolution in England* (Cambridge, 2002) which stresses the importance of the trade with West Africa. E. Williams, *Capitalism and Slavery* (London, 1944) remains a great classic, brilliantly written and full of insights. R. Pares, 'Economic Factors in the History of the Empire', *Economic History Review* 7, 2 (1937) and R. Pares, *Merchants and Planters* (Cambridge, 1960) describe the business practices and mentality of the 'mercantilist' era by one of the great scholars of Caribbean history. For the East India Company, Holden Furber, *Rival Empires of Trade in the Orient 1600–1800* (Minneapolis, 1976) and H. V. Bowen, *The Business of Empire: The East India Company and Imperial Britain 1756–1833* (Cambridge, 2006) are essential. M. Greenberg, *British Trade and the Opening of China 1800–1842* (Cambridge, 1951) remains unsurpassed for the period up to the first opium war. H. S. Ferns, *Britain and Argentina in the Nineteenth Century* (Oxford, 1960), D. C. M. Platt (ed.), *Business Imperialism 1840–1930: An Inquiry Based on the British Experience in Latin America* (Oxford, 1977) and P. Winn, 'Britain's Informal Empire in Uruguay in the Nineteenth Century', *Past and Present* 73 (1976) describe the British commercial penetration of South America. A. G. Hopkins, *An Economic History of West Africa* (London, 1973) is unmatched as a regional study and sets the European impact in a longer perspective. J. F. Munro, *Maritime Enterprise and Empire: Sir William Mackinnon and his Business Network, 1823–93* (Woodbridge, 2003) is a treasure trove. Cecil Rhodes's business empire is dissected in C. W. Newbury, *The Diamond Ring* (Oxford, 1989), which shows how the profits from De Beers paid for the invasion of what is now Zimbabwe in 1890. C. van Onselen, *Chibaro: African Mine Labour in Southern Rhodesia 1900–1933* (London, 1976) unsparingly depicted the brutal regime on which mine profits depended. N. H. R. Crafts, *British Economic Growth during the Industrial Revolution* (Oxford, 1985) is essential reading for the sources of British industrial success. K. H. O'Rourke and J. G. William, *Globalization and History: The Evolution of a Nineteenth-century Atlantic Economy* (London and Cambridge, MA, 1999) provides the context and explains the rhythms of trade and migration. C. Feinstein, 'British Overseas Investments in 1913', *Economic History Review* 43, 2 (1990), 288–95 is the authoritative computation. S. Chapman, *The Rise of Merchant*

Banking (London, 1984) examines a crucial evolution in British mercantile activity. G. Jones, *Merchants to Multinationals: British Trading Companies in the Nineteenth and Twentieth Centuries* (Oxford, 2000) is a marvellous survey of the astonishing range of commercial enterprise. D. Kynaston, *The City of London* (5 vols., London, 1994–2001) offers an unrivalled portrait of the City from the early nineteenth century until recent times. A. Dilley, *Finance, Politics and Imperialism: Australia, Canada and the City of London c. 1896–1914* (forthcoming 2012) is a superb reconstruction of the often fraught relations between the City and two of its largest borrowers. D. Headrick, *The Tools of Empire: Technology and European Imperialism in the Nineteenth Century* (Oxford, 1981) and the essays in T. G. Otte and K. Neilson (eds.), *Railways and International Politics: Paths of Empire, 1848–1945* (London, 2006) illuminate the technological transformation that underpinned the huge expansion of trade.

7. GOVERNANCE

Fundamental to the study of imperial governance is the monumental work of F. Madden (ed.), *Select Documents on the Constitutional History of the British Empire and Commonwealth* (8 vols., Westport, CN, 1985–2000), which provides not only a massive selection of original documents but a detailed commentary that serves as a constitutional history of all the various colonial territories as they became part of the empire. J. Henretta, *'Salutary Neglect': Colonial Administration under the Duke of Newcastle* (Princeton, 1972) explains how and why London avoided systematic interference in colonial affairs before the 1760s. B. Bailyn, *The Origins of American Politics* (New York, 1968) examines the working of the colonial assemblies. The crisis of governance is traced in P. Marshall, *The Making and Unmaking of Empires: Britain, India and America c. 1750–1783* (Oxford, 2005). J. M. Ward, *Colonial Self-Government: The British Experience 1759–1856* (London, 1976) and P. Buckner, *The Transition to Responsible Government: British Policy in British North America 1815–1850* (Westport, CN, 1985) explain the adoption of 'responsible government'. G. T. Chesney, *Indian Polity* (esp. 3rd edn, 1894) and J. B. Fuller, *The Empire of India* (London, 1913) convey the British officials' view of their role as the 'guardians' of India. A. Seal, *The Emergence of Indian Nationalism* (Cambridge, 1968) and J. Gallagher, G. Johnson and A. Seal (eds.), *Locality, Province and Nation* (Cambridge, 1973) show the connection between new forms of British rule in India and the rise of nationalism. E. T. Stokes, *The English Utilitarians and India* (Oxford, 1959) and T. R. Metcalf, *Ideologies of the Raj* (Cambridge, 1995) explore British thinking. C. A.

Bayly, *Empire and Information: Intelligence Gathering and Social Communication in India 1780–1870* (Cambridge, 1996) discusses the efficiencies and deficiencies of British political intelligence. R. J. Moore, *The Crisis of Indian Unity* (Oxford, 1974) describes the British discovery of the attractions of federation in inter-war India. M. Perham, *Lugard: The Years of Authority 1898–1945* (London, 1960) is a generally admiring biography of the proconsul to whom the invention of 'indirect rule' is attributed. R. Owen, *Lord Cromer* (Oxford, 2004) shows how the British deployed a 'veiled protectorate' to manage Egypt, strategically one of the most vital components of their imperial system. J. Cell, *Hailey: A Study in British Imperialism 1872–1969* (Cambridge, 1992) follows the career of the most influential twentieth-century British proconsul. L. Benton, *A Search for Sovereignty: Law and Geography in European Empires 1400–1900* (Cambridge, 2010) emphasizes the instability and uncertainty of colonial law-making.

8. REBELLION

B. Bailyn, *The Ideological Origins of the American Revolution* (Cambridge, MA, 1967) and his *The Ordeal of Thomas Hutchinson* (Cambridge, MA, 1974) examine the world-views of both rebels and loyalists in the American revolution. D. H. Fischer, *Paul Revere's Ride* (Oxford, 1995) brilliantly conveys the rebellious atmosphere in Massachusetts. Marshall, *Making and Unmaking* analyses the British reaction. A superb account of how the American struggle impinged upon Indian societies is Alan Taylor, *The Divided Ground: Indians, Settlers and the Northern Borderland of the American Revolution* (New York, 2006). M. Jasanoff, *Liberty's Exiles: The Loss of America and the Remaking of the British Empire* (London and New York, 2011) describes the fate of the 60,000 loyalists, red, white and black. For slave resistance and rebellion, M. Craton, *Testing the Chains: Resistance to Slavery in the British West Indies* (Ithaca, NY, 1982) and K. Morgan, *Slavery and the British Empire: From Africa to America* (Oxford, 2007). For Pontiac's rebellion on the eve of the American revolution, C. Calloway, *The Scratch of a Pen: 1763 and the Transformation of America* (Oxford, 2006). J. Monet, *The Last Cannon Shot: A Study of French-Canadian Nationalism 1837–1850* (Toronto, 1969) explains the moderate outcome of the French-Canadian revolt in Quebec. E. T. Stokes, *The Peasant Armed: The Indian Rebellion of 1857* (ed. C. A. Bayly, Oxford, 1986), K. A. Wagner, *The Great Fear of 1857: Rumours, Conspiracies and the Making of the Indian Uprising* (Oxford, 2010) and W. Dalrymple, *The Last Mughal: The Fall of a Dynasty, Delhi, 1857* (London, 2006) are key accounts of the Indian Rebellion of 1857. N. Collett, *The*

Butcher of Amritsar: General Reginald Dyer (London, 2005) contains a forensic examination of the circumstances in which nearly 400 Indians were shot in cold blood. J. B. Peires, *The Dead Will Arise: Nongqawuse and the Great Xhosa Cattle-killing Movement of 1856–57* (Johannesburg, 1989), P. Delius, *The Land Belongs to Us: The Pedi Polity, the Boers and the British in the Nineteenth-century Transvaal* (London, 1984), J. Guy, *The Maphumulo Uprising: War, Law and Ritual in the Zulu Uprising* (Scottsville, 2005) and the same author's *Remembering the Rebellion: The Zulu Uprising of 1906* (Scottsville, 2006) offer highly sophisticated histories of African resistance in South Africa. K. Sinclair, *The Origins of the Maori Wars* (Wellington, 1957) should now be compared with J. Belich, *The New Zealand Wars* (Auckland, 1986). M. Shadbolt, *Season of the Jew* (London, 1986) is a brilliant fictional reconstruction of Te Kooti's rebellion in New Zealand.

9. CULTURE AND RELIGION

The modern debate about the relationship between empire and culture really began with E. Said's manifesto, *Orientalism* (London, 1978), itself an application of the ideas of Michel Foucault. John MacKenzie was the pioneer of the cultural history of empire: see among others J. M. MacKenzie (ed.), *Imperialism and Popular Culture* (Manchester, 1985); J. M. MacKenzie, *Propaganda and Empire: The Manipulation of British Public Opinion 1880–1960* (Manchester, 1984); J. M. MacKenzie, *Orientalism: History, Theory and the Arts* (Manchester, 1995) and J. M. MacKenzie, *Museums and Empire: Natural History, Human Cultures and Colonial Identities* (Manchester, 2009). C. Hall and S. Rose (eds.), *At Home with the Empire: Metropolitan Culture and the Imperial World* (Cambridge, 2006) and B. Porter, *The Absent-Minded Imperialists: Empire, Society and Culture in Britain* (Oxford, 2004) represent sharply opposing views of the way empire shaped British culture at home. Porter's book was a powerful counterblast to loosely argued and methodologically incoherent claims. R. Price, 'One Big Thing: Britain, its Empire and their Imperial Culture', *Journal of British Studies* 45 (2006) offers a balanced critique of all sides. S. Potter, *News and the British World: The Emergence of an Imperial Press System 1876–1922* (Oxford, 2003) was a pioneering examination of how news circulated around the empire.

A. N. Porter, *Religion versus Empire? British Protestant Missionaries and Overseas Expansion 1700–1914* (Manchester, 2004) is now the authoritative study of the Protestant missionary enterprise. N. Etherington (ed.), *Missions and Empire* (Oxford, 2005); E. Elbourne, *Blood Ground: Colonialism, Missions and the Contest for Christianity in the Cape Colony and Britain,*

1799–1853 (Kingston, Ontario, 2002); R. Price, *Making Empire: Colonial Encounters and the Creation of Imperial Rule in Nineteenth-Century Africa* (Cambridge, 2008); T. Jeal, *Livingstone* (London, 1973); J. Cox, *Imperial Fault Lines: Christianity and Colonial Power in India, 1818–1940* (Stanford, 2002) describe different facets of missionary activity. The study of British humanitarianism is currently in a state of revival. Older books include S. Drescher, *Capitalism and Anti-Slavery: British Mobilization in Comparative Perspective* (Basingstoke, 1986) and D. Turley, *The Culture of Anti-Slavery, 1780–1860* (London, 1991). An introduction to the extensive debate about the role of women and gender can be found in P. Levine (ed.), *Gender and Empire* (Oxford, 2004), C. Midgley, *Women against Slavery: The British Campaigns, 1780–1870* (London, 1992), and A. L. Stoler, *Carnal Knowledge and Imperial Power: Race and the Intimate in Colonial Rule* (Berkeley, 2002).

10. DEFENCE

A. T. Mahan, *The Influence of Sea Power on History* (1890) was a hugely influential interpretation of the naval foundations of British world power. J. Corbett, *Some Principles of Maritime Strategy* (London, 1911) reflected the strategic debates of the Edwardian period. D. H. Cole, *Imperial Military Geography* [1924] (8th edn, London, 1935) gives an insight into inter-war military thinking and teaching. B. H. Liddell Hart, *The British Way in Warfare* (London, 1932) was written against the huge continental commitment of the First World War. A small sample of the colossal literature on imperial defence should include P. M. Kennedy, *The Rise and Fall of British Naval Mastery* (London, 1976), a wonderful survey; G. S. Graham, *The Politics of Naval Supremacy* (Cambridge, 1965); R. Pares, 'American *versus* Continental Warfare, 1739–1763', *English Historical Review* 51, 203 (1936), 429–65; C. J. Bartlett, *Great Britain and Sea Power 1815–1853* (Oxford, 1963); N. A. M. Rodger, *The Command of the Ocean: A Naval History of Britain 1649–1815* (London, 2004) – a magisterial study; N. Tracy, *Nelson's Battles: The Triumph of British Seapower* (London, 1996); A. J. Marder, *The Anatomy of British Seapower: Naval Policy in the Pre-Dreadnought Era* (New York, 1940); and *From the Dreadnought to Scapa Flow: The Royal Navy in the Fisher Era* (5 vols., London, 1961–70); G. Kennedy (ed.), *Imperial Defence: The Old World Order 1856–1956* (London, 2008); K. Neilson and G. Kennedy (eds.), *The British Way in Warfare 1688–2000: Essays in Honour of David French* (Farnham, 1990); H. Strachan, *European Armies and the Conduct of War* (London, 1983). The strategic anxieties of the aftermath of the First World War are brilliantly conveyed in K. Jeffery, *The British Army and the Crisis of Empire 1918–1922* (Manchester, 1984). M. Howard, *The Continental Commitment: The Dilemma of British Defence Policy in the Era of Two World Wars* (1972) remains fundamental.

11. THE END OF EMPIRE

The interested reader can now see a large sample of the official documents in which the British retreat from empire was anticipated, argued against, justified, planned for, deferred, fudged and misunderstood in the superbly edited series *British Documents on the End of Empire*. There are volumes dealing both with the view 'from the centre' and with the particular experience of some of the colonies, including Ghana, Nigeria, Malaya, the West Indies and the Central African Federation among many. Each volume has a substantial introductory essay. For India, the monumental equivalent is N. Mansergh (ed.), *Constitutional Relations between Britain and India: The Transfer of Power 1942–1947* (12 vols., London, 1970–83); for Burma, H. Tinker (ed.), *Constitutional Relations between Britain and Burma: The Struggle for Independence 1944–1948* (2 vols., London, 1983–4).

The most brilliant short treatment can be found in J. Gallagher, *The Decline, Revival and Fall of the British Empire* (Cambridge, 1982). R. F. Holland, *European Decolonization 1918–1981* (Basingstoke, 1985) sets British experience in the European context and offers an explanatory framework. Some of the present writer's views can also be found in J. Darwin, *Britain and Decolonisation: The Retreat from Empire in the Post-war World* (Basingstoke, 1988). M. Shipway, *Decolonization and its Impact: A Comparative Approach to the End of the Colonial Empires* (Oxford, 2008) reverses the usual perspective to ask how decolonization affected the colonized. The chapters in W. R. Louis and J. Brown (eds.), *Oxford History of the British Empire: The Twentieth Century* (Oxford, 1999) trace the course of British withdrawal in different parts of the world. Amid the huge literature on the end of the Indian Raj, Y. Khan, *The Great Partition: The Making of India and Pakistan* (London, 2007) stands out as a fresh and fascinating treatment. The desperate tangles of Britain's Middle Eastern interests, even more tangled after 1945 than before, are revealed in W. R. Louis, *The British Empire in the Middle East 1945–1951* (Oxford, 1984). For the critical episode of Suez, K. Kyle, *The Suez Conflict* (London, 1989). There is a growing literature on the 'dirty wars' of British decolonization. D. Anderson, *Histories of the Hanged: Britain's Dirty War in Kenya and the End of Empire* (London, 2005) meticulously examines the evidence in one of the most controversial cases. The gradual pulling apart of the 'white dominions' from their old 'British' identity was a neglected aspect of the decolonization process. S. Ward, *Australia and the British Embrace* (Melbourne, 2001) was a pioneering study of this side of the 'end of empire'. The conventional finale of British imperial ambitions was the decision in January 1968 to withdraw from 'East of Suez' by 1971. The fierce political struggle in London over whether and when to leave Southeast Asia militarily can now be followed in P. L. Pham, *Ending 'East of Suez': The British Decision to Withdraw from Malaysia and Singapore, 1964–1968* (Oxford, 2010). The white settler view has rarely been given a sympathetic hearing by historians. Some of its bitterness can be gleaned from J. R. T. Wood, *The Welensky Papers: A History of the Federation of Rhodesia and Nyasaland* (Durban, 1983), based as the title suggests on the voluminous archive of the federation's second and last prime minister. The same writer's *So Far and No Further: Rhodesia's Bid for Independence during the Retreat from Empire 1959–1965* (Johannesburg, 2005) and *A Matter of Weeks Rather than Months: The Impasse between Harold Wilson and Ian Smith: Sanctions, Aborted Settlements and War 1965–1969* (Trafford, 2008) were similarly based on 'unfettered access' to the papers of Ian Smith.

Index